GOLAZO!

GOLAZO!

The Beautiful Game from the
Aztecs to the World Cup:
The Complete History of How Soccer
Shaped Latin America

Andreas Campomar

RIVERHEAD BOOKS
New York

RIVERHEAD BOOKS
Published by the Penguin Group
Penguin Group (USA) LLC
375 Hudson Street, New York, New York 10014

USA • Canada • UK • Ireland • Australia • New Zealand • India • South Africa • China

penguin.com

A Penguin Random House Company

GOLAZO!

An application to register this book for cataloging has been submitted to the Library of Congress.

First Riverhead trade paperback edition: May 2014
ISBN: 978-1-59448-586-2

PRINTED IN THE UNITED STATES OF AMERICA

10 9 8 7 6 5 4 3 2 1

Cover design by Gregg Kulick
Cover photograph: Popperfoto/Getty Images
Book design by Tiffany Estreicher

For my mother,
who showed me how I might find
identity through culture;
and
for my father,
who taught me how to watch fútbol.

In Latin America the border between soccer and politics is vague. There is a long list of governments that have fallen or been overthrown after the defeat of the national team.

—Luis Suárez

Tell me how you play and I will tell you who you are.

—Eduardo Galeano

Football is popular because stupidity is popular.

—Jorge Luis Borges

Whoever invented football should be worshipped as a god.

—Hugo Sánchez

Poverty is good for nothing, except for football.

—Jorge Valdano

That Latin America is unique, because there exists no other Latin America except this one, does not mean that it is one, in the sense that there is unity. Disunion does not exclude identity. Neither does diversity.

—Mario Sambarino

CONTENTS

ACKNOWLEDGMENTS

It is a strange paradox that one only learns how to write a book once it has been written. By then, it is usually too late. Fortunately, I have been able to rely on the wisdom and generosity of others for guidance. There are many who gave of their time and knowledge, and to whom I am indebted. Moreover, I am equally thankful to all those who took an interest, however fleetingly, in my attempt at an interpretation of the Latin American game. Any errors in this book are mine, and mine alone.

My first thanks go to my agent, Matthew Hamilton of Aitken Alexander Associates, and my publisher, Jon Riley at Quercus, both of whom saw early promise in this project. When I first suggested a book on Latin America football to Matthew, he replied, "Great, now who can we get to write it?" I dispensed with my publisher's judgment and put myself forward. Matthew and Jon both encouraged, even when there seemed to be no end in sight. Thank you to my U.S. editor, Laura Perciasepe at Riverhead, who understood what I was trying to achieve and was ever patient as the clock ticked toward a tight deadline. And to Ricardo Sabanes, publisher at Club House in Buenos Aires; in the words of Gustavo Cerati, "¡Gracias . . . totales!"

I am especially grateful to Josh Ireland at Quercus, a prince among editors, without whose good counsel and smart judgment this project would never have made the finish line. My thanks also go to Séan Costello, for his swift copyediting, Emma Thawley, Flora McMichael, Corinna Zifko and everyone else at Quercus.

The idea for the book resulted from from an essay I was commissioned to write—on the image of Uruguay through Eduardo Galeano's work—by the brilliant Ivor Indyk at *Heat*, the Australian literary magazine. A version of that essay appears as an introduction to this book. Thank you, Ivor.

Special thanks go to Jason Wilson, an academic in the very best sense, whose encyclopedic knowledge of the Río de la Plata helped shape this book.

Outside Latin America, I would like to thank Olga Tomé, Francisco

Panizza, Carlos Aguirre, Richard Giulianotti, John Crace, Leo Hollis, Peter Parker, Nick Robinson, Pete Duncan, Charlotte Macdonald, David Wood, Ian Preece, Rick Gekoski, Peter Russell, Tom Pemberton.

In Latin America, I encountered a generosity of spirit that reflected the very best of a much-maligned continent. In Montevideo, my thanks go to my family, in particular Jorge Ciasullo, Martina Campomar, Pia Ciasullo, Jacqueline Campomar, Luis Campomar, Walter Lockhart. And also to Jorge da Silveira, Juan Carlos Luzuriaga, Gerardo Caetano, Rafael Bayce, Julio María Sanguinetti, Felipe Arocena, Alfredo Etchandy, Jorge Figueroa and Mario Romano.

In Buenos Aires: Federico Ciasullo, Julio Frydenberg, Carlos Yametti, Ezequiel Fernández Moores, Pablo Alabarces, Roberto Di Giano, Rodrigo Daskal, José Garriga, Oscar Barnade, Ariel Scher, Vanesa Fernández.

In Lima: Gerardo Álvarez, Aldo Panfichi, Luis Arias Schreiber, Victor Vích, Sergio Markarián, Martín Benavides, Wilmer del Águila Ochoa.

In Santiago: Konstantinos Simonidis, Danilo Díaz, Jorge Iturriaga, Eduardo Santa Cruz, Sebastián Salinas, Edgardo Marín, Cristián Muñoz.

In Mexico: Marcelo Assaf, José Samuel Martínez López, Roger Magazine, Miguel Ángel Lara, Carlos Calderón, Abraham Patinio.

In Brazil: Nacho Cerezo, Edgardo Martolio, José Renato Santiago, José Paulo Florenzano, Ricardo Weiss, Alvaro do Cabo, Édison Gastaldo, Leonardo Affonso de Miranda Pereira, Felipe Soutinho, Michel Jamel.

In Asunción: José María Troche.

I would also like to thank the staff and the resources at Biblioteca Nacional de Chile, Biblioteca Nacional de la República Argentina, Biblioteca Nacional de Uruguay, British Library, British Newspaper Library, Senate House Library and Ibero-Amerikanisches Institut.

And last but not least, thank you to the wonderful Gina Rozner, without whose love, patience and support this book would never have been written. I cannot thank you and Broo (*el super gato*) enough.

COMO EL URUGUAY NO HAY

(There's No Place Like Uruguay)

My father and I are watching the last match of the 2010 World Cup that we will see together. Not for us the hyperbole of a World Cup final, for this is *our* final, Uruguay's final: an essentially meaningless affair for third place.

"*Mira . . . mira como lleva la pelota*. Look . . . just look at that ball control," my father says with approval, though I can detect a hint of malice in his voice that sounds more like justification.

Football is the passion that my father and I share. While we differ on so many issues, many of which further that gentle father-son antagonism, here we come together. We applaud the flashier, more articulate aspects of the game: a deft back-heel, a neat flick, the weighted pass and, of course, the art of dribbling. (My father especially approves of the audacity of dribbling in one's own penalty area, an approach much frowned upon by the ever-cautious *sajónes*, Anglo-Saxons.) I realize that his attitude toward football is not dissimilar to that of the Uruguayan polemicist and football fanatic Eduardo Galeano. But then they were born in the same city, Montevideo, a decade either side of Uruguay's World Cup triumphs, and both retain nostalgia for the way the game should be played. I am reminded of the "author's confession" in *Soccer in Sun and Shadow*, Galeano's poignant love letter to the beauty of the game: "I've finally learned to accept myself for who I am: a beggar for good soccer. I go about the world, hand outstretched, and in the stadiums I plead: 'A pretty move, for the love of God.'"[1] Nevertheless, this love of good football is actually a passion for the Latin American game—or more to the point, for River Plate football (*el fútbol rioplatense*). It was what Galeano calls "the second discovery of America," when Uruguay brought her own inimitable style of play to the 1924 Summer Olympics in Paris.

"*Suárez, che, no sos un boludo.* Hey, Suárez, don't be an idiot." My father gesticulates at the television as the young player tries for goal from an unlikely angle. I can't help but agree with him.

According to my father, and for that matter every other Uruguayan to whom I have recently spoken, the fact that we have come this far shows that we can still compete at the highest level; that *la garra charrúa* ("the Charrúa claw") is still alive. I, on the other hand, have never believed in *la garra charrúa*: that spirit of the Uruguayan national team—La Celeste—which allows it to snatch victory in the face of overwhelming defeat. (It somehow seems disingenuous to identify ourselves with those poor seminomadic Charrúa Indians, the last of whom were betrayed and vanquished in 1832, leaving the country without any semblance of an indigenous culture.) Nevertheless, our run to the playoffs, which has been born of good fortune rather than great skill, has allowed Uruguay to prove that it is not an irrelevance—even in terms of the rest of Latin America—and that, as Uruguayans, we earn the right to exist. Moreover this success is an indication, despite our checkered past both on and off the pitch, of our better selves.

As with many small nations, Uruguay has developed an exaggerated sense of self. During the opening decades of the twentieth century, the Latin American republic channeled her sense of inferiority and was transformed into a modern social democracy; the first in Latin

America. Nevertheless Uruguay's inception had been inauspicious. By the time it was created as a buffer state between Argentina and Brazil with the help of British mediation in 1828, it had suffered varying degrees of occupation at the hands of her neighbors. Moreover, independence did not herald maturity, for the rest of the nineteenth century was played out through a cycle of wars. It was only in the first decades of the twentieth century, under the twin presidencies of the enlightened José Batlle y Ordóñez that Uruguay began to prosper. An ardent opponent of militarism, having witnessed the near destruction of the nascent nation through civil war, Batlle y Ordóñez sought to implement a number of social reforms to fulfill his vision of a proto-European Uruguay. Sustained immigration from the Old World throughout the late nineteenth century, which led to the rapid urbanization of the port capital, Montevideo, encouraged the development of football within the poorer parts of the city. Moreover, the development of public playing fields, from two in 1913 to 118 in 1929, allowed for a new generation of skilled players to emerge. It was due to this generation, which included the country's black minority, that the country was able to secure gold medals at the 1924 and 1928 Olympics. Hosting and winning the inaugural 1930 World Cup confirmed the country's sporting supremacy.

By the middle of the twentieth century, Uruguay had one of the highest standards of living on the continent. "In no other country do people live as we do . . . no other people on earth currently enjoy achievements such as ours," was the roseate view furthered by President Luis Batlle Berres in a 1949 speech.[2] A year later the country secured its second World Cup, thereby intensifying its inflated self-image. While Brazil had played with flair and assurance, Uruguay had relied on sheer strength of character to win games. The competition from European football, which the Second World War had all but obliterated, lacked the cutting edge it would later regain.

This golden age of prosperity, together with unparalleled successes on the football pitch, gave rise to a variety of self-aggrandizing and self-deluding epithets. In 1951, the *New York Times* praised Uruguay as the "Switzerland of the Americas" on account of its foreign trade boom and the large sums of flight capital (especially pure gold) that made its way there.[3] Montevideo, once regarded as a parochial city, had become the "Athens of the River Plate"; while the slogan *Como el Uruguay no hay*" (There's no place like Uruguay) became a self-serving mantra for all Uruguayans. In half a century the country had emerged from a civil-war-riven agrarian backwater to become a modern social democracy. The concept of Uruguayan exceptionalism was born. Nevertheless the country's euphoria would be short-lived. When Uruguay was truly tested by a mesmeric Hungary in the 1954 World Cup semifinal, she lost. What the country failed to recognize at the time was that this match would be the turning point in her sporting fortunes.

. . .

Lack of political foresight coupled with an entrenched view that the outside world would have to adapt to the country rather than vice versa meant that Uruguay began to stagnate. Things were no better on the pitch. For the ensuing decades the epithet of the "Switzerland of the Americas" was to prove a curse and became a sick joke when, after years of economic decline and guerrilla insurrection, the country finally succumbed to a military coup in June 1973. (Though, as early as 1968, a state of emergency had been declared under a civilian presidency, which became known as "the dictatorship that dare not speak its name" [*la dictadura que no osa decir su nombre*].) The ensuing twelve-year dictatorship, which had the unenviable record of incarcerating more political prisoners per capita than any other country, put paid to the idea that Uruguayans were somehow "superior" to their fellow Latin Americans. Even non–Latin Americans saw the country for what it was. In *The Return of Eva Perón*, V. S. Naipaul skewered the Uruguayan psyche: "Uruguayans say that they are a European nation, that they have always had their back to the rest of Latin America. It was their great error, and part of their failure. Their habits of wealth made them, profoundly a colonial people, educated but intellectually null, consumers, parasitic on the culture and technology of others."[4]

Uruguay had become a self-satisfied, middle-class "medio-cracy," mired in its own history, an overbureaucratized country that had seen its wealth slowly evaporate. Regrettably, it retained unrealistic expectations in relation to the game that had helped form its identity. Uruguay now worked on precedent: that it had won two World Cup finals meant that it might win again. The unnerving graffiti daubed on a wall at the airport—*EL ÚLTIMO QUE SALGA QUE APAGUE LA LUZ* (the last person to leave must put out the light)—said it all: the country was prostrate.[5]

My father is now on his feet. Edinson "El Matador" Cavani, having slipped his markers, slots the ball in the right-hand corner of the net to bring us on level terms with Germany. "*Epa! Ahora mira como juegan. Uruguay—siempre impredecible.* Hey! Now look how they're playing. Uruguay—always unpredictable."

Like many Uruguayans from the more genteel neighborhoods, my father supported Nacional, which sported the red, white and blue of the country's great *libertador*, José Artigas. I, on the other hand, became a fan of Peñarol, a working-class club that had originally been founded as the Central Uruguay Railway Cricket Club in the final decade of the nineteenth century. (Nacional fans have always prided themselves on being truly Uruguayan, whereas Peñarol is seen as an immigrant club; hence the Italianate sobriquet "*mangare merda*" [shit-eaters].) My uncle, whose fault this blatant act of perfidy was, had been shrewd enough to buy me my first football strip: a cheap polyester-and-nylon affair consisting of a black-and-yellow-striped shirt, black shorts and fluffy yellow socks, all emblazoned with the number 9. This number belonged to Fernando Morena, who would become the greatest goal scorer in the country's first division. Morena was *un crack*—a term used for players of exceptional ability—having scored seven goals in one match against Huracán Buceo in 1978. Unfortunately he was also known as "El Pajama," having developed an undeserved reputation for not traveling well and only performing at home ties. On the back of Peñarol's 2–0 drubbing of Aston Villa in the 1982 Intercontinental Cup, I wore my football kit with pride. This match, which at the time I had taken in my stride, changed the way I thought about football forever. I desired panache and flair rather than work rate. I never saw the European game in the same light again.

Whereas my father had caught the tail end of Uruguay's glory years—having witnessed Peñarol overpower Real Madrid over two legs in the 1966 Intercontinental Cup—I have only caught glimpses of what has been a great tradition. And yet it has been a tradition based less on fact than fantasy. For a country so proud of its prowess and so ready to tether its identity to two World Cup triumphs, failure has dogged the national team since her semifinal defeat against Brazil in the 1970 World Cup. I was too young to have followed Uruguay four years later, though my father assured me that her performance in Germany was abject: the team played without shame (*sin vergüenza*), losing two matches and drawing one. Nevertheless, it was not until the 1986 FIFA World Cup that I really understood what playing *without shame* meant.

Having been on the receiving end of a 6–1 rout by a dynamic Denmark, Uruguay had to show its mettle. Loss of confidence in the aftermath of her golden era had prompted the country to adopt a physically aggressive style of play rather than revert to the finesse for which it was once renowned. And in Omar Borrás the country found a manager who saw football in proto-martial terms. (Unsurprisingly, Borrás had colluded with the dictatorship in order to further his managerial career.) He had also shown his hand early by coining the phrase *grupo de la muerte* (group of death) for a group that included West Germany, Denmark and Scotland. Before the tournament, Morena passed sentence: "Borrás' team doesn't take risks, underutilises its good players and has neither a tactical plan nor its own style. It'll be a disaster, just like in '74, due to lack of competent management."[6]

When ex-Peñarol defender José Batista scythed Gordon Strachan from behind and was shown a red card after fifty-six seconds, Uruguayan football had sunk to a humiliating low. The rest of the match, which was fraught with foul play, ended in a goalless draw. Despite making it through to the next round, the Latin Americans were unable to go quietly. The Uruguayan journalists spat at the Scottish press, while accusations of lying and cheating were leveled at Borrás by the Scottish officials. The Uruguayan manager, on the other hand, kept his bile for the French referee, by calling the latter an *asesino* (murderer). For the match against Argentina, Borrás was expelled from the dugout. (Throughout the tournament, Uruguay's star player, Enzo "El Príncipe" Francescoli, failed to make the impression that had been expected; something he would sometimes do when he played for the national team; though it seemed to me that he would save his best for River Plate.)

At the 1990 World Cup, Uruguay promised much in its opening match, outplaying Spain in a one-sided encounter. (Rubén Sosa did, however, sky a penalty.) Toward the end of the match, television viewers could hear the Uruguayan manager shout, "*Dale, muchachos, están cagados.* Come on, lads, they're [the Spanish are] fucked." It would be Uruguay's turn next when it was subjected to another European primer in fast-flowing football, this time at the hands of the Belgians in a 3–1 defeat. Against South Korea, a goal in the last minute of the match allowed the former world champions safe passage in the last berth of third-placed teams. The hosts were waiting, though it took until the sixty-fifth minute for Schillaci to breach the Uruguayan defense. Defeat had been imminent: Uruguay had had her luck.

Apart from a spectacular win against Brazil in the final of the 1995 Copa América—aided by a penalty shoot-out, the underdog's twelfth man—success on the international stage was hard to come by. Three years later, Brazil did not make the same mistake and dispatched Uruguay by three goals to nil. Thereafter the country had to rely on its neighbors to see it through World Cup qualification. In the last match of the 2001 qualifiers, Uruguay had to draw against Argentina in order to secure a place in the playoffs. For a nation that has self-obsession as one of its better character traits, the end of the match saw the Argentine players display a hitherto-concealed altruistic nature. When Verón played for time on the touchline to see out a 1–1 draw, the crowd shouted its appreciation, *"¡Ay, gracias Verón! Hey, thanks Verón!"* Uruguay's great nemesis, with whom it had shared a great footballing tradition, had finally come to its aid. Another mediocre display in the 2002 World Cup did little for the country's image at home or abroad; though it showed a glimmer of former glories, when it made a strong comeback with three second-half goals against a hitherto rampant Senegal. Uruguayan football had come a very long way from its auspicious beginnings.

"Dale, Forlánnnnn. Come on, Forlánnnnn," my father shouts, but his voice peters out as our hero hits the bar with the last kick of the match.

We lose by three goals to two, though Diego Forlán—our best player and the best player of the tournament—has nearly carried the hopes of the continent into extra time. Typical Uruguay, I think to myself, so near and yet so far. But then this is what being Uruguayan has been like these past forty years—a peculiar mix of masochism and nostalgia. We can't help ourselves: football continues to reinforce our identity as Latin Americans; it has made us who we are. As Galeano points out, "Every time the national team plays, no matter against whom, the country holds its breath. Politicians, singers and street vendors shut their mouths, lovers suspend their caresses, and flies stop flying."[7]

The beautiful game has achieved what a succession of third-rate dictators and craven presidents have never been able to do: to instill the continent with a sense of self-belief and a historical narrative of which it can be proud, and thereby cast off those heavy shackles of colonialism.

London—Montevideo—Buenos Aires—
Lima—Santiago—Asunción—São Paulo—
Rio de Janeiro—Mexico City

2011–2013

CORTÉS AND THE BOUNCING BALL

The man who sent the ball through the stone ring was surrounded by all. They honoured him, sang songs of praise to him, and joined him in dancing.

—Fray Diego Durán, *Book of the Gods and Rites* (c. 1576–1579)

The 1986 FIFA World Cup in Mexico will forever be remembered for the duality of "El Pibe de Oro" (The Golden Boy), Diego Armando Maradona. By turns footballing genius and pantomime villain, Maradona held a mirror to both the potencies and shortcomings of his native Argentina. Though his self-confessed Hand-of-God goal against England may have appalled sporting purists—Latin Americans take a more evenhanded approach when it comes to their own failings—his crime was assuaged by a goal of such sublime beauty that it represented the heights to which the continent might aspire.

By the time Maradona lifted the World Cup trophy above his head in front of over 114,000 spectators, after having helped dispatch West Germany 3–2 in the final, it represented vindication and maintained the unbroken series of Latin American triumphs in World Cups held in the Americas. The connection was not lost on other Latin Americans, who, despite their misgivings about Argentinian ethnic snobbery, saw the victory as communal. And yet there was something more primal at play, something that went to the very soul of the continent.

A few miles away from the Estádio Azteca, buried under modern-day Mexico City, lay Tenochtitlán—a city described by Hernán Cortés as the most beautiful in the world—whose memory stands witness to an Aztec (Mexica) ancestry from which not only Mexicans but also all Latin Americans should claim cultural heritage. In his Nobel lecture, delivered four years after Maradona had led the Argentines to glory, the Mexican poet Octavio Paz sought to explain what most Latin Americans instinctively felt but, for the most part, could not express: "Hispanic eccentricity is reproduced and multiplied in America, especially in those countries such as Mexico and Peru, where ancient and splendid civilizations had existed . . . That history is still alive: it is a present rather than a past. The temples and gods of pre-Columbian Mexico are a pile of ruins, but the spirit that breathed life into that world has not disappeared; it speaks to us in the hermetic language of myth, legend, forms of social coexistence, popular art, customs."[1]

Among Tenochtitlán's ruins, which rest under the Metropolitan Cathedral of Mexico City, can be found a ball court dating to the 1480s. More than a hundred years later, Fray Bernardino de Sahagún would compile his *General History of the Things of New Spain*, a primer of Amerindian practices for clerics coming to the New World. The seventy-eight buildings documented in the book include a description of two ball courts: "The thirty-second edifice was called *Tezcat-lachco*; this was a ballcourt, in it they killed some captives as devotion when the sign *omacatl* [an Aztec deity associated with specific calendar dates or signs] reigned."[2]

Notwithstanding their use as theaters for human sacrifice—which played a significant role in Mesoamerican religion often through live heart extraction, mutilation and decapitation—it was on these ball courts (*tlachtli*) that the most renowned variation of the ball game took place. *Ullamaliztli*, as witnessed by the Spanish conquistadors in the sixteenth century, was played throughout the Aztec empire. In his memoirs, *Primeros Memoriales*, the Franciscan de Sahagún sought to capture the essence of this peculiar pursuit:

Then the playing of the ball game began. And the spectators sat above the ball court on both sides; all the noblemen, or lords, or seasoned warriors sat divided into two sections. And on each side above the ball court, each on his own side, sat the contenders to whom the ball game pertained. And to each side of the court was attached a [circular stone] called tlachtemalacatl, which had a hole [in the center]. And he who put [the ball] through it, won the game . . . And it was said that the ball game was like war . . .[3]

At the game's peak, over 16,000 rubber balls were exported each year from the lowland provinces to Tenochtitlán as royal tribute. (The Castilloa elastica—from which latex sap was gleaned, mixed with the extract of the morning glory plant and fashioned into rubber balls—grew wild from the lowlands of southern Mexico down through to present-day Colombia.) Nevertheless, the game that the conquistadors encountered had not been limited to the Aztecs. From what is now southern Arizona down through Mexico and into Central America, an area of a million square miles, the ball game had been played for over two millennia until the fall of the Aztec empire in 1521. (Over 1,500 ball courts have been unearthed.) Since its inception in 1600 BCE by the Olmecs (known as the "rubber people")—to which time rubber balls from El Manatí, on the Gulf of Mexico, have been dated—the game gradually evolved. Although Pan-Mesoamerican in spirit, the ball game took on diverse meanings and traditions according to region.

By the advent of the Spanish conquest, *ullamaliztli* had become a largely secular and highly popular pastime. Not a true sport in the modern sense, the ball game was a combination of competing functions: part ritual and part recreation, on which large wagers would be placed. Yet popularity—the game was played relentlessly—did not herald conformity. The Mesoamerican ball court varied in size, between one hundred and two hundred feet in length, twenty to thirty feet in width, and eight and eleven feet in height, though all courts retained the shape of a Roman *I*. Ball games were played as singles, doubles, and with up to eleven players. Teams did not have to be evenly matched: there were instances of matches where two players were drawn against three. The most important players, on either team, stood in the center of the court as if primed for battle.

There seem to have been variations in scoring points, the ability to send the ball through a ring, secured to the side of the central court, which won the game instantly:

> *The Spectators seeing the Ball so drove through the Hole, which they look'd upon as miraculous, tho' it was only an accident, were wont to affirm, that the Man who did it was certainly a Thief, or an Adulterer, or would dye very soon, since he so fortunate, and this Success was talk'd of for a long time, till the like hapning [sic] again it was forgot.*[4]

This necessitated both skill and good fortune: the knee, buttock and hip were all used to propel the ball, while employing other parts of the body would incur a foul. Belts and padding, fashioned from leather and wood, were used to protect the players' hips and thighs. Moreover, the rings were at times either the same size or fractionally smaller than the ball, which made scoring even more problematic. According to Fray Toribio de Benavente Motolinía, "A man, throwing it by hand from close range could not put it in once in one hundred tries, nor in two hundred."[5]

Rubber balls were usually the size of a skull, and both quick and heavy. As one Spanish chronicler observed: "Jumping and bouncing are its qualities, upward and downward, to and fro. It can exhaust the pursuer running after it before he can catch up with it."[6] Or as the seventeenth-century Spanish historian Antonio de Herrera y Tordesillas succinctly pronounced: "The balls made thereof tho' hard and heavy to the hand, did bound and fly as well as our footballs."[7]

Given that it was lauded for its belligerence, it is unsurprising that the ball game often resulted in death and injury. Too often balls rebounded with such speed that players were unexpectedly caught in the face and stomach. The fortunate had to have their bruises cut open in order to have the blood clots removed. The less fortunate were struck dead instantly by the sheer force of impact. There was an art to playing the game well that provoked admiration in one of the great Spanish chroniclers, Fray Diego Durán:

> There were those who played it with such skill and cunning that in one hour the ball did not stop bouncing from one end to the other, without a miss, [the players] using only their buttocks [and knees], never touching it with the hand, foot, calf, or arm. Both teams were so alert in keeping the ball bouncing that it was amazing.[8]

Durán applauded the panache with which Indian males—highborn or low—played the game, also remarking on "the skill and lightness with which some play it, how much more are to be praised those who with such cunning, trickery, and nimbleness play it with their backsides or knees!"[9] In the manuscript of the *Book of the Gods and Rites*, the Dominican friar dedicated a chapter to the ball game in what must be one of the finest accounts of Aztec culture. Admonished during his lifetime for seeking to understand Aztec society and practice, and subsequently forgotten for over three hundred years, Durán chronicled a civilization that was on the verge of vanishing.

While applauding the noblemen for playing the game for "recreation and sport," he balked at those who played it "for profit and as a vice."[10] (Though the Spanish were not immune to the pleasures of gambling themselves.) The Aztec nobility, who took to the courts with great skill, often employed the services of proto-professional players, who were made to play each other on feast days. Gambling on ball games was rife, and with it came the obligatory superstitions. The ball, an object of reverence, was subjected to incantations and the creation of spells, so as to increase the chances for success on the court. Priests, "black as those who come from Hell,"[11] would consecrate ball courts by throwing the ball across the court four times; while games were played at midnight, especially on days of auspicious omen. In many cases there was a personal cost:

> *These wretches played for stakes of little value or worth, and since the pauper loses quickly what he has, they were forced to gamble their homes, their fields, their corn granaries, their maguey plants. They sold their children in order to bet and even staked themselves and became slaves, to be sacrificed later if they were not ransomed.*[12]

Though for the nobility the stakes could be even higher. The tyrannous ruler of Azcapotzalco, Maxtla, who eventually met his death on a ball court, was reputed to have lost the Tepanec empire in a ball game. While Axayacatl, monarch of Tenochtitlán, gambled his annual income, together with duty revenue, against Xochimilco. When Xihuitlemoc, ruler of Xochimilco, won the match, he was duly assassinated by his quondam ally. This was no game: this was war by proxy.

Cortés returned from the New World to the court of Charles V with a team of *ullamaliztli* (ball game) players who were drawn by the German painter Christoph Weiditz juggling various objects with their feet. (Although there is no evidence of the ball game having been played at court, López de Gómara disdainfully records that the team only included "eight tumblers, several very white Indian men and women, and dwarfs and monsters."[13]) Nevertheless, it was not long before the game that had charmed the very earliest conquistadors and that Motecuhzoma Xocoyotl had introduced to Hernán Cortés with such delight, was prohibited "because of the Mischief that often hapned [*sic*] at it."[14] Motecuhzoma should have listened to the portents long before the arrival of the Spanish. Nezahualpili, ruler of Texoco, had construed a comet, which had been observed in the east, as an ill omen: namely, the destruction of the empire. Motecuhzoma, however, failed to believe Nezahualpili's prophecy, so a ball game was held to test its validity. Motecuhzoma duly lost the game, and history took its course.

Tragically, by 1585, all 556 ball courts in the region had been destroyed, a process accelerated by the Iberians' proselytizing impulse. The Franciscan Motolinía, who believed Mesoamerican religion to be in effect devil worship perpetrated by Satan himself, saw the ancient ball game as a form of witchcraft. He recorded how the ball courts were destroyed because of their idolatrous nature. *Tchatali* had all but been eradicated.

.   .   .

By the twentieth century, all that was left were the shadows. In *Itinerary*, his intellectual memoir, Paz recalls Chichén Itzá, where in his youth he spent a week among the ruins:

> *One morning as I was walking through the Ball Game Court in whose perfect symmetry the universe seemed to rest between two parallel walls, under a diaphanous and impenetrable sky, a space where silence converses with the wind, a game field where constellations battle, altar of terrible sacrifices: on one of the reliefs that grace the sacred rectangle one can see a defeated player, on his knees, his head rolling on the ground like a sun decapitated from the heavens, while from his severed throat sprout seven jets of blood, seven rays of light, seven serpents . . .*[15]

The significance of the Grand Ball Court was not lost on the young Paz, who marveled at the explicitness of the Mayan bas-reliefs. It was here, in what had been one of the largest Mayan cities, which boasted thirteen ball courts, that the Spaniards would have "encountered history as well as geography."[16] And while death may not have been a prerequisite of the Aztec ball game, the Mayan variant (Pok-Ta-Pok) was steeped in chthonic mythology where death and the game had become inextricable. Even the court itself, architecturally configured so that it rested lower than the surrounding pyramids, may have represented a portal to Xibalba (Place of Fear), the terrifying underworld where the Lords of Death would be encountered.

The myth-historical narrative of the Quiché Mayan, contained in *Popol Vuh* (*Book of the People*), is arguably the most important Amerindian text that survives. Transcribed and translated into Spanish by Fray Francisco Ximénez at the beginning of the eighteenth century, the book recounts the creation myth of the Quiché and the gods' various attempts to create a conscious human being. Yet what makes the text even more remarkable is the importance of the ball game and its significance in Mayan culture.

Divided to into five parts, opening with the beguiling "This is the beginning of the Ancient World" and ending with the tragic finality of "This is enough about the being of Quiché, given that there is no longer a place to see it,"[17] the central myth in part three of the book records the various ball games played against the Lords of Death in Xibalba.

When the terrestrial ball games of Hun Hunahpu and Vucub Hunahpu, the sons of the divine grandparents (the oldest gods), disturb the Lords of Death, four messengers in the form of grotesque owls are dispatched from Xibalba. The message from these dark lords, who among their number include Demon of Pus, Demon of Jaundice, Scab Stripper, Blood Gatherer and Demon of Filth, is a firm challenge to a ball game in Xibalba. The brothers take up the offer and make their way across rivers of blood and pus and past a torrent of scorpions into the Underworld. Nevertheless, it is after a night in the Dark House, where they are given two cigars and a torch and told not to exhaust them, that Hun Hunahpu and Vucub Hunahpu are sacrificed for failing the trial. They are buried in the ball court, though the decapitated head of Hun Hunahpu is put in the fork of a calabash tree, which then duly bears fruit. When Blood Moon, the daughter of a Lord of Death, passes the tree, the severed head spits into her hand. Discovering she has fallen pregnant, Blood Moon is expelled from Xibalba through a hole in the ground. On earth she gives birth to the hero twin boys, Hunahpu and Xbalanque.

Once the hero twins discover a ball-game kit hidden in their house, they become accomplished players. Their games, like those of their father, upset the Lords of Death, who summon them in seven days. The message, however, is sent to their grandmother, who dispatches a louse to bid the boys into the Underworld. Unlike their fathers before them, the hero twins manage to outwit the Lords of Death, both on and off the ball court. Deception through illusion, however, allows the Lords of Death to be defeated, when Xbalanque decapitates Hunahpu and brings him back to life. Two Lords of Death, who are overly impressed by this trick, ask to be mock-sacrificed, only to die at the hands of the hero twins.

There have been numerous interpretations of the significance of the ball game and its centrality to Mayan culture. The ball, with its mysterious flight through the air, is thought to have reflected the movement of the sun and the solar system. While the transition from the terrestrial to the underworld is certainly the battle between light and darkness, day and night, good and evil as well as life and death. The ball court, on the other hand, represented both the removal and renewal of life: a place where the shedding of blood would bring rebirth and fertility. The very nature of the game meant that fortunes could be reversed at any point. While decapitation (of figures such as Hun Hunahpu) came to symbolize the maize god and the sacrifice of defeated players the crop harvest. Skull racks (*tzompantli*), such as those at Chichén Itzá, were placed adjacent to the ball courts: a timely reminder of those that had been sacrificed. The pitting of two opposing forces in a game of both skill and chance, where sacrifice was the endgame, acted as the harbinger of seasonal change.

While the Mesoamerican ball game may have been the most highly developed in the Americas, it was not the only ball game played by the Amerindians. As far south as Patagonia, *tchoekah* proved a popular pastime, played as a forerunner of hockey. A variety of rubber-ball games were played in what is now Colombia, Venezuela, Ecuador, Bolivia and the western heartland of Brazil. According to Eduardo Galeano, even "the Indians of the Bolivian Amazon say they have been kicking a hefty rubber ball between two posts since time immemorial,"[18] though this is more likely a tongue-in-cheek view of Latin American hegemony in all things football.

From the Otomac in the Venezuelan *llanos* (plains), who mostly used their shoulders to play, to the Amniapä of Brazil, who liked to wager arrows, the ball game flourished wherever there was rubber. The Apinayé, who live between the Amazonian rain forest and Brazil's savannah, played the rubber-ball game as part of an initiation ceremony into adulthood. The game's mythology tells the story of a madman who uses a leg bone to attack villagers at night. The villagers manage to capture the man and cut off his head, only for it to roll away and return in the light to exact its revenge. The head is tricked into a hole, whereupon it is covered with earth. In time a rubber tree grows from the burial site, and the sap is used to create the first rubber balls.

Even as late as the first decades of the twentieth century, explorers found that Amazonian Indians were playing with balls "not unlike football."[19] "In some parts of the Putumayo the author has seen the Indians at their games with these balls of caucho, and their cleverness with them was really remarkable as they passed the ball from one to the other, impelling it by means of their knees, hands and heads."[20]

Despite the conquistadors' efforts to drive it into extinction, variants of the ancient Aztec game survive to this day. (In Sinaloa, Mexico, a variation is still played as *ulama*; while in Michoacán, a nocturnal game is played, whereby the ball, symbolizing the sun, is set alight and moved around with sticks.) Nevertheless, in the writings of Durán and his fellow Iberian chroniclers, the evidence of this ancient ritual is still alive. The Dominican friar may have been unable to persuade a group of Aztec elders to play a game for him, but he remained captivated by "the games, tricks, and skills which these people performed with their feet, hands, and bodies."[21] Durán seemed to foretell what would be made clear for the world to see in the twentieth century: "I venture to say that there is not and never has been another nation in the world which has practiced greater and cleverer skills than these."[22]

PART ONE

THE DISCOVERY OF THE AMERICAS

1800–1950

CHAPTER ONE

NOT QUITE CRICKET

1800–1900

If I should die, think only this of me: That there's some corner of a foreign field that is forever England.

—Rupert Brooke, "The Soldier" (1914)

Put the bum, the gaucho, the peasant, the basic element of our population, through all the transformations of the best systems of education; in one hundred years you won't make of him an English worker, who works, consumes and lives in dignity and comfort.

—Juan Bautista Alberdi, *Bases and Starting Points for the Political Organization of the Argentine Republic* (1852)

The Cricket Clubs of Rio Janeiro and San Paulo had a set-to last month, the latter being the challenger. Each side won a match. The games were played in Viscount Maua's demesne at S. Paulo. The San Paulo club gave a grand banquet of 50 covers, and the toasts were eloquent and numerous.

—*The Standard* (June 3, 1875)

I t is commonly, but mistakenly, held that the first team sport the British introduced to Latin America was association football. It was, in fact, cricket.

On February 3, 1852, a cricket match was played in Buenos Aires. The pitch, even by mid-nineteenth-century standards, was notorious for its treacherous bounce, so much so that "swift bowling was apt to inflict wounds."[1] As the shadows began to lengthen on that late summer afternoon, the players, all of whom were of British extraction, could make out Federalist troops in the distance. These Argentines, defeated by their own countrymen at the Battle of Caseros, had fought for Juan Manuel de Rosas, the authoritarian *caudillo* dictator, who would shortly board the HMS *Locust* and spend the next twenty-five years in exile on a farm outside Southampton. When the battle-weary men filed past the ground, the cricketers stopped play and gave a gentlemanly round of applause. After a few minutes, the match was quietly resumed. Six years later, during the siege of Buenos Aires by General Justo José de Urquiza, who sought to reintegrate Buenos Aires into the Confederation, the cricket ground was cut off from the city. Oblivious to yet another internecine war and disgusted by the potential loss of a day's cricket, the British players successfully petitioned the besieging commander and were allowed safe passage across enemy lines to play their match. As one contemporary travel writer noted: "It was a very risky proceeding for a few men to spend the day surrounded by such characters as might be expected in the rear of Urquiza's army."[2]

Cricket matches such as these, often played in fantastic and improbable circumstances, were not exclusive to the Argentine republic. When W. H. Bullock traveled across Mexico in the mid-1860s, he was surprised at what he found at the "head-quarters of cricket," the village of Napolés.

During the voyage out from England I had heard that cricket was played in the country, but supposed it would turn out to be cricket of that degenerate sort which one finds occasionally played by the English residents in different parts of Europe. So that when I got to the ground, and found an excellent pavilion, a scoring-box, visitors' tent, the field marked out with flags, with the well-known letters M.C.C. (Mexico, not Marylebone, Cricket Club) marked upon them, and some eighteen or twenty players in flannels and cricket shoes, I was not a little astonished, and soon found out that I had to do with a very different sort of cricket to what I had expected.

Perhaps the most surprising part of the performance was that the best player on the ground was a Mexican, whose bowling and batting did infinite credit to the training which he received at Brice Castle School.

Among the English players were several gentlemen close upon sixty years of age, who all expressed to me their conviction that they owed much of the health and energy which they still possessed, in spite of forty years' residence in Mexico, to having stuck, through thick and thin, to their Sunday cricket. They assured me that they had never allowed political events to interfere with their game, which they had pursued unconcernedly, more than once, in view of the fighting going on in the hills around them.[3]

The game had also been played in the grounds of Latin America's only royal castle, the neoclassical Castillo de Chapultepec. Two years before his execution at the hands of a firing squad in 1867, the Austrian archduke Emperor Maximilian I of Mexico posed with Sir Charles Wyke, the British ambassador, for a surreal photograph, both wearing cricket "whites." In Rio de Janeiro, Emperor Dom Pedro II "the Magnanimous" was frequently seen at matches. Chilean cricket, however, was far less sophisticated. While a British Royal Navy lieutenant was heartened to see that Valparaíso possessed a cricket club, he lamented the poor ground and slope on which the game took place.

Wherever the British settled in Latin America, sporting—especially cricket—clubs were quickly established. As early as 1827, mine owners and businessmen founded the Mexico Cricket Club in Mexico City. In 1842, the Victoria Cricket Club, its name a tribute to Britain's young queen, was established by a group of Englishmen in Montevideo. Lima's Salon de Comercio, conceived three years later, would become the Lima Cricket and Lawn Tennis Club. Meanwhile, in Chile, the Valparaíso Cricket Club was inaugurated 1860, the second club to be formed there. Rio de Janeiro boasted a number of clubs—including the Anglo-Brazilian Cricket Club, British Cricket Club, Rio British Cricket Club and Artisan Amateurs Cricket Club—though matches seem to have been played on an ad hoc basis. (George Cox, whose son Oscar would be instrumental in establishing football in the Brazilian city, founded the Rio Cricket Club in 1872.) Clubs such as these, where expatriates could reinforce their culture and maintain their contacts, provided civilized respite from the hardships of day-to-day life in Latin America.

Cricket's popularity was not exclusive to the Spanish-speaking Americas. In the 1850s and 1860s, clubs blossomed in the United States. Fred Lillywhite, the cricketer-cum-entrepreneur, noted that "Cricket in Philadelphia has every prospect of becoming a national game"[4] when he toured Canada and the United States in 1859. Enthusiasm for this most English of sports in the United States would be short-lived, as baseball began to capture the nation's imagination. This would also be true for the northern Latin American republics, where baseball was the favored pastime among Yankee workers. Proximity proved an unfair advantage for the United States, so that her influence from the mid-nineteenth century onward stretched from Mexico, through Central America, and into Colombia and Venezuela. Cricket in Mexico, though popular within the expatriate communities of Pachuca, Puebla and Monterrey, could never compete with baseball. (Baseball would later usurp football in Nicaragua, Panama, as well as along the coastal regions of Colombia and Venezuela.) Even the myth that Abner Doubleday invented baseball, for which there is scant evidence, has a curious Mexican provenance. During the occupation of Mexico City in the Mexican-American War, Doubleday was said to have encouraged his cadre to play the game in the Halls of Montezuma. With no other bat to hand, an Illinois army volunteer employed General Antonio López de Santa Anna's wooden leg, which had been requisitioned as war booty.

With her commercial interests displaced by the United States in the northern republics, Britain would have to settle for exerting her considerable influence over Brazil, Uruguay, Argentina, Chile and Peru. Her attitude to these Latin republics—which would always be imbued with certain high-handedness—differed little from that of Spain. The quest for "El Dorado" remained, though it now spoke a different language. Under Iberian rule, South American trade with imperialist Britain had been a somewhat erratic affair. Initially independence failed to ignite local investment, and though in 1808 40 percent of British exports found their way to Latin America, it proved to be an arrant overestimation of what was an unknown market. By the late 1810s, these nascent republics had started to attract foreign investors, who could provide the necessary expertise for developing infrastructure and mining projects, especially in Mexico and Peru. By 1822, Latin American governments had started to float bonds in London. Gran Colombia was the first republic to do so, followed by Chile and Peru. Such was the appetite for Latin American investment that the fictional Republic of Poyais, invented by a Scottish adventurer, issued a bond. After three years, the loan bubble finally burst when the Bank of England raised the lending rate. The defaults now came in quick sucession: Peru, Gran Colombia, Chile, Mexico, Argentina and the Federal Republic of Central America. This lesson in financial mismanagement would set the tone for the next two centuries.

· · ·

By the 1860s and 1870s, foreign investors began to flock back to the region despite the inherent trading risk. The products varied from country to country. Argentina and Uruguay produced meat, wool and hides; nitrates and guano were exported from Peru; coffee, sugar and rubber from Brazil; copper and nitrates from Chile. The British, ever keen to act the mediator, provided banking, insurance and other services. Fortunes were made as quickly as they were lost. Investors were particularly drawn to infrastructure projects, in the form of railway and utility companies, which would give the British greater influence than the size of her expatriate communities would suggest. In the 1880s, the British began to exert a commanding presence in the railway market, having bought both railway lines and concessions from Latin American governments. The Santos–São Paulo Railway in Brazil became one of the most lucrative ventures on the continent, dominating coffee exports. These railway networks that radiated from capital city across the continent, for the most part operated and manned by the British, would be instrumental in advancing football in the late nineteenth and early twentieth centuries. Railway workers, both local and British, across the continent formed teams, and the ease with which the new lines allowed swift movement between hitherto remote locations encouraged the development of competitive matches. By the outbreak of the First World War, Argentina would have the largest network on the continent, which would give her a sense of national cohesion, if not identity. The Argentinian version of "Manifest Destiny"—Roca's Conquest of the Desert (Conquista del Desierto) in the 1870s and 1880s—may have been genocide under the guise of civilization, but it catalyzed the railway industry.

Industrial superiority, coupled with a perceived moral ascendency derived from their vast empire, afforded British immigrants and workers a position in society that was closed to those who had emigrated from the poorer European nations. The continent, especially on the Pacific coast, where riches were thought to be most abundant, proved a draw for many speculators, scrupulous or otherwise, who sought to take advantage of natural resources and cheap labor. In the 1870s, an English traveler in Peru discerned a distinct lack of ethics among the country's new rich, which was not untainted by snobbery: "Men who would never have been anything but lackeys in their own country have become masters of land and money in Peru . . . [they]

were noted for neither moral nor intellectual capacity, utterly innocent of any culture or regard for it."[5] Over thirty years later, the British were still being accorded an astonishing degree of respect,
regardless of their social class or education. "From the moment of his
arrival on Brazilian soil, an Englishman, even the very humblest
specimen of his race, in scholastic parlance, 'goes up one.' He is transformed from Bill Jones to Senhor. His views are respected, and, however profound his ignorance concerning the world and its inhabitants,
he will not be told peremptorily to 'shut up.'"[6] Britain stood for industry, modernity and progress, something that could not be said for the
agrarian economies of the Iberian Peninsula and Italy.

The late nineteenth century had witnessed immigration to South
America on a substantial scale. Immigrants may have come looking
for the life that their home countries had failed to provide, but some
were sorely disappointed. Many even returned. In Brazil, the coffee
plantations attracted workers, especially from Italy. The conditions
that greeted many of these workers were so bad that in 1885 the Italian government published a leaflet warning against migration to Brazil. In London, *The Times* warned its readers of the dire conditions to
which Yorkshire workers were exposed in São Paulo. Immigration
could also be selective, with immigrants tending to congregate where
their fellow countrymen had already settled. The Welsh settled in
Patagonia, while the Germans and Italians opted for southern Brazil.
Indentured Koreans worked the henequen industry in Mexico and
Chinese laborers worked the sugar and cotton plantations in Cuba
and Peru. Between 1870 and 1900, Latin America more than doubled in population, growing from 25 million to 62 million. During
this period Brazil, a country that actively sought immigration, grew
from 3 million to 18 million. With the abolition of slavery, cheap
labor was sought, especially for the coffee plantations. And yet it was
Buenos Aires that became the first city in Latin America whose population broke the million barrier. By 1914, this port city had a
foreign-born population of 30 percent. In a century, Buenos Aires

had been transformed from a colonial city, which under Iberian rule had contributed little in terms of commerce, into a proto-European metropolis.

The *criollo* (creole) upper classes, always susceptible to European values that could be worn as a badge of ascension, mimicked those whom they saw as their betters in both belief and custom. Though relatively small in number, the British were able to maintain a profile that belied their size. Thus, when it came to sporting events, the local *criollo* population could not afford to ignore what were seen initially as the outlandish antics of the British.

The British would attempt to consolidate their position in one country in particular. Of all the republics, Argentina proved to be the closest the British ever came to establishing a colony in the region. In the 1890s, a United States consul, posted in Buenos Aires, wryly observed: "It almost seems that the English have the preference in everything pertaining to the business and business interests of the country . . . They are 'in' everything, except politics, as intimately as though it were a British colony."[7] Paradoxically, it would be the very country that would endure the most fractious relationship with Britain over the next century that would also be the first to take up football.

The Lands That England Lost

The myth that football was introduced to South America by uncouth sailors who played free-for-alls on the docksides of the continent as they waited to pick up their cargo is so good that it has become accepted as truth. In his paean to the beautiful game, *Soccer in Sun and Shadow*, the Uruguayan polemicist Eduardo Galeano poeticizes the story told by his fellow countryman:

> *Outside the madhouse, in an empty lot in Buenos Aires, several blond boys were kicking a ball around.*

"Who are they?" asked a child.

"Crazy People," answered his father. "Crazy English."

Journalist Juan José de Soiza Reilly remembers this from his childhood.[8]

Football, however, was born of the British club, where it would supersede cricket as the game of choice. The idea that sport in Latin America was somehow propagated by the local working-class criollos watching sailors on shore leave remains rooted in myth. In the nineteenth-century cricket, football and rugby were the preserve of expatriates, who in turn were aped by the *criollo* elites. Nevertheless this bewildered attitude toward the "crazy" English—Englishness and Britishness to this day remain interchangeable in Latin America—obtained even as late as 1896 in Rio de Janeiro, where a Brazilian journalist observed: "In Bom Retiro, a group of Englishmen, a bunch of maniacs as they all are, get together, from time to time, to kick around something that looks like a bull's bladder. It gives them great satisfaction or fills them with sorrow when this kind of yellowish bladder enters a rectangle formed by wooden posts."[9]

In turn, British attitudes to Latin America had always been ambivalent at best. And their early dealings with the viceroyalty of the Río de la Plata—culminating in the humiliating conclusion to Sir Home Popham's ill-fated and unsanctioned expedition to Buenos Aires and Montevideo in 1806–1807—exemplified the British government's confusion regarding its policy toward the continent. Popham had sought to conquer this part of the Spanish empire by provoking unrest in Buenos Aires. Yet he underestimated the local *criollos*, who would fight valiantly against the invaders and refuse to submit to another colonial power. Even before the British withdrawal, Lord Castlereagh had dismissed "the hopeless task of conquering this extensive country against the temper of its population."[10] While *las invasiones ingleses* (the British invasions) may loom large in the annals of Argentine and Uruguayan history, reinforcing the myth of *criollo* exceptionalism, they are all but forgotten on the part of the British. Failure to take the Río de la Plata (River Plate) did not end British interest in the region. Unable to exert its dominance on Argentina directly, Britain sought a more "informal" route—through commerce. And with commerce came the British obsession with ball games. The Río de la Plata proved especially fertile ground for these most English of pursuits.

Cricket had come to Argentina early. The Buenos Aires Cricket Club was founded in 1831, with a membership of twenty-five, but it was not the first time the country had witnessed the game. During *las invasiones ingleses*, the British troops had found time to revive "the national diversions of horse-racing, and cricket, for which we always carried the materials."[11] By the 1850s, the Buenos Aires Cricket Club was established as the preeminent club in the capital and would play ad hoc matches against visiting elevens, made up of British naval officers on shore leave. In 1864, the club thrashed an eleven from the HMS *Bombay* by seven wickets, only for the ship to be destroyed by fire off the coast of Uruguay. Three years later a cricket match took place that would set the tone for one of the most fiercely fought rivalries in sporting history. Montevideo's proximity to Buenos Aires—together with her shared history under the viceroyalty of Río de la Plata until the second decade of the nineteenth century—had formed an uneasy bond between the two countries. (Uruguay, dwarfed by both Argentina and Brazil and whose independence was abetted by British intervention, would later shape its identity through football.) In 1868, the Buenos Aires Cricket Club, captained by the British consul Frank Parish, played the Monte Video Cricket Club (MVCC) in the Uruguayan capital. The match would have been held as early as 1864, but political upheaval in Uruguay led to its being postponed. Although the match was played by "11 B. Ayreans contra 18 Montevideans," all the players were British. The Uruguayan president Pedro Varela believed that even though both teams consisted of Englishmen and sons of Englishmen, who never wished to be considered anything else, "in the thing they loved the most, which was sport, they took Uruguayan and Argentine nationalities."[12] The following year a second "international" took place in Buenos Aires. Between 1868 and the Second World War, twenty-nine such matches were played between these Río de la Plata rivals, of which Argentina lost only six.

Cricket, however, remained an acquired taste for the *criollo* population and a recherché sport for the elites. (Argentine cricket was played to subcounty standards in the 1920s and 1930s.) Even in the second half of the twentieth century, by which time Argentina had cemented its identity, the game continued to be seen as a symbol of British imperialism. When the Buenos Aires Cricket Club's pavilion burned down in 1946, bad luck was not deemed to have played its part: rather the hand of the Peronist government was suspected. Worse was to come in 1953, when the majestic Jockey Club also fell victim to Peronist arsonists. Several masterpieces, including Goya's portrait of Don Antonio de Porcel, together with the 50,000-volume library, were destroyed. When the fire brigade was telephoned, the reply was unnervingly curt: "We have no instructions to put out a fire at the Jockey Club."[13]

.   .   .

In 1867, the Football Association's Laws of the Game—which had been codified in December 1863 after heated debate and sought to unify the game and differentiate it from rugby—were sent to the editor of *The Standard* in Buenos Aires. The editor, Edward Mulhall, forwarded the rule book to Thomas Hogg, a keen games player. Six years earlier, Dublin-born Mulhall and his brother had established an English-language newspaper in order to serve the needs of the Anglo community, which was largely made up of English, Scottish and Irish immigrants. On May 6, the following announcement was printed in *The Standard*:

Foot Ball

A Preliminary Meeting will be held on Thursday evening next, at 7.30 p.m., in Calle Temple, opposite No. 46, for the purpose of making rules and regulations for Foot Ball Matches, to be played on the Cricket Ground, during winter.

All persons interested are requested to attend.

BY ORDER.

Buenos Ayres, May 6, 1867[14]

The match, scheduled for May 25, the republic's national day, had to be postponed due to a waterlogged pitch at the Boca Junction railway station. And so on June 20, 1867, the first official football match was played in Latin America, though it is possible that it had been played informally beforehand. Employing the Football Association's 1863 rules, "with some slight modifications," and playing in red and white caps respectively, the Blancos (whites) ran out 4–0 winners against the Colorados (reds) over one hundred minutes. The players were all British, except for William Boschetti, who had been born in St. Lucia. *The Standard* expected a large attendance, weather permitting. Walter Heald, the club's secretary, recorded the match day in his diary:

June 20th, Thursday. This being a holiday and the football match day, J. Hogg and I went out by the 10 [o'clock] train to Palermo to mark out the ground as we had settled to play on the cricket ground, after having placed all the flags we adjourned to the Confitería and had some bread and cheese and porter and soon after that, the rest of the players came out by the 12 o'clock train; we could not muster more than about 8 on a side and that made the work very heavy, we played for about 2 hours and then shut up, being utterly exhausted; we returned by the 3.30 train and I forthwith proceeded to dress for the L. as I was going out to dine with Barge previous to the meeting; my back was very painful and indeed seemed to take away all my appetite as I could hardly touch a thing at dinner; we dined at the Louvre with Kohman and had champagne and claret; I had to hold out [sic] 7 o'clock as our Lodge opened at that hour and they are very punctual in commencing business, particularly as it was the installation of W. M night; they were nearly a 100 present and the proceedings lasted until about 10 o'clock, I being made S.; on leaving the Lodge I went straight back to Temple and then at once to bed, but alas! Not to sleep as my back was so very painful that I got very little sleep that night as I could not rest long in any one position and there was no doubt that I was injured internally (probably in the region of the kidneys) from a severe blow in the side that I accidentally received from J. Hogg in a charge.[15]

Football may have come to Argentina early, but despite the club's promising start, it was short-lived. Rugby Union Laws were soon adopted by the club, only for the sport to be banned by the government in 1875 because of the number of injuries suffered by its participants. Even *The Standard* took up against the game, only for its rival, *The Buenos Ayres Daily News and River Plate Advertiser*, to come out in the game's defense: "Football is a capital game, as all Britishers know . . . although our friends *The Standard* run it down, and think it impossible to play without getting a rasper on the shin bone, or a bang in the eye."[16]

By the early 1870s, yellow fever and cholera, exacerbated by the lack of adequate sanitation, had depleted Buenos Aires. Civil wars, blockades, disease proved difficult conditions in which to conduct business. Published in 1870, Mansilla Fuentes's *Una excursión á los indios Ranqueles* (*A Visit to the Ranquel Indians*) paints Buenos Aires as "a vertiginous agitation, in the middle of narrow, muddy, dirty, fetid streets that block out the horizon and the clean, pure sky . . . all crowded together by egoism, like a bunch of disgusting shell fish."[17] Moreover, there was the inherent corruption of successive governments with which to contend. (A game at which the British were especially proficient.)

In June 1875, however, *The Standard* ran an editorial that would change the course of Argentinian football forever: "A meeting of the members of the Foot-ball Club was held . . . it was decided that the rules of the Foot-ball association should be adopted in lieu of Rugby rules under which the game has hitherto been played." It even provided a comical explanation for the uninitiated: "The game is essentially one of the legs."[18] Three years later, the Spanish-language *El Nacional* acknowledged the sport for the first time in its editorial, pronouncing, "this English game, it will not be long before we get used to it."[19] Hogg and his peers may have been the first to establish the game in Argentina, but it is to a Scot that the Argentinians still look as their founding father.

Born in Glasgow's Gorbals, a working-class area prone to emigration, and educated at the University of Edinburgh, Alexander Watson Hutton arrived in Buenos Aires on February 25, 1882. His early life had been blighted by the death of his parents and his brothers, the latter having been stricken by consumption. In Buenos Aires—now a burgeoning city of immigrants—Watson Hutton taught at St. Andrew's Scots School, but swiftly fell out with the school's board when it failed to grant his request for a playing field and gymnasium. In 1884, he established his own school, the English High School, where physical education would become part of the curriculum. Two years later William Waters, the son of Hutton's former landlady in Glasgow, arrived in the Argentine capital with a bag of leather balls. (Waters would later establish himself as one of Argentina's foremost importers of sporting goods.) When he brought the deflated footballs into the country, the customs officers found it impossible to classify what they thought to be wineskins or leather caps. An officer cleared the matter up by stating, "Things for the crazy English."

Watson Hutton's insistence on sport, especially football, may have been in part due to the tragic ill health of his immediate family. Nevertheless, the fervor with which he sought to proselytize his charges showed the influence of Arnoldian Muscular Christianity, which had been propagated through sport by the Reverend George Cotton, master at Rugby School under Arnold and later headmaster at Marlborough College. Manliness and physical health would be the ideal antidote to idleness and torpor. Moreover, having been set up as a bilingual and coeducational establishment, the school would be able to bridge the gap between the Latin and Anglo-Saxon: educating young Argentine men and women schooled in the English tradition. By the turn of the twentieth century, the school had produced hundreds of young men for Argentina's "leading commercial institutions and banks."[20]

The *criollos* also saw the transformative benefits of physical education. In October 1875, Domingo Faustino Sarmiento, the polemicist and ex-president of the republic, was made an honorary member of the Buenos Ayres Cricket Club. In his thank-you letter to the club secretary, Sarmiento was full of praise for the British and their pastimes: "When I saw the students of Oxford and Cambridge compete for their famous rowing prizes and the virile cricket matches, athletics and other games that the young in England practise, in order to exercise and develop their physical strength, I understood how 20,000 clerks and civil servants in India managed against 200,000 insurgent Sepoys, maintaining British dominion over 150 million inhabitants, until the arrival of the line troops."[21] Sarmiento believed that the favored pastimes of a nation were somehow reflected in its public virtues and history, while athletic games conserved the vigor of a race. In *Facundo: Or, Civilization and Barbarism*, one of the defining texts of nineteenth-century Latin America, Sarmiento sought to embrace the political liberalism of the Enlightenment and stem the flow of barbarism that he felt emanated from the pampas. (That these nascent republics would somehow regress to their pre-independence states would remain a defining anxiety well into the twentieth century.)

Football continued to be played, though it was not without its detractors. In the early 1890s, over four hundred deaths and injuries associated with the game were recorded in Britain. This news made its way across the Atlantic. Advertisements in the English-language press began to offer special insurance policies for those taking part in both football and polo matches. *The Standard* warned parents that, given football's violent nature, they should refrain from allowing their children to play it. Watson Hutton responded by stating that association football was one of the most healthy and least dangerous pastimes. While Watson Hutton had made a success of the English High School, out of whose alumni would be formed one the greatest teams in Argentina's history, it remained one of many English establishments in the city. (The fact that it was bilingual was due to the competiveness of the educational market rather any integrationist agenda on the part of the headmaster.)

Like the many other Scots who ended up teaching in Latin America—Alec Lamont became headmaster at St. Andrew's School in Buenos Aires, and Andrew Gemmell took a position at Mackay and Sutherland in Chile—Watson Hutton not only brought the game with him, but also brought a distinctive style of play, one that would come to define Latin American football. The English game's obsession with dribbling, which meant keeping the ball close to one's boots while a mêlée ensued, was verging on the solipsistic. The pass, at which the Scots excelled, was discouraged, often vehemently so. While playing for his country against Scotland in 1877, the Honorable Alfred Lyttleton was upbraided for not having passed the ball. His reply merely confirmed his social rank: "I am playing purely for my own pleasure, Sir!"[22] Queen's Park, a club Watson Hutton must have seen play in Glasgow, had developed a sophisticated "combina-tion" technique, in which dribbling and passing were combined into an art form. More important, this style of play allowed the players to work together as a team rather than eleven individuals. The pass not only put paid to the more aggressive aspects of the game, but in time would put an end to the cult of the amateur.

In 1887, the Buenos Aires Football Club played Ferro Carril Gran Sur (Southern Railway), a club attached to a railway company, in what is believed to be the first match in Argentina to be played strictly under football association rules. Given that the railwaymen were "mostly Rugby Union players," it is not surprising that the club from the capital ran out 2–0 winners.[23]

Until the 1890s, football in Argentina had been a sporadic affair, organized on an ad hoc basis, while utilizing a number of codes. It was only when Watson Hutton, following Alec Lamont's failed attempt to set up a championship, established the Argentine Associ-ation Football League (AAFL) with five teams in 1893 that the game in the republic developed any structure. Such was the popularity of the league that by 1899 a second division was added. It would not be the English High School that would dominate but Lomas Athletic Club, five-time winners between 1893 and 1900. The team won forty-six games. And yet those whom the gods wish to destroy they first call promising. In 1909, the team suffered the heaviest defeat in Argentine footballing history, succumbing 18–0 to Atlético Estudi-antes. This tawdry performance proved to be the last game the club ever played: that day Lomas Athletic switched codes to rugby.

Football had now moved up-country. In 1892, a football club was founded in the agricultural district of Lobos, one hundred kilometers from Buenos Aires, in order to alleviate the boredom of pampas life. Lobos Athletic Club would become one of the finest teams in the Argentine, narrowly losing to Lomas Athletic in a playoff for the championship six years later. In 1899, Lobos Athletic toured Mon-tevideo, thus becoming the first Argentinian club to do so. Having dispatched Central Uruguay Railway Cricket Club (CURCC) 2–0, the players had to seek asylum on a Royal Navy warship when political upheaval broke out. Nevertheless, the club's days were numbered. The two-hundred-kilometer round trip to play Lobos Athletic was beginning to wear on the *Porteño* (those who live by the port, i.e., Buenos Aires) clubs. In 1900, the AAFL restricted the league to playing facilities within a fifty-mile radius of the city. The *equipo de campo* (country team) duly folded.

A similar problem occurred three hundred kilometers northwest of Buenos Aires in Rosario, where the Central Argentine Railway Athletic Club (Ferrocarril Central Argentino) had been founded for the company's employees. Unfortunately the city's remoteness meant it was tough to find much in the way of decent opposition. Thus each morning a company board member would trawl the port in order to find a crew willing to play the railway team.

.   .   .

Where Argentina went, Chile duly followed. Though unlike Argentina, which had labored under the autocratic Rosas, the country had acquired a reputation for democracy early on. (This status, seldom established on the continent, would evaporate with the death of Salvador Allende in 1973.) The continent's great liberator, Simón Bolívar, saw Chile's potential early: "If any American republic is to endure, I am inclined to believe it will be Chile. There, the spirit of liberty has never waned; the vices of Europe and Asia will come late or never to corrupt the customs of that far corner of the world . . . in a word, Chile can be free."[24] By the twentieth century, such was the country's belief in its democratic tradition that it came to define Chilean culture. At the same time an anglophile tendency was not lost on fellow Latin Americans. "[Chile] is governed by an intelligent, renewable, and progressive aristocracy, similar to the English aristocracy," noted a Uruguayan scientist at the end of the century.[25] The preponderance of foreign interests led a Cuban diplomat to remark on the country's distinct lack of Hispanic characteristics.

Valparaíso had all the makings of a British city, in which a sense of English decorum obtained. The city proved pivotal to Atlantic-Pacific trade in the nineteenth century. Tragically the 1906 earthquake devastated the city, and this, followed by the opening of the Panama Canal eight years later, would provincialize what had hitherto been an international city. Yet it was here that football was first played in the 1880s. As in Argentina, British clubs, businesses and academic institutions furthered the game along similar lines. In 1892, Valparaíso Football Club was founded by David N. Scott, an English journalist who would become Chilean football's founding father. The club might have been established sooner had it not been for the civil war that had taken place the previous year.

Despite pockets of enthusiasm, the game languished in the Chilean capital. (Although a team of *criollos* did form the Santiago Wanderers, the first club to emerge from the Chilean barrio rather than from a quondam British club.) In 1893, a scratch Santiago team—Santiago Club—was put together in order to play the port city. Judging by the names of the players, there was little in the way of *criollo* influence in either team:

Valparaíso FC: Webb, McNaughton, Reynolds, Roberts, Bailey, Crangle, Baldwin, Woodgate, D. Scott, Fleming, Simpson.
Santiago Club: P. Scott, McColl, Coast, Madden, Rogers, Anderson, Hood, Melrose, V. Scott, Jones, Allan.

Valparaíso thrashed its opponents 7–2 and 5–0 over the two legs. Later that year a Valparaíso eleven played an international fixture against a Buenos Aires eleven at Viña del Mar. (Though it would not be until 1910 that a Chile national team would play an international.) The club would gain a reputation for high-scoring matches. When Santiago National Athletic was beaten 8–1, the team, with revenge in mind, hastily asked for a rematch. The following day Valparaíso showed no mercy: Santiago National capitulated by 9–0.

In 1894, a "committee of sports," including representatives from MacKay and Sutherland Athletic, Colegio San Luis, Victoria Rangers, Chilean, and Valparaíso FC, was convened to discuss the viability of an association. Chile became the second country in Latin America to establish a football association when the Foot-Ball Association of Chile (FAC) was formed in 1895.

After the foundation of the FAC, football began to boom. In the capital a host of teams were founded including Santiago City Club, Santiago Athletic Club and Santiago Rangers Football Club. Moreover the trend for teams to amalgamate had begun. In 1897, Santiago Athletic Club and Santiago Rangers, who because of their religious beliefs played only in the mornings and on special holidays, formed Atlético Unión under Juan Ramsay and his four brothers. The club would be given the flattering sobriquet "El Invencible" (The Invincible). Juan Ramsay was an iconic figure in the history of Chilean football. He would be described as "calm of temperament, with great enthusiasm . . . one of the purest and most brilliant backs that has performed on the pitch." Although he was Chilean by birth, the Spanish-speaking press extolled his Anglo demeanor: he was "English in all the acts of his glorious career."[26] By the end of the century, football had made its way to regional towns such as Coquimbo and Concepción, and even as far north as Iquique. The decade, however, belonged to Valparaíso FC. Unfortunately, history was not to prove kind to this most British of clubs. By 1918, the club had to be disbanded. Of the many Valparaíso FC players that had volunteered to fight for the British in the First World War, only one returned.

.   .   .

If ever there were two capital cities in Latin America that would enjoy a symbiotic relationship, it was Buenos Aires and Montevideo. Proximity may have strengthened cultural and financial ties between the cities, yet the Uruguayan capital could never truly rid itself of the parochial image that a flourishing Buenos Aires had foisted upon it. Football would allow the city to emerge from the long shadow cast by her neighbor.

British interests in the region's buffer state had always been robust. During the 1830s, the French blockade of Buenos Aires had driven foreign investment to the other side of the Río de la Plata. With foreign investment came the British. Thus the history of football in Uruguay unfolded along similar lines to that of Argentina. While sailors from the British ships, docked in Montevideo, may have played kick-abouts, it was more formal institutions that established football in the country. The Montevideo Cricket Club and its local rival, the Montevideo Rowing Club, both took up football but only as a secondary sport. (Montevideo Rowing practiced the art of "dropkicking the football.") For the game to flourish, the country required a proselytizer, who, like Watson Hutton in Buenos Aires, could impart the rules of the game. That role fell to a Cambridge-educated Englishman, William Leslie Poole.

Founded in 1874, the English High School closely resembled similar establishments across the Río de la Plata. It was here that Poole—by all accounts an accomplished athlete, excelling at football, rugby, rowing and cricket—took up a teaching post when he arrived in Montevideo in 1885. In 1891, an eighteen-year-old of Anglo-Brazilian-Alsatian parentage founded the country's first football club, Foot Ball Association. Henry Lichtenberger, an alumnus of the English High School, had learned the game under Poole's watchful eye. Paradoxically one of the club's statutes decreed that foreigners were barred from membership, even though all existing members were Uruguayan-born of British parentage. The first performances were underwhelming: 3–1 and 6–0 losses to a Montevideo Cricket Club that included Poole. Subsequently, the club changed its name to Albion Football Club and accepted foreigners, one of whom was Poole.

In the same year as Lichtenberger put together his team of friends and alumni, a sports club was conceived that, in the following century, would become one of the greatest teams to grace the game. Eleven kilometers from the city center, in the working-class suburb of Peñarol, Central Uruguay Railway Cricket Club (CURCC) was founded by the railway company's workers. Of the 118 founding members, seventy-two were British, forty-five Uruguayan and one German. The club's players sported a black-and-yellow-striped kit, based on the colors of George Stephenson's Rocket steam locomotive. The standard of football in these early years remained low. (The Montevideo Cricket Club dispatched Albion and CURCC 10–0 and 8–0 in a nascent round-robin tournament.) By 1895, CURCC had appointed its first *criollo* captain. Skilled in the art of dribbling and an early idol of the stands, Julio Negrón could play in every position on the field. (He later went on to win four polo championships with Hurlingham in Buenos Aires.) The notion that the *criollos* might take to the game and better it was now not inconceivable. In the 1890s, a young boy watched a match at the Montevideo Cricket Club, where his father worked as a grounds-man. During the match he was heard to say: "I could play better than they can. If only they would let me play, they'd see." This young boy, Juan Peña, would eventually play outside right for Peñarol, winning the championship in 1900, 1901 and 1905, before transferring to Belgrano in Buenos Aires. He scored the first official goal for the club after the Uruguay Football Association League was founded. But it was the sheer force of his shot that made him famous. One of Peña's penalties was said to have killed a goalkeeper.

Although Uruguayan football failed to develop as quickly as the Argentinian game, proximity to its neighbor would prove invaluable. Whereas other Latin American countries would have to content themselves with domestic football alone, competitive internationals between Uruguay and Argentina started early. In August 1889, the first international outside of the United Kingdom was played at the Montevideo Cricket Club, where Buenos Aires FC beat Montevideo FC 3–1. Throughout the last decade of the nineteenth century teams from either side of the Río de la Plata played a yearly match. These encounters tended to be one-sided affairs with the Argentinian elevens running out clear winners. (In 1892, the Montevideo FC went down to ten men because one of the fullbacks could not play with an abscess in his eye.) In 1898, the Albion FC played five matches against three Argentinian teams (Belgrano Athletic Club, Lobos Athletic Club and Lomas Athletic Club), managing to salvage a draw on only one occasion. At the end of the century, despite all the progress the country made, it seemed that Uruguay would have to wait a long time to compete against its neighbor.

.   .   .

By the beginning of the twentieth century, the British in Lima had shrunk to some four hundred residents, compared to the three thousand Italians now living in the capital. This was a far cry from the late 1850s, when the British boasted a sizable community in the country. Football had been played as early as 1870, having been brought to Lima from England by one Alexander "Alejandro" Garland. Nevertheless, the Guerra del Pacífico (War of the Pacific 1879–1883), in which Peru and Bolivia were challenged by Chile over the exploitation of nitrates in the region, stemmed the development of any sporting activity in the country and it was not until 1892 that the first official football match was played in Peru. According to the Spanish-language *El Callao*:

FOOTBALL

—On Sunday, August 7, a football challenge will take place between *Limeños* and *Chalacos* [inhabitants of Lima and Callao respectively] in Santa Sofia, Lima, organised by Messrs Larrañaga and Foulkes, starting at three in the afternoon.[27]

A year later Unión Cricket was founded with the express intention of playing cricket and tennis. These sports were usurped when Pedro

Larrañaga and John Conder introduced football to the club. By 1895, regular matches were played between the Lima Cricket and Football Club, which still flew the British flag, and Unión Cricket, whose membership included both foreigners and Peruvian gentleman of Lima's grander families. The seriousness with which the game was taken was evident when, in 1896, Unión Cricket imported turf from Britain in order to improve its playing facilities. A year later, such was the game's popularity that spectators were asked to pay admission. (When the HMS *Leander* played a Peruvian selection, there were over two thousand spectators.) By the late 1890s, clubs such as Association Football Club, Unión Foot Ball and Club Foot Ball Perú were being founded exclusively to play the game. It would be at schoolboy level that the game would gain momentum. In 1899, the football final of the Campeonato Atlético Nacional (National Athletic Championship) drew 20,000 spectators when President López de Romaña attended. The winning school, Nuestra Señora de Guadalupe, was entirely *criollo*.

Football and the Battlefields of Paraguay

In the twentieth century, Paraguayan sides would regularly prove to be among the toughest, most intransigent opponents on the continent. Yet in many respects Paraguay was also the most underrated footballing republic, overshadowed by the more obvious technical ability displayed by Uruguay, Chile and Peru. The country's fighting spirit—or *garra*—which made them so awkward to play against, can be traced to the second half of the nineteenth century.

While the authoritarian Rosas may have seen Uruguay and Paraguay as little more than insubordinate provinces of Argentina, Francisco Solano López had greater ambitions for his country. Independence had failed to establish democracy within this landlocked country. Moreover, a succession of dictators had sought to further an isolationist policy, whereby the country remained perennially alert against potential aggressors. (Dr. José Gaspar Rodríguez de Francia had sought to close the frontiers and make the country self-sufficient.) This was not undue paranoia but a function of the country's vulnerable geographical position in the center of the continent. Yet it was from here that Solano López sought to realize his dreams of creating an empire with Asunción at its center.

Propagating Paraguay's interests in a region where Brazil and Argentina sought hegemony and tiny Uruguay provided the buffer state between these two rivals, may have been inherently sensible, but all-out war was folly. An unhealthy interest in Uruguay led to the seizure of a Brazilian vessel on the Río Paraguay by Paraguayan forces. And instead of cultivating Argentina, Solano López made an incursion into Argentine territory in order to subjugate the south of Brazil and ultimately Uruguay. Tragically, Solano López's actions forced Brazil, Argentina and Uruguay into an uncomfortable and often fractious alliance that would nevertheless prove near fatal to his country. The Paraguayan War (or the War of the Triple Alliance) lasted for more than five years; even though the Argentine statesman Bartolomé Mitre impulsively exclaimed at the outset: "Tonight to the barracks, in eight days Corrientes, in two months Asunción."[28] Paraguay's only hope of success was to achieve a quick victory. Solano López, however, was merciless even with his own troops: officers, who fought under the legend "conquer or die," were executed if defeated. As the war drew on, Solano López became more unreasonable and mistrustful, especially of his own men. In the end the diminutive dictator was undone by a bullet to the thorax at the Battle of Cerro Corá.

The War of the Triple Alliance all but eviscerated the Paraguayan population. Only 28,746 men remained out of a surviving population that had been reduced from 525,000 to 221,079. The cost to the country was heavy, not only in terms of Paraguayan lives but also in territory. Paraguay would have ceded more of its territory to Brazil and Argentina had the rivalry between the latter two not been so heightened. Peace did not bring stability. The republic suffered numerous *golpes* (coups d'état) and saw thirty-two presidents between 1870 and 1932. Paradoxically, the slaughter reinforced Paraguay with a sense of heroism in the face of great odds, which has long since become ingrained in the country's culture and football. The words of Solano López's teenage son, killed by a lance, have echoed through the republic's history: "A Paraguayan [colonel] does not surrender."[29]

The aftermath of war, coupled with Asunción's geographical isolation, would delay the adoption of the English game. (Though, as early as 1886, a match was played in the capital.) One of the teams, made up of British railway workers, decided to call themselves "Everton" as a tribute to the Liverpool-based team. Yet, it took a Dutchman to bring football to this landlocked country. Wilhelm (William) Paats is regarded as the father of Paraguayan football, having brought the game to a country that lacked any formal practice of sport. Born in Rotterdam, Paats went to Argentina at eighteen in order to overcome a pulmonary illness. He moved upriver to Asunción, where he was offered a post as an accountant and became something of a polyglot (he is said to have spoken nine languages). It was on a trip to Buenos Aires that he bought a football at Harrods. Back in Asunción he would walk down the street with the ball in his hands, every now and then kicking it in the air. This act, which Paats felt would encourage the sport, provoked marked curiosity among children and adults alike. The "restless sphere" would then be passed around the onlookers to see whether they enjoyed playing with it.

Whether Paats in fact brought the "McGregor" football (endorsed by the founder of the English Football League, William McGregor) into the country remains open to conjecture. A similar story obtains, though this time with the great Paraguayan intellectual Juan Silvano Godoi as protagonist. Godoi is said to have purchased the "McGregor" at Harrods for twelve pesos, and then given it to his son. Lucio Sila Godoi, who would become president of Club Olimpia between 1902 and 1904, used the ball in Paraguay's first competitive match in the Plaza de Armas. Even the Asunción-based newspaper *La Tribuna* commented on the popularity of the game among the pupils at the Escuela Normal de Maestros who played "in their school uniform and returning home perspiring and wet, exposed themselves to harsh colds."[30]

By the end of the century, football had begun to penetrate the central and northern republics. Even though the influence of the British was not as marked here as elsewhere on the continent, *criollos*, educated abroad, were beginning to bring football home. In Ecuador, Juan Alfredo and Roberto Wright established the game in Guayaquil, the city in which they had been born. After living in England, the brothers settled in Lima, where they became members of the Unión Cricket de Lima. On moving back to Guayaquil, they brought with them a leather ball and subsequently founded the Guayaquil Sport Club in April 1899. In Bolivia the construction of the railways that helped exploit the country's natural resources brought the game with it. By the early 1890s, workers from the Antofagasta (Chile) and Bolivia Railway Company, which transported natural mineral resources between Pulacayo and Antofagasta, played football four thousand meters above sea level. The altitude gave the Bolivian Indians, who were used as cheap labor, an advantage over their European masters: they did not suffer *"muyu-muyu"* (local disease). In 1896, the Oruro Royal Football Club became the country's first football club, founded by *criollos*, some of whom had played the game in Chile. The founding articles stated that the object of the club was "to find a useful distraction . . . for the young and later to install a gymnasium."[31] The first match, in which only one Englishman played, pitted the "Reds" against the "Blues": the latter lost 7–4. Thirty-four years later at the inaugural World Cup, held in Montevideo, the Oruro Royal Football Club would form the basis of the Bolivian national team.

Corinthians in Brazil

For a country whose identity seems inextricably linked with the beautiful game, football failed to develop early in Brazil. Even so, the
country's sporting trajectory would closely resemble that of her
neighbors, despite her Portuguese heritage and cultural distinction
from the rest of Latin America. As with Brazil's neighbors it was the
British and their fondness for club cricket that laid the foundations
for football. Clubs were founded in the cities where the English
tended to settle, such as Rio de Janeiro, São Paulo and Bahia. But
unlike Argentina, Chile and even Uruguay, sport in Brazil, despite
its sizable British communities, somehow managed to lag behind the
rest of the region. Travelers to the country in the 1860s could not fail
to witness the paucity of culture and lack of physical exercise: "A
great want in Brazil is the out-door games, the debating clubs, the
cheap concerts, the lectures, the periodicals, and all the various appli-
ances which the European at home has at his command, to strengthen
and improve both mind and body."[32] Even fifty years later there were
still—mainly British—detractors who believed that sport could not
take hold in the country given that "tropical conditions . . . are not
conducive to a substantial expenditure of physical energy."[33]

As late as 1894, sport fell victim to geographical remoteness and
the lack of infrastructure. A letter sent from the Honorary Secretary
of Santos Athletic Club to "Cricket: A Weekly Record of the Game"
summed up the position of sport in Brazilian society.

*Thinking it might interest you to hear how cricket is carried on in these
warm regions by the "balance" of the English and Americans left over
from the ravages of the "Yellow Jack," I take the liberty of sending you
herewith our cricket fixture card for the coming season. As you will
see, we have to arrange or rather manufacture matches between the
members on account of the distance to any other cricket-playing community, the only outside matches we are able to play being against Rio de*

Janeiro, São Paulo and Campinas. Our club was only started in August 1890, so is not a very old institution, but there is plenty of enthusiasm, cricket being looked forward to as only Englishmen can look forward to it, even with the great difficulties we have to overcome, the greatest being that we are obliged to play on the sea beach, which is luckily very hard and makes a really good and true pitch with cocoa-matting laid down.[34]

In that same year, however, Charles Miller would arrive from England and change the course of Brazilian sport forever. Although born in São Paulo to a Scottish father and Brazilian mother, Miller was afforded a private school education at Banister Court in Hampshire, where he excelled at both cricket and football. Playing up front, as a center-forward and on the left wing, Miller tried out for Hampshire and St. Mary's in Southampton. It was for Hampshire that he played against an all-powerful Corinthian side—one full of England caps—only to lose by 6–3. Unlike the founding fathers in neighboring Latin American republics, Miller had had experience of the footballing boom in England. He had played the game to a high standard and had loved it. Thus, after his arrival, in Brazil, he would attempt to re-create what he had experienced in Hampshire. In 1927, shortly before his fifty-third birthday, Miller gave an interview in *O Imparcial*. He recounted his arrival from England all those years before:

On the quay at Santos, solemn, as if he were at my funeral, my father was waiting for me to disembark holding my degree certificate. But in fact I appeared in front of him with two footballs, one in each hand . . . The old man, surprised, enquired:

– What is this Charles?

– My degree, I replied.

– What?

– Yes! Your son has graduated in football . . .

The old man, in good spirits, laughed. I was off the hook.[35]

Whether Miller's rather roseate rendering was meant to be tongue-in-cheek will never be known. Surely it couldn't have been a mistake? Miller's father could never have welcomed his son off the boat, given that he had died eight years before in Glasgow. In constructing a narrative for its footballing history, Brazil needed a "beginning" and Miller seemed to have provided it. While much has been made of Charles Miller as the founder of Brazilian football, this, like so many other Latin American myths, may only be partly true. Football had been played the year before Miller's arrival in 1894 in Juiz de Fora, some two hundred kilometers from Rio de Janeiro, where it was overseen by Episcopalians. Indeed, as early as 1872, priests are said to have taught their charges the Eton Wall Game at the Colégio São Luís. Two years later sailors were seen playing a variation of the game on Gloría Beach in Rio de Janeiro.

In 1895, Miller organized a football match for the São Paulo Athletic Club (SPAC) shortly after the end of the cricket season. The players, who in the main worked for the London and Brazilian Bank, the São Paulo Railway and the city gas company, played eleven a side; though in the end only sixteen were actively engaged, while the others failed to display sufficent stamina to carry on. Yet football was not just a game for the British. The following year Mackenzie College, an American school in the city, started playing the game after a basketball was used as a football. In 1897, Hans Nobiling arrived in the city from Hamburg, with a set of rules from his quondam club. He sought out the local German community and its gymnastics club, and subsequently founded Hans Nobiling's Team. In 1899, after having had the name Sport Club Germânia rejected in favor of the more cosmopolitan Sport Club Internacional, Nobiling founded his own Sport Club Germânia.

.   .   .

Clubs consisting of German expatriates were not exclusive to Brazil: Atlético Aléman played in Chile, while in Montevideo the Deutscher

Fussball Klub was one of the founding teams of the Uruguayan league. The Germans, though not as numerous as the British, were sometimes found in the more remote areas of the continent. A British traveler in the late 1870s observed: "At present it may be said there is no English community in Caracas or any where else in Venezuela . . . the Club here, is entirely composed of Germans, who have also clubs at La Guayra, Puerto Cabello, Maracaybo and Ciudad Bolívar."[36]

.   .   .

By the end of the century football remained, for the most part, the preserve of the British. Though the influence and power they exerted within the continent were less than met the eye. While its citizens may have had a hand in everything from tin mining in Mexico to the construction of railway networks in Brazil and Argentina, Britain's sphere of influence would steadily diminish as that of the United States grew. Nevertheless, a roseate view of football in the late nineteenth century, even with its British, non-*criollo* roots, still obtains on the continent. Though thoroughly British in style—and devoid of the technical ability that would later come to define the Latin American game—nineteenth-century football is regarded as unsullied by commerce and corruption, characteristics that would later come to be seen as endemic in the region.

In Uruguay, where a fitful civil war would persist until 1904, the century played out with a tragedy on the pitch. Born in Brighton in 1871, Henry Stanley Bowles played center-forward for Preston North End before sailing for Montevideo, where he took up an accountant's position in the London and Brazilian Bank. Having scored the first international goal for his adopted country in 1890, Bowles would have his life cut short nine years later. On August 15, 1899, a tornado swept across the field at Punta Carretas and destroyed the makeshift wooden huts that served as dressing rooms for the players. Poor Bowles, in the wrong place at the right time, had been changing into his football kit.

Lack of allegiance to an empire, especially an English-speaking one, suggested that association football would never take hold in Latin America. It had even failed in the Dominions and other Anglophone territories, though cricket had succeeded in its stead. (In the West Indies, the shallow structure of society would allow the black working class to take up the sport and make it its own.) The sport that P. F. Warner had called "more than a game" laid the foundations for the beautiful game. The president of the Marylebone Cricket Club considered cricket to be "an institution, a passion, one might even say a religion. It has got into the blood of the nation."[37] Everything Warner believed cricket to be would also be true of football. In the twentieth century, football would become both a passion and a religion that would get into the blood of the whole of the continent.

CHAPTER TWO

BATTLES OF THE RIVER PLATE

1900–1920

The sport the world made its own was association football, the child of Britain's global economic presence, which had introduced teams named after British firms or composed of expatriate Britons (like São Paulo Athletic Club) from the polar ice to the Equator. This simple and elegant game, unhampered by complex rules and equipment, and which could be practised on any more or less flat open space of the required size, made its way through the world entirely on its merits.

—Eric Hobsbawm, *Age of Extremes:*
The Short Twentieth Century: 1914–1991 (1994)[1]

I have never seen such enthusiasm for the game as shown by the two Republics [Argentina and Uruguay] and everywhere one sees the hold it has taken on the people.

—Sam Allen, Secretary-Manager, Swindon Town FC (1912)[2]

It would be true to say that wherever the railways went, that was where football was introduced, as much in Argentina as Latin America.

—Alfredo di Stéfano (2002)

By the turn of the twentieth century, the Anglo-Saxon attitudes that had found expression on the pitch were seemingly absent off it. After nearly a century of independence, the nascent Latin American republics, many of which had found it difficult to establish peace within their borders, were still struggling to forge a coherent sense of identity. In 1900, the Uruguayan man of letters José Enrique Rodó published an essay that would change the way in which Latin Americans thought about themselves. Though in many ways a victim of its own oratorical grandiloquence, *Ariel* sought to construct a sense of pan–Latin American identity. This call to arms, whose popularity would endure for decades, pitted Ariel (the spiritual in the form of Latin civilization) against Caliban (the utilitarianism and materialism of the United States). Latin American identity, brittle at best, was being fashioned through a French interpretation of the classical ideal, while maintaining a staunch anti-*yanqui* position. And yet Rodó remained conflicted: "As for me, you have already seen that, although I do not love them [United States], I admire them."[3] This would reflect the ambivalence of U.S.-Latin American relations in the twentieth century. The Spanish defeat at the hands of the United States in Cuba two years before had understandably hardened the region's intellectuals against what they saw as North American aggression. Two poets, the Nicaraguan Rubén Darío and Cuba's José Martí, had taken a similar stance but were far more eloquent in their execution. Rodó, who had failed to recognize his own country's historical whitewashing of its indigenous past, might have been better critiquing his own continent with the same vigor he had applied to the United States. For intellectuals, such as the Peruvian García Calderón, it was fear that had undermined the continent's relationship with her northern neighbor. "To save themselves from Yankee imperialism the Latin American democracies would almost accept a German alliance, or the aid of Japanese arms. Everywhere the Americans of the North are feared."[4] The question of identity would continue to exercise the continent's greatest minds for the next century.

Where identity could be swiftly acquired was on the pitch. Nowhere was this more evident than in Buenos Aires, the game's birthplace on the continent. Immigration—by 1914, the capital's population had swelled to 2,035,031—and rapid urbanization provided the catalyst for the foundation of a host of football clubs. Spain and Italy had provided the country with the majority of its immigrants, yet there were also sizable influxes from the Middle East as well as those refugees escaping the pogroms of Eastern Europe. Immigrants tended to retain their ethnicity, in some cases preserving their customs and language as a badge of honor. For many the promise of an agrarian paradise with high wages had failed to materialize: the country being too vast and remaining in the hands of too few. There were the Italian *golondrinas* (swallows), agricultural laborers who flitted between Europe and Latin America, and made hay while the sun shone in both hemispheres. The dearth of purchasable land forced many farmworkers to find work in the capital. Argentina would become a land of polarities: in Europe "rich as an Argentine" would become a byword for the affluent, while at home the urban poor, of which there were many, lived in *conventillos* (tenements), usually in terrible conditions.

During the first decade of the new century, numerous football clubs, established by young men regardless of their social background, began to flourish. Such was the enthusiasm for the game that by 1904 *La Argentina* reported, "The clubs that do not form part of the league have multiplied . . . over 400 and a number more than 6,000 enthusiastic *foot-ballers.*"[5] Middle-class students were as likely to set up a club as those from the expanding working classes. With its attendant symbols of belonging—grounds, colors and rules—the football club could provide a firm identity for those whose sense of who they were had been blurred by immigration. The Argentinian game laid its roots locally in the barrio (a defined neighborhood, which would retain its own character and identity), a place from which it would never truly be extracted. River Plate and Boca Juniors, which were founded in 1901 and 1905 respectively, were both from the barrio of La Boca, though the former would move in the early 1920s. From Mataderos to Avellaneda, the industrial heart of the capital where Racing and Independiente were established, the expanding metropolis offered clubs' local fans a sense of belonging that would even trump national loyalty.

It was regular international competition that allowed River Plate football to develop more quickly than elsewhere. The geographical proximity of Montevideo to Buenos Aires—two capital cities with such similar customs and traditions that they might have belonged to the same country—meant that an amicable rivalry was established early on. In 1901, Albion Football Club hosted its Argentinian rivals, Belgrano Athletic Club, and held a postmatch dinner that would not have shamed the grander tables of London and Paris.

MENÚ

Albion Football Club

Montevideo

Dinner given in honour of the Belgrano Athletic Club

On Sunday June 23 est. 1901

HORS D'OEUVRE

Assortis à la Bienvenue / Canapé d'anchois à la Bonne Amitié

POTAGE

Tortue Américaine à la Belgrano

RELÈVE

Brotola Normande «Aux Vainqueurs»

ENTRÉES

Petits pâtés de foie gras au Xme. Anniversaire /

Filet Durandaux, Cresson au Football for ever /

Bécassines bandées à la Referee

RÔTIS

Poulets santés Lyonnaise à l'Albion

LÉGUMES

Petits pois à l'anglaise à la Prensa Uruguaya

ENTREMETS

Boudin al Kirsch à l'Argentine

DESSERT

Fruits de saison à l'Uruguayenne

VINS

Sauternes—Château Margot—Médoc

Café à la Brésilienne—Liqueurs à la Parisienne
Cigares à la Cubaine
7.30 p.m. Rôtisserie Severi[6]

No other two nations in the history of the game would play each other as often as Uruguay and Argentina. In 1905, Sir Thomas Lipton, the Glasgow magnate who had grown up in the same city as Watson Hutton, bequeathed a cup open only to native-born players of both countries. The inaugural match of the Lipton Cup ended in a goalless draw, in spite of extra time having been played. As visitors, the Uruguayans were awarded the cup. Not to be outdone by Lipton, Nicanor Newton started his own cup competition the following year. The Argentinians ran out 2–1 winners, with Eliseo Brown managing to dribble past a record number of six players in a virtuoso performance.

The English Are Coming . . .

The British had introduced football to South America, but they were never keen proselytizers. While the game had moved on since its inaugural match in Palermo, it had hitherto lacked proper instruction. When English teams began to embark on Latin American tours in the first decade of the twentieth century, it would be the beginning of a process that would change the game forever. Not only would it be a primer in how to play à l'anglaise but it would also help develop the game into a spectator sport.

In 1904, Southampton, which plied its trade in the Southern League, was the first British team to make the arduous journey south. Seeking to expand the activities of the Sociedad Hípica (Equestrian Society), Baron Antonio De Marchi had invited the professional club to play a series of matches in Buenos Aires. Born in Italy, De Marchi had become the son-in-law of Julio Argentino Roca, the president of the republic. The first match, in which Alumni was beaten 3–0, resembled a society function, with all the best families of Buenos Aires turning out, rather than a sporting event. Southampton made light work of the capital's opposition, before crossing the River Plate to thrash a Uruguayan eleven 8–1. Southampton, especially the intelligent play of England international George Molyneaux, had certainly impressed the creoles.

The following year Nottingham Forest made its way to Montevideo, Rosario and Buenos Aires. The players, who were due to play seven matches, kept themselves fit on the passage over by playing cricket on deck. For the English team, the tour was an unmitigated success. The score lines reflected their superiority: Liga Uruguaya was beaten 6–1, Británicos 13–1, Liga Argentina 9–1. Even the great Alumni team was thrashed 6–0 in front of 10,000 spectators at the Sociedad Sportiva ground. By the end of the tour, Nottingham Forest had scored fifty-one goals and only conceded two. Such was the esteem in which Nottingham Forest was held that Independiente copied the club's red strip. Scoring at will, however, would prove less easy for the English club when they returned home: at the end of the following season they were relegated to the Second Division on goal difference.

In what would become an annual event, the Argentine Football Association now looked to Britain's dominions. The South African Football Association was invited to participate in a three-way tournament, which would include an English side. In the end Fulham FC failed to make the journey to Buenos Aires, allowing the South Africans to embark on a twelve-match tour of Argentina, Uruguay and Brazil. South African football may have developed along similar lines to that in Latin America—established by Anglo settlers and the British army during the closing decades of the nineteenth century—but it was further advanced. This was due in part to the Corinthian tours of 1897, 1903 and 1907, which had helped improve the level of the South African game. While the South Africans—many of whom were from Great Britain—may have been below the standard of the British, they were too good for many South American teams. In Buenos Aires a university eleven (Universitarios) was hammered 14–0, the highest winning margin for a touring side, while in Montevideo a combined side (Combinados) went down 6–1. Brazil provided little more in the way of competition when the Scratch-Team Paulista, an eleven that included Charles Miller, lost 6–0 in its first tour match. The "representatives of the Dark Continent,"[7] who happened to be Caucasian to a man, had proved a triumph both on and off the field. It would be against the Alumni that the South Africans lost their only game by the narrow margin of one goal. The match, played in front of 12,000 spectators including the president of the republic, would be a turning point in Argentina's sporting history. Politics had yoked itself to the game. The rematch, however, failed to live up to expectation when the South Africans won by two goals to nil.

In spite of the popularity of the South African touring side, no foreign team would tour the region for another three years. In 1909 Everton and Tottenham Hotspur made the 11,000-kilometer trip to the Río de la Plata. The Everton director, E. A. Bainbridge, saw both teams as "pioneers of football in foreign lands." Tottenham, recently promoted to the First Division, had the heavier schedule, playing seven matches including two exhibition games against Everton. Shortly after the teams had disembarked, the two touring sides played each other in front of the president of the republic. The first match ended in a 2–2 draw, with Walter Tull scoring for Tottenham. Tull, who would make ten appearances for the North London club, became the first black player to play in South America, just as he had also been the first black outfield player to play professional football in England. The spectators quickly took to the young striker. "Early in the tour Tull has installed himself as favourite with the crowd," reported the *Buenos Aires Herald*.[8] Tragically Tull died in action in 1918, having survived the battles of the Somme and Ypres. Although Tottenham Hotspur lost the second leg 4–0 to Everton, it won all its other matches. The Uruguayan League and Rosario were dispatched 8–0 and 9–0 respectively, though it could only score five against an Alumni team that comprised six players called Brown. Everton, the reigning runners-up of the First Division, only managed to beat the Uruguayan league by two goals to one, and blamed an under-whelming performance on a substantial lunch that had been eaten prior to the match. Though the tour proved a success, the exhibition matches between the English sides were not as popular as those they played against the local teams. Partisanship had started to take hold with the *criollo* spectators cheering on their own. On the way home Tull acquired a parrot in Brazil, only for the bird of ill omen to die on the day that the club's North London rival, Arsenal, was pro-moted to the First Division in its stead.

. . .

By the time the legendary Corinthians toured Brazil in 1910, they were a team on the wane. The successful tours of South Africa, Canada and the United States as well as Germany, Hungary and Austria were consigned to the past. The establishment of the Amateur Foot-ball League in 1907 had put paid to what had been the most famous football team in the world. Nevertheless, the Brazilian tours of 1910 and 1913 showed the Latin Americans how football might be played. The opening match of the first tour might have yielded a shock result when a championship-winning Fluminense—founded by Oscar Cox, a young upper-class Brazilian, whose idea the tour had been—opened the scoring after a minute. Normal service was resumed shortly thereafter when the British side put ten goals past the Flumi-nense goalkeeper. No quarter was shown in the following match when Corinthians beat Rio 8–1. Associação Atlética das Palmeiras was brushed aside by two goals to nil, though by now these matches had became more of a social event: "There was a great number of people . . . There were also private cars, straw hats, blasting of horns and French perfume in the air. An extremely fashionable event, that first Corinthian game on Paulista ground. To watch football was 'the thing to do.'"[9] In the following match against Paulistano, passions would run high: "On one occasion the referee was strongly criticised for giving the Corinthians a goal when the ball struck the cross-bar and bounced in and then out again. A small nigger boy was so incensed at this that, evidently stirred by patriotic feelings, he assaulted Timmis in the correct place with his bare foot. His retreat was so rapid that, to the intense amusement of the Corinthians, the victim could do nothing."[10] The last match, against a SPAC side turning out as *Os Estrangeiros* (the Foreigners), was played in front of a crowd of 10,000.

. . .

By the 1910s, the cordiality afforded touring teams was beginning to sour. When Swindon Town toured Uruguay and Argentina in 1912, it attracted 20,000 spectators in its opening match against combined "Norte" (North) eleven, but the level of aggression on the pitch was met with disappointment by the local press. Two years later Exeter City became the last English team to tour the region before the outbreak of the First World War. The club was by no means fashionable, plying its trade in the Southern League. Yet, in spite of its lowly status, the club won six of the eight matches it played in Argentina. Exeter, though no strangers to unprepossessing football, played Racing in a match that would foreshadow the darker side of the Latin American game. After Exeter had scored three goals against the Avellaneda side, the highly strung club secretary ran onto the pitch with a revolver. Once the referee was persuaded to continue the match, he immediately awarded a penalty in favor of the Argentinians. Though the games were well attended, the Argentinians came to appreciate the English game for what it was—rough and inelegant. This, however, was not the first time that the English had had their gainsayers: the great Corinthian touring sides had also been accused of overly aggressive play. The Argentinians, on the other hand, were offered some advice from a British point of view. The Exeter manager thought the players "clever in dribbling and fast, but their weak point is that they are individualists and try to shine each above their fellows. They will never achieve real success until they recognise that it takes eleven men to score a goal."[11] Individualism had come to the Argentinian game early. It was a vice that the game could never truly eradicate.

Culturally more at home with Latin opposition, Torino and Pro Vercelli were the first Italian sides to tour the continent. When São Paulo's LBF league invited Torino, which was also due to play in Buenos Aires, in 1914, the competing APEA league, together with Rio's AMEA, quickly summoned the Piedmontese. Torino was too strong for the Brazilians, though the club fared less well in Argentina, where it slumped to defeats against a magisterial Racing side and a national eleven.

Alumni and the Shock of the New

One of the enduring myths in Argentina—one more likely propagated by the amateur–professional divide—is that the history of football began with the introduction of the professional game on May 31, 1931. Whether this has more to do with an Argentinian denial of the game's Anglo-Saxon roots than any intrinsic snobbery regarding amateurism remains unclear. The game had not changed overnight: it would be hard to believe that three decades of the century passed without players having received some kind of recompense for their services. In Buenos Aires and Montevideo, certain players were amateurs in name only. A certain Zanessi played for Dublin Montevideo, where he excelled. During the week he traipsed around the streets of the capital, making a meager living as a street vendor, but came into his own on the pitch on Sundays. By Mondays, however, he was so exhausted that he could not work. He proposed that the club pay him the two pesos that he might have earned on the Monday so that he could play on Sunday. Otherwise he threatened to quit. Even if many of the players involved were amateur in name only, these decades remain fundamental to the creation of what would be seen as *lo criollo* (the creole) or *la nuestra* (our game).

On October 3, 1898, one of the greatest teams ever to play football in Argentina was founded. The English High School Athletic Club was created to bring together the school's alumni, many of whom had ended up playing for a variety of clubs, including Palermo, Belgrano, Lanús and Bánfield. The Argentine Association Football League—which would have another three incarnations before becoming the Asociación del Football Argentino in 1934—had already experienced teething problem with clubs poaching players from their rivals. (A rule was introduced stating that no player would be allowed to play for a competing team without giving the league a month's written notice.) In 1899, the club entered the Second Division, gaining promotion a year later. In the same year, the club, which was essentially a team of players rather than a formal organization, won its first championship. With the foundation of a third tier for the under-seventeens, a new rule was implemented that no club could use the name of an educational institution. (This was deemed advertising and, therefore, incompatible with amateurism.) Newly retitled as "Alumni," they would win ten championships between 1900 and 1911, missing out in 1904 and 1908. Even in its early years, Alumni proved popular. The *Buenos Aires Herald* inaugurated the Herald Trophy by asking its readership to vote for the most popular club. The English High School ran out winners with 6,942 votes (Qilmes coming in second with 3,467). While being the first domestic side to beat a touring team further enhanced the team's reputation. It was, however, the Brown brothers, five of whom also played for Alumni, who captured the public's imagination. The eldest, Jorge Brown, who would captain both club and country, was the stalwart of the team, changing position from gifted striker to solid defender. Eliseo Brown, who scored twenty-four goals in the 1907 season, was said to have a terrifying shot from thirty to forty meters.

In 1909, Alumni scored seventy-four goals while conceding only nineteen. In that season, its only defeat came from a surging River Plate. The year before, River had played Racing for promotion to the First Division. When River scored its second goal, the fans ran onto the pitch to celebrate. This infraction caused the match to be replayed. River made sure of the result and scored seven goals.

While Alumni may have had Anglo-Saxon roots—a fact that has made it proto-British in the eyes of modern-day Argentinians—the team was in effect *criollo*. The Browns, who were fourteen siblings in all, were born in Argentina, as was their father, Don Diego, who grew up in Quilmes.

Although they were *criollos*, Alumni played as they had been taught, both on the field and off it. Imbued with a sense of fair play, moral correctness and fortitude, the team swept all before them. So potent was the team's forward line that its goalkeeper, Laforia, was quoted as saying that he did not really play for Alumni because the team did not need a goalkeeper. In 1921, Jorge Brown openly declared a preference for the British game in *El Gráfico*, the very magazine that would come to create the notion of *lo criollo*:

> *The football I cultivated was a real demonstration of handiness and energy. A game more brusque, but virile, beautiful, vigorous. The modern football is weakened by an excess of passing close to the goal. It is a game that is more fine, perhaps more artistic, even apparently more intelligent, but it has lost its primitive enthusiasm. With the present style the scores are more modest compared with the results of the old style. It is important to keep in mind that football is not a delicate sport . . . It is a violent and strong game in which physical resistance and the muscles of the players are what is proved. This style has unfortunately disappeared.*[12]

The British game, of which he spoke in glowing terms, was in effect the "long ball" game or "kick and run." This style of football was more to his liking because it was the game that he had known and played to a high level, rather than any negation of *lo criollo*. Commenting on a match in 1930, Alberto J. Olivari, a midfielder who had played for San Isidro and Argentina in the 1910s, shared Brown's discomfort: "That wasn't football of my times, all vigour and strength. They looked like young ladies playing tennis."[13]

Andrés Arturo Mack, a Cambridge graduate who would return to Britain to fight in the First World War, had taught football at the Buenos Aires English High School. He had placed great emphasis on playing with courage and not succumbing to fear on the pitch. Forty years on, Angel Bohigas, in his foreword to Escobar Bavio's roseate history of the club, sought to contextualize the potency of Alumni: "Because with due respect to all opinion—without excluding those who slightly pour scorn on Alumni's game without ever having witnessed it and proclaim the superiority practised by the professionals—I have to say that never has such a brilliant demonstration of technical football been seen on our pitches like that which was offered to us at Quilmes in the final of the *Copa de Competencia* [the Knockout Cup] in 1906. Belgrano A. C. was the other team. And we know they were beaten 10–1."[14]

Moreover, Alumni played as a team rather than succumbing to the cult of the individual that would dog the River Plate game. Carlos Lett, who played inside left, would later remember, "The secret of [Alumni's] success owed to the friendship that existed between the players, rather than the ability of its components. In this game a drop of bad blood, between two of the players, immediately affects all of the team, something that never happened, due, for the most part, to the character of the Brown brothers, and especially Jorge."[15]

Alumni were never a niche team appealing solely to the dwindling British community. Their status as champions transcended both class and community. The team's success was even used for political gain. The writer and fan of San Lorenzo Osvaldo Soriano realized years later that when José Figueroa Alcorta and Alfredo Brown embraced each other, it was "the first time that a president had used football for popular ends."[16]

. . .

By November 1911, Alumni had played its last match. Time had caught up with both the players and the team. Although Alumni had attempted to structure itself as a formally organized club, it had failed where other clubs were beginning to succeed. The largest crowds may have come to see Alumni play, but it played on rented grounds, since the club had no ground to call its own. Moreover, gate receipts and other profits were donated to worthy causes such as the Hospital Británico. The club's final balance, $12,322.29, was donated to eight charities. In 1936, having dedicated most of his life to the sports he loved, Jorge Brown died. Two months later, the founding father of Argentine football, Watson Hutton, followed his charge.

The demise of Alumni did not herald the death of Anglo-Argentine football. Quilmes won the title the following year with a team that included many ex-Alumni players. By this time, however, unity in the Argentine game had given way to schism. In 1903, the Argentine Association Football League (AAFL) had rechristened itself the Argentine Football Association (AFA) and translated the laws of the game into Spanish. Nine years later, the association would Hispanicize itself as the Asociación Argentina de Football, though the Anglo essential element remained. "Football" was not translated into *fútbol* until 1934, though Tobías Garzón took the liberty of Hispanicizing "football" to *fútbol* in his *Diccionario Argentino* twenty-four years before.

Unhappy with the terms that AFA was offering on gate receipts, especially for high-grossing international matches, the Club de Gimnasia y Esgrima de Buenos Aires left the association in 1912 and formed the Federación Argentina de Football with a number of other dissenting clubs. Although it would not be the last time that Argentinian football was riven with factionalism, the schism was short-lived: two years later the associations were reconciled.

Rising above the internal wrangling, one team reigned supreme in the 1910s. Between 1913 and 1919, Racing Club de Avellaneda won seven consecutive titles, losing only five league games during that period. Carlos Isola, the River Plate goalkeeper who acquired the sobriquet "El Hombre de Goma" (The Elastic Man), said that the team was the only *máquina* (machine) that he had ever seen. And this in spite of having witnessed the sheer beauty of River Plate's La Máquina of the 1940s. The club had taken its name from Racing Club de France after seeing a feature on the team in a Parisian magazine. For once Eduardo Wilde's maxim "the Argentines imitate everything, we're ridiculous, especially because we copy badly" did not obtain.[17] Alumni may have been the country's founding team, but Racing reflected its Argentinian soul. In 1914, the club would play thirteen matches, of which it won twelve, scoring forty-five goals. The club was nicknamed "La Academia" (The Academy) due to the lessons in how to play the game they handed out to other teams.

In Juan Ohaco, Racing had a striker of exceptional talent. Sporting a white cap, under which he would skulk, Ohaco became a player of legend. He may have become the club's leading scorer with 244 goals in 278 matches, but the shady figure that he cut on the pitch only fueled rumors of a former life as a murderer or thief. Ricardo Lorenzo—the Uruguayan *El Gráfico* journalist, who wrote under the pseudonym of Borocotó and would invent the notion of the Argentine game—considered Ohaco "the first 'Man-orchestra' of Argentine football in that he performed well in any position."[18]

In 1928, the Buenos Aires weekly *El Gráfico* looked back at this era as the turning point not just for Argentinian but also Latin American football: "When football began to spread, the stars [*los cracks*] with British names gave way to those with purely Latin, especially Italian and Spanish surnames like García, Martínez, Ohaco, Olazar, Chiappe, Calomino, Laforia, Isola, etc."[19] Football had been nationalized, but the railways that had been so instrumental in furthering the game would have to wait until 1948 for the heavy hand of Perón to wrest them from British ownership.

The Heirs of Artigas

On the eastern shores of the Río de la Plata, the game was developing at a tempo that belied Uruguay's provincial nature. In 1899, students from the Universidad de la República formed the continent's first genuinely *criollo* club, Nacional. In order to reinforce its nationalist origins—a direct response to CURCC's overt Anglo roots—the club played in red, white and blue. The colors, though ostensibly British, reflected the flag of José Gervasio Artigas, the country's liberator. Yet, unlike Artigas—who had sought to create an inclusive society, one in which *zambos* (Afro-Indians), blacks, Indians, creoles and gauchos might live in harmony—the middle-class club would be selective and not field a black player until the next decade.

The River Plate game had long employed strength over skill on the field. The ferocious long-range shots, positional play and bodily contact were all tenets of the English game. Nacional now sought to be different. Although glowing in its assessment of the early days of the Uruguayan game, *Del fútbol héroico* describes how Nacional had to change its style of play: "Made up in the main by smaller and quicker players . . . physically inferior compared to its rivals, [Nacional] abandoned physical encounters that were allowed back then . . . They chose dribbling, fast and short passes, quick sprints."[20] This style of play proved a success with the spectators, who enjoyed finesse rather than brutality. Guile and skill would always trump Anglo tenacity and courage, owing in part to the influence of Italian *bella figura*, that of making an impression. Showing off, especially in front of an expectant crowd, elicited more applause. Once fees were charged at the gates, players had turned into performers, playing to an audience. Writing later in the century, Eduardo Galeano, a Nacional fan, voiced what every Latin American football fan knew: "I've finally learned to accept myself for who I am: a beggar for good football. I go about the world, hand outstretched, and in the stadiums I plead: 'A pretty move, for the love of God.'"[21]

Three brothers would come to define the amateur era of

Uruguayan football. In 1902, Amílcar, Bolívar and Carlos Céspedes formed the spine of the Nacional side that had become champions. Amílcar, the eldest, had started his career as a center-half before ending up in goal; but it was Bolívar, quick with a furious shot, and Carlos, elegant and a fine dribbler, who were heroes to the terraces. The following year, all three siblings played in the country's first international triumph over Argentina, when Nacional fielded the international side. Before the match, their father famously said, "We know that we cannot win; we came as brothers to do our duty."[22] With the country in the final throes of an erratic civil war that had long dominated her short but turbulent history (when the dictator Latorre resigned the presidency in 1880, he declared the country "ungovernable" and left for Argentina), the siblings fled Montevideo for Buenos Aires, where they played for Sporting Barracas. They were not the only foreigners to play for the club. A few years later, Barracas fielded a one-armed Irishman in goal.

The 1903 Campeonato Uruguayo had ended with Nacional and CURCC tied on points. It was decided, because of civil war, to hold the deciding match the following year. CURCC, many of whose foreign players were exempt from conscription, expected to face a depleted Nacional side of inexperienced youngsters. Moments before the start of the match, however, the brothers, having returned from Buenos Aires, appeared on horseback. Nacional ran out 3–2 winners, securing the championship with two goals from Bolívar and one from his younger brother. Triumph turned to tragedy when, the following June, Bolívar succumbed to smallpox and died. His brother Carlos followed three weeks later. Amílcar, against the strict orders of his football-mad father, had had himself vaccinated.

If Nacional had given the Uruguayan game its *criollo* spirit, then C.U.R.C.C. was its English teacher. From the closing decades of the nineteenth century, CURCC had tended toward the physicality of the British game. But a Scotsman would change all that. John Harley had been born in Glasgow in 1886, and had made his way to

Argentina to work on the railways. For two years he had played for Ferro Carril Oeste before moving across the River Plate. CURCC had been so impressed by Harley that they suggested the Central Uruguay Railway make him an offer of a job (a not uncommon occurrence where good players were concerned). He would captain the club for eight years. Harley also become the national side's first center-half and brought some Scottish erudition to the passing game. By the time he retired from the game in 1920, Uruguayan football was about to enter its golden age.

In the first four years of the century, Nacional and CURCC shared the championship between themselves. During the rest of the amateur era, even if clubs such as Wanderers, River Plate and Rampla Juniors managed to win the championship, either Nacional and CURCC (who changed their name to Penarol in 1913) would invariably finish the season in first or second position. The Uruguayan championship would become even more of a two-horse race in the professional era until 1976, when Defensor secured its first title. Uruguay's political history in the twentieth century would be the perennial struggle between Colorados ("Reds") and Blancos ("Whites"). The Uruguayan mind seemed unable to entertain anything but this simple duality.

. . .

In 1912, Uruguayan football emerged, albeit briefly, from the shadow of the Argentinian game. Héctor Rivadavia Gómez, a Uruguayan politician and president of Montevideo Wanderers, had put together a national team of the best players rather than a scratch eleven. From August to October, the two countries played four games for four cups: the Copa Lipton, Copa Premier Honor Uruguayo, Copa Premier Honor Argentino and Copa Newton. The Uruguayans did not lose a single match. The highlight was a 3–0 win in Montevideo, where Dacal, Scarone and Romano all hit the net. Uruguay had played like *una máquina* and shown just how competitive she had become. When the Copa Lipton was played the following year, normal service was resumed. Uruguay lost by four goals to nil: the Estudiantes forward, Maximiliano Susán, scoring all four.

But there was one Uruguayan in particular who had shone throughout that spring. Ángel Romano would move from Nacional to Boca Juniors for only two seasons, returning to Montevideo in 1915. He was a magnificent footballer, with the ability to dribble past players at will and play in every position (including goalkeeper) on the pitch. He was also famed for dribbling past goalkeepers and forgetting to score. Boca had managed to lure Romano with a home, clothing and employment at Bunge y Born, a cereal company. The investment would pay off: Romano became a hero to the Boca fans. Amateurism remained but a question of smoke and mirrors.

By the 1910s, passion for the game ran high. Had Jorge Luis Borges had any interest in football, he might have written a short story about Abdón Porte. (Though, in 1918, Horacio Quiroga would publish the biographical "Juan Polti, Half-back.") From 1911 to 1918, "El Indio" (The Indian) Porte played over two hundred games for Nacional. By 1918, however, this combative center-half found that he was unable to perform at the level that had made him an idol to the terraces. His last match was a 3–1 victory over Charley, in which he played well. In the early hours of March 5, 1918, Porte stole into an empty Estádio Gran Parque Central, where in the center of the pitch he shot himself through the heart. In the straw hat that lay by his side were two letters, one of which was addressed to the president of the club.

> *Dear Dr José Maria Delgado, I only ask that you and the other colleagues of the board do for me as I have done for you: do it for my family and for my dear mother. Goodbye dear friend from life*
>
> *. . .*
>
> *I will not forget for a moment*
> *How much I loved you*
> *Goodbye forever . . .*[23]

Porte's love for his club had been so great that when he realized his legs were beginning to fail him, he could not bear to live with the condition. His final request was to be buried in the barrio of La Teja, in the same cemetery as Bolívar and Carlos Céspedes.

Los Negros con el Alma Blanca (The Blacks with the White Soul)

From its very inception, football in South America had been imbued with a sense of exclusion. Born of the private sporting club and British reserve, the game had developed along class and ethnic lines. Creoles may have felt themselves to be a class apart, and when they took over the game little seemed to change. Where the British had sought to exclude certain elements of creole society, it was now the turn of the *criollo* to dictate who could and could not play the game. But certain countries were better at integrating black (*negro*), *mulato* or *pardo* (half-caste) players than others.

In 1916, Argentina hosted the first South American championship, Campeonato Sudamericano de Selecciones. The tournament, which would later become the Copa América, had been the brainchild of Héctor Rivadavia Gómez six years before. As part of her centenary sporting celebrations in 1910, Argentina hosted the three-way Copa Centenario Revolución de Mayo in which she beat Uruguay 4–1 in the final match. "Arnoldo" Watson Hutton, the son of Argentinian football's founding father, scored the third goal. He had come to the game early, debuting for Alumni at fifteen years of age. Rivadavia Gómez had conceived of an inclusive competition between all the *países hermanos* (fraternal countries) of South America. Moreover, he wanted an organization that would unify the federations of the continent and act "as a powerful governing centre which would reduce the danger of the kind of breakaway currently seen in Argentina."[24] Although it may have defied Jules Rimet, the founding father of the World Cup, and his concept of FIFA as the ultimate governing body for the game, it gave the South American

game the impetus it needed. Who would look after South American
football's interests if not the South Americans themselves? By the time
CONMEBOL (Confederación Sudamericana de Fútbol: South American Football Confederation) was founded in 1916, the administration
of football on the continent had been completely taken out of the hands
of the British.

The inaugural tournament, which was played as a round-robin
competition between Uruguay, Argentina, Brazil and Chile in 1916,
was not without incident. Both the opening and closing matches
highlighted unsavory aspects of the burgeoning South American
game. After Uruguay thrashed Chile 4–0 in the opening match, the
Chilean delegation made an official complaint that Uruguay had
fielded two "African slaves" rather than Uruguayans. Juan Delgado
and Isabelino Gradín, both Afro-Uruguayans, became the first black
players to play international football. They played under the sobri-
quets "El Negro Juan" and "El Negro Gradín," though the latter was
also known as "El Negro con el Alma Blanca" (the black with the
white soul). Famed for his speed, Gradín would win gold in the 200
and 400 meters at the 1919 South American Athletic Championship
(Campeonato Sudamericano de Atletismo). The other two goals were
scored by Gradín's fellow Peñarol player José Piendibene, who would
become Uruguay's leading goal scorer against Argentina. Such was
Piendibene's artistry on the pitch that he was lionized with a number
of nicknames including "King of the Pass," "Emperor of the Dummy,"
"Monarch of the Header," and "Sultan of the Dribble."

The closing match of the tournament, between Uruguay and
Argentina, ended before it had even started. After five minutes the
match had to be called off due to overcrowding at the Gimnasia y
Esgrima ground. When an ensuing riot broke out among the spectators, the wooden terraces were set alight with naphtha taken from car
headlights. Although the match was rescheduled at Racing Club's
Avellaneda ground, it ended in a goalless draw. Uruguay was crowned
champions on points. Brazil, however, went home disappointed by

the aggression of both the Chileans and Uruguayans. The Brazilian press coverage maintained a predictable Anglo position to her defeat:

> *The score of matches does not always express the valour of the adversaries: victories can afterwards be discredited as defeats, but chivalry during the match, courtesy, the good, the true, calm, rational and intelligent game, without violence, with energy, the force of determination, with all of this together, finally, in the qualities which our compatriots implanted in Buenos Aires and which were rewarded with moral victory in all of the matches, this impressed because it is not the work of chance, this endures because it is not the fruit of materialism, this elevates, honours, dignifies and glorifies not only our foot-ballers but all of us, Brazilians, because it is the reflection of our culture, the expression of our character, the essence of our race.*[25]

Although Brazil possessed the largest Afro–Latin American population on the continent, the country would not come to terms with color and race until the 1950s. The Brazilian writer Mário Filho credited Pelé and the 1958 World Cup winners with having "completed the work [the abolition of slavery] of Princess Isabel."[26] Yet, only a century before, slavery obtained in a Brazilian empire where racism was endemic. The Haitian revolution of the late eighteenth century had propagated the fear among the white elites of a similar slave revolt. In 1846, the superintendent of the Royal Botanic Gardens of Ceylon had taken the temperature of this postcolonial society, in which blacks formed the lowest stratum of society: "A general rise of the black population is much dreaded in Brazil, which is not unreasonable, when the great proportion it bears to the white is taken into consideration . . . I believe the time is not far distant, when Brazil will share the fate of the other South American states. In such an event the white population will be sure to suffer from the savage rapacity of the mixed races, especially those with African blood in them . . . they are mostly free, and bear no good will toward the whites."[27]

Abolition of slavery had come to the country late. In 1888, Princess Isabel, acting for her father Dom Pedro II, sanctioned the "Lei Áurea" (Golden Law). The law, which made Brazil the last civilized country in the Western world to abolish the practice, was not without its detractors. Rio de Janeiro, where slavery was still deemed economically valuable, provided the majority of deputies who voted against the bill. Two years before, the abolitionist Joaquim Nabuco reflected on the deleterious effect of slavery upon the country: "It is a system which prevents our incorporation into modernity."[28] Abolition may have ushered in freedom, but it did not improve the plight of many ex-slaves. In the late nineteenth century, waves of European immigrants who sought work in the New World only helped push Afro-Brazilians further down the social ladder, making them into something of an underclass. And with France and Britain providing the cultural focus for many white elites, the divisions in Brazilian society would remain clearly marked.

The football clubs of Rio de Janeiro and São Paulo, having been founded by the elites in each city, merely reflected these divisions. Thus it was inevitable that Brazilian football would fail to integrate fully its working-class, black and mulatto players until the 1930s. When, in 1902, members of the Rio Cricket and Athletic Association established Fluminense Football Club, there was no change in the social climate of the club. The newly established club would preserve the values of upper-class *carioca* (inhabitants of Rio de Janeiro) society. Only those from the highest echelons of Rio society needed apply. Members would sport the club's colors on their hatbands as a discreet badge of distinction. Until the mid-1960s, the club refused to admit members who were not of European descent. Mário Filho sought to capture what membership might entail:

> *In order to join Fluminense the player had to live the same life as an Oscar Cox, Félix Frias or Horácio da Costa Santos, a Waterman, a Francis Walter, or an Etchegary, all established men, chiefs of firms, first-rate*

employees of big companies, sons of rich fathers, educated in Europe, used to spending money. It was a hard life. Those who did not have access to a constant supply of ready money couldn't stand the strain.[29]

Two years later, Botafogo, hitherto a rowing club, was founded in the well-heeled barrio of the same name. And yet in spite of its status as an elite pastime, indeed maybe because of it, football managed to capture the imagination of the urban underclass. Flamengo was established when a group of players seceded from Fluminense and joined the Clube de Regatas do Flamengo. Because Flamengo possessed no ground of its own and played instead in the open spaces of Rio, it attracted a working-class fan base that followed the team around the city. Bangú, on the other hand, had an altogether different social setup, one that had been forced upon the club by circumstance. Established by the British management of the textile concern Companhia Progresso Industrial do Brasil, the club found that it could not field enough British players to form a squad. When Brazilian workers were asked to represent the club, it gained a working-class following. (Bangú would become the first club in the professional era to win the Rio state championship, albeit in the pirate Liga Carioca de Football.) A letter written in 1904 by Charles Miller to his old school captures the enthusiasm with which the sport had been adopted by Brazil's poorest inhabitants:

A week ago I was asked to referee in a match of small boys, twenty a side. I told them it was absurd them playing twenty a side; but no, they wanted it. I thought, of course, the whole thing would be a muddle, but I found I was very much mistaken. They played two half-hours, and I only had to give two hands. The youngsters hardly spoke a word during the game, kept their places and played well; even for this match about 1,500 people turned up. No less than 2,000 footballs have been sold here within the last twelve months; nearly every village has a club.[30]

Obsession with race and class, however, did not stop Brazil from choosing a light-skinned mulatto as its first football idol. Arthur Friedenreich was born to a German father and an Afro-Brazilian mother, and his darker complexion and wiry hair would always mark him out. The green-eyed mulatto had started his career at the German immigrant club, Sport Club Germânia, moving back and forth between various clubs, including Flamengo, before settling at Paulistano. Friedenreich had been coached by Hermann Friese, a German émigré whom, in 1903, *O Estado* called the greatest player of all time. Friese had played football in Hamburg, but had also been an outstanding athlete, having competed at the 1500, 800 and 400 meters. When, in 1906, Friese's Germânia won the Campeonato Paulista, the inevitable was beginning to take shape. Those that had founded the game in São Paulo would soon be left behind. The nadir came in a match between SC Internacional and the São Paulo Athletic Club (SPAC), in which Charles Miller, now playing between the posts, let in nine goals.

Friedenreich was a goal-scoring machine. By the time he hung up his boots in 1935 at the age of forty-three, he had found the net 1,329 times. (In age of statistical inexactness, especially where football was concerned, this has always been open to question.) He was a curious, though highly effective, combination of classical English center-forward and Afro-Brazilian suppleness. In a society where race was highly demarcated, "Fried" was neither black nor white. He may have been accepted by the white elite, but would also be picked to play for black elevens. Such was Friedenreich's readiness to hide his Afro-Brazilian roots, and evade racism, that he would straighten his hair to give himself a side parting before taking to the field. But it took the 1919 Campeonato Sudamericano to make Friedenreich a national hero.

Now in its third edition, the championship was becoming repetitive. Uruguay had been crowned twice, while Brazil had come in third behind Argentina on both occasions. An epidemic of Spanish flu in Rio had delayed the tournament by a year. The opening match proved auspicious for the hosts with Chile giving her usual craven performance. Friedenreich scored a hat trick, while Neco, the Corinthians striker, managed a brace in a 6–0 thrashing. With both Brazil and Uruguay tied on points, after a 2–2 draw, the neighbors met each other in a playoff. Goalless in normal time, the match went into extra time but failed to provide a winner. Finally, in the 122nd minute, Friedenreich made no mistake when the ball came off a Uruguayan defender. The best player of the tournament had scored the winning goal. For the Uruguayans the championship would be marked by tragedy. In Uruguay's 2–0 victory over Chile, Roberto Chery, the young Peñarol goalkeeper, suffered a strangulated hernia during the match. He died the day after Uruguay lost the playoff. Solidarity was shown for Uruguay's fallen hero with a memorial match, in which the Argentinians played in Uruguay's colors and Brazil in those of Peñarol.

The following year normal service was resumed when Chile hosted the championship in Viña del Mar. It was now Brazil's turn to receive a drubbing, this time by the Uruguayans, who scored six. The night before the final match against Chile, a stranger turned up at the hotel where the Uruguayan delegation was staying and asked for Piendibene. When introduced to El Maestro, he threatened to kill him should the hosts lose. The following day, the man returned only to be physically assaulted by the Uruguayan players.

For the Brazilians, embarrassment would turn to anger when they broke their journey in order to play a "friendly" in Buenos Aires. There, a Uruguayan-born journalist, now resident in the Argentine capital, allowed his wit to be infected by overt racism in a *Crítica* article entitled "Monkeys in Buenos Aires." The Brazilians failed to see the humor in such sentences as: "The little monkeys [Brazilians] are already on Argentinian soil. This afternoon it will necessary to put on the light at 4pm to see them. We have seen them jumping down the streets."[31] Moreover, the article featured a cartoon of monkeys dressed for football. The article divided the Brazilian dressing room, with certain players deciding not to play the friendly. When the Porteño crowd realized that the Brazilian eleven included a number of Argentinians, the players were pelted.

Not that the Brazilian press was any less prejudiced. During the 1919 championships, *O Imparcial* went so far as to state "the black in Brazil does not want to be black."[32] This attitude was not solely confined to Brazil. Miguel Rostaing, an Afro-Peruvian who would play for Alianza Lima in the 1920s and 1930s, believed that the Afro-Peruvian male looked for lighter-skinned women in order to better his race. Even as an Afro-Peruvian himself, he felt that "blacks don't want to be blacks."[33] Poor Carlos Alberto, the first mulatto to have turned out for Fluminense, applied rice powder (*pó-de-arroz*) to his face in order to conceal his darker skin. When perspiration caused the powder to run, the opposing fans booed the player.

Nor was racial prejudice solely a Latin American vice. Shortly before giving up the game in the late 1920s, Club Athletico Paulistano undertook the first European tour by a Brazilian club. Along with Friedenreich, Joaquim Prado was the only mulatto player in the squad. Class outweighed race in these matters, for Prado was a member of an eminent São Paulo family and cousin of Paulistano's president, Antônio Prado Júnior. During a match in Paris, a French relative of Prado Júnior inquired as to the name of "that monkey." Prado Júnior replied curtly: "That is no monkey, that is your cousin."[34]

While clubs in Rio de Janeiro began to attract black players in the 1920s, it was not until the next decade that São Paulo followed suit when segregation became untenable. In 1923, Vasco de Gama won the Rio championship with an eleven composed of blacks, mulattoes and illiterate whites. Four years later it seemed that little in the way of social progress had been made. On May 13, the anniversary of the abolition of slavery, a match was played between *pretos* (blacks) and *brancos* (whites). *O Combate* reported, "The great mass of spectators chose its favourite, which was the Black team . . . It seemed that the crowd's every effort was bent on seeing the black team win, and that it saw in that victory a question of honour."[35] When the black eleven won again the following year, *A Gazeta* reported, "The white team included the names most in evidence in the principal division [of the local league]. Among them were four players from last year's championship team; we don't understand how such a strong team was defeated."[36]

Brazil's attempts to replicate a European ideal were, according to Gilberto Freyre, "as artificial, as ridiculous, and as absurd as the use by a tropical people of ice skates in order to appear as civilized or fashionable as the Swiss, the Scandinavian, or the British."[37] Uruguayan football, on the other hand, had embraced its black players early. This would be reflected in the country's domination in international football for over a decade. Racist though the diminutive republic was, her small size forced her to show a degree of tolerance, if only for the sake of expendiency.

Los Íntimos de Lima

The War of the Pacific had left Peru physically and psychologically devastated. When, in 1881, the Chileans captured Lima, there was no administration with which the victors could negotiate peace. The country was on her knees. Manuel González Prada, the Peruvian politician and critic, laid the blame at the door of the elites: "We fell because Chile, which watches while Peru sleeps, caught us poor and without credit, unprepared and poorly armed, without an army or a navy."[38] Economic damage would in time be repaired, but the humiliation of defeat would never truly fade. Pusillanimity—that character flaw that every Latin American republic, eager to show its strength, feared—had embedded itself in Peru's identity.

By 1895, the "Aristocratic Republic" had taken over the reins of power and the country entered two decades of economic and political stability. Prosperity did not, however, beget equality. In certain quarters, feudalism, which had been prevalent in the nineteenth century, had not fully disappeared. In 1910, Roger Casement, the infamous British consul who would later be executed for treason, wrote in his diary: "Peru has got to deal with this hideous evil [Indian slavery in the Putumayo], or stand the consequences of loss of prestige and reputation."[39] Under the tyranny of the rubber baron Julio Arana, Indians were starved and flogged, young girls raped, while fathers, who were too old to work, were shot in front of their sons. From Lima, which had finally burst its colonial walls and was beginning to transform itself into a modern Latin American city, an elite ruled the country. Labeled the "Twenty-four Friends," these men included the two presidents of the era. While political power remained in the hands of the few, the growth of an urban working class in the capital gave rise to labor movements and repeated strike action. In 1912, the inaugural season of the Peruvian Football League (Liga Peruana de Football), the country's first national workers' federation was founded. Among the disparate unions that made up the Federación Obrera Regional Peruana (FORP) were the textile groups from working-class barrios such as La Victoria and Vitarte. It would be these factory workers who formed the clubs that later came to dominate Peruvian football.

In the first few years of the new century, football remained the preserve of the Anglo-Peruvians and *criollo* elite. As one traveler to the country observed: "Football seems to have an altogether extraordinary fascination for Latin-Americans, although it was a game entirely unknown to them before it was introduced from England. Lima and Callao are very severely 'bitten' with the mania for furious football, and during the months of October–May it is played perpetually. Most enthusiastic are the players; and, moreover, they play extremely well. The Callao team have a very competent captain in Mr. Joseph Dodds . . . The Lima Cricket and Football Club is another well-patronized coterie of sport-loving men, and their games are watched by considerable crowds of interested spectators composed of both sexes."[40] Lima Cricket and Football Club and Association Foot Ball Club had furthered the creation of the Peruvian Football League. Not that encounters prior to the league's inception had been at all gentlemanly. Brawls and their ensuing injuries were not uncommon, nor for that matter was a loose interpretation of the rules.

The league, which comprised two divisions, included a number of working-class clubs. Sport Inca, Sport Progreso and Sport Vitarte originated from the capital's largest factories. Yet it was Sport Alianza—founded by a group of stable workers belonging to Augusto B. Leguía's stud—that would become one of Latin America's greatest clubs. Success, however, did not come early: Alianza had to wait until 1918 to secure its first championship. The anglophile Lima Cricket, on the other hand, was crowned the league's inaugural champions, though its days as a competitive team would soon be numbered. Four years later, the club decided to hang up its boots and concentrate on less popular sporting activities. Elite teams across the continent would suffer the same fate. Unlike working-class clubs, which found an ever-expanding pool from which to choose their players, membership in the established Anglo clubs began to stagnate. The league, however, restricted itself to Lima. Clubs from the neighboring port of Callao had to wait to join, though when they did so, violence would become a regular part of the intercity game.

For many working-class players across the continent, football was learned early and in a similar fashion. The ubiquitous *pelota de trapo* (rag ball)—socks or stockings filled with rags and a weight—was used in place of a proper football. To play with a manufactured leather ball was the dream of every working-class *pibe* (kid) on the continent. In 1948, Leopoldo Torres Ríos would direct the seminal Argentinian film *Pelota de trapo*, about a group of young boys who endeavor to purchase their own football. Neighborhood games would take place in *potreros* (fields) and empty lots with five to eleven players making up a side. It was here that the art of *picardía* (craftiness) was acquired. This was not "slyness" for its own sake; rather it was a way of evading any injury at the feet of the tackling player. (As games became increasingly violent, players had no option but to learn how to evade contact.) Part of the game was also learning how to retaliate with subtlety. For those who made the transition from *pibe* to player, these skills represented the difference between success and failure.

Miguel Rostaing, known as "El Quemado" (The Burned One), having been branded in a domestic accident, played for Alianza Lima from 1919 until 1936, winning six championships with Los Blanquiazules. Rostaing remembered football in Lima in the 1910s:

> *My first team was Huáscar. We formed it in the neighbourhood in 1914 among friends. We were players and founders of Huáscar. Most of us used to train after work. Between five and seven at night we would run and do calisthenics. Some who couldn't go in afternoon trained in the morning. Those who could went in the afternoon, and others trained at night. On Huáscar every team member paid monthly dues, I think fifty centavos, to maintain the club . . . Sometimes we had to buy shoes too. There were times that some players didn't have enough for the shoes, and we had to help them out . . . When I played, I played every position. I was like a one-man orchestra, to be exact. I played right forward, left forward, left wing, right wing, right half, left half, and once I even played center half. And I also played defense. They always changed me around to different positions. I played them all the same. After all, the ball is round everywhere on the field.*[41]

It was while playing for clubs such as these that players formed a bond of friendship. Nowhere was this sense of camaraderie more pronounced than at Sport Alianza (later Alianza Lima). The club, which would become known as the Intimos (Close Friends) or Compadres (Mates), was conceived on the basis of friendship. Moreover, it would come to represent the working-class barrio of La Victoria. Although the barrio was home to a high proportion of the capital's black population, only one Afro-Peruvian appears in an early photograph of Sport Alianza. (The club would later come to be known as "Alianza Lima, Equipo de los Negros" [Alianza Lima, Team of the Blacks].) Despite the firm barrio allegiances, Alianza's reputation began to draw fans from other areas of the city. "Our fans were from different neighbourhoods," recalled Rostaing:

> *Of course, the largest quantity from La Victoria, from Abajo el Puente, from Malambo, from all those places. I used to think: "I'm a player; I'm not making any money at this." I guess I played, at least in part, because the people applauded me . . . The fans would start to buzz, and as you were playing you would start faking out your opponent, dribbling around him. They would call you, for example, "Quemado Rostaing!" "Villanueva!" "Lavalle!" They would call to us, and we would dribble by the other guy. Uf! We would pass to somebody else. Sometimes he would let the ball go to another teammate. The game opened up there. It was, in fact, the fans who made us do that.*[42]

Though not all fans exerted such a positive effect on the game. By the early 1920s, the fans from Callao (Atlético Chalaco), who were mostly fishermen by trade, had gained a terrifying reputation. "They came with dynamite, and the Lima fans couldn't stand up to them . . . They almost blew up a back that we had. He was going to throw in the ball, and they threw a stick of dynamite at him, and they almost blew him up, ball and all."[43] In a match against Atlético Chalaco, the Alianza Lima goalkeeper, Eugenio Segalá, had to be taken off the pitch and given medical attention (five stitches) when an opposing fan knifed him through the back of the net. The assault had had the desired effect: Segalá turned to meet his assailant, only for Atlético Chalaco to take advantage and score.

El Gráfico: The Magazine That Changed Football in América

If the publication of Rodó's *Ariel*, and its ensuing *arielismo*, had cat-alyzed the search for identity at the start of the twentieth century, the end of the 1910s would see the foundation of a magazine that would come to define Latin American identity through football. Originally conceived as an illustrated magazine, *El Gráfico* was first published in Buenos Aires in 1919.* A photo-story on the South American cham-pionships, held in Brazil, provided the first mention of the game. (The matches were so popular that "capacity was always insufficient for the crowds.")[44] Two years later, however, the general articles on culture, politics and society had given way to sport. Although pri-marily dedicated to football, articles on other sports in which Argen-tina excelled were published. The weekly would become the "Bible of sports in South America,"[45] selling in every major city on the conti-nent, from Lima to Montevideo and from La Paz to San José.

By the 1950s, the magazine had reached its zenith with a contin-ental circulation of over 200,000 copies. Each issue of *El Gráfico* may have been eagerly awaited, especially in those countries where sport-ing coverage was sporadic, but it effectively reinforced Argentina's hegemony in the region. Alfonso Senior Quevedo, the first president of Bogotá's Millonarios, who changed the face of the continental game, would later remember, "I played football because when I was a boy, magazines or newspapers would arrive by boat from Argentina or Spain, and I read them."[46] It may not have been overt cultural colo-nialism, but who could gainsay the effect of editorials that waxed lyrical on *el fútbol rioplatense* (River Plate football) or the statistics of Porteño (Buenos Aires) players?

---

* On the cover of the first issue, a photograph showed the country's bright future—the alumni of Buenos Aires's schools—parade past La Casa Rosada, the presidential palace.

Argentinidad (Argentine-ness), a notion that was delicate at best, had found its voice in the most unlikely quarter. In 1913, on his return from Europe, the poet Leopoldo Lugones gave a series of lectures at the Teatro Odeón in Buenos Aires. These now-celebrated lectures, which President Roque Sáenz Peña attended, reclaimed José Hernández's epic gaucho poem, *Martín Fierro*, as Argentine heritage. Published in 1872 to popular acclaim, though failing to capture the imagination of the literary elite, *Martín Fierro* recounts the story of a gaucho army deserter and his life of freedom among the Amerindians. Lugones, who had been brought up in the provinces and remained an outsider to Porteño society, saw the mixing of races—the pride of the Spanish mixed with the self-sufficiency of the Amerindian—as the distinguishing feature of the *criollos* compared to the Europeans. Even biological determinism, though its advocates were just as misguided in South America as were those in Europe, had become creolized. Lugones put paid to the theory—held by nineteenth-century intellectuals such as Sarmiento and Alberdi—that Anglo-Saxon immigration would somehow improve the inferior Indian and Spanish bloodlines. In 1924, Lugones gave his infamous *la hora de la espada* (the time of the sword) speech, in which he called for a return to militarism. He now turned to the fascist right and supported the 1930 coup d'état. But for a man who had sought to invest the republic with an identity, Lugones came to a pathetic end. In 1938, he took his own life with a heady mixture of whiskey and cyanide. The cause was not known, though it was said that he had tired of Argentine politics.

A preoccupation with race and identity was not limited to Argentina. Emboldened by her victory in the War of the Pacific and the pacification of the Mapuche at home, Chile sought to exert a sense of *Chilenidad* ("Chilean-ness"). Nowhere was this more evident than on the football pitch. While footballers from Valparaíso were seen as firmly European, having kept English as the language of the sport, and therefore white, Santiago's players were deemed more "Chilean":

a mixture of *criollos* and mestizos (those of Spanish and Amerindian heritage). By the 1910s, the question of identity was beginning to be constructed within the crucible of international football. The myth, now propagated by the sporting pages, was that Chilean players were different from their neighbors, the mixture of Indian and Spanish blood making them more reliable. Deviation from a Chilean norm was seen as undesirable. No wonder the Chilean delegation complained that Uruguay had fielded two black players at the inaugural Campeonato Sudamericano de Selecciones.

Geography—squeezed into a thin strip between the Pacific Ocean and the Andes—had not favored her football. Unlike the River Plate and Brazil, Chile had not attracted European teams, which continued to lend her football an air of parochialism. Factionalism had not helped the game either. The Football Association of Chile, which had been founded in Valparaíso, was a national association in name only. By the beginning of the twentieth century, other cities, such as Coquimbo, Iquique and Santiago, followed suit and established their own associations. Moreover, the foundation of a government-backed Federación Sportiva only sought to complicate matters and thwarted any authority that the Football Association of Chile might have had. In stark contrast to the nation's otherwise ordered society, years of footballing chaos ensued, with various competing leagues playing the game in Santiago.

The country's inflexible attitude toward professionalism further retarded the Chilean game. The Chilean historian Sebastián Salinas has stated that the country "from the very creation of the Football Association in 1895, exhibited a completely adverse stance to any form of professionalism, clinging on to amateurism with [a sense of] pride that cost years of backwardness."[47] Not that the Chileans were the only country to take this stance. In 1907, the Ministry of Justice and Public Education received a letter from the Argentine Football Association warning against the perils of professionalism. "Our Association considers professionalism to be the gangrene of this

virile sport in Europe, and is resolved to fight, until the last, its introduction into the Republic."[48]

This backwardness was demonstrated when Chile hosted the
Campeonato Sudamericano de Selecciones, now the continent's most
important sporting event, in 1920. The host country managed only a
draw against Argentina and lost all her other matches. The postmor-
tem proved sobering: it called into question not just the team's technical and tactical ability but also its claims of racial superiority. This
led President Alessandri to issue a counterargument in an interview:
"The Araucanian race that populated this land in the era of the Spanish conquest was the strongest of all natives on the continent and also
fought against the bravest and strongest Spanish captains, because
only they would arrive to the most distant and impoverished of the
discovered countries. From the struggle between these two races our
people came forth, strong, vigorous, enduring and virile."[49] The
nation's weakness in front of goal had been spotted by the Uruguayan
Rivadavia Gómez in 1917. "The Chileans possess great capacity for
power, speed and strength. They only lack the ability to develop these
aptitudes, since success does not depend on how they show off indi-
vidually, but rather rests in the team."[50] Unfortunately for Chilean
football, this weakness would be chronic.

.   .   .

In 1910, Georges Clémenceau, France's future prime minister, toured
Latin America. He observed societies that, in seeking out Western
sophistication, had looked mainly to France rather than Italy or Spain
for their cultural compass. This may have had more to do with the
fact that France provided an "otherness" (a sense of a better, idealized
version of the self that Latinity could achieve) that Spain and Italy,
cultures from which most immigrants into the continent came, could
not. "Englishness" (or "British-ness," the words were used inter-
changeably) would remain alien to the Latin mind: an awkward culture, easily aped, but intrinsically unfathomable.

A decade later, the founding clubs of the continent had all but disappeared, and so too had the vestiges of an Anglo game. Brazil would look to the future and make the game her own, but for the *rioplatenses* the fact that the game was inherited continued to irk them. *El Gráfico* became somewhat father-fixated—obsessed not only with outdoing but also outclassing the force and industry of British football. The great postwar clashes between England and Argentina would be heightened by ongoing disputes regarding the sovereignty of Las Malvinas, but the antipathy was formed early. In 1928, the weekly set out its thesis:

> *Inspired in the same school as the British, the Latins soon began modifying the science of the game and fashioning one of their own, which is now widely recognized . . . it is different from the British in that it is less monochrome, less disciplined and methodical, because it does not sacrifice individualism for the honor of collective values . . . [British football] is monotonous because it is always uniformly the same. River Plate football, in contrast, does not sacrifice personal action entirely and makes more use of dribbling and generous personal effort, both in attack and defense, and for that reason is a more agile and attractive football.*[51]

And yet, there remained a part of *el fútbol rioplatense* that would be forever British. The weekly did not make the connection between the aggression and physicality its teams displayed—often taken to extremes—and the English game from which these traits had been inherited.

In the closing pages of his River Plate odyssey, *The Purple Land That England Lost*, published in 1885, W. H. Hudson has his protagonist turn on the English and keenly observe: "I cannot believe that if this country had been conquered and recolonised by England, and all that is crooked in it made straight according to our notions, my intercourse with the people would have had the wild, delightful flavour I have found in it. And if that distinctive flavour cannot be had along with the material prosperity resulting from Anglo-Saxon energy, I must breathe the wish that this land may never know such prosperity . . . We do not live by bread alone, and British occupation does not give to the heart all the things for which it craves . . ."[52] In response to which the Argentinian writer Ezequiel Martínez Estrada, would later write, "The final pages of *The Purple Land* express . . . the supreme justification of America in the face of Western civilization."[53] The same could now be said of *el fútbol criollo*.

CHAPTER THREE

THE RETURN OF THE NATIVES

1920–1930

We are Europeans yet we are not Europeans. What are we then? It is difficult to define what we are, but our works speak for us.

—Octavio Paz, "La búsqueda del presente," Nobel Lecture (1990)

As one man was drawn into the play, another covered his position so that at all times Uruguay was protected as few teams are.

—*New York Times* (March 21, 1927)

If Paris did not exist, Latin American writers would have invented it.

—Cristóbal Pera, *Modernistas en París* (1997)

In 1924, the South Americans arrived in Europe early. The Uruguayan delegation, en route to the VIII Olympiad in Paris, had scheduled a series of friendlies against Spanish opposition. Though this had more to do with funding Uruguay's Olympic odyssey—a concern for the Uruguayan authorities that bordered on obsession—rather than mere preparation for the games. After the opening match, in which the Uruguayans dismissed Celta de Vigo 3–0, the Galician newspaper *Faro de Vigo* exclaimed, "We have now seen the South Americans play. And how they play!"[1] The Basques, however, were less than welcoming. Aggressive play, born of the club's British roots, coupled with a host of statuesque players, had made Athletic Bilbao a formidable force in Spanish football. During one of the game's numerous scuffles, Jésus Larraza turned to the Uruguayan midfielder José Vidal and barked, "Look kid! This isn't a

game for young gentleman."² Sarcasm did not sit well with the Uruguayans: the Spaniard was later seen limping off the pitch. Praised for their
agility, good positioning and precision passing, the South Americans did
not disappoint. Uruguay won all nine matches and conquered Spain. *El
Eco* extolled the virtues of the Uruguayan teamwork: "This homogeneity
has its tradition in the combined game which they carry out, full of
method . . . a true collective and moreover possessor of the tactic of rarely
lifting the ball from the ground. Fast . . . very open, great movement.
But the truly captivating in these South American champions is the
quality of the pass."³ Early on in the tour, Nacional's talented forward,
Pedro "El Vasco" (The Basque) Cea, had visited his grandmother, whom
he did not know, in a small town near the Portuguese border. South
American football had had to travel far in order to find its way home.

. . .

By the 1920s, Latin American intellectuals had begun to celebrate,
and thereby redefine, their *mestizaje* (mestizo) heritage. Identity would
now be realized from within rather than from without. In Mexico, the
secretary for education, José Vasconcelos, employed the talents of
Diego Rivera, José Clemente Orozco and David Alfaro Siqueiros to
paint monumental public murals to the glory of Mexico's Amerindian
heritage. Vasconcelos had sought to create some kind of order out of
the chaos of the revolutionary war. Moreover, he sought to mine his
country's past for the sake of its future: "Tired, disgusted of all this
copied civilization . . . we interpret the vision of Cuauhtémoc [the last
Aztec ruler] as anticipation of the . . . birth of the Latin American
soul . . . We wish to cease being [Europe's] spiritual colonies."⁴ This
was a far cry from the positivism—especially its unhealthy fixation on
the negative aspects of the mixing of races—that had so consumed
nineteenth-century liberal thought. In 1861, Sarmiento had voiced his
loathing of Argentina's creole culture in a letter to the future president
Bartolomé Mitre, "Do not try to economize the blood of gauchos. It
is fertilizer that must be made useful to the country. Their blood is the

only part of them that is human."⁵ Sarmiento's negation of his country's traditions was by no means uncommon in a region troubled by its identity. (The Argentinian litterateur Jorge Luis Borges would later reclaim gauchesque culture through his short stories.) This was not without reason. For many Latin American intellectuals, the notion of the Amerindian and Negro as inferior was coupled with a distaste for that quixotic Iberian trait: indolence married with pride. (Even in the sixteenth-century picaresque novella *Lazarillo de Tormes*, the Spanish nobleman, though starving, is far too lazy and dignified to work.)

In 1925, Vasconcelos published his infamous *La Raza Cósmica (The Cosmic Race)*, which employed social Darwinism to justify the triumph of the mestizo race. Racial purity was the product of inbreeding and therefore deemed weak. Eccentric theories such as this were nothing new. Two decades previously, Nicolás Palacios had written *La Raza Chilena*, which put forward an outlandish thesis: Chileans could claim kinship to German Visigoths, who had made their way to Chile via Spain, and had had their bloodline mixed with the Mapuche. Chileans were therefore superior to Europeans as well as to their South American neighbors. Unsurprisingly, certain intellectuals found this obsession with *raza* (race) to be an indication of the continent's inferiority complex. In 1923, the Salvadoran essayist Alberto Masferrer saw through the fanfare and bombast: "If one gives attention to our journalistic literature and in belligerent and nationalistic poetry—so prolific in Hispanoamerica—one will find that hardly a day passes without an article, a harangue, an ode, a sonnet, dedicated to celebrating the merits of *la raza*, the defence of *la raza*, the future of *la raza*; which, veiled or openly, always allude to the United States of the North."⁶

In addition to the preoccupation with race, there remained the question of regional difference. Independence in the nineteenth century had created artificial borders, which in turn forced the nascent societies of South America to differentiate themselves from their neighbors. (To this day, Argentina and Uruguay maintain similarities in both custom and speech; so much so that the former sees the latter as a proto-province rather than a separate nation-state.) Celebration of race was one thing, progress and modernization another. Comparisons to the Old World—that tool of self-advancement and aggrandizement for every developing country—were always going to be employed as a means of defining differences in a continent that was finding it difficult to define itself. Certain republics touted themselves as the Athens of the Americas (Colombia and Uruguay), whereas Paris was invoked as a byword for elegance and sophistication (Buenos Aires and Guatemala). Though its conceit may have indicated otherwise, no city or country would be truly satisfied with its own identity. For many countries in the region, football had begun to create a sense of "otherness": a discrete psychological identity where previously one had not existed. (Uruguay's *garra charrua*, Brazil's *futebol arte*, Argentina's *la nuestra*, Peru's *el toque* would later reflect identities as it was felt they should be rather than as they actually were.) The game would become such an intrinisic part of the psychology of these republics that history would have to be rewritten. By the early 1940s, one historian sought to capture the defining feature of Uruguayan football as a "synthesis of racial fortitude, a tangible and spiritual manifestation of Latin mental agility and physical virility."[7] Notions such as this, which were always biogenetically framed, were not limited to Uruguayan football. Similar ideas of *criollo* exceptionalism were expounded across the region, each republic providing its own version of a super race in footballing terms. Football still desperately needed an "other" against which to define itself. Now that the Anglo-Saxon strain had faded from the South American game, identity would have to be sought elsewhere. It was time for South American football to travel to Europe.

The Quest for European Gold

Expectations on the thirty-hour train journey to Paris had been high among the Uruguayans. In the South American mind, Paris epitomized all that Latinity could achieve: a sense of a better, idealized self, which could compete with the Anglo-Saxon on equal terms. While the attractions of the French capital surpassed all Uruguayan anticipation, the *village olympique* proved a disappointment. The poor facilities and crowded conditions ensured that the South Americans would not stay long. Despite a limited budget, a villa was found close to the Colombes Stadium in Argenteuil, where the delegation was looked after by the curiously named Madame Pain.

With twenty-two teams competing for gold, competitive international football had come of age. The only other non-European countries to have entered were Egypt, Turkey and the United States. Great Britain and Germany had both declined to participate. The extent to which Uruguayan football was a known entity in Europe remains unclear. The successful Spanish tour had brought *el fútbol rioplatense* to a wider audience, but it was nonetheless rumored, in a legend that has now passed into history, that the Uruguayans were poor, obscure tradesmen. (According to Galeano, "Pedro Arispe was a meat-packer. José Nasazzi cut marble. 'Perucho' Petrone worked for a grocer. Pedro Cea sold ice."[8]) France certainly knew the status of the Uruguayan squad. "The French press has published news of the imminent arrival of the Uruguayan Olympic team. There are great hopes in Paris—where the reputation of the South American Champions is very popular—to see whether the Uruguayan squad can measure up to the French Olympic team."[9]

Not that this was evident from the low attendance figures of 3,025 for Uruguay's first match. Yugoslavia was promptly dispatched 7–0, after having spied on the Uruguay's mock training session, during which the Latin Americans pretended that they could not play. The United States followed by losing three goals to nil. In the quarterfinals, Uruguay encountered the hosts, who were soundly beaten 5–1 in front of 30,000 spectators. The *New York Times* claimed there was no stopping these "small but sturdy bronzed men,"[10] while *Le Figaro* praised "the precision, speed and good combinations of their football,

supported by a marvellous defence of the backs, Arispe and
Nasazzi."[11] When asked by the press how Uruguay had managed to
run rings around its opponents, the country's right half, José Leandro
Andrade, who would die penniless and alcoholic, stated that the
team practiced by trying to catch chickens.

The Netherlands, under their English coach, would prove tougher
opposition. After scoring in the first half, the Dutch played
defensively—a tactic that exposed the highly organized Uruguyan
team's lack of flair on this occasion. Nevertheless, two goals by Uruguay in the second half, one of which was a disputed handball penalty
in the eighty-first minute, proved to be the difference. The Dutch duly
complained to the Olympic committee, but the Latin Americans' victory was upheld. Now it was the Uruguayan delegation's turn to protest
when a Dutch referee was announced for the final. The decision was
overturned, not that a partisan referee would have a made a difference.
In the final, Uruguay swept aside a courageous Swiss side 3–0. It was
said that in the second half the Uruguayans played with a panache that
had never graced an Olympic football pitch. Gold had been secured in
Latin America's spiritual capital, Paris. Such was the popularity that
this Latin American side had secured after their sparsely attended
opening match that 10,000 spectators had to be turned away from the
Stadium Colombes. "Popular enthusiasm as was seen today has never
before been equalled in the annals of international sporting competition in Paris," was the view from the United States.[12]

For many Uruguayans, the reception of the Olympic gold medalists
in the foreign press was more important than the ensuing fanfare at
home. Plaudits rained down on the champions from *La Vanguardia de
Barcelona* to *La Gazzeta dello Sport*. Gabriel Hanot, a French footballer
whose career had been curtailed by the First World War and then
ended in an aviation accident, could barely contain his admiration:

> *The principal quality of the victors was a marvellous virtuosity in
> receiving the ball, controlling it and using it. They have such a complete*

technique that they also have the necessary leisure to note the position of
partners and team mates. They do not stand still waiting for a pass.
They are on the move, away from markers, to make it easy for team-
mates . . . To an impeccable technique is added a stout foot and a good
eye . . . The Uruguayans are supple disciples of the spirit of fitness rather
than geometry. They have pushed towards perfection the art of the feint
and swerve and the dodge, but they know also how to play directly and
quickly. They are not only ball jugglers. They created a beautiful football,
elegant but at the same time varied, rapid, powerful, effective.[13]

Nevertheless, Hanot, who would later become editor of *L'Équipe*,
could not help but compare this free-spirited team with Anglo-Saxon
professionalism: "Before these fine athletes, who are to the English
professionals like Arab thoroughbreds next to farm horses, the Swiss
were disconcerted."[14] Even the British, whose own Football Association had declined to enter on the grounds that the definition of
amateurism had not been settled with FIFA, were ready to congrat-
ulate "this really wonderful team of Uruguayans, from the other end
of the world, on their great victory. Those, who understand the technique of the great dribbling game, and who witnessed their matches,
will agree that their play reached the highest standard."[15] Certain
quarters proved more circumspect in their assessment. Gabriel Bon-
net, the vice president of FIFA, praised the Swiss as true amateurs,
thereby casting aspersions on "professional" Uruguay.

Footballing success had even greater significance off the pitch,
something that was not lost on Enrique Buero, Uruguay's elegant
minister plenipotentiary to Berne: "A victory for the Uruguayan team
in the 1924 Olympics would have great repercussions in the sporting
world, which nowadays links all the politicians and leaders of these
old societies."[16] But it was *El Día*'s special correspondent in Paris,
Lorenzo Batlle Berres, who voiced what every Uruguayan felt: "You
are Uruguay. You are now the motherland, boys . . . the symbol of
that little dot, nearly invisible on the map . . . which has been getting

larger, larger, larger."[17] The triumph of the undiscovered team from a hitherto unnoticed country would become a potent myth. In *Beyond a Boundary*, his exquisite treatise on cricket, C. L. R. James would argue that the game had changed the world's perception of the West Indies: "Clearing their way with bat and ball, West Indians at that moment had made a public entry into the comity of nations."[18] So had football for diminutive Uruguay. Her seemingly innate ability to master the round ball had changed the face of the sport. In many ways, the game would never be the same. Nor, for that matter, would Uruguay. The country would become inconceivable without football.

While the Europeans were astounded by the skill with which the Uruguayans played the game, the latter's style was a product of regular competition. Freguent tournaments, both at local and international level, had catalyzed the playing of game in the Río de la Plata. Moreover, the First World War, which effectively stopped the European game for four years, allowed a generation of footballers to flourish in the southern hemisphere while their counterparts were being butchered on the Western Front. It had been during these years that Latin American football was allowed to cast itself in its own image without the help of foreign influence.

Bad Neighbors

While the press in Latin America celebrated Uruguay's Olympic gold as a victory for the continent, Argentina claimed it as a victory for *el fútbol rioplatense* (River Plate football). And yet there was a feeling that an opportunity had been missed. This was certainly true for the Argentine players. The great Boca Juniors goalkeeper of 1910s and 1920s, Américo Tesoriere, commented: "The campaign carried out by the Uruguayans is magnificent and it rejoices me. I would have liked to be in Paris with the Argentine team to play the Olympic tournament's final match . . . It is essential that our officials learn once and for all. They have to choose a team in due time without thinking of useless factions in order to reach the unity of action."[19] Factionalism, which infected Latin American domestic football in the 1920s, also poisoned the selection of an Argentinian Olympic football squad. Even with the republic's international sporting reputation at stake, the Comité Olímpico Argentino and the Confederación Argentina de Deportes could not come to an agreement.

Jules Rimet, however, took a diplomatic approach, echoing what Enrique Buero had written to the Uruguayan Ministry of Foreign Relations: that a victorious team "is the best propaganda for any country, specially for the new countries little known in Europe."

Uruguay, which had long been tired of being patronized by her overbearing neighbor, now espoused fraternal harmony. *La Nación* went so far as to print a florid Uruguayan editorial:

> *The Argentine soul and the Uruguayan soul have vibrated in unison in these times of clamorous jubilation. The hearts of these two peoples have had palpitations that have made it seem, at times, that only one heart was beating. Before now, it often upset us [Uruguayans] . . . that we were referred to as an Argentine province. But this time we have happily embraced that misunderstanding: with pleasure we have wanted to show the world that the two countries on the shores of* La Plata *are brothers, not in a trivialized externalization of a merely courteous formula, but in the profound and cordial fullness of unmatched affection.*[20]

Cordiality, however, remained superficial. With an eye on the main chance, Argentina challenged the world champions to a two-leg "final." The matches would confirm who the true champions really were. The first, in Montevideo, was a close-run affair: the Argentinians were the better team on the day and unlucky to be held to a 1–1 draw. The return leg, however, proved an historic encounter and would change the Latin American game. In Buenos Aires, the

Estádio Sportivo Barracas had capacity of 40,000 spectators, though 52,000 had managed to gain entry. Such was the fervor of the crowd that it began to stray onto the pitch once the match had started. After five minutes, the game was postponed until the following week. The Uruguayans had felt unease at the cordon of police holding the football supporters at bay. For the replay, a twelve-meter-high fence was erected around the pitch at the stadium. This one act would provide a barrier between the fans and the players that stands to this day. One moment of brilliance apart, the match was a master class on the darker side of the River Plate game. This time the Argentinians were not wholly at fault. The Uruguayans, frustrated at their lack of possession in the second half, took to the more physical side of the game. The Argentine Adolfo Celli had his tibia fractured. When stones were thrown at Andrade, certain Uruguayan players took to throwing them back. Scarone lost his temper and kicked out at a policeman, only to end the day at the police station. The match descended into farce when the Uruguayans left the field five minutes from time, despite having been asked to play on. The Argentinians waited and the match was theirs: they had beaten the world champions. By the end of the game, the individual brilliance of Cesáreo Onzari's goal might have been all but forgotten. After only fifteen minutes, Huracán's left-winger curled a corner directly into the Uruguayan goal. (The law on scoring from corners had only just been changed.) From that day on, any goal scored in this way would be known as an "Olympic goal" (*gol olímpico*).

The perennial Uruguay-Argentina confrontation had become a grudge match. Violence, which had crept into the Latin American game, began to overshadow the sport. In November 1924, however, Latin American football would suffer its first tragedy. The Campeonato Sudamericano that year was held in Montevideo but not under the auspices of the Asociación Uruguaya de Football.

Lacking the infrastructure for an international tournament, the Paraguayan Football League (Liga Paraguaya de Fútbol) offered to

host the championship in Uruguay, as an honor to the world champions. (The healthy gate receipts would fund the renovation of Asunción's Estádio de Sajonia, which was later renamed "Uruguay.") The
final match would pit Argentina against Uruguay, with the Uruguayans only needing a draw to clinch their fifth title. In the aftermath of
the goalless draw that secured Uruguay's triumph, a group of Argentine fans went to the Hotel Colón in Montevideo, where the Argentine squad was staying, in order catch a glimpse of their heroes.
When the players appeared on the hotel balcony, much cheering
ensued. This high-spiritedness came to an abrupt end when a drunken
Uruguayan began to hurl insults at the Argentine players, who in
turn threw bottles at the aggressor. By now the fracas had taken to
the street, where another Uruguayan, Pedro Demby, took off his
jacket and squared up to Argentines in the manner of a boxer. At that
moment a passerby pulled out a revolver and shot Demby in the neck
and throat.

South Americans on Tour

Victories at a continental level had failed to give Latin American
football the sense of identity it craved. Thus, paradoxically, European
affirmation was needed in order to make these teams truly Latin
American. This would take the form of the tour (*gira*), transforming
these teams into mythical entities. Success abroad brought with it not
only a place in history but also a mythology for future generations.
Latin American football could not—and would not—exist solely
within its own sphere of influence. It needed to show its potency not
only within the region but also in the Old World. The ties that once
bound the continent to Europe have never been cut, no matter how
many governments have sought an autonomous path.)

The First World War put an end to foreign tours by European

clubs, which forced the Latin American game to develop organically. The continuing influx of immigrants into the region, especially into the burgeoning port capitals, fed the game with players and supporters. The English game, in which stamina and strength were considered paramount, had been usurped by a more fluid and elegant football. For Uruguay, Olympic gold had given the country what a century of independence could not: a sense of the exceptional had helped crystallize her identity. This was reinforced in 1925 when Nacional undertook a European tour of epic proportions. Thirty-eight games—of which the Montevidean club won twenty-six, drew seven and lost five—were played in front of over 800,000 spectators. The Uruguayans were not the only team from Latin America to make the journey across the Atlantic. Three days before the squad boarded its steamer for Europe, Boca Juniors had already embarked on a tour of its own. CA Paulistano would leave three days after Nacional and play ten matches in France, Switzerland and Portugal. This would be the defining year of the decade: a year in which both the Hispanic and Lusophonic (i.e., Portuguese) South American cultures would combine to outshine European football.

For Nacional, the tour had an inauspicious start. Manuel Varela was not able to cope mentally with leaving home and disembarked in Santos, where he joined Palestra Italia on its tour of the Río de la Plata. After arriving in Paris from Genoa, the Uruguayans played a combined Paris eleven in front of 40,000 fans. Complaints were made about the state of the pitch, and Andrade grumbled, "I am frozen to my bones. It's terribly cold. I couldn't move."[21] Nevertheless, Nacional ran out 3–1 winners, with *El Día* praising Castro's goal as "a marvellous piece of dribbling."[22] In the next match against a Normandy eleven, the home team had acquired the services of an English goalkeeper in order to negate the Uruguayans' attacking strength. Such was the ferocity of "Perucho" Petrone's shot that on one occasion the ball took the goalkeeper into the net. That day Petrone scored all five goals. The Argentinian press was more circumspect in praising its neighbors, especially after a fight took place between two Nacional players (a trait that would become characteristic of the Uruguayan game). *Crítica*, in an editorial on *les sauvages sudamericains* (the Savage South Americans), worried that Argentinians would be tarnished by Uruguayan bad behavior: "Quarrels and resentments should be aired at home, not on foreign soil . . . [Europeans] might wrongly suppose that beneath the polite and cultured appearance of a South American lies a wild and savage Indian . . . The fact of being a good football player is not a reason for being ill-mannered."[23]

By the time Nacional suffered its first defeat, at the hands of the Catalonian Esportiu Europa, the Uruguayans had won five games and drawn one. With twenty-two goals in favor, and one against, Nacional's forwards were scoring at will. Before the match against Roubaix, the club president promised his players prize money should they win by a superior goal margin than CA Paulistano, who had beaten the France eleven 7–2 the week before. Petrone notched up another five goals in a 7–0 thrashing. Yet his days on the tour were numbered. After scoring fifteen goals, he suffered a knee injury against Barcelona that would keep him out of the game for over a year.

In Rotterdam, a Netherlands eleven, still smarting from its Olympic semifinal defeat, sought revenge. Héctor "El Mago" (The Wizard) Scarone, who had scored the decisive eighty-first-minute penalty to send the Dutch out of the competition, now added a brace in an emphatic 7–0 win. El Mago, whom Zamora called "the symbol of football," would be the club's leading scorer on tour, with twenty-six goals in twenty-three games. Short and lively, with two good feet, Scarone was renowned for his exquisite finishing. Despite his stature, Piendibene later remarked, "You need to position yourself in the air and head [the ball] like [Scarone]."[24] The following year, El Mago became the first Uruguayan to play for a European club when he signed for Barcelona; he would go on to play for Inter Milan and

Palermo in the early 1930s. Such was the depth of the squad that on May 17 Nacional played three matches in three countries. While one eleven played in Paris against a Franco-Swiss side, another lined up against a Brussels team in the Belgian capital. Later that day, Nacional was held to a 0–0 draw in the Copa Uruguaya in Montevideo.

For Argentina, which had not sent a team to the 1924 Olympics, Boca Juniors' tour was a way of stealing a march on Uruguay's burgeoning reputation. An editorial in *Crítica* reminded readers just what lay in store for both club and country: "It is the first time an Argentine team goes to the Old World, whence many people [in Argentina] have arrived . . . Boca Juniors' trip abroad has the potential of obtaining the biggest success yet for that institution, for the sport, and for our country."[25] Populist and sensationalist—the paper even ran regular features on the Porteño obsession with psychoanalysis—*Crítica* sought to propagate its notion of *argentinidad* (Argentine-ness) through publication of the tour's dispatches. Not all the papers took a jingoistic stance. Traditionally more conservative in its politics, *La Nación* was indifferent to "famous triumphs" abroad; rather it believed that Boca's task was "to maintain the gentlemanly tradition of the Argentine sportsmen."[26] Footballers, especially from an immigrant barrio such as La Boca, would never resemble the polo team—with its roster of upper-class Anglo-Argentine surnames: Kenny, Miles, Nelson and Naylor—that had won gold at the 1924 Olympics. Though the squad for the most part comprised players of Italian extraction, expressions of *argentinidad* would not only manifest themselves on the pitch. *Crítica*'s football correspondent wrote a glowing piece about how beautiful the tangos, to which the players listened, sounded during the Atlantic crossing. Moreover, the *himno nacional Argentino* (Argentinian national anthem) was always sung after matches.

The tour, which was initiated by a group of businessmen, would take in thirteen matches in Spain, five in Germany and a final game against a combined French eleven in Paris. As with Nacional, the squad was strengthened with players from other clubs. Footballers from Rosario joined other guest players, including Cesáreo Onzari (Huracán), Manuel Seoane (El Porvenir) and Luis Vaccaro (Argentinos Juniors). Seoane and Vaccaro were fundamental to the success of the tour, though they were very different players. Vaccaro was renowned for his ability to run continuously for ninety minutes, and such was his presence that when he did not play, Boca was invariably defeated. Seoane, on the other hand, did not have the physique of a footballer. Naturally stout, with a fluctuating weight problem for which he would be long remembered as "La Chancha" (The Pig), he had started playing for the factory team of Campomar before moving to Independiente and gaining a reputation as a striker of exceptional flair. In 1923, his involvement in an altercation with the referee in a match against River Plate was punished by a yearlong suspension, which initiated his subsequent move to the rival Asociación Amateur de Football. Renato Cesarini, the Argentinian who played for Juventus and Italy, later said of La Chancha, "[Seoane] was a player of results, not of the team . . . the best that I ever saw. I have no doubt."[27] During the tour he proved to be Boca's top scorer, hitting the net twelve times in sixteen matches. Once his ban ended, he returned to his former club and became its leading scorer in the amateur era.

While the press, for the most part, saw Boca Juniors as Argentinian ambassadors abroad, it was apt to turn on its own. After the successful Madrid leg, during which Boca won all three of its matches, the Porteños suffered two humiliating defeats in Bilbao to Real Unión de Irún (4–0) and Athletic Club (4–2). *La Razón* was quick to negate the club's Argentine-ness: "Boca Juniors is not the highest expression of Argentine soccer . . . What does the prestigious club represent, at the end of the day? At most, *porteño* soccer—a branch of porteño soccer, not an Argentine one, because Buenos Aires is not the nation."[28]

The final match of the tour proved to be the club's crowning moment when Seoane scored a hat trick against a combined Paris eleven. Boca had triumphed where its neighbor had dazzled the sporting world the year before. After the match, Américo Tesoriere paid with what little money he had left for his teammates to ascend the Eiffel Tower, then the tallest building in the world. It was a fitting end to what had been a highly successful tour.

While CA Paulistano may have played the shortest of the three tours, it was in many ways the most successful. The team from São Paulo lost only one of their ten games. The first match, against a French eleven, set the tone for the tour. Arthur "El Tigre" (The Tiger) Friedenreich, displaying "lightning speed" and his dribbling skills, scored a hat trick in the 7–2 thrashing.[29] *Le Journal* hailed the Brazilians as "Les Rois du Football," which must have irked the Uruguayans, who were in effect touring as Olympic champions.[30] Quick to draw comparisons with their fellow Latin Americans, *L'Écho de Paris* stated: "The Brazilian players have made a great impression. Their game is less brilliant than that of their rival Uruguayans, but at least as effective. Their shots along the ground are the most dangerous that exist."[31] Nevertheless, the team lacked the assurance and solidity in defense that made the Uruguayans such a potent force. Mário—who in 1922 had played against amateur British opposition and had dribbled "through the entire defence, rounding the keeper and planting the ball in the net"—was the leading goal scorer after Friedenreich, who notched up eleven. The last match against Portugal had to be curtailed so that the team could board the steamer on time. In what little time they had been allotted, Paulistano managed to score six goals. Even the Portuguese press praised the exceptional play of the Brazilians. When CA Paulistano arrived in Brazil, the team was feted as returning heroes. Once the usual banquets and victory parades had passed, a monument was commissioned to honor the victorious team.

Though the three teams approached their respective tours in different ways, they all saw themselves as ambassadors for their respective republics. The myth of each tour went deep: for Nacional, it was the longest and greatest tour ever undertaken; whereas for Paulistano the moniker acquired in Paris—the Kings of Football—would always remain. The creation of a positive image abroad, which had been historically difficult for so many of these republics, had now been achieved through football. Maintaining it would be a different matter.

. . .

For many visiting teams, a stop-off in Brazil proved a diversion before and after the exigencies of Argentinian and Uruguayan football. Rio de Janeiro, more than any other Latin American city, appealed to European visitors, and not without reason. The city adhered to the notion of a tropical paradise that led the English travel writer Philip Guedalla to comment: "Anyone might be excused for doubting Rio. Its air is heavy with unreality; and cautious travelers, habituated to landscapes couched in a more normal idiom, justifiably refuse to believe a word of it . . . The hand of Nature (powerfully aided by the hand of man) stuns new arrivals into a sort of happy dream where anything may happen."[32] Distraction, in the form of a vibrant night-life, did little to instill a competitive edge in the visiting teams.

By the late 1920s, Brazilian football was emerging from the long shadow cast by the Río de la Plata. Carioca (Rio) football was proving highly effective, as Motherwell came to learn in the Brazilian leg of its South American tour. In front of 50,000 spectators, Motherwell played to a tie with Rio de Janeiro, though the match will forever be remembered for Oswaldinho's goal. Starting from the halfway line, the center-half dribbled past five players before scoring. Brazil's leading football historian, Tomás Mazzoni, believed it to be one of the greatest goals ever scored in the country. Three days later a combined São Paulo–Rio eleven, which constituted the Brazilian team, thrashed the Scottish side 5–0.

Adherence to the rules—always a poor second to displays of panache and guile—proved difficult for many South American sides. When Chelsea toured the region in 1929, the Second Division team was subjected not only to the "black arts" of the Argentinian game but also to the partisanship of "unfair play." Luis Monti, who would underperform in the 1930 World Cup final, kicked a Chelsea player in the groin only to be egged on by the crowd with shouts of *"muy bien Monti"* (well done, Monti). If player-on-player violence was not enough, an Argentinian spectator hit the Chelsea captain in the face. It came as no surprise that the Chelsea management complained to the football association that "non-observance of the laws of the game hindered real football."[33] Moreover, the touring team's coach was vandalized. In the same year, an Anglican bishop, who had spent twenty-five years in South America, displayed a similarly high-handed Anglo-Saxon attitude:

> *There is now a Saturday half-holiday (called the "English Saturday," by the way) and clubs abound. The game is played on Saturday afternoon and most of Sunday; it is as universally popular, and there are the same crowds and excitement, as at home. I have spoken to one who witnessed what was perhaps the first game played in a certain suburb of Buenos Aires, by Englishmen of course, and he heard the comments of some of the few Argentine spectators, "How brutal! How barbarous!" and now they are as football-mad as we are. It is a salutary madness, however, even though they have still much to learn. It is hard for Latins to keep their tempers and take a beating in a sportmanlike spirit. But undoubtedly South Americans are the better for the boating, tennis and football which they have learned from us British.[34]*

Violence apart, the game in the region had developed its own idiosyncrasies. When Motherwell toured Brazil, the spectators were astonished to find that the Scottish goalkeeper employed the goal kick.

Football in the Land Without Men

The First World War had been good to Paraguay. European demand for her natural resources—which included beef and cotton—had helped provide certain stability after years of political turmoil. More-over, the landlocked republic was no longer as geographically isolated as it had once been. The expansion of the railway lines connected her to Argentina in the south; while foreign investment proved the catalyst for modernization. Over four decades of immigration had bolstered a population decimated at the hands of the Triple Alliance. Staunchly conservative and Catholic, Asunción remained a backwater compared to other capitals. This was not helped by her oppressive and humid climate, which gave the whole city an air of listlessness. Moreover, the country's mix of Guaraní and European cultures made Paraguay different from many of her neighbors. As a bilingual republic—not unlike Peru's Quechua bilingualism—she was truly exceptional in the region.

For Paraguay, international competition would be critical to the development of the game. In 1919, an Argentinian squad had made its way up the Río Paraguay to Asunción to play four matches. Although the Paraguayans improved from their 5–1 rout, they lost all four matches. It would be another two years before Paraguay would celebrate her first victory in international football (unless one counts the decidedly weak opposition provided by the sailors from HMS *Petersfield* in the intervening years). In the same year as her first victory, the Paraguayans traveled to Buenos Aires to take part in the 1921 Campeonato Sudamericano de Selecciones. Not that they were taken seriously by their River Plate rivals. The team's Buenos Aires–born manager, José Durand Laguna, was told by his Uruguayan counterpart, "Don't worry, *Negro*,* if you want I'll tell my boys not to attack too much so as not to thrash you." The Argentinian responded in true Paraguayan fashion: "On the pitch it's eleven *versus* eleven . . . we are not afraid of you and we'll play you to the death."[35] And play they did, stunning Uruguay 2–1.

---

* The term *negro* in Uruguay does not always equate to the derogatory "nigger." It can be a good-humored nickname for anyone of dark skin, swarthy complexion or even for those with dark hair.

Stability could not last and the rest of the decade was played in the shadow of political factionalism and war. In 1922, civil war put an end to the domestic game, and Paraguayan football had to seek its opposition abroad. Despite the treasury having stipulated that "the Paraguayan State does not have money for balls," a national squad was sent to the 1922 Campeonato Sudamericano in Brazil.[36] (The minister who signed the document would later die of gunshot wounds after becoming embroiled in a love triangle.) With Paraguay, Brazil and Uruguay having managed five points from four games, a playoff would decide the championship. Uruguay, however, abandoned the tournament, after having two legitimate goals disallowed by the Brazilian referee in its 1–0 defeat to the Paraguayans. It was a game too far for Paraguay, who also complained of partisan refereeing in her 3–0 defeat, and went home as runners-up. In the same year, a team, playing under the handle *Nda recoi la culpa* ("I am not to blame"), toured Argentina in order to raise money for the Red Cross.

. . .

While Argentina, Uruguay and Brazil set the pace for the game on the continent, in other countries it was far slower to develop. The reasons for this varied from country to country, though geography and politics were often to blame. Football was effectively quarantined for a decade during the Mexican revolution (1910–1920). What the Mexican novelist Martín Luis Guzmán so eloquently termed *la fiesta de las balas* (the fiesta of bullets) would arrest the development of the domestic game. In 1923, the Mexican ambassador to Guatemala, Juan de Dios Bojórguez, organized the nation's first international tour. Three matches would be played in Guatemala, though *la selección mexicana* looked suspiciously like the starting lineup of Club de Fútbol América. When only four Mexican-born footballers were selected for the national team, the furor that ensued forced the authorities to reselect the eleven. In the event, Mexico beat the hosts two games to one. Later that year, a Guatemala eleven traveled to Mexico DF, where it was beaten 2–0 in a three-match rubber. Between these two tours, Pancho Villa finally fell foul of yet another assassination plot and died in a hail of bullets in his American car. For years, the country's geography would compromise her football: physical proximity to the United States would be offset by cultural distance, while cultural proximity to Latin America was offset by physical distance.

Competitive international football, in the form of foreign opposition, came to Bolivia late. Ever since La Guerra del Pacífico (The War of the Pacific) the country had been hamstrung by her geography. And geographical isolation only furthered a sense of cultural isolation. By the late 1920s, first-rank teams were no longer willing to travel to Bolivia. In 1927, Unión Coquimbo FC de Chuquicamata from Chile played seven matches in La Paz, Oruro and Cochabamba. Boca Juniors may have played the Strongest, Bolivar, Club Bolivar Nimbles and an Oruro eleven four years later, but it was a local team from Antofagasta and not the great club from Buenos Aires. (River Plate fans, never afraid to employ Argentinian racial superiority in their chants, would famously sing: "The area of La Boca is filled with Bolivians, who shit on the pavement and wipe [their asses] with their hands.") For a country whose loss of territory would be a constant source of shame, it must have been disconcerting when some of the touring teams came from towns that had been annexed by Chile.

In the same year, Club Almagro, the first Porteño team to tour, was beaten 1–0 by La Paz's The Strongest in front of 20,000 spectators. After Bolivia's pathetic display in the 1926 Campeonato Sudamericano, where the hosts, Chile, had ripped her apart 7–1 in her first international, followed by similar humiliation at the hands of Argentina (5–0), Paraguay (6–1) and the eventual champions Uruguay (6–0), Bolivian football finally had something of which to be proud. The leading scorer of the tournament, David Arellano, had found the net four times for Chile in the opening match against Bolivia. He would make an even greater impact the following year.

Death in Valladolid and the Birth of Colo-Colo

The century that had passed since Independence—during which time politics across the region had been played out under the watchful portraits of the great *libertadores*—only served to crystallize notions of exceptionalism. Taken in by European flattery, certain republics saw themselves as set apart. In 1864, the conservative statesman Antonio Varas sought to distinguish Chile from her neighbors: "I have such a poor idea of the . . . sister republics that . . . I regret we have to make common cause with them."[37] Inflated ideas of Chilean superiority still obtained into the 1920s. It was difficult, however, to reconcile this attitude when the River Plate republics were so far advanced in footballing terms and Chile had clearly failed to impose herself in the international arena. The 1924 Campeonato Sudamericano had been a disaster for the Andean republic. In the first match against their Uruguayan hosts, the Chileans were thrashed 5–0, which included a hat trick by the peerless Pedro "Perucho" Petrone. Further losses to Argentina and Paraguay sent Chile to the bottom of the table. It was somehow prescient that the only Chilean goal of the tournament was scored by David Arellano. The young physical education teacher would be instrumental in changing the course of his country's footballing history.

Arellano had been a gifted forward for Club Magallanes, which had been one of the leading teams in the Asociación de Football de Santiago. Nevertheless, he had now experienced at first hand the progress of *el fútbol rioplatense*. The game in Argentina and Uruguay, where clubs not only trained but also "looked after" their players, was professional in all but name. When Arellano sought to implement a degree of professionalism at Magallanes, the directors turned against him. (Moreover, he had been overlooked as captain due to an arbitrary change of the rules by the board.) He believed that amateurism had held Chilean football back. In April 1925, Arellano left the club and took ten players with him. Thus Colo-Colo, which would become one of Chile's greatest clubs, was founded.

Colo-Colo would give expression not only to Arellano's vision but also to a sense of Chilean identity (*chilenidad*). The club, born of rebellion, had taken its name from a sixteenth-century Amerindian chief who had masterminded the defeat of the Spanish, though in Araucanian myth it was a nocturnal lizard that fed on human blood. This was a bold move for a country that had never come to terms with her Mapuche heritage. Having established obligatory training sessions and employed the use of tactics, Colo-Colo won the Liga Central de Football in its first season. When, in 1926, the club toured the south of Chile and traveled as far as Ancud, it acquired a national fan base outside of the capital. Under Arellano, Colo-Colo was seen as progressive, even "scientific," in its approach to the game. The club's middle-class roots, however, were still evident in its notions of "fair play." (If the team was winning with ease, penalties would be deliberately missed.) Yet what this modern club needed was international competition.

In 1922, after a hiatus of eight years, European sides had begun to make the journey back to Latin America. One of the first teams to play in the Río de la Plata and Brazil was a combined Basque squad (Federación Guipuzcoana). The team included José María Belauste, who was called up from France, where he had been exiled for political reasons. (He would later leave Franco's Spain to manage in Mexico.) Belauste had entered Spanish mythology when he forced a goal against Sweden at the 1920 Olympics, taking four Swedish players with him into the net. Spain would win silver and, thus, the legend of *la furia española* (the Spanish fury) and its accompanying aggression was born. Walter Harris, an Englishman who had started his career with Coventry City before moving in Spain, coached the touring side. A year later, the quondam Scottish champions, Glasgow's Third Lanark, won four of its eight matches in Argentina and Uruguay. For the Scots, most of whom had not been abroad before, the trip was not without incident. In Buenos Aires, objects (which were said to include firecrackers and knives, not uncommon in the region) were thrown onto the pitch as one of the Glaswegians was preparing to take a corner. Third Lanark walked off the pitch. While in Montevideo, Peñarol complained about the hard-tackling Scots. (By the 1986 World Cup, the boot would be on the other foot.)

In 1926, Barcelona's Real Club Deportivo Espanyol would attempt to reestablish Spanish dominion in the New World. Among the touring side was Ricardo Zamora, whom *El Gráfico* would put on its front cover with the legend "The Marvellous Spanish Goalkeeper."[38] Nicknamed "El Divino" (the Divine), Zamora combined both bravery and dominance between the posts. These attributes—together with the elegance that his white polo-neck sweater and tweed cap bestowed—endeared him to the *bella figura*–obsessed Latin American crowds. In Chile, Arellano imposed his philosophy on a Zona Central de Chile eleven, which beat the first European side to tour 4–3 and 4–1. Nevertheless, the high point of the tour was in Montevideo. After having beaten Nacional by one goal four days before, Deportivo Espanyol now took on Peñarol. The match played out as a duel between the thirty-six-year-old José "El Maestro" Piendibene and Zamora. Although a passionate Nacional supporter, Galeano recognized the beauty in the game's only goal:

> *The play came from behind. Anselmo slipped around two adversaries, sent the ball across to Suffiati and then took off expecting a pass back. But Piendibene asked for it. He caught the pass, eluded Urquizú and closed in on the goal. Zamora saw that Piendibene was shooting for the right corner and he leapt to block it. The ball hadn't moved, she was asleep on his foot: Piendibene tossed her softly to the left side of the empty*

net. Zamora managed to jump back, a cat's leap, and grazed the ball with his fingertips when it was already too late.[39]

Like all touring sides in the 1920s, Deportivo Espanyol had offered the hosts the opportunity to experience a different style of playing. And yet, without anyone knowing it, the tour had achieved more than that. As well as participating in competitive football in the region, the Spanish had inadvertently challenged the very essence of River Plate football: not just how the *rioplatenses* played but in effect who they were.

Surprisingly, the illustrated sporting weekly *El Gráfico* chose to invoke the Spanish game instead of the British, to develop its theory of *lo criollo* (the creole). Without any sense of irony in its condescension—ever the Porteño way—*El Gráfico* damned Spanish football with faint praise:

> *We feel that the quality of the football played in our country is very high—so high that we consider that only the football played by British professionals is superior to it—and it is thus within a very strict definition of technique that we respect the merits of our guests . . . and we conclude that football in Spain has made surprising progress that puts it almost on a par with our own. We say almost on a par since we are convinced that our own play is technically more proficient, quicker and more precise: it perhaps lacks effectiveness due to the individual actions of our great players, but the football that the Argentines, and by extension the Uruguayans, play is more beautiful, more artistic, and more precise because approach work to the opposition penalty area is done not through long passes upfield, which are over in an instant, but through a series of short, precise and collective actions: skilful dribbling and very delicate passes.*[40]

For the *rioplatenses*, dribbling was now deemed the highest form of football: the expression of *criollo* artistry. The cult of the individual had replaced any team ethic that might have existed previously. But then this was the very aspect of the game at which Argentines and Uruguayans excelled. The differences between the Old World and the New were evident when the Deportivo Espanyol players were taken to see Lanús versus Independiente. When interviewed about the Argentine game, the Spanish players questioned the reluctance to shoot on goal—though they were courteous enough to praise the clever dribbling and the precision of the passing game. (Though the Chilean game also had a tendency to prevaricate in front of goal.) Ernesto Sábato, in his novel *Sobre héroes y tumbas* (*On Heroes and Tombs*), identified the cult of *bella figura* ("cutting a beautiful figure"), which by the 1960s had begun to disappear:

> But the world is like that and in the end it's all about goals. And in order to show you what these two methods of playing were, I'm going to tell you an illustrative story. One afternoon, at half time, la Chancha [the "Pig": Seoane] said to Lalín: "Cross it to me, old man, and I'll come in and score." The second half starts, Lalín indeed crosses the ball and el Negro [the "Black": Seoane's other nickname] takes it, moves in and scores . . . Running toward Lalín with open arms, Seoane shouts: "You see, Lalín, you see." And Lalín replies: "Yes, but I'm not enjoying it." Here, if you like, is the problem with criollo [Argentinian] football.[41]

In 1926, Santiago hosted the Campeonato Sudamericano for the first time. On this occasion, as opposed to previous competitions in all of which it had placed at the bottom of the group, Chile came third. The Bolivians were now the region's whipping boys, conceding twenty-four goals in four matches. Chile managed to secure a 1–1 draw against Argentina, which in the former's eyes amounted to a win. As in 1923 and 1924, Uruguay was crowned champion at Argentina's expense. Arellano was the competition's top scorer with seven goals, having helped himself to four at the expense of a hapless Bolivia in her 7–1 thrashing. Chileans had long favored boxing over football; Colo-Colo's 1927 tour of the Americas and Europe would change that.

The precedent for ambitious foreign tours had been set two years previously by Nacional and Boca Juniors. In Carlos Cariola, a playwright and erstwhile president of the Federación de Fútbol de Chile (FFC), Colo-Colo had its champion. The tour would be beneficial for Chile both diplomatically and educationally, though the idea was that it should be financially lucrative. Moneys came via the Ministry of Education, so that the players would not have to forgo their salaries. Nevertheless, wages were not equitable: some players were paid for the duration of the tour, while others had to make do with a few months' salary. On the first leg of the tour, between January and March 1927, Colo-Colo played a series of matches in Ecuador, Cuba and Mexico before heading for Europe. The competition was not of the first rank: in Mexico Colo-Colo unsurprisingly won ten of its twelve matches. The Spanish, however, would prove stronger opposition. In the capital, Atlético de Madrid outclassed the Chileans and ran out 3–1 winners. The Madrid-based newspaper *ABC* praised the "clean and proper" game in which "gentleman players . . . fought with honour." (Unlike their River Plate rivals, who would be more aggressive in their conduct on pitch, Chile gained a reputation for fair play.) Evenhanded in its assessment of the Chileans, the report admired the speed of the outside forwards while pointing out the team's defects. "We like the defensive trio less. The back is weak and the goalkeeper delivers nothing more."[42] What the European tour would demonstrate was that Chilean football still lacked confidence in front of goal and exhibited a tendency to prevaricate.

The following match, against Real Unión Deportiva, showed a decisiveness that had been lacking when Colo-Colo won by six goals to two. The victory celebration would, however, be short-lived. The Spaniards, eager to show that defeat had been an aberration, challenged the visitors to a match the following day. Strengthened by additional players that had been recruited locally, Real Unión

Deportiva only managed to secure a 3–3 draw. The turning point for Chilean football came in the thirty-fifth minute of the match. Arellano went for up for a header against David Hornia and took an accidental blow to the stomach. Colo-Colo's talisman had to be taken off the pitch with an injury. The following evening, after having suffered excruciating pain, Arellano died. The doctors had failed to diagnose peritonitis. Only the day before, Arellano had decided not to play, but had been persuaded otherwise by his teammates. A similar incident had befallen the Paraguayan game in 1923. Oscar López de Filippis, a talented forward for Olimpia, collided with the goalkeeper of Sastre Sport and also died of peritonitis.

Arellano's untimely death was a national tragedy. *Los Sports*, the Santiago sporting magazine, ran the headline ¡DOLOR! with a picture of the grinning footballer underneath.[43] The extended obituary, which detailed the death, burial and eulogies, rendered Colo-Colo's captain in proto-martial terms. In defending Chile abroad, Arellano now not only belonged to Colo-Colo, he also belonged to the country.

The rest of the tour was played out in solemn fashion, with the squad donning a black armband that would become part of its strip. The 5–4 victory against a Barcelona eleven proved a high point, though the squad would be brought back to the harsh realities of River Plate football when it lost three games in a row by significant margins in Montevideo. The squad, now desperate to return home, were given a final lesson at the hands of Peñarol (6–1) and Boca Juniors (6–0).

Death, both untimely and abroad, had nationalized Arellano. The myths were quick to start. Arellano was now credited with having invented *la chilena* ("the Chilean"), the theatrical overhead bicycle kick that he ably performed. The inventor of this deft move was, however, another Chilean, Ramón Unzaga. Born in Bilbao, in Spain, Unzaga became naturalized after migrating to Chile with his parents. He began executing *la chilena* while playing for Club Atlético y de Fútbol Estrella de Mar in Talcahuano, and the move gained popularity in the region when he played for his adopted country in the 1920 Campeonato Sudamericano. He too would be nationalized.

. . .

By 1927, Nacional had embarked on another grueling *gira*, though this time the club had decided to pit itself against teams from North America and Cuba. The United States was, however, unknown territory for the Montevideans. Anticipating the arrival of the Uruguayans, John Kieran alerted his readers in his *New York Times* editorial to what amounted to soccer invasions and reminded them of how Sport Club Hakoah Wien's tour had "awakened [the United States] to the possibilities of soccer as an international sport . . . a little more of the same won't do any harm."[44] Unfortunately, the goodwill engendered by the Viennese, who were about to embark on their second tour of the country, would ultimately evaporate. (Tragically, the club was shut down and had its assets seized after the Anschluss in 1938.) Nacional's first match, a 6–1 defeat of an American Soccer League eleven in front of 20,000 spectators, was lauded by the *New York Times*: "Attacking with fury . . . as the game progressed their splendid passing combinations became more and more effective." Andrade was singled out for his "flashing play."[45] First impressions did not last. By the third match, against the mediocre Newark Skeeters, the Uruguayans were finding it difficult to control their tempers. After they conceded the only goal of the match, police intervention was needed when the referee was punched in the face and had to be taken off the pitch by three policemen. The manager of Nacional, not averse to what had become a national tradition of laying blame at the feet of the referee, complained that his team had been discriminated against. Not for the first time the Uruguayan consul general, José Richling, would be an apologist for his country's players. He later denied having stated that he would send the team back "if there were any future disturbances."[46] Moreover, he excused the players on account of the language difference and the American interpretation of the rules.

(The American game was unrefined and more physical, even by Latin American standards.)

Now that this had all been explained to the Uruguayan players, the tour could progress with ease. After dispatching an All-Star U.S. team with panache, Nacional would endure the worst match of its tour. In Boston, a fight between the players ensued after a Uruguayan struck an opposing player. Taking advantage of the situation, two thousand spectators left their seats and made for the melee on the pitch. While the police rescued the Uruguayans, two U.S. players were knocked unconscious. Richling was quick to exonerate, blaming the referee. By the end of the U.S. leg, Nacional had played thirteen games in front of nearly 90,000 spectators and had only been beaten three times. Nevertheless, these disturbances had only reinforced the hackneyed notion in the U.S. press of "Latin-ness" and that Latin America remained a politically backward continent. The Uruguayans may at times have been their own worst enemies, but they did not deserve the melodramatic editorial that saw them instigate "so many rousing riots that the Uruguayan Consul General took the ball away from them in order to prevent open warfare between the United States and the whole of South America."[47]

Amsterdam, 1928: Battle of the River Plate

Having made the mistake once, and thereby forgoing what she thought to be rightfully hers, Argentina sent a delegation to IX Olympiad in Amsterdam. Though the field was smaller than four years previously, seven non-European teams entered, including Mexico and Chile. The reigning champions were strong favorites but made hard work of reaching the final. Nevertheless, this high-scoring tournament had the Latin Americans dishing out the punishment as well as taking it. Argentina had the better draw, making light work of an inexperienced United States team 11–2. Chile fell at the first hurdle, having been 2–0 up against Portugal within thirty minutes. Portuguese resolve and fitness prevailed—the very thing that would fail them when they lost to Egypt in the quarterfinals—and the Chileans were beaten 4–2. The left-winger, José Miguel Olguin, would later say, "It was the first serious lesson that we had about the value of organized football . . . The Portuguese went well prepared."[48] Mexico, whose development of football had been arrested by the Mexican revolution, was thrashed 7–1 by a Spanish side keen to reproduce its former glories. Spain's swift march to the quarterfinals would be abruptly halted when she conceded seven goals in the replay against Italy. Argentina remained the in-form team. Against a plucky Belgian side, the Argentinians scored three goals within the first ten minutes, leading one newspaper to note that "the Argentines early in the game seemed to toy with their opponents."[49] Once Belgium drew level, Argentina scored another three goals. In the semifinals, Egypt conceded six goals without reply. Argentina—whose squad was a roster of predominantly Italian names that might have passed for an Italian side—would have to wait and see if the mother country could overcome her neighbor.

For the gold medalists, the route to the final had not been an easy one. In the opening match, against the Netherlands, the hosts sought to exact revenge for the perceived injustice of 1924. Special trains were laid on for the Dutch supporters, who had come from across the country to watch their countrymen defeat the South Americans. Tickets, now in short supply, were selling at over twelve times their cover value. This time Uruguay kept a tight defense and easily overcame the Dutch. The 2–0 margin might have been greater but for some excellent saves by the Dutch goalkeeper. Facing Germany in the next round proved a daunting task. The match was an ill-tempered affair—so much so that the Egyptian referee sent off two Germans and José Nasazzi, Uruguay's stalwart defender and captain. The German press was outraged: "A hard contest full of unsportsmanlike behavior. Is this the purpose of the Olympics?"[50] Years later, Nasazzi would remember the match, which Uruguay won 4–1, as one of the hardest he ever played. "[The Germans] had a fantastic team of very quick and strong giants, who were frightening . . . if ever there was a time I felt fear it was in that [game]."[51]

The semifinals against Italy would showcase the best of both continents. Vittorio Pozzo, who would lead Italy to two World Cup championships in the 1930s, wrote in *La Stampa*: "The magnificent passionate Italians are defeated by bad luck."[52] Pozzo singled out José Andrade as the Uruguayans' "ace," a rock in defense but dangerous in attack. "La Maravilla Negra"—or *merveille noire* as Andrade was christened in Paris four years previously—had nearly not made the trip to Europe. When his request to be paid was declined, he refused to play. Fortunately for Uruguay, he changed his mind when he saw his fellow players leave Montevideo on the steamer. He was quickly booked a passage and reunited with the delegation in Rio de Janeiro.

Familiarity had not bred contempt, but it did lead to a rather a muted final. Despite the packed Olympic Stadium—there had been over 250,000 requests for tickets—the match did not meet expectations. The Spanish sports newspaper *El Mundo Deportivo* found this "was not the brilliant [match] that was anticipated due to the [teams'] excessive knowledge of each other's game."[53] After the 1–1 draw, the secretary of the Argentine delegation was unusually sportsmanlike about the outcome: "If there is another tie we would like to declare ourselves both Olympic champions, but as this is not permitted under the Olympic rules we will have to play a third game."[54]

The replay merited its status as a final. Scarone, whose absence in the first match was noted by the press, was joined by Borjas and Figueroa, while Castro, Petrone and Campolo sat on the bench. The winning goal merited a gold medal on its own. "El Vasco" Cea— about whom Nasazzi said "the team lines up with *el Vasco*, me and nine others,"[55] floated a delicate pass to Borjas, who headed the ball into the path of Scarone. With an open goal in front him, El Mago made no mistake. The Uruguayans were worthy champions. After winning gold, Peñarol's Álvaro Gestido—whose brother Óscar would become a military general and briefly serve as Uruguay's president before dying in office—remembered feeling very alone before the Chileans turned up crying tears of joy. Though Chile had lost the consolation final to the Netherlands on the toss of a coin, the Dutch had declined to accept third place and granted Chile the win. South America now had two champions.

. . .

At the end of the decade, it was the turn of Rampla Juniors, who had been crowned Uruguayan champions in 1927 and runners-up a year later, to visit the Old World. European appetite for Latin American football had only been whetted by a second Olympic gold. After a couple of warm-up matches in Brazil, where the Uruguayans won and tied against Rio and Paulista selections respectively, the squad headed to Spain. It was an inauspicious start to the tour when Rampla Juniors went down 3–0 to a Selección Militar (Military Eleven), composed of players from the Spanish national team. After victories against Atlético Madrid and Valencia, the Uruguayans notched up impressive victories against Schalke '04, Red Star and Olympique de Marseille, before beating Ajax 2–1. The second leg of the tour would be remembered for all the wrong reasons. Rampla Juniors returned to Spain to be hosted, over two legs, by Sevilla, whose stadium had recently been inaugurated with a friendly between Spain and Portugal. (The Spanish, captained by Zamora, outplayed the Portuguese, netting five goals in a whirlwind forty-five minutes.) The Uruguayans, however, did not honor the newly constructed Estádio de la Exposición. Violence was once again part of the Uruguayan repertoire, especially where penalty decisions were concerned. When Magallanes, the Rampla Junior midfielder, struck the referee, the game was all but lost. The expulsion that followed only escalated the ill will and the Uruguayans walked off the pitch. Crowd trouble and police intervention ensued, only for Rampla Juniors to play out the match with ten men.

After four and half months, during which time Rampla Juniors played twenty-two matches, it was time to return home. The journalist who covered the whole tour wrote an elegiac closing article that captured the club at its zenith: "We have lived through events, whose memory will never be erased from our minds. Faced with all the obstacles: struggling against every kind of inconvenience, enduring the cold and the heat; snow or rain . . . crisscrossing Europe in every direction and experiencing 289 hours by train, the team sent to Europe won marvellous victories, amazed numerous fans and wrote, for the club's history, perhaps its finest pages."[56] Unfortunately, the year of the stock-market crash would be the club's finest hour.

Heading for a Crash

During the previous decade, the game in Latin America had thrown off the last vestiges of its British origins and replaced them with a robust and assertive *criollo* identity. But the South American countries' hegemony on the pitch was not matched by their influence off it. By the beginning of the First World War, the United States replaced Great Britain as Latin America's primary trading partner. Their sphere of influence, originally limited to Central America and the Caribbean, now extended itself farther south. The Monroe Doctrine of 1823 may have excluded the European powers from subjugating the Latin American republic, but it did not temper ideas of Manifest Destiny. Said one U.S. senator in the 1840s, "The Mexican is an indigenous aborigine, and he must share the fate of his race."[57] The ties to the Old World had not been fully severed: European interests in the region still demanded that dividends and loan repayments be honored. Moreover, the surplus of U.S. imports, coupled with war debts, had Europeans looking closely at their investments abroad. Thus dollars moved from the United States to Latin America and on to Europe, before making their way back to the United States. With American bankers outdoing each other in foisting loans on the region, not to mention the appetite with which Latin American governments took up this credit, the decade became known as the "Dance of the Millions." The availability of credit had New York overtake London as the region's financial center. Unscrupulous enticement was not unknown. The son of the Peruvian president Juan Leguía received $520,000 from a New York investment bank for "facilitating" loan contracts. Examples such as this were far from rare. Although loans were used to fund municipal infrastructure projects, from hospitals to motorways, they were also politically and financially beneficial for the creole elites. It was clearly an insupportable system and Latin American economies had already begun to slow down two years before the time of the Wall Street crash in October 1929.

Football, however, continued to flourish despite the shadow cast by the economic situation. Uruguay may have been world champions, but the team was shown no quarter at the 1929 Campeonato Sudamericano. Paraguay opposed the Uruguayans in the opening match of the tournament in front of a partisan Argentinian crowd. When Ramón Viccini was stretchered off with a broken leg after twelve minutes, Paraguay was reduced to ten men. The underdogs proved worthy 3–0 winners, despite the aggression the world champions meted out. (Petrone acted more like a boxer against the Paraguayan defense than a striker.) In the final match, which the Uruguayans had to win by a significant goal margin, Argentina took the crown by hitting the net twice.

Though they were reigning world champions, defeat came as no surprise. Earlier that year, Ferencváros had stunned Uruguay 3–2, having been three goals up at halftime. Although a talented side, the

Hungarians were not quite the side they would become in the 1960s. MTK Budapest FC had dominated the 1920s, winning the championship seven times; though Ferencváros managed to secure the championship from 1926 to 1928, the same year in which Hungary won the Mitropa Cup. The Hungarians had started their tour in Brazil with a 2–1 win over São Paulo, before drawing 1–1 with Fluminense in Rio. Yet on its return to São Paulo, Ferencváros met its match in Palestre Italia (who would later change its name to Palmeiras). When the Italo-Brazilians beat the Hungarians by five goals to three, *Folha da Manhã* ran the front-page headline THE CHAMPIONS OF CENTRAL EUROPE UNDERGO, IN SÃO PAULO, ONE OF THE HARDEST SETBACKS IN ITS SPORTING HISTORY.[58] Defeats to Argentina and São Paulo at the end of tour reinforced just how strong the South American game was.

Football has a way of subverting the norm, of championing the underdog, of rebuffing the favorite. The 1920s should have belonged to Argentina. Beyond the shores of the British Isles, she was one of the few countries that had integrated football into society. Her football was by far the most advanced in South America and matched the game in several European countries. And yet the decade was dominated by that diminutive republic that had been conceived as nothing more than a buffer state. Uruguay, however, would remain an anomaly: a country that should never have come into being but for an historical quirk of fate. (Even her great *libertador*, José Gervasio Artigas, whose portrait hangs in every public office, opposed succession from the United Provinces of the River Plate.) For Uruguay, two Olympic gold medals had shown the world her potential. Even better was to come.

CHAPTER FOUR

CHAMPIONS OF THE WORLD

1930–1940

The Rise and Fall of the Oriental Empire

When does football cease to be a game? What is the dividing line between a game and a conflict?

—*Buenos Aires Herald* (1929)

South American players are usually gifted ball players . . . it is almost a gift of their environment, but they are careless of physical condition . . . and they like to romance with the game, rather than approach it with a thoroughly professional determination.

—Alfredo Di Stéfano, "For the Love of the Game,"
The Real Madrid Book of Football (1961)

It has been suggested by cynics that football is almost as great a danger to the peace of South America as the politics of soldiers, students and artisans. Both sports are flavoured with a fanaticism only equalled by the Inquisition.

—Rosita Forbes, *Eight Republics in Search of a Future: Evolution and Revolution in South America* (1933)

The infamous Chelsea tour of Brazil and the Río de la Plata had not been without repercussions. Predisposed to short-termism, a trait that had come to shape the continent's history, the Latin Americans had sought to win by any means possible without thinking of the consequences. The British Embassy in Rio de Janeiro was embarrassed: not so much by the nature of the two defeats, but by the resultant crowing: the Brazilians "claim as a nation to have beaten England" was the message home.[1] Further invitations to tour the region were not encouraged.

For Uruguay, a British presence at the inaugural FIFA World Cup would have given the competition the approval it craved. It was not to be. Despite the Uruguayan chargé d'affaires' entreaties, the football association remained adamant, while the Foreign Office in London tactfully evaded responsibility. The Uruguayans may have felt slighted, but they were not an exception in such matters. The football association had taken similar positions in the past. Robert Guérin, who would become FIFA's first president, had stated that dealing with the FA was akin to "slicing water with a knife."[2] For the British, there was much to lose: not least maintaining that paternal aura as the founding father of the game. Losing to a surgent Latin American team—even if they were the Olympic champions—would not do. Therefore, the British authorities remained "rather chary of seeking to promote the despatch of British football teams abroad, especially those composed of professionals, as we have had some unhappy experiences recently in Europe in which such teams had not only disgraced themselves, but had caused much disappointment to their opponents and their supporters."[3] Isolationism would not serve British football well. And this attitude was not the sole preserve of the British. Certain Latin American republics would take up a similar position, the most famous example of which would be the 1958 FIFA World Cup where Czechoslovakia exposed the insularity of Argentinian football in its 6–1 thrashing. (Until that tournament, the Argentines had not played a World Cup match for twenty-four years.) Argentina, according to Fontanarrosa and Sanz, was "the country where until 1958 everyone believed that they had invented football."[4]

Disappointment with British attitudes was compounded by the rejection by a number of European countries with closer cultural ties to the diminutive republic. This, however, did little to affect what would become one of the defining moments in Uruguayan history. And yet, was La República Oriental del Uruguay (The Oriental Republic of Uruguay, her formal name) what Jules Rimet and Henri Delaunay had in mind as a host nation when the tournament was conceived? The 1928 Olympics proved that Uruguay's meteoric rise to the heights of world football was no fluke. If the country could not compete with larger nations economically—which led to an inferiority complex of which it would find it difficult to rid itself—then it would redefine itself through the game. Securing the inaugural World Cup, however, would not be an easy task for the world champions.

In 1926, Delaunay voiced what everyone at FIFA already knew: "Today international football can no longer be held within the confines of the Olympics; and many countries where professionalism is now recognized and organised cannot any longer be represented there by their best players."[5] Yet it was not until the 1928 FIFA Congress in Amsterdam that the work of the association's special committee came to fruition. Though the format of an international tournament had finally been decided upon—open to any country whose players were amateur or professional—a host country was needed. While talent had served the Uruguayans well, now luck and timing were needed. As things turned out, the Wall Street crash and the ensuing Depression would play into their hands.

The eighteenth FIFA Congress, which was held in May 1929, proved crucial for Uruguay's hopes. On the second day of the gathering, the Argentine delegate, Dr. Adrián Beccar Varela, demonstrated his country's solidarity with the Olympic double-gold medalist. The arguments recorded in the congress's minutes were as much a declaration on Uruguay's behalf as an assertion of Latin American superiority.

1. the excellent results obtained by that country in the two last Olympiads;
2. [the] enormous development of football in South America and Uruguay;

3. [the] celebration of the centenary of Uruguay's political indepen-
   dance [*sic*] in 1930;
4. in charging Uruguay with the organisation all the South American Associations would feel honoured.[6]

The honor of the continent may have been at stake, but the delicate
subject of financing the tournament had not been determined, especially its division of spoils. Rodolphe Seeldrayers, the future president
of FIFA, expressed concern that "football has already frequently been
accused of being led by financial considerations so we must be careful
not to give fuel to such ideas."[7] Not for the last time would FIFA take
a Janus-like stance in relation to money. It was, however, Uruguay's
willingness to finance a tournament, and take on any liabilities, that
proved decisive. The financial proposal put forward by the Uruguayan
delegation did not allow for profits: all earnings would be plowed
back into the tournament. FIFA would take 10 percent of the gross
receipts, while the municipality of Montevideo and the Uruguayan
government would fund the travel and accommodation expenses of
the participating nations. Unable to compete with the Uruguayan
proposal, the other candidates unsurprisingly now favored withdrawal.

The field was left open for Uruguay. Nevertheless, the republic's
pride in securing the inaugural World Cup was couched as a Pan-
Latin American endeavor. Enrigue Buero, who believed in national
aggrandizement through sporting success, stated, "We have given a
heart-warming example of intercontinental solidarity, and I'm sure it
made a truly positive impression."[8] For the Uruguayan delegation, the
hard work had only just begun: Montevideo had a year in which to
construct a stadium and organize a tournament that would be the
envy of Europe.

Now that Uruguay had won the bid, the Europeans proved indifferent. All five losing candidates—Hungary, Italy, Netherlands, Spain
and Sweden—snubbed the tournament. Two months before the opening

ceremony, no European nation had decided to enter. With the British unaffiliated to FIFA, and Germany, Austria, Czechoslovakia and Switzerland having declined to participate, there were few countries left. Uruguay was in danger of hosting a Campeonato Sudamericano de Selecciones (South American championship) dressed up as a World Cup. The situation forced Buero to take drastic action. He not only implored the European associations to attend but also offered compensation to those professionals whose livelihood might be affected by spending two months abroad. Diplomatic entreaties failed to make an impression. The secretary of the FA, Frederick Wall, refused to bother to even make up an excuse in his response: "I am instructed to express regret at our inability to accept the invitation."[9] Rumors of a Pan–Latin American boycott of FIFA and any future competition held in Europe did little to engender interest.

In the end, political pressure needed to be applied. Rimet coerced the French to enter, though the squad would not be at full strength. Lucien Laurent, France's inside right, later recalled: "The French Federation had great difficulty putting a team together . . . Several of the players who were contacted were forced to decline because their bosses didn't want them to leave for two months."[10] The only other European countries to enter were Belgium (under pressure from the Belgian Seeldrayers), Romania (whose squad was chosen by King Carol II) and Yugoslavia (a mediocre team of the third rank). The European footballing superpowers had stayed away, and FIFA lacked the authority to compel them to play. At least the United States had shown a sense of Pan-American solidarity and had joined Argentina, Chile, Mexico, Brazil, Bolivia, Peru and Paraguay. Uruguay would exact her revenge on Europe four years later when she declined to participate in Italy's Campionato Mondiale di Calcio. (Italy would not be outbid a second time: a 3.5-million-lire investment would trump Sweden's bid.)

Despite Uruguay's footballing prowess, Montevideo lacked the infrastructure to hold the tournament. Buero may have shown Rimet

the plans for a new stadium during the congress, but work on the Estádio Centenario (Centenario Stadium) would not commence until February 1930. Influenced by Le Corbusier—who had given a lecture tour
the year before and famously commented that Buenos Aires geographically turns its back on the Río de la Plata and presumably, by extension, on Latin America—Juan Scasso and his team of architects had
designed a stadium to match the country's ambition. Constructed out
of imported, reinforced concrete on the outskirts of Montevideo, this
elliptically shaped stadium would be large enough to fit the Roman
Colosseum. (The concrete, however, would not be able to withstand
the brine of the South Atlantic air.) Forsaking the Anglo-Saxon preference for standing close to the action, Scasso surrounded the pitch by
a water-filled ditch to keep out the spectators. Yet it was the art deco
grace of the hundred-meter Torre de los Homenajes (Tower of Hom-
age), with its sleek wings and ship's prow, that transformed the Estádio
Centenario into much more than a stadium: this secular, modernist
country had built a temple to the game. With the July opening ceremony looming, three teams of workers had to toil in shifts so that
construction could continue twenty-four hours a day. The work, however, was not completed on time: the elements had been beyond the
young Scasso's control.

Thus the first match of the inaugural FIFA World Cup was played
in front of four thousand spectators at Peñarol's Estádio Pocitos.
France ran out 4–1 winners against Mexico, with Lucien Laurent
scoring the first goal with a well-taken volley in the falling snow.
Despite the tournament's ultimate success, it would be marred by
eccentric decisions taken by the referees. In her next match against
Argentina, France succumbed to a late free kick by Luis "Doble
Ancho" ("Double Wide," for his ability to cover the pitch) Monti,
after the Argentinian had spent the match bullying the opposition.
Six minutes from time, with Marcel Langiller clear on goal for an
epic equalizer, the Brazilian referee ended the match. While the
French remonstrated with the referee, the Uruguayan spectators

booed their Argentine neighbors. The match was restarted, though the Uruguayan government would have to assuage (and not for last time) the hurt feelings of the Argentinians.

Bolivia may not have had high hopes for the tournament, but the team showed its esteem for the host nation by having each player sport a letter on his jersey that spelled out VIVA URUGUAY. This deference, however, had no effect on the Uruguayan referee in Bolivia's match against Yugoslavia. The landlocked republic may not have won an international, but it did not deserve to have several goals disallowed. Despite holding on for sixty minutes, the Bolivians in the end crumbled, conceding four goals. (Yugoslavia would succumb to the hosts in the semifinal, having received a questionable offside decision for what would have been the equalizer.) As if to redress the balance, the Bolivian referee, Ulises Saucedo, awarded five penalties in Argentina's match against Mexico. The great Argentine Guillermo Stábile, who would become the tournament's top scorer, netted a hat trick; the second player to do so after the United States' Bert Patenaude had dismantled Paraguay two days before.

It was not until July 18, 1930, on the centenary of the signing of the country's constitution, that Uruguay played her first match. The completion of the Estádio Centenario had been beset by numerous setbacks, the most alarming of which was the bedding down of the newly laid pitch. In spite of the delay, Rimet was not unimpressed by the new stadium: "It's the best in the world. I've been to most of them, if not all, and this is by far the most complete one."[11] Peru proved worthy opponents for the Olympic gold medalists, despite having lost 3–1 to Romania in a match blemished by having the first-ever player—Plácido Galindo—sent off in a World Cup. Alianza Lima's charismatic black right wing, José María Lavalle, toyed with the Uruguayan defender, Gestido, to such an extent that he earned himself the sobriquet "La Sombra de Gestido" (Gestido's Shadow). Lavalle epitomized the agility and *picardía* (cunning) of Peruvian football, though this exasperated his teammates: "When he found a halfback who wasn't too good, who you could easily dribble around, he would have a [field day] with him. He laughed at him, and he danced the *marinera* [a traditional Peruvian dance] around him. He ran, he stopped, he gave him the ball and took it back. He would spin him around the field. When this happened he wouldn't let go of the ball for anything. Those things hurt the team. He didn't centre the ball, and the team couldn't make goals. And he just laughed."[12] Fortunately for Uruguay, the indefatigable Cea combined with the one-armed Héctor "El Divino Manco" Castro to spare the hosts' embarrassment. Peru may have only gone down 1–0, but this loss, so tantalizingly close to victory, would help engender a neurosis in the Peruvian game that the sociologist Aldo Panfichi would call *la historia del casi* (the history of near misses).

By the semifinals, both teams from the Río de la Plata had hit their stride. This time the United States fared better than its humiliating 11–2 Olympic defeat to Argentina two years previously. Despite fielding six British players and losing Raphael Tracy to a broken leg after ten minutes, the Americans managed to keep the deficit to one goal by Monti. Yet, in the second half, the floodgates opened and the Argentinians scored five goals in forty minutes, with Stábile adding a brace to his tally. On the following day, Yugoslavia, who had put paid to Brazil's hopes in the first round, in spite of the latter's individual flair, scored quickly against the hosts, only to be overwhelmed by six goals. The scene was set for a repeat of the 1928 Olympics final, though the buildup to Uruguay's finest hour would be far from amicable. The press on either side of the River Plate did little to stem the animosity. For Argentina, the two years since her defeat on the world stage had only inspired feelings of revenge. Moreover, the recent emergence in the public consciousness of an Argentinian style of play—*la nuestra* and *lo criollo*—only heightened a sense of the difference between the two nations.

On the day before the final, tensions reached a fever pitch with Porteños shouting "Death to Uruguay" in the streets of Buenos Aires.

The solidarity shown to their neighbors prior to the tournament had all but disappeared. As the steamers, crammed with football fans, left the docks for Montevideo, those who stayed behind gave voice to jingoistic slogans such as "Argentina yes, Uruguay no! Victory or death!" Over 15,000 Argentinians made the short crossing, though only a small portion would manage to enter the stadium. The rich and well connected chartered yachts or commissioned boats: six politicians requisitioned a government barge that was hauled across by a tugboat. But the fog and rain of the River Plate winter would play havoc with the crossing. (On their return, the Brazilians had made their excuses. Russinho, who played for Vasco da Gama, rued plain "bad luck," while Fausto "Maravilha Negra," the Black Wonder, complained that the cold "was a terrible thing, leaving us nearly frozen.")[13] Six hundred fans from Rosario arrived in Montevideo, hungry and exhausted, after severe delays, only to see the Uruguayan navy flying its masthead pennants in celebration. Those who did make the Uruguayan capital in time were further delayed by customs officers, who worked to the dictum "Not one Argentinian revolver should enter Uruguay."[14]

The River Plate's obsession with identity—furthered by an inherent fear of its absence—would also manifest itself off the pitch. Carlos Gardel, one of the great interpreters of the tango, whose iconic status is as much a part of Argentinian identity as that of Eva Perón, had become the object of a River Plate custody battle. Although born the illegitimate child of French parents in Toulouse, Gardel was said to have confirmed Tacuarembó, a city in northern Uruguay, as his place of birth. The confusion was aggravated by an interview he gave to a Colombian magazine, *Caretas de Antioquia*, in which he was quoted as saying: "My heart is Argentinian, but my soul is Uruguayan, because that is where I was born." On the eve of the final, Gardel remained impartial, at least in public, as to who might lift the trophy. When asked who he thought it might be, he found an elegant solution to an awkward question: "Soccer is more difficult to judge than a horse-race, and we all know that at the racetrack nobody ever gets it right . . . But . . . leaving aside the

Brazilians and the Yankees—I just don't know about them as sportsmen—I would say that the River Plate teams will be the most difficult to beat. If they get to the final, we shall simply have to toss a coin to see who will win. Both teams are good and play marvellous and artistic soccer."[15]

In private, however, he would remain an Argentine partisan, though *el turf* (horseracing) surpassed any love he might have had for football. He joined the Argentinian team at the Hotel La Barra, where he sang a selection of tangos. Ever the bird of ill omen, Gardel had similarly entertained the Argentinian team two years before. He is said to have sung "Dandy" just before the final of the 1928 Olympics. Argentina succumbed to Uruguay. For superstitious Uruguayans this was evidence enough: Gardel was in fact Uruguayan. Not that it mattered. In 1934, a year before his tragic death in an airplane crash in Colombia, "El Mago" (The Magician) released the swooning "Mi Buenos Aires querido" ("My Beloved Buenos Aires"). While Gardel's status as Argentinian cultural idol had hitherto been pretty secure—he had embodied that Porteño ideal: dandyism and machismo as one—it was now cemented.

The morning of the final was fraught with tension. Before the match the Belgian referee, John Langenus, sought assurances for his safety, and it was not until midday that the Royal Belgian Football Association allowed Langenus to referee the final. Dressed in a pair of knickerbockers and a coat and tie, Langenus made his way out onto the field with two footballs. The two republics had failed to reach an agreement as to whether the final should be played with an Argentinian- or Uruguayan-manufactured ball. In the event, both footballs were used: one in each half. Uruguay opened the scoring in front of over 80,000 spectators, through Dorado's twelfth-minute goal. Yet by the end of the first half the country's hopes of securing a third world title were hanging by a thread. The Argentinians were proving superior to their neighbors. With its players employing pace and intelligent positioning, goals had come from both Peucelle and Stábile, though Nasazzi accused the latter of being offside when he scored. It was left to Pedro Cea, the only player to have seen action in every match in both Olympics and this World Cup, to equalize after a superb piece of dribbling. His penchant for scoring when Uruguay was a goal down justified his reputation as the "Olympic equalizer." And yet, before the tournament, Cea had effectively retired from the game, until his late call-up. Another two goals followed, the last in the penultimate minute by "El Divino Manco" (The Divine One-handed) Castro, who had lost half his arm to an electric saw as a teenager. Castro had not been above using his stump as a bludgeon to gain an unfair advantage, and had injured Juan Botasso, Argentina's substitute goalkeeper, as he put the ball in the net.

The year after the death of José Batlle y Ordóñez, the president who had reinvented this coastal republic, Uruguay had achieved its greatest triumph. Not only had the country managed to host the inaugural FIFA World Cup successfully, she had withstood Argentinian pressure. The match, according to the Argentinian writer Juan Sasturain, may have been "the biggest neighborhood final [*final de barrio*] in the world," but it would become Uruguay's defining moment.[16] The relief and exaltation was palpable. Celebrations carried on through the night and the Uruguayan president declared a national holiday. In a letter to his friend Julio E. Payró, Juan Carlos Onetti would ironically recall:

> *There's no news—except that I have been retained as a ticket seller at the Estádio [Centenario] or Nacional ground . . . Can you conceive of a more autochthonously Uruguayan job? In front of me, the people; above me, the proud mast where the national flag flutters on those days that now belong to the bronze of history; the glorious afternoons of 4–0, 4–2 and 3–1, the glory between screams, hats, bottles and oranges.*[17]

In Buenos Aires, the Uruguayan consulate and the Oriental Club were stoned, and in certain quarters Porteños made halfhearted attempts at drumming up national fervor in the face of international defeat. This response—a potent admixture both of the country's inferiority and superiority—would become a national characteristic. Rumors of Argentinian hubris quickly circulated in Montevideo. The Argentinian players had allegedly worn shirts emblazoned with ARGENTINA CHAMPION under their strip.

Uruguay had been both ruthless and aggressive, harrying its larger neighbor into submission. The team had once again been led to a final by José Nasazzi, "El Gran Mariscal" (The Great Marshal), setting the precedent for future *caudillo** captains. (Uruguayan teams, no matter how talented the squad, would only flourish under strong leadership.) After the match, Nasazzi summed the game up succinctly: "In the days leading up to the Final, you could already tell that the Centenario would be completely packed. We knew that it was our big chance to beat Argentina, with whom we enjoyed a fierce rivalry at the time. And that's what happened. The atmosphere and our fighting spirit overwhelmed the Argentinians. Even Luis Monti, who was one of their key players, didn't kick anybody and played like a gentleman."[18] This was not lost on the Argentinian press. *La Prensa* felt that the national team should be composed of players who had nothing wrong with them physically or mentally and that "lady-players should be eliminated."[19] "El Cañoncito" (The Little Cannon) Varallo later remembered the match with a certain bitterness: "We ran out of steam, to tell you the truth . . . I aggravated my injury when hitting the bar with a shot that could have won it for us . . . From that point on they [Uruguay] started to get stronger and, with all due respect to my teammates, we weren't gutsy enough. How I cried that day. Even now when I look back it still makes me angry."[20] Varallo had been told by a local doctor not to play, but had not trusted him because he was Uruguayan. Gianni Brera, the Italian sports journalist, would later

---

* A leader of men. The Latin American obsession with the *caudillo* can be traced back to the military leaders in the wars of independence.

write: "Between the two 'rioplatense' national teams, the ants are the Uruguayans, the [grasshoppers] are the Argentinians."[21]

Monti, Argentina's brutal enforcer, who had been picked over the elegant Adolfo Zumelzú of Racing Club, had all but disappeared in the final. For *El Gráfico*, Zumelzú embodied the aristocratic side of Argentinian football: "noble . . . neat sidestep, a short passer . . . complete intelligence." Whereas Monti was a "fighter . . . strong in bitter struggles . . . a battler": the Argentinian as pugilist. But in this match courage had failed him. Two Italian agents, sent to "scout" at the behest of Mussolini, had not only threatened his life but that of his mother. By all accounts, he was so terrified before the match that he could not lift his legs for trembling. At halftime, the San Lorenzo defender had been in tears. Argentinians, ever fond of finding a scapegoat for their shortcomings, looked to Monti for their failure. He would later say, "All the Argentinians had made me feel like rubbish, a maggot, branding me a coward and blaming me exclusively for the loss against the Uruguyans."[22]

For many Latin American observers, Uruguay's triumph represented a victory for all Latin Americans. *El Liberal* in Asunción may have employed hyperbole in its editorial, but it was heartfelt: "Paraguayan sport is on its feet and, as well as its South American brothers, in these solemn times, overwhelmed by the most frank joy and happiness."[23] At the post-tournament banquet for the foreign delegations, the president of the Asociación Uruguaya de Football sowed the seeds of exceptionalism: "If every one of us makes in our own sphere what these boys have done in theirs, we will be able to say, without vanity and without arrogance, that Uruguay is the first nation among all the nations on Earth."[24] Unfortunately for the River Plate republic, it would misconstrue these words of praise: world champions in football would mean just that, nothing more. Triumph on the pitch would plaster over the cracks of a society already in denial. Looking back on the decade, the Uruguayan historian Lincoln Maiztegui would write: "When conditions became unfavorable, starting with the great crisis of international capitalism in October 1929, the 'model country' revealed her true face; her economy declined, social reality became extremely troubled and democratic stability, pride of that society, broke like a twig in the wind."[25] The sun was about to set on what Sasturain called the "Oriental Empire." Uruguay's golden age had lasted less than a decade.[26]

Una Faccia, Una Razza ("One Face, One Race")

Uruguay may have been world champions in name, but in truth, the balance of power in the Americas had already crossed the Río de la Plata. By 1932, the River Plate neighbors had broken off diplomatic relations after a Uruguayan vessel was inspected in Buenos Aires. To a British traveler, though, "the breaking off of relations between Argentina and Uruguay in August 1932, may be traced to the bitterness on one side and the impolitic rejoicing on the other which followed the defeat of the larger republic in the stadiums of Montevideo."[27] After Argentina's fourth title at the 1929 Campeonato Sudamericano (South America championship), winning the World Cup had looked assured. And yet, in spite of the country's poor showing in the final and the resultant criticism, Argentinian football would come to dominate the continent for the next two decades. Professionalism would be the catalyst behind the country's success.

It was not only Latin America that sought to fashion identity through sporting prowess. In Italy, unification (Risorgimento) had been achieved in the mid-nineteenth century, but successive governments had done little since to engender a cohesive sense of national identity. The country remained culturally fractured and economically backward, thus accelerating mass immigration to the Americas. By 1914, it is estimated that six million Italians lived outside the country. Fascism, under Mussolini, would seek to employ *calcio* (soccer) for its own ends. Yet success on the international stage would highlight differences, as much it would present an Italian ideal. Unlike German ideas of racial purity, which were extreme in their narrowness, fascism sought to bolster an Italian population that had been decimated by migration, war and poor health. Those with Italian connections who had moved away—mostly to Brazil, Argentina, Uruguay and Paraguay—were now welcomed home.

The first Argentinian player to sign for a European club was Julio Libonatti, who transferred from Newell's Old Boys to Torino in 1925. Four years earlier, El Matador had scored the only goal against Uruguay, securing Argentina her first South American championship. Such was Libonatti's prowess in front of goal that the Torino chairman signed him while conducting other business on a trip to Buenos Aires. Libonatti did not disappoint for either his new club or country: as an *azzurro* (Italian) striker he managed fifteen goals in seventeen appearances. His extravagance was legendary: he would buy twenty-five shirts instead of a couple. Ricardo Zamora thought him the best striker in the world. Could other Argentinian players follow where Libonatti had succeeded? The introduction of the Carta di Viareggio (Viareggio Charter) in Italy in 1926, which unequivocally excluded foreign players, seemed to stand in their way. The solution to this legal problem was simple as it was elegant: the creation of dual nationality. Those born abroad of Italian parents would remain Italians, even though they possessed the citizenship of another country. The *rimpatriato* (repatriated) was now free to play as an Italian. And in welcoming the *rimpatriati*, Fascist Italy could issue a stinging rebuke to those governments that were responsible for creating the Italian diaspora.

The 1928 Olympics had proved to be something of a showcase for *el fútbol rioplatense*. Raimondo Orsi shared the same Genoese heritage as Libonatti; though it was Orsi's ability on and off the ball that had so impressed the president of Juventus, Edoardo Agnelli. Fortunately for Orsi, Agnelli believed that players should be

incentivized in a professional manner. The transfer fee from Independiente was 100,000 lire, a package that included a Fiat 509 and a
monthly salary of eight thousand lire. Orsi was now credited for having "discovered Italy for the Argentinians."[28] Some of the Buenos
Aires press did not take kindly to what it saw as underhandedness on
the part of Italy: "The Italians want to form a national team at the
cost of Argentine football . . . The Fascist government, impressed by
the value of Argentine players and wanting to make Fascist football
appear the best in the world, has set its eyes on well known Creole
players and wants to tie them to Italian clubs to make them Italian
players."[29]

For that arbiter on all matters *criollo*, *El Gráfico*, the *rimpatriati*
were in effect acting as diplomats: "[They] go, actually, in their capacity as ministers of Latin American football in Europe."[30] Indeed
there was more than a hint of Argentinian proto-colonialism in the
editorial. "We must not be egotistical. Orsi, Cesarini, Stábile and all
those crossing frontiers in search of better horizons, on the way to
countries that need them . . . They leave to conquer other lands. The
country is now a little small for us, and a good football lesson given
on one of our pitches no longer dazzles anyone. For many years we
have held the Chair in dribbling and in scoring goals. For that reason, it is necessary to go outside; the good players that do us proud
abroad are working patriotically. Stábile goes to Italy, not to defend
football in the peninsula, but to defend *criollo* football, since he is a
criollo player."[31]

In a column entitled "The Boys Who Emigrate," the journalist
"Sobrepique" questioned the notion that Italian clubs looked after
their players better than their equivalents in Argentina. Tempted by
the lire on offer, players of Italian extraction were lured back to the
very country that had forsaken their parents. Italy was now considered the land of opportunity, where players would be paid hand-
somely and not discarded as a result of injury, as they were in Latin
America. On many occasions the *rimpatriati* were the Italian clubs'

best ambassadors, as was the case with Renato Cesarini. While playing for Juventus, the midfielder wrote to his former Chacarita Juniors teammate Eugenio Castellucci, telling him to drop everything and head for Italy, where Cesarini would look after him. Castellucci made the trip, but only played two matches for the Italian champions. Renato Cesarini had himself been helped by Orsi to secure a contract with Juventus. Unlike many *rimpatriati*, Cesarini was born in Senigallia, near Ancona, though his family immigrated to Argentina when he was a year old. Although he had already played for Argentina before his return, he would go on to make eleven appearances for the Azzurri. In 1931, he became famous for scoring in the last minute of an international against Hungary, which gave rise to the saying *Zona Cesarini*: this was finding the net in extremis.

The creative genius of the South Americans was not always welcome. The art of dribbling, which was considered the epitome of the game, was lost on Italian football, which viewed it as an unreliable extravagance. Whereas uncompromising players like Monti, whose courage had failed him when playing for Argentina, could be trusted to achieve what was required. In the late 1930s, *Lo Sport Illustrato* compared the two styles: "The Italian player . . . tends to simplicity, the quick game, the result obtained by the direct route . . . the art of the South American is to play the game, our art is to resolve the game."[32]

When Demaría returned to Argentina to complete his national service, or *colimba* (an amalgamation of the words *corre* [run], *limpia* [clean] and *barre* [sweep]), the question of dual nationality was brought to the fore. The *Gazzetta Della Sport* now referred to certain *rimpatriati* as "steamer-Italians." The image of the *rimpatriati* was further tarnished when Guaita, Scopelli and Stagnaro were caught at the French border, trying to avoid conscription for the Ethiopian War. *Il Littoriale* reprimanded the Roma trio as "twice robbers . . . because they stole our money as well as our confidence."[33] In its bid to include the Italian diaspora, Fascist Italy had not counted on the

Latin American instinct for self-preservation. The very thing that had brought these players to Europe would eventually take them back.

Amílcar Barbuy, one of the first Brazilians to play in Italy, having moved from Palestra Itália to Lazio, spoke for a generation of players who sought their fortune elsewhere: "I'm off to Italy. I am tired of being an amateur in football when such a condition has stopped existing a long time ago, masked by a hypocritical system of [bonuses] which clubs give to their players while keeping most of their income for themselves. For twenty years I have offered my modest services to Brazilian football. What has happened? The clubs got rich and I have nothing. I am going to the country that knows how to pay for the players' skill."[34]

In 1931, Barbuy would be joined at the Rome club by seven other Brazilians. Unsurprisingly, the club invited the moniker "Brasilazio." Nevertheless, adapting to life in Italy was harder for the Brazilians than it was for their River Plate neighbors. Prone to homesickness, they were more likely to return home. The tragic death through injury of Lazio's Otávio Fantoni, who played with two cousins and became known as Fantoni II, did little to attract more of his countrymen. Brazilian players now stayed away. Reactions to the South Americans were mixed. Perceived as saviors when they arrived, they were just as likely to return home having played a handful of matches: talent was not the only requirement.

Criollo identity had become universal. This new conception of Latin-ness would now allow for dual citizenship, and representing a second country was not seen as an act of treason. Nowhere was this more evident than at the 1934 World Cup. Although more professional in its organization than the Uruguayan tournament, Mussolini's Campionato Mondiale di Calcio still failed to attract the best footballing nations. Enrique Buero's desperate attempts to entice the Home Nations to play in the inaugural World Cup were echoed four years later. Charles Sutcliffe, vice president of the football league, took an isolationist stance in relation to the game. Having voted for the withdrawal of the Home Nations from FIFA in 1928, he famously wrote, "I don't care a brass farthing about the future of the game in France, Belgium, Austria and Germany."[35] The 1934 World Cup was deemed "a joke," while he believed "the national associations of England, Scotland, Wales and Ireland have quite enough to do in their own International Championship which seems to me a far better World Championship than the one to be staged in Rome."[36] Uruguay refused to defend her title, ostensibly in retaliation for having been snubbed by the Europeans four years earlier, though it was more likely that, in the midst of the Depression, traveling to Italy was not a priority. With Peru and Chile having withdrawn, Brazil and Argentina qualified automatically, but sent weak teams. Both countries were dispatched in the first round: Brazil, without fielding any Paulistas, went down 3–1 to Spain, continuing her bad form at international level, while Argentina, fielding a team without any survivors from 1930, lost to Sweden 3–2. The tournament was, on the face of it, a washout for the Latin Americans.

Yet, playing in the blue of Italy, Latin America would flourish. Vittorio Pozzo, who had lived in England before the First World War, called up four Argentinians in Orsi, Monti, Demaría and Guaita, together with Guarisi, a Brazilian from São Paulo. Not averse to employing martial metaphor to rouse his players before matches, Pozzo was blunt: "If they can die for Italy, they can play for Italy."[37] Although crucial goals from Guaita and Orsi helped Italy clinch the title, they were not decorated for their sporting prowess. Orsi had equalized in the eighty-first minute with a swerving shot that eluded the Czech goalkeeper. On the following day, he tried to reproduce the shot for the cameras, but was unable to create the same effect.

. . .

The onset of the Second World War in 1939 did little to diminish the number of Latin American players heading for the Italian leagues. In the 1939–1940 season, there were nineteen Argentinians and eleven Uruguayans playing in Serie A and B. Miguel "Michele" Andreolo, a Uruguayan who had played for Nacional, would make his life in Italy, playing for the national team from 1936 to 1942. He would be remembered for his bad manners on the pitch, having spat at the English referee in an England vs Rest of Europe match in 1938. After the "Phoney War," however, numbers began to tail off, so that by 1942–1943 there were no *rimpatriati* playing in Serie A. By 1946, however, the great South American export had begun to flood the European market.

La Guerra de la Sed (The War of Thirst)

The War of the Triple Alliance had failed to thwart Paraguay's ambitions or dim its national pride. For a country whose population had been decimated, she retained a sense of glory in inverse proportion to the scale of her loss. Bolivia, on the other hand, had been humiliated in the War of the Pacific, whose peace settlement left her without access to the coast. Not only was she poor: she was now landlocked. By the beginning of the twentieth century, yet more of her territory, this time in Acre, was annexed by her eastern neighbor, Brazil. Failure to adapt to the twentieth century would invite the unflattering moniker of "the beggar on the golden throne." And her determination to secure access to open water would render Bolivia almost suicidal.

It was not until the late nineteenth century that the semi-arid Chaco region gained any importance in the eyes of Paraguay. Foreign investment from Argentina had bolstered the country's economy, though it gave her neighbor undue influence in Asunción. (Ever wary of the creeping hand of British colonialism, Argentina was not above exerting proto-colonial influence wherever her interests lay.) By the

1920s, the Chaco question became a national priority for Bolivian and Paraguayan intellectuals. After the inevitable saber rattling, war broke out in 1932 and was fought in the heat and aridness of the region. As a surviving soldier would later recall of "La Guerra de la Sed" (The War of Thirst): "Someone should open a window somewhere to let in the air. The sky is an enormous stone under which the sun is imprisoned."[38] Although heavily outnumbered, the Paraguayans knew the territory over which they were fighting and possessed a heightened sense of patriotism; a sentiment that was absent in their enemy. Commanded by the tactically incompetent Prussian Hans Kundt, the highland Indians were unaccustomed to fighting in such punishing terrain. For all her technical superiority, Bolivia failed to match the guerrilla tactics of her neighbor. In June 1935, an armistice was declared just as Bolivia planned to surrender.

For Paraguay, this moral victory only exacerbated her sense of exceptionalism. The writer and politician Justo Pastor Benítez deemed the war a necessity, despite the loss of 30,000 to 40,000 Paraguayans: "The country needed a landmark to indicate the termination of decadence and to conclude the process of territorial demarcation; a victory, which would revive the faith that had been slumbering and which would waken the moral forces that lie in the depths of history."[39] Latin American commentators sought to explain the war's origins in terms of the exploitation of oil resources, furthered by the regional interests of Royal Dutch Shell and New Jersey's Standard Oil. This would give the Chaco War an anti-imperialist veneer, though the causes were far more complex. With her territorial ambitions now in check, Bolivia began to turn inward. The end of the old political order would produce a more reflective climate in which questions of land ownership and universal suffrage would be addressed. Nonetheless, Argentinian attitudes to Bolivia remained disparaging. In his psychological study of Argentina, *X-Ray of the Pampa*, Ezequiel Martínez Estrada did not spare the neighboring republic: "[Bolivia's] people are the farthest removed from Europe . . .

she believes that only by looking to water as a substitute for iron can she defend herself . . . Beyond all sentimental and diplomatic reasons, Bolivia is an absurdity."[40]

The Chaco War put an end to the domestic game in both republics, but it did at least allow Paraguayan football to flourish abroad. In the 1930s, Argentina may have possessed the best league on the continent, but its most talented player was Paraguayan. Arsenio Erico was a footballing god. Between 1934 and 1946, he played 325 matches for Independiente, scoring 293 goals, an all-time record for Argentinian football, but this phenomenon had only come to the attention of the Argentinians by a quirk of fate.

At the beginning of the war, many of the country's best players had volunteered for military service. When Erico joined his unit in Puerto Casado, he was promptly sent back to Asunción by his commanding officer. It was decided that Erico would better serve his country on the pitch than on the battlefield. He promptly joined the Red Cross squad that had been assembled by the Liga Paraguaya de Fútbol (Paraguayan Football League). In order to raise money for the war effort, the squad would tour Argentina and Uruguay, playing twenty-six games. During the Argentinian leg of the tour, Erico so impressed Independiente that the Avellaneda club paid five thousand pesos for his transfer. Erico donated the money to the Paraguayan Red Cross.

Other players had already made the journey south. In 1927, Manuel Fleitas Solich became the first Paraguayan to play in Argentina. "El Brujo" (The Wizard) played for Boca Juniors, where he dominated as an impenetrable midfielder, inspiring the club to win the 1930 championship. His playing career, however, would be curtailed by an injury, though he would carve out a successful second career as manager of Flamengo and Real Madrid. In 1934, Constantino Urbieta Sosa, who had moved to Argentina to play for Newell's Old Boys three years before, traveled to Italy to play for Argentina. Delfín Benítez Cáceres also missed the war, but became a hero to the terraces of Boca. By 1934, he had swapped the *albirroja* (red and white) shirt for the *albiceleste* (sky blue and white), playing for Argentina. Fluid attitudes to nationality not only applied in Italy. Nevertheless, there were those who stayed behind. Aurelio González, the top scorer in the 1929 Campeonato Sudamericano, turned down a lucrative offer to play for San Lorenzo. His Olimpia teammate, Rogelio Etcheverry, distinguished himself as a pilot, shooting down a Bolivian ace in a dogfight. With the cessation of hostilities, a friendly was played between Paraguayan soldiers and Bolivian prisoners in Pirayú. On this occasion, the Paraguayans ran out winners, and the players ended the match by embracing each other. For the Bolivian soldiers, who came back from the war, the welcome was muted. By contrast, the country's athletic delegation, which came in last at the medal table at the inaugural 1938 Juegos Bolivarianos (Bolivarian Games), were received as returning heroes.

The decade belonged to Erico, "El Paraguayo de Oro" (The Golden Paraguayan), who was Alfredo Di Stéfano's hero. As the Argentinian would later remember: "He was a master goalscorer, a dancer, a genius for headers and back-heels. Erico didn't run; he glided . . . Erico was acrobatic, and moved like a dancer when he ran . . . he could out-jump everyone, and he could place the ball in the net like the gods."[41] Top scorer in the Argentinian league from 1937 to 1939, Erico brought a majesty to the game that even eluded great players like Perdernera, Bernabé and Masantonio. His trademark: the back-heel.

In 1937, River Plate secured the championship, despite Erico's scoring forty-seven goals for Independiente. The following season, Piccardo, a local tobacco company, set the goal scorers of the league a challenge: a prize of two thousand pesos to the player who scored exactly forty-three goals. ("Cigarillos 43" being the brand of cigarette.) By the last match of the season, the Paraguayan had scored forty-one goals and needed two against Lanús. Fortunately, the remaining goals came quickly for Erico, who, desperately trying not to score again, spent the rest of the match creating chance after chance for his teammates in an 8–2 rout. The prize money was shared among the team.

"The Crafty Berlin Decision"

By the mid-1930s, the goodwill that had attached itself to the Latin American game was beginning to tarnish. In March 1936, a Montevideo select eleven, composed of Club Atlético River Plate players, offered Parisian spectators a different face of Uruguayan football. Despite its status as one of the capital's less fashionable teams, River Plate had boasted a squad that included Severino Varela. "La Boina Fantasma" (The Phantom Beret) would play for Boca Juniors, with whom he scored a goal in 1943 that *Crónica* called *el golazo del misterio* (the mystery supergoal). Arriving from nowhere to meet a cross that looked as if it were going out of play, Varela scored with a diving header of such audacity that River Plate's defense was taken by surprise. (By 1945, Varela would be making the weekly journey across the Río de la Plata in order to keep his job at the Uruguayan state energy company, before returning to Montevideo to play for Peñarol.)

The Montevidean squad made quick work of what was expected to be a successful European tour. The eleven years of goodwill that had passed between the legendary European tours of Nacional and Boca Juniors were wiped out by a game of such hostility that *L'Écho de Paris* ran the headline, A LAMENTABLE MATCH AT THE PARC DES PRINCES: *After a Game Spoilt by Violent Incidents, the Teams of Paris and Montevideo Played a Null Match: 1–1.*[42] The Uruguayans had squared up to a combined Paris eleven in more ways than one, with the game being marred by a plethora of Uruguayan infractions: "brawls, fisticuffs, trip-ups, malicious kicks aimed at opponents, dangerous hacking, deliberate handball, argument without end, intervention by the stewards, frequent interruption of the game, referee insulted and hit, furious crowds . . ."[43] In the second half, the referee awarded the French a penalty only to be punched by a Uruguayan player. Disgusted by the blatant aggression of the touring team, the Belgian referee flung his whistle to the ground and marched off the pitch. A Franco-Uruguayan player had to take charge of the rest of the match in front of a braying crowd of 30,000 Parisians. No wonder the French press compared the "hooligans" of 1936 with the artistry of Andrade, Scarone and Petrone in 1924. What must Jules Rimet have thought as he sat in the stands and watched these quondam world champions? The Royal Dutch Football Association, however, thought better of playing their two matches against the Uruguayans and promptly canceled them.

Yet it was not only the Latin Americans who were guilty of overt "professionalism" in their play. The opening match of the 1936 Summer Olympics, between Italy and the United States, was an ill-tempered affair that would set the tone for the rest of the tournament. An American player received a kick to the stomach, while another suffered torn knee ligaments when he was pushed off the pitch. The German referee had no choice but to send off Achille Piccini after the latter had punched an opposing player. When Piccini refused to leave the pitch, his fellow teammates surrounded the German referee, held his hands to his sides and covered his mouth. Piccini played on, and Italy won by the one goal. No wonder Winston Churchill was driven to say, "The Italians lose wars as if they were games of football; and lose games of football as if they were wars."[44] Despite being managed by Vittorio Pozzo, the architect of her 1934 World Cup triumph, Italy's team was no longer the same side that had beaten Czechoslovakia. Nor was Austria the *Wunderteam* of the early 1930s, a fact that Peruvians would later conveniently overlook.

Outside of the two Río de la Plata nations, Peru produced some of the most elegant and accomplished football on the continent. Her football would come to mirror the flair of Brazil rather than the pace of

Chile. The perennial problem for the Andean republic—as for other countries that suffered from geographical isolation—was a dearth of international competition. Peru may have had the talent, but irregular fixtures against foreign teams would hinder her chances of developing into one of Latin America's strongest footballing nations. Ultimately, as near miss followed near miss, her successes would become more a matter of imagination rather than of reality.

Peru would have to travel to find competition. In August 1933, the Combinado del Pacífico (Combined of the Pacific) undertook a tour of epic proportions, starting in Curaçao and ending in Spain by way of Panama, Ireland, Scotland, England, the Netherlands, Czechoslovakia, Germany, France and Italy. Two businessmen—Jack Gubbins from Peru and the Chilean Waldo Sangüeza—had overcome their republics' historical differences to assemble a squad mainly comprising players from Lima's Universitario. The club's fierce rival, Alianza, provided the brilliant saver of penalties Juan Valdivieso and the outstanding forward Alejandro Villanueva. Shortly before the tour, in a match against Sportivo Unión, Valdivieso had to replace the injured Villanueva up front. The goalkeeper scored seven goals in an 8–1 thrashing. Colo-Colo provided the only three Chilean players. Combinations of the squad played as the "Peru-Chile XI," "All-Pacific" and "South American Team," sometimes on the same day. As the All-Pacific eleven were being trounced 10–1 by a Madrid team, the Peru-Chile XI went down 4–1 against Barcelona. The tour may not have been ostensibly successful—the defeats against the better teams tended to be heavy—but it gave the Peruvians an indication of how they might fare on the international stage. The players were financially compensated for the games they played, which gave lie to their professed amateur status.

In 1935, Peruvian football succeeded where its military had failed fifty years before. Alianza Lima undertook a seven-match tour of Chile and put the country's teams to the sword. In a maneuver that would swiftly become familiar, Alianza supplemented its squad with players from rival clubs. The first match ended in a 3–1 defeat of Magallanes, which had just won the First Division title for the third year in succession. The following match against Colo-Colo saw Alianza, "El Rodillo Negro" (The Black Knee) in full flow, scoring four goals. The conservative broadsheet *El Diario Ilustrado* compared the slow pace and discipline of the Peruvians to the physical exertion of the Chileans. Later in the tour, Santiago's *El Mercurio* complained of the "rough play of the Peruvians" after "Lolo" Fernández was sent off for fouling a defender. Alianza would end the tour without loss, aided by the phenomenal efforts of Valdivieso, who saved four penalties in seven matches. Moreover, the club succeeded despite having a reputation for carousing the night before a match. (Players such as Domingo García were known to play drunk.)

By the 1936 Olympics, Peru had a strong, attacking side that could dribble at will. Could the Peruvians reproduce the form that had so nearly embarrassed Uruguay six years before? Against Finland in Peru's opening match, Lolo Fernández blasted five goals in a 7–3 drubbing. Peru's euphoria, though well earned, was misplaced. The Finns were not one of the stronger teams in the tournament, and the high goal tally was by no means an exception. (Only two days before, Germany had beaten Luxembourg 9–0.) Expectations were understandably high, but nothing could prepare the Latin Americans, even by their own fantastical standards, for what would come next. Luck, that delicate link between talent and timing, would somehow elude Peru.

The quarterfinals pitted the Peruvians against Austria, an amateur side that had beaten Egypt in the previous round. Peru started the match slowly and by the thirty-seventh minute had conceded two goals. Fortune favored the Peruvians in the second half when the Austrian striker Adolf Laudon was taken off injured, allowing the South Americans the chance to score two goals in quick succession. The equalizer set off Latin American celebrations, which ended in a pitch invasion. In extra time, Peru scored five goals, of which the

Norwegian referee only allowed two. Peru had won 4–2 and reached the semifinals . . . or so she presumed.

After the match, the Austrian Football Association lodged a formal complaint with FIFA's Jury of Appeal arguing that the game had been unlawfully interrupted. The official report (*Organisationskomitee für die XI. Olympiade Berlin 1936: Amtlicher Bericht*) confirmed that:

> *There existed factors hampering the normal course of events during the match, and that technical objections could not be made, but that the material organization of the tournament as provided by the customary rules, failed through unforeseen circumstances, so that it was impossible to prevent spectators from jumping into the field and impossible to prevent one of these spectators from kicking one of the players; also considering the fact that this caused a decrease of the fighting energy of the team, and that such an incident cannot be reconciled with the spirit of good sportsmanship.*[45]

In order to avert further embarrassment, the Jury of Appeal held that the match should be replayed in an empty stadium. Outraged at the decision, the Peruvians failed to show, so the game was rescheduled for the following day. With no team to play against once again, Austria was handed a "walk-over." The Peruvians were now on their way home. Such was the belief in the team that the minister of foreign relations, Dr. Alberto Ulloa, addressed congress on the subject and stated: "The path to total victory of the Peruvian team has been obstructed."[46]

In Lima, large crowds gathered outside newspaper offices, only to move on to La Casa de Pizarro (the House of Pizarro: Government Palace) in order to vent their frustration. *Time* magazine reported that "President Oscar Benavides of Peru . . . addressed an angry crowd. Said he: 'I have just received cables from the Argentine, Chile, Uruguay and Mexico solidifying the Peruvian attitude against the crafty Berlin decision." The crowd, which had already torn down an

Olympic flag, surged on to listen to more speeches in the Plaza San Martin. Later it proceeded to the German consulate to throw stones at the windows until police arrived in trucks. At Callao, the seaport near Lima, workmen on the docks refused to load two German vessels."[47] Latin American solidarity, though, would be short-lived: only Colombia followed Peru's lead and withdrew from the games.

As with all perceived sporting injustice, Peru's Olympic odyssey became shrouded in myth. Eduardo Galeano later conceived of the team's short-lived tournament as a Latin American tragedy played out on the fields of Berlin. In Peru, those with a conspiratorial cast of mind tried to make sense of what many would have put down to plain bad luck. The most prevalent fiction was that Hitler, whose interest in the game was minimal, had watched Norway beat Germany, only to transfer his affection to Austria. When Peru beat Austria, the *Führer* was so upset that a team composed of what the writer Guillermo Thorndike called "mestizos, barely white, also blacks and browns . . . all mixed with Quechua"[48] should have defeated an Aryan team that he ordered the match to be replayed.

For a tournament in which Peru had only played two matches, including one against a weak amateur Austrian side, and didn't even reach the semifinals, the 1936 Olympics remains a hyperbolized event in the country's footballing history. The myth, furthered by Peruvians, that Hitler transferred his affections, having watched Germany succumb 2–0 to Norway, is wishful thinking; so too the very idea that the replay was politically influenced by the Nazi regime.

Hyperbole was not the sole preserve of the Peruvians. The *Daily Sketch* overplayed its reporting of the pitch invasion. The image of "1,000 Peruvian supporters" flooding the pitch with "iron bars, knives and even a pistol" may have entertained readers in the United Kingdom, but it exaggerated the incident. The *Daily Mirror* went further still: "On Saturday Dr. Peter Bauwens, famous German referee, was compelled to strike down a Peruvian spectator who tried to draw a revolver on him."[49] The number of pitch invaders has always remained vague, though it is highly unlikely that there were a thousand Peruvians at the games, let alone in Europe. (Until the 1930s, the Olympic Games, because of their amateur status, retained very much a middle-class spectatorship, unlike football, whose demographic stretched across class boundaries.)

The Peruvian players were the victims of events outside of their control, a combination of plain black luck and poor judgment. Whether the team, talented though it was, would have secured another Latin American gold in the sport is unclear. (Football has a habit of playing havoc with the fortunes of pretournament favorites.) The team was not only failed by FIFA but also the Peruvian delegation, which might have sought a better solution for a frustrating problem. Even the short journey to the Hotel Russicher Hoff, where the members of FIFA were entertaining appeals, was fraught with disaster. In his report to the Peruvian FPF, the head of the delegation, Claudio Martínez, wrote: "The Peruvian delegates left the Olympic Villa at 9 a.m., but seeing as the cycling event was using the motorway at the time, we had to let the cyclists pass . . . The buses had been instructed to stop . . . This meant one could not leave until 10 a.m. and the bus took more time than usual."[50] It was not until 11:30 a.m. that the Peruvians reached the hotel, which did little to endear them to FIFA.

Paradoxically, Peru's tragedy provided Benavides's dictatorial regime with the fillip it needed to gain credibility in face of looming elections. The United States' chargé d'affaires in Lima was particularly perceptive: "President Benavides has found this to be a splendid opportunity to take action to endear him to the populace, particularly the labouring element which largely holds more radical views, and it is evident that the Peruvian Government has not neglected to take full advantage [of this incident] to reap political prestige from this affair."[51] The political aftermath of the match has tended to overshadow the brilliance of Peru's performance.

Near misses would become the country's forte. Before Peruvian football faded from view in the next two decades, its team demonstrated what they were truly capable of. As hosts of the 1939 Campeonato Sudamericano, Peru finally became champions of the continent; though the absence of Brazil and Argentina weakened the field. Ecuador, a new entrant to the competition, was now the region's whipping boy. Much was expected of the Paraguayans, until they fell out with their management before the tournament had even started. (Acts of vandalism took place on the steamer from Valparaíso to Callao.) The Peruvians, on the other hand, were well served by their English manager, Jack Greenwell, who outthought Uruguay tactically in the final match. He had played for Barcelona in the 1910s, only to stay in the country after his playing career had ended. When the Spanish Civil War ended his successful managerial career in Spain, during which time he coached Barcelona, Espanyol and Valencia, he moved on to Peru. Ever the journeyman manager, Greenwell would move on to Colombia in the following year. That would be his final stop.

The Invention of *Futebol* (*Arte*)

For decades, Brazilian football had been its own worst enemy. The nation's shortsightedness regarding the integration of its black and mulatto players saw its footballing development lag behind the River Plate republics. In the seventeenth century, the word had been that the country was "a hell for Blacks, a purgatory for Whites, and a paradise for Mulattoes," but this seemed hardly to obtain any longer.[52] Attitudes to race remained for the most part colonial, as if they were unabashed by the shame of having abolished slavery so late. Rodrigo Octávio may have been premature, when, in 1912, he announced to an audience in Geneva that Brazil was a "new country without history or traditions, where a new nation is rising without any aristocracy or any prejudices."[53] This was manifestly untrue in the 1910s, and in certain quarters little had changed two decades later. Intellectuals such as Oliveira Viana may have bemoaned a lack of national unity and identity, while advocating the mixing of races at the expense of black culture. Published in 1933, Viana's *Evolução do povo brasileiro* advanced the theory that "between the Negro's mentality and that of the Caucasian lies a substantial and irreducible difference which no social or cultural pressure no matter how long it may be continued, can possibly overcome."[54]

And yet a different voice was beginning to be heard, one that championed Brazil's racial diversity. Published in the same year as *Evolução do povo brasileiro*, Gilberto Freyre's groundbreaking *Casa grande e senzala* (*The Masters and the Slaves*) sought to turn the country's perceived (black) weakness into its strength. Rather than having them "whiten" themselves, Freyre believed the mulattoes' racial superiority should be recognized and the mixing of races embraced. Pride might then replace the country's inferiority complex. Theory and practice, though, would prove to be difficult bedfellows. (Brazil would come to think herself as racially democratic; the reality would be otherwise.)

It was not long before Freyre applied his theories to football. The day after Brazil's semifinal defeat to Italy at the 1938 World Cup, he wrote in the *Diários Associados*: "Our football style seems to contrast with the European due to qualities such as surprise, skill, cleverness, speed and, at the same time, individual brilliance and spontaneity . . . Our passes . . . our flourishes with the ball . . . there is something that reminds one of dancing and capoeira, making the Brazilian way of playing football a trademark, which . . . sweetens the game invented by the English and played so stiffly by them. All this seems to express in a very interesting way, for psychologists and sociologists, the flamboyant Mulatism and the trickery which are nowadays part of the true affirmation of what Brazil is."[55] In the next decade, the sociologist would warm to his theme, making the case for football and dance: "The Brazilians play [football] as if it were a dance. This is probably the result of the influence of those Brazilians who have African blood or are predominantly African in their culture, for such Brazilians tend to reduce everything to dance, work and play alike, and this tendency, apparently becoming more and more general in Brazil, is not solely the characteristic of an ethnic or regional group."[56]

While Brazil was attempting to change attitudes to race from within, she was not helped by the spiteful reminders of her heritage from without. Argentina nearly provoked a diplomatic row during the 1937 Campeonato Sudamericano when, throughout the tournament, the Brazilian players had to endure racial abuse from the Argentine crowds. Not content with casting aspersions on the modernity of Brazilian cities (players were asked whether there were telephones in Rio de Janeiro), the Brazilians were called *macaquitos* (little monkeys). For Argentina, the assertion of her racial superiority was becoming a national pastime. In *X-Ray of the Pampa* (1933), his analysis of Argentine identity, Ezequiel Martínez Estrada proffered a simple theory: "Argentina distrusts other countries because she considers them to be the residence of the Indian who no longer exists in her territory, the repository of her taboos."[57] Even as late as the early 1970s, there had been no change in attitude. While completing the research for his incisive essay on Argentina, *The Return of Eva Perón*, V. S. Naipaul jotted a few thoughts in his notebook: "*Un prejuicio racial integral contra* todos [a built-in racial prejudice against everyone] . . . *Dios es argentino* [God is Argentine]."[58] Casual hyperbole this may have been, but Naipaul was not wrong.

In a high-scoring tournament that ended with Brazil and Argentina even on points, a playoff was arranged in order to decide the winner. Argentina had already beaten Brazil by one goal to nil, so held the psychological advantage. Unfortunately, the match would illustrate the dark side of the South American game. Various incidents, which necessitated police intervention, marred a tight contest. When the Brazilian defender, Carnera, brought down Varallo, the

Boca Juniors goal machine used his boots on his opponent to show his displeasure. Such was the ill temper of the match that the *Jornal dos Sports* observed that it was "characterised by violence that one cannot describe in all its details." The paper was outraged when the Argentinian police "brought down their swords on the shoulders of various of our patricians."[59] The Brazilians left the field of play in protest, but returned once their safety was guaranteed. In extra time, Independiente's Errol Flynn lookalike, Vicente de la Mata, scored a brace. Two years later, in 1939, de la Mata would score one of the greatest goals in the history of Argentinian football against River Plate. Having received the ball from his own goalkeeper, de la Mata dribbled past half of the opposition before slotting the ball between keeper and post. *El Gráfico* called the move *gambeta diabolica* ("diabolic dribble").

The match, which had been broadcast by radio in Brazil, would live long in the Brazilian imagination as the "match of shame." It even warranted an entry in the diary of the president, Getúlio Vargas.

Yet again Brazil's lack of resolve had ceded victory to her steelier neighbor. Charges of the same reticence could not be leveled at the country's head of state. When Getúlio Vargas took office in 1930, few thought that he would still be the head of state a decade and a half later. His rise to power had been the product of conspiracy, both on his part and that of his opponents. The presidential victory of Júlio Prestes had been tainted by fraud, though this failed initially to provoke a coup. When João Pessoa, Vargas's vice-presidential candidate, was shot at point-blank range in a patisserie by João Dantas, the co-conspirators were forced into action. After a short-lived coup, during which a military junta took power, Vargas was handed the reins of power. In true *caudillo* fashion, he rode into Rio de Janeiro and tethered his horse to the foot of the city's obelisk. For the next seven years, Vargas ruled as a constitutional president before establishing himself as a dictator.

Born in the southern state of Rio Grande do Sul, Vargas

possessed a different outlook than the oligarchies of São Paulo. Freyre deemed him a product of his region:

> *The men . . . are not typical gauchos in behavior, but, having more Indian blood than the typical gauchos and being the descendants of Indians . . . they have in them something of their Jesuit masters: they are silent, introspective, subtle, realistic, distant, cold. They have also something of their brave ancestors, the "mission" Indians . . . They are telluric, instinctive, fatalistic, proud, dramatic . . . Vargas seems to be a sort of Dr. Jekyll and Mr. Hyde in that he has in him something of the Jesuit but something also of the Indian. He is avid for power and domination, but he had also stood for the common people and for revolt against sterile conventions and power plutocratic groups.*[60]

The Depression was keenly felt in the region, especially by Bolivia, Chile and Peru, in spite of commodity prices having already started to fall before the crash. Nevertheless, the Depression allowed these republics to focus on the domestic market rather than on imports. Self-reliance in many ways allowed the region to mature economically. Import-substituting industrialization (ISI), which had been employed prior to the crash, was now implemented through certain tariff and exchange-rate changes catalyzed by the fall in commodity prices. In Brazil, the price of coffee had plummeted to such an extent that Vargas was forced to burn coffee beans in order to stabilize prices. Imports were now cut by two-thirds, forcing the country to supply its own domestic market. This proved the catalyst for the Brazilian economy. During Vargas's first seven years in power, industrial production increased by approximately 50 percent. In the shadow of global economic uncertainty, Brazil had begun to master her own potential. The same could not be said of her football.

Professionalism, which the leagues in São Paulo and Rio de Janeiro introduced in 1933, had not been without its detractors. Hypocrisy reigned in certain quarters, where the passing of the amateur era was equated with the mercenary nature of the black and mulatto player. It had been conveniently forgotten that as early as 1917, tickets had been sold for matches. Moreover, players had been handed incentives (not quite a salary on which to live) to turn out for their clubs. Although the game at club level had become more egalitarian, blacks were still not trusted to perform roles like goalkeeping. International football, however, retained an obvious color bar. To play for Brazil as a black or mulatto was the exception rather than the rule.

Fausto dos Santos was a black midfielder of exceptional ability. Born in Codó, which had gained a reputation for harboring escaped slaves, to a poor family, he had overcome his circumstances to play first for Bangu before moving on to Vasco. At the 1930 World Cup, he dazzled the spectators in spite of his country's mediocre showing. Fausto may have earned the epithet "Maravilha Negra" (Black Marvel), but this had long been the unimaginative label applied to any talented black player. (The Uruguayan José Andrade had been christened with the same moniker in the 1920s.) Criticism of his fellow players in the face of international opposition at the 1930 World Cup did little to endear him to the authorities Yet he remained an idol to the fans. On a tour of Spain in 1931, Fausto broke with Vasco and signed for Barcelona. He wished to be treated as a professional. *El Diluvio*, the Barcelona newspaper, had been astounded by the player's energy: "Fausto works like a slave. Is it possible that all the Brazilian centre-halves work like slaves? Is that the reason why all of them are black?"[61] The Catalan transfer proved short-lived, so Fausto moved to Young Fellows in Switzerland before heading for Montevideo's Nacional. Disqualified for having played professionally in Europe, he did not take part in the 1934 World Cup. Fausto had become that legacy of professionalism: the journeyman player. Now dogged by ill health, he signed for his old team, Vasco, before moving on to Flamengo. In 1939, at the age of thirty-four, the Maravilha Negra died of tuberculosis. Even in his last years, he had played magnificently, though had at times been let down by his headstrong nature. His family, after all, had come from a town of escaped slaves.

Another player who had come up through Bangu was Domingos da Guia. Strong, elegant and with an incisive footballing brain, Domingos epitomized the new brand of fullback. He excelled in the Copa Río Branco (played solely against Uruguay) of 1931 and 1932, which brought him not only to the attention of the Uruguayans but also to the Brazilians. "I am going to have that *crioulo* [nigger] plated in gold," shouted a Carioca fan in admiration.[62] Exceptional in defense, Domingos was now known as "The Fortress" and "the best full-back on the entire continent."[63] He followed Fausto's lead of signing for Vasco, though by 1934 had followed the money to Nacional in Montevideo. Financially astute in his signings, Domingos returned to Vasco before moving on to Boca Juniors, where he won his third championship title in as many countries.

For black players such as Domingos, footballing skill had been born out of a desire for self-preservation: "When I was still a kid I was scared to play football, because I often saw black players, there in Bangu, get whacked on the pitch, just because they made a foul, or sometimes for something less than that . . . my elder brother used to tell me: the cat always falls on his feet . . . aren't you any good at dancing? I was and this helped my football . . . I swung my hips a lot . . . that short dribble I invented imitating the *miudinho*, that type of samba."[64] This was not only true of black players in Brazil but also in Lima and Montevideo. As well as developing an array of evasive maneuvers, Domingos sought to distance himself from "blackness" and present himself as a mulatto. He kept his curls under a cap; and once he dispensed with it in the mid-1930s, he took to straightening his hair. He even distanced himself from his fellow Flamengo and Seleção teammate Leônidas da Silva. In 1995, Domingos recalled, "[Leônidas] had a real disadvantage . . . [because] he was black, black, black as tar . . . [even] with his money he remained that *crioulinho* [little nigger]. Not me, I am mulatto, so I was treated differently."[65]

Leônidas da Silva, according to Nelson Rodrigues, epitomized the Brazilian player: "He had the imagination, improvisation, mischievousness, and sensuality of our typical *crack* [star player]."[66] The Brazilian creator of the *bicicleta* (bicycle kick) may have shone as the "Diamente Negro" (Black Diamond), but he had suffered appalling racial abuse from the crowds. "Being black, [he] believed he always had to do more to have his worth recognised," recalled Leônidas's wife. "Back when he was playing, a large part of the athletes were still the sons of high-class families."[67] Abuse (which also took the form of death by lynching) was compounded by racial discrimination, when the president of the Confederação Brasileira de Desportos (CBD, Brazilian Sports Confederation) argued not to call him up for international duty. Brazil was not the only country in the region embarrassed by the image that its black players might convey. At the turn of the decade, the Peruvian magazine *Toros y Deportes* commented, "How are we going to send a team of blacks to a championship! . . . They will say we are a country of that race!"[68] And yet, those very players, of which Brazil had been ashamed, would be instrumental in forcing Brazilian football from the long shadow cast by her River Plate neighbors.

The Seleção had fared badly at the 1930 and 1934 World Cups, falling at the group stage and first round respectively. Lack of preparation, coupled with a naive attitude to playing international competition, belied the depth of talented individual players in the squads. Without Argentina and Uruguay to upstage it, the 1938 FIFA World Cup would be the turning point for Brazilian football.

The only other Latin American team to travel to France was Cuba, whose qualification was eased by the withdrawal of Colombia, Costa Rica, Dutch Guiana, El Salvador, Mexico and the United States. In their first match against an experienced Romania, the Cubans managed to draw 3–3 after extra time. Carvajales, whose outstanding goalkeeping had kept Cuba in the match, covered the replay as a radio commentator, so sure was the manager of winning the match. Romania succumbed 2–1 to allow the Cubans to progress to the quarterfinals, where Carvajales's prowess between the posts eluded him. He let in eight goals.

For Brazil, it would be an auspicious tournament: the promise of what her football might become. Moreover, the squad, for the first time, had become inclusive, with black, mulattoes and whites playing together. Poland would, however, provide stiff opposition in the first round. Frustrated by the state of the waterlogged pitch, Leônidas took off his boots, only to be reprimanded by the Swedish referee. The match, which was played at a slow pace, went into extra time, with Leônidas adding a brace to his opening goal. The 6–5 score line demonstrated that the days of using two defenders were numbered. Nevertheless, Domingos had been excellent in spite of running a high fever.

The quarterfinal against Czechoslovakia showed the brutal side of Brazilian football. For all their elegance on the ball, a *rioplatense* attitude seemed to have taken hold of the team. Three players were sent off, including Říha and Machado, for trading blows. The prolific Sparta Prague striker, Nejedlý, went off with a broken leg, while the Czech goalkeeping captain Plánička, known as "The Cat of Prague," played on with a broken arm. With the match having ended in a 1–1 stalemate, the replay was played two days later. Leônidas scored yet again to bring his tally in the tournament up to five. The semifinal pitted Brazil against the reigning world champions, Italy.

Even five years afterward, with Europe in the midst of terrible conflict, Brazil had not forgotten the injustice they believed themselves to have suffered. FIFA was again reminded that the squad had not been given enough time to rest before the semifinal. The CBD had conveniently forgotten that the Brazilians had been so sure of success that they'd booked tickets for the final in Paris. More damaging, Leônidas and Tim were rested in for a match on which Italy duly had stamped its authority. Overconfidence had taken the place

of underachievement: poor Domingos, who had been feted throughout the tournament by the French press, brought down Piola in a
disputed decision. As Meazza was about to take the penalty, his
shorts fell down. Unruffled by the potential embarrassment, he pulled
them up and fired the ball past the distracted Brazilian goalkeeper,
Walter, who had a reputation for making saves. The Europeans ran
out 2–1 winners. Domingos would later excuse his actions by stating
that he had not known the rules of the game.

Failure, even at the penultimate hurdle, only seemed to reinforce
the nation's newfound belief in its sporting prowess. Moral victors, or
"kings without a crown," as Mário Filho called the returning players,
they may have been at home, but Europeans remained unconvinced.
Writing in the early 1940s, the German philosopher Karl Loewenstein did not observe a population equipped for the game: "The foreign observer cannot fail to notice the apparent lack of physical fitness
in the population. This may be due to the tropical climate which mil-
itates against strenuous physical exertion . . . and, last but not least, to
the deplorably insufficient diet of the poorer classes, which live mainly
on *arroz e feijan*—rice and beans, with some fruits—the staple food of
the Brazilian masses."[69] How wrong he would be.

War Clouds Gather

Argentine football had always been partial to the more physical side
of the game. Violence on the pitch tended to be reflected in the
stands, where passions ran high. In 1939, the game had claimed its
first fatality in a match between Lanús and Boca Juniors. The game
had succumbed to the inevitable. When a fight broke out between the
players, the Boca fans threatened to invade the pitch. Shots were fired
in order to control the crowd, but tragically, a trigger-happy officer
discharged his weapon directly into the crowd and killed two fans.

The state of the Argentinian game even reached the Ministry of Information (MOI) in London:

> *It would be fatal if a team went out from here to play football in the Argentine, as nothing arouses the passion of the locals so much as this perfectly sound form of exercise. When one knows that the spectators have to be wired in and that the police are armed with tear-gas bombs, and that shootings have been known to occur, there is little need for me to enlarge upon the inadvisability of sending a team out.*[70]

In order to stamp its authority on the game, the Asociación del Fútbol Argentino (Argentine Football Association) had in fact looked to the country that had invented its rules. In 1937, Isaac Caswell, a retired referee from Blackburn, was chosen to bring the Argentine game under control. Even on the crossing, he was warned off by his fellow Anglo-Argentine passengers: "Most of them advised me to go back to Blackburn. They believed I was undertaking a dangerous task. Some of them said that I would probably lose my life! This didn't scare me. I was intent on seeing things through."[71] In order to understand the local game, Caswell scouted the league matches, where he was given a warm reception of claps and cheers. He was alarmed by what he saw. "Visualize an Argentine ground. All the bigger enclosures—and the largest, the River Plate club's stadium, holds 150,000 people—are surrounded by a high wall . . . Enclosing the playing-pitch is a wire fence ten feet high . . . barbed at the top. Mounted police are on duty outside and, in some cases, inside the ground while foot police are held in reserve and, at times, a fire-brigade as well . . ."[72] Caswell persevered, though, without much success.

> *Changes had to be administered in careful doses. There was rough play, incessant whistling by referees, frequent stoppages for injuries (accompanied often by about a dozen persons rushing on the field to give the player water), constant arguing with the referee, fights on the field and*

interventions by police. Often, there were free fights among spectators, some of whom waited after the match to threaten or throw missiles at the referee. For six months my work was heartbreaking.[73]

Matters came to a head in a match between Boca Juniors and Racing Club, where the English referee sent off a player for continuing to admonish his teammate, even when told to stop. The police came onto the pitch in order to escort the player off, while the spectators took to throwing stones. Retribution by the crowd also took place off the field. When Caswell called off a match for stone throwing—the goalkeeper and fullbacks having been pelted by the home crowd—angry fans slashed his car tires. Even the Asociación del Football Argentino (AFA) took stringent action and closed the stadium for six weeks. Peruvian football was equally lawless. A visitor to Lima observed that "spectators have a playful habit of firing blank revolver shots to put a penalty-kicker off his aim! I saw them roll newspapers into a ball, set them alight and throw them down among the rival supporters."[74] But in spite of the violence and against the advice of the Ministry of Information, the British government entertained an invitation in 1940 from the president of the AFA, Adrián Escobar, to send English and French teams out to the River Plate—though this had more to do with keeping the region on the side of the Allies than furthering competitive football. With the "Phony War" about to give way to the German invasion of the Low Countries, a wartime football tour was an expensive if not dangerous luxury. Yet again, Latin American football would have to fend for itself while Europe tried to destroy itself.

CHAPTER FIVE

IN SPLENDID ISOLATION

1940–1950

Latin America in the Shadow of Argentina

One plays against La Máquina with the full intention of beating them, but as a football fan, I would sometimes prefer to sit in the stands and watch them play.

—Ernesto Lazatti, Boca Juniors[1]

São Paulo is like Reading, only much farther away.

—Peter Fleming, *Brazilian Adventure* (1933)

For the abundance of gold which he saw in the city, the images of gold in their temples, the plates, armours, and shields of gold which they use in the wars, he called it El Dorado.

—Sir Walter Raleigh, *The Discovery of the Large, Rich, and Beautiful Empire of Guiana* (1596)

Europe was still the continent where Latin American dreams were fashioned. Third place at the 1938 World Cup, a tournament the country felt she should have won, had given Brazilian football an overinflated sense of itself. After all, Flamengo's "Black Diamond," Leônidas da Silva, had top-scored with seven goals and shown the dexterity of the Brazilian game. The Second World War, which, as with its predecessor, would not be without economic reward for many Latin American republics, would delay Brazil's hopes of hosting the tournament she so coveted. The country would have to wait, though when her time came, the footballing gods had other ideas in mind. The decade that now followed belonged to one country in the region; it was not, however, to be Brazil.

By 1939, it had been sixteen years since the Copa Roca had last been contested. The tournament, which had taken its name from Julio Argentino Roca, Argentina's former president and ambassador to Rio, had first been played in 1914. Initially conceived as a three-match contest between Brazil and Argentina over three years, the 1915 edition was never held and the idea seemed to have been quietly abandoned. When relations between AFA and CONMEBOL broke down, Argentina decided not to participate in Lima's 1939 Campeonato Sudamericano. It was the first time the country had missed the tournament. Instead of traveling to Lima, the Argentinians went to Rio de Janeiro—the Brazilians had also withdrawn—to resurrect the bilateral trophy.

In Vasco da Gama's São Januário Stadium, Argentina started with a forward line of Peucelle, Sastre, Masantonio, Moreno and García. In a score line that would have been unthinkable before the match, the bewildered Brazilians were thrashed 5–1. Carlos Peucelle, a brilliant dribbler of the ball who had played in the 1930 World Cup, remembered, "On the other Argentinian wing was Moreno and 'Chueco' García. These two, as always, wore out the ball. Besides, they had already gained a fabulous reputation as a wing. They also looked like they had been together all their lives . . . Nevertheless, the Brazilian newspapers said, about that match, that you have never seen a game like ours, and it wasn't possible to know which of the two was the winger and who was the wide midfielder. We did it all instinctively."[2] Both players had once made such a fool of the great defender Schubert "Mono" (Monkey) Gambetta that the Uruguayan had to change his position to save face. "Have some respect, the gentleman is a musician," shouted one to the other.[3] For Moreno, Brazil's weakness had been clear enough: though Argentina had merited her victory, the Brazilians might have tempered the embarrassing score line had they played calmly. Panic under pressure would dog Brazilian football. For a long time this would prove a psychological advantage for the River Plate republics. Before the 1958 World Cup final, George Raynor, Sweden's English manager, famously said that if Brazil were to concede a goal, they would "panic all over the show."[4]

For the rematch the following week, Brazil made four changes that would serve them well. With the score level at two all, Brazil was awarded a penalty toward the end of the bruising encounter. When Argentina's Arcadio López, whose precision passing had led to two goals in the first match, verbally abused the referee, the police accompanied him off the pitch. In a gesture of solidarity, the rest of the team made for the dressing room. Without the safe hands of San Lorenzo's Sebastián Gualco—who was renowned for cutting out crosses—with which to contend, or any other Argentinian player for that matter, Brazil put the ball into an open net to draw the series level. With a third match unlikely, now that the affronted Argentinian delegation had decided to return home, the rematches were postponed until the following year.

Not that a year would make any difference to the deadlock. This time Argentina traveled to São Paulo, where she was held to a 2–2 draw at Palestra Itália's Parque Antárctica. With the winner yet to be decided, a further match was arranged a week later. This time Argentina made sure of the 1939 Copa Roca with three goals from Baldonedo, Zorilla and Fidel. Eight days later Brazil found herself playing the first of a three-game rubber in Buenos Aires. It took Argentina only a few minutes to score, though the second half would witness a Brazilian surrender of epic proportions. The 6–1 drubbing would be her heaviest defeat against her neighbor, though not quite the six–nil thrashing Uruguay had given her in 1920. Brazil did hold out high hopes for the second game, even if it was highly unlikely that they'd repeat the same score line. In the event, Peucelle, who had scored a hat trick in the match before, could not repeat his performance, and Brazil ran out 3–2 winners. With the series now squared, normal play was resumed in front of 80,000 spectators. The Argentinians, who, unlike their prevaricating rivals, were not afraid to shoot on goal, managed four goals before halftime. The 5–1 victory had the Brazilians complain about having to play in the strong afternoon sun, though São Paulo's *Folha da Manhã* was quick to admit in its lead article that the score "confirm[ed] once again the real superiority of Argentinian football."[5] Brazil had failed to play her own game, one which Américo R. Netto described twenty years before: "The Brazilian school states that shots be taken from any distance, the precision of the shot being worth more than the fact that it is made close to the target . . . it's enough for two or three players to break away with the ball, which, by its devastating speed, completely unexpected, disorientates the entire rival defence."[6] Revenge would come in time, but not until after the war had ended.

The Brazilians returned home deflated. Not only had they lost to Argentina, but they had lost by significant margins. The following month, the country would host her diminutive neighbor for the two-match Copa Barón de Río Branco, which Brazil had won on each of the two occasions the cup had been played. In the opening game Uruguay edged her hosts 4–3 in a thrilling match, in which Peñarol's Severino Varela scored a brace. In the second match, "La Boina Fantasma" (The Phantom Beret), the moniker Varela acquired at Boca Juniors, scored Uruguay's only goal in a one-all draw.

It was not without reason that Brazil now declined to take part in an unofficial Campeonato Sudamericano that Chile organized to celebrate Santiago's foundation by Pedro de Valdivia in 1541. By now, the Ecuadorians were the whipping boys of the continent, having first participated in the tournament two years before. After four matches, Ecuador had conceded eighteen goals, though she would improve on that tally. Both Argentina and Uruguay put six goals past the hapless Ecuadorian goalkeeper, who would end the tournament having retrieved the ball twenty-one times from the back of his net. The only Ecuadorian goal came against the eventual winners, Argentina. Uruguay, on the other hand, had managed not to concede any goals until she met her neighbor. The match, which was won by a single goal from Sastre, would be remembered (only by Uruguayans) for the Chilean official's biased refereeing. Shortly before the end of the match, Uruguay managed an equalizer. The goal stood at first, only to be disallowed as a result of the traditional pressure applied by the Argentinian players on the referee.

Chile, in spite of hosting the tournament, had only managed third place. Three years before, the country had built her own temple to the game, the Estádio Nacional. The plan for the stadium, which cost 23 million pesos, had taken two decades to come to fruition. Even before its inauguration, the Chilean president, Arturo Alessandri, remained unconvinced of its necessity for the nation: "The only thing I wish for is that one day this white elephant can fill itself,"[7] he said. By the early 1940s, however, Chile was so confident of her own sporting ability that she sought to emulate *El Gráfico* but in her own voice. In the first issue of *Estádio*, the editorial ran along populist lines: "Domestic sports, for the good of our race, have in the past few years greatly improved. All the social classes of our people practise sport." And yet, in spite of her sporting prowess, there remained that barely veiled sense of inferiority. "Chile, our thinly populated, small country, on more than one occasion has caused her name to vibrate throughout the whole world through her sportsmen."[8]

Failure abroad would not be confined to Brazil's Seleção. In the summer of 1941, at the end of the season, Flamengo and Fluminense took part in a nocturnal round-robin competition with San Lorenzo, Huracán, Independiente and a combined Rosario squad composed of Newell's Old Boys and Rosario Central players. While great rivals at home, in Argentina the two Rio-based teams would be reconciled by their own poor form. Fluminense would lose all its matches by the same four-goal margin. Flamengo suffered a 7–0 defeat in its first match, though went close in a 6–5 encounter against Independiente. San Lorenzo was the only Argentinian team to be beaten by a Brazilian club. Fortunately, for the players, there would not be the ignominy of a Fla-Flu derby to contest the wooden spoon: Independiente had won the tournament early.

Loss of form on the pitch roused the country's hitherto dormant inferiority complex in the face of *el fútbol rioplatense*. The run of disastrous results would inflate the worth of River Plate players in the eyes of the Brazilian public. Clubs sought to buy Argentinian players in order to strengthen their squads. Mário Filho would later deem this *platinismo* (River-Platism) a form of admiration for the Argentinian player rather than for the River Plate game. The great playmaker Antonio Sastre, who had played with Erico and de la Mata at Independiente, moved to São Paulo Futebol Clube in 1942. In Rio, where most of the Argentinians naturally gravitated, Flamengo and Fluminense were especially active in the transfer marker. In reality, though, this was nothing new: players had been moving between the two countries since the 1920s.

From the first decade of the century, Brazilian football had had to contend with the superiority of Argentina and Uruguay. In 1908, São Paulo and Rio de Janeiro hosted a combined Argentinian squad, the first to play a series of matches in that country. The inaugural match may have ended in a two-all draw, but the Paulistas would lose the next two matches 6–0 and 4–0. The Argentinians, imbued with a sense of British "fair play" and their 2-3-5 formation, rested some of their best players to make for a fairer contest. In Rio, the score lines were equally shaming for the Cariocas: 3–2, 7–1 and 3–0. Brazilian football had much to learn.

Political machinations, exacerbated by the geographical and cultural distance between Rio de Janeiro and São Paulo, had not helped the Brazilian game keep up with its neighbors. The rivalry between Cariocas and Paulistas in many ways reflected the antagonism between the political authority of the capital and the economic power of São Paulo. In 1927, Vasco da Gama had hosted Santos Futebol Clube to celebrate the inauguration of the São Januário Stadium. In front of the president and five ministers of state, Santos relished beating its rivals 5–3. After the match, Araken wryly said, "They build a ballroom, and we put on a show."[9] Later that year, President Washington Luís returned to watch the Federal District take on the Paulistas. He received a three-minute ovation from the crowd. "I have never received such applause in my life. Nor in my country."[10] Approbation from the masses, however, could not save him from being ousted in a coup three years later.

The game, which had promised much, was a tense affair. Fifteen minutes from time, with the score at 1–1, the Cariocas were awarded a penalty. Where the traditional *rioplatense* response might have been to resort to violence, the Paulistas walked off the pitch in disgust. When the president ordered play to continue, the players sent a message back saying that they, not him, made the decisions on the pitch. The penalty was finally taken, though there was no goalkeeper to make a save.

. . .

It was not until the introduction in 1937 of the Estado Nôvo (New State)—which borrowed its ideology from both Mussolini's Fascist Party and Salazar in Portugal but dispensed with the more authoritarian aspects of totalitarianism—that Getúlio Vargas tied his social policies to the corporatist state, the ideal of a unified national culture. National inclusion, which envisaged the country as a Brazilian family with Vargas at its head, was furthered by an effort to eradicate what were deemed to be un-Brazilian characteristics from daily life. Radio broadcasting would help further Vargas's ideas of national unity. *Hora do Brasil* (Brazil Hour), which covered topics of national interest from commerce to culture, was broadcast to the republic every night at eight. Not that this governmental intrusion was always welcome. In certain cities the local broadcasters failed to retransmit the program. By 1939, Vargas had implemented a campaign of *brasilidade* (Brazilization), which sought to cement national identity. The year before, he had reinforced his ideas on nationhood in a May Day speech: "A country is not just the conglomeration of individuals in a territory; it is, principally, a unity of race, a unity of language, a unity of national thinking."[11] Vargas now became concerned with immigrant communities—especially those from Germany and Italy, where cultural ties with their home countries were stronger—that might pose a national security risk. Newspapers, foreign-language schools and non-Brazilian organizations were closed down. Popular Brazilian culture—such as Rio's Carnival and samba schools—were promoted as symbols of Brazilian culture. Football was also seen as an important prop of national identity, and the country's unique mix of Amerindian, African and European cultures was wholly encouraged. It was not long before the game became the responsibility of the state.

In 1941, the Conselho Nacional de Desportos (CND) was created by decree in order to "orient, finance, and encourage the practice of sport of in all of Brazil."[12] The game, which had struggled to instill professionalism in the previous decade, had all but become nationalized. The game's popularity was not lost on Brazil's shrewd *caudillo*, who sought to strengthen government control over both the working classes and their employers. Vargas now took to making public addresses in the country's football stadiums: football and politics had come together. He had announced the first minimum-wage legislation at Corinthians' São Januário Stadium in 1940. That same year Vargas inaugurated the Estádio do Pacaembu, which had been constructed in order to mollify local interests. Family members began to hold key positions within the country's sporting infrastructure. In 1942, Vargas's nephew, Manoel do Nascimento Vargas Netto, became president of Rio's Federação Metropolitana de Futebol (FMF). The following year it was the turn of Vargas's son, Getúlio Vargas Filho, to run the São Paulo federation, Federação Paulista de Futebol.

During the late 1920s and 1930s, no one had done more to propagate the game among the masses than Mário Filho. The son of a newspaper owner, Filho had seen the potential in sports journalism early on. With the establishment of the short-lived newspaper *Crítica*, Filho sought to popularize football, finding the epic qualities in these weekly matches and shortening the long Anglo names of the clubs. In 1931, he founded *O Mundo Esportivo*, which would also enjoy only a brief life, since it was launched at the end of the season. Without any sporting activities to cover, Filho turned Rio's carnival into a proto-sporting activity with its own groupings and judges. By the time he had moved on to *O Globo*, Filho had started to establish footballing rivalries, especially between Flamengo and Fluminense. ("Fla-Flu" would become the country's most famous contest, though some tension between the clubs had always existed.) And yet, in spite of popularizing the game as a diversion, Filho believed in professionalism and in the emancipation of the Afro-Brazilian through football. Moreover, football had become instrumental in creating a coherent national identity, something the country had hitherto lacked. In 1947, Filho wrote the ground-breaking *O negro no futebol brasileiro* (*The Black in Brazilian Football*), which sought to emphasize the achievements of the black and mulatto in the context of the Brazilian game. This was football as social history.

The Second World War would help realign the Americas, largely as a result of the pragmatic behavior displayed by the Latin American republics. Nevertheless, nineteenth-century tensions—usually in relation to boundary disputes—between certain republics resurfaced. In July 1941, Peruvian forces overpowered Ecuador in less than a month over the latter's territorial claims. For Argentina, who had always seen herself as superior to her neighbors in the region, now had to contend with Brazil as the continent's leading power.

With most of Europe under German occupation and the British actively blockading the Atlantic, the Latin America republics had to look to their northern neighbor for an export market. By 1940, exports—especially the flow of commodities from the south to the north—with the United States had reached over 40 percent. The republics closest to the United States were the first to join the Allies. Strained diplomatic relations between Mexico and the United States, caused by the nationalization of the former's oil resources under General Cárdenas, would become cordial once the European market evaporated. Brazil shrewdly played the United States off against Nazi Germany, with Vargas securing American dollars to finance the Volta Redonda steel mill in return for allowing air bases to be constructed in the country to aid the Battle of the Atlantic. Cheap dollars would also help finance a number of other infrastructure projects. In August 1942, Brazil declared war against the Axis powers and sent 25,000 troops to fight in Europe. But many of the republics in the region would hold on to their neutral status until late in the war. Argentina waited until early January 1944 to break her ties with Berlin and Tokyo.

.   .   .

Until 1940, Palestra Itália's Parque Antárctica was the largest stadium in São Paulo. The club had dominated Paulista football in the 1930s with championships from 1932 to 1934, and again in 1936 and 1940. By 1942, however, the club's name and overt Italian origin were no longer acceptable. The Ministry of Justice declared that no club could use the name of an enemy power. In March, the club played as Palestra Itália for the last time in a 2–2 draw against Flamengo. Palestra Itália had become Palestra de São Paulo. Unfortunately for the club, the change in name was still not deemed satisfactory. Ejection from the league and seizure and transfer of the club's assets, which were not insubstantial, were threatened unless the club made a further change of name. Palmeiras was born. By the final match of the season, against São Paulo Futebol Clube, the newly christened team followed an army captain onto the pitch with the Brazilian flag to rapturous applause. São Paulo failed to acknowledge this patriotic gesture, and an ill-tempered match ensued. With Palmeiras 3–1 up in the second half, a penalty was awarded against São Paulo. Unable to disguise their disgust at the referee, São Paulo left the field in act of bad sportsmanship. Palmeiras was crowned champions.

São Paulo's time would come the following year. With the brilliant Leônidas da Silva at the heart of the team, the club would win the title in 1943, 1945, 1946, 1948 and 1949. Known as the "Rolo Compressor" (Steamroller), São Paulo's lineup of Leônidas, Mesquita, Sastre and Remo was a goal machine. But as successful as Brazil's steamroller may have been, there was only room for one *máquina* (machine) on the continent.

The Man-Made Machine

On October 19, 1941, River Plate hosted Boca Juniors in the penultimate match of the season. Boca, the reigning champions, had waged, by their own high standards, a lackluster campaign, and would only manage fourth place. River Plate, on the other hand, was a contender for the championship. And yet few could have foreseen the humiliation that Boca would have to endure at the hands of its fiercest rival. With River up 3–0 at halftime, *El Gráfico* interviewed the British ambassador, Sir Esmond Ovey, who declared, "Watching this match, once again one understands why football had achieved such dissemination . . . Here [the sport] is practised in accordance with the *criollo* character, that is, the Argentinian player is not mechanical but shows his ingenuity, his tendency for the aesthetic."[13] By the end of the match, Boca had succumbed 5–1, and River effectively secured the title. Boca had been taken apart by "La Máquina" (The Machine).

Argentinian football had come a long way from the *potrero*, that mythical patch of wasteland, as yet given over to the city, which had served as makeshift pitch for a generation of players. During the first two decades of the century, local teams had transformed themselves into clubs, which offered their members other sporting and social activities besides the spectacle of a weekly match. By the 1960s, a European visitor could not believe his eyes. "When one walks beneath the impressive gateway of the [River Plate] club, it is like entering another world, with almost its own sky. The golf course, gymnasium, athletic track, swimming pool and towering stadium, patronised by thousands of club members."[14] River Plate had only numbered seven hundred members in the mid 1910s, but by the end of the following decade, membership had grown to over 15,000. In 1938, River Plate, now one of the country's biggest clubs, moved to a sparsely populated area of Buenos Aires known as the "Siberia of Núñez." The club had returned to the *potrero*, though it now took the shape of a grand modern stadium, El Monumental.

Conceived by the club's president, Antonio Vespucio Liberti, who would later lend his name to the stadium, the horseshoe-shaped El Monumental held 70,000 spectators. To mark its inauguration, River Plate entertained Montevideo's Peñarol in a one-sided match that ended in a 3–1 win for the hosts. After thirty minutes of the game, the referee halted play and asked for a minute's silence to commemorate those who had contributed to the club's success. Without governmental assistance, which had taken the form of a soft loan of 2.5 million pesos from President Justo, the stadium might never have been completed. Earlier that year, Boca Juniors had received a loan of 1.6 million pesos for the construction of the La Bombonera, which took two years to build. This was less surprising, seeing as Justo had declared himself a fan of the club. In his extended essay *La cabeza de Goliat* (*Goliath's Head*), Ezequiel Martínez Estrada recognized what the capital had become: "The population of Buenos Aires is divided into clans, according to football clubs."[15] Politicians now fully understood the power of the game.

On the pitch, the first half of the decade was dominated by one of the greatest teams ever to have kicked a football. Now for the most part forgotten outside of the continent, where Brazil's 1970 World

Cup squad epitomizes *futebol arte*, River Plate played "total" precision football. They started the 1941 season with a vengeance, scoring five against Atlanta without reply; however, results throughout the campaign were uneven. After River had put Boca to sword, *El Gráfico* dedicated fourteen pages to the match, but the newspaper also questioned why the club had not played the whole tournament in a similar fashion. The goals came from Labruna, Moreno, Deambrosi (a brace) and Pedernera. In *Crítica*, José Gabriel called the forward line *una maquinita* (a little machine).[16] Moreno was the man of the match. Walter Gómez would later say of "El Charro": "The greatest, better than Pelé, was Moreno . . . what mastery of the ball, what strength, what precision, what style! Pelé broke into a sweat, [but] Moreno played in tails."[17]

It was in the following season that River Plate truly became La Máquina. The team played with such swagger that they became increasingly difficult to beat. Although River may have been the best club on the continent, the players were not infallible. When the club played in Chile, the local sporting weekly *Estádio* did not seek to flatter: "River Plate has disappointed the Chilean public, since its performance was a far cry from what we expected from a champion team."[18] The football may have disappointed, but the tour would be remembered for the first performance of the Colo-Colo club anthem. Ferenc Plattkó, a Hungarian goalkeeper who had played in Spain in the 1920s, had successfully coached the Chileans to the championship. By 1940, he had been contracted by River Plate, only to leave halfway through the season. Seven losses in seventeen games had sealed his fate. Plattkó would continue to flit between clubs in Santiago and Buenos Aires, before managing Barcelona in the 1950s.

It was another Hungarian who had a less ephemeral effect on River Plate's style of play. Emérico Hirschl, a journeyman coach, had started his Latin American odyssey with La Plata's Gimnasia y Esgrima in 1932. He had become the first foreign coach to manage a club in the professional era. In the 1920s, the Hungarian, who would become known as "El Mago" (The Magician), had played for Ferencváros. In 1929, the Budapest side had undertaken a South American tour, during which he had supposedly fallen in love with Buenos Aires. Yet, not unlike that of his countryman Plattkó, Hirschl's introduction to the Argentinian game was far from an easy one.

Founded in the late nineteenth century, the provincial city of La Plata had become the capital of the province of Buenos Aires. For three years, until the exile of Perón in 1955, it would become Ciudad Eva Perón (Eva Perón City), having been rechristened after her untimely death. In 1933, Gimnasia y Esgrima powered through the opening games of the season. It was not until the sixth match that the club was held to a draw. *Crítica* labeled the team "El Expreso Platense" because it resembled "a train that demolishes everything put before it and manages to elevate itself among the powerful [clubs]."[19] The club, however, would be made to feel less than welcome by the big five (River, Boca, Racing, Independiente and San Lorenzo) and some biased refereeing.

After the first round of the season, Gimnasia led the field with twenty-seven points. This was in part due to the brilliance of Arturo Naón, the club's greatest scorer, who would end the season with thirty-three goals. When the management of the club failed to honor its promise of a reward for having topped the table, the players went on strike. With negotiations at an impasse, the reserve team took to the field against Estudiantes and won with the only goal of the game. The turning point came against Boca, a match the Platenses should have won. Two early goals by Gimnasia should have been enough to see them through, but abject refereeing on the part of De Dominicis allowed Boca to win 3–2. It is perhaps a measure of the scandal his decisions prompted that, even in a league that was used to debatable decisions, De Dominicis was suspended for bias. Gimnasia won the next fixture, but the rot had set in. Against San Lorenzo, Gimnasia fell victim to another bout of abysmal refereeing, this time from the whistle of Rojo Miró. With San Lorenzo 2–1 in front, the visitors had a clear-cut penalty awarded as a free kick outside the area. This injustice turned to farce when the Gimnasia goalkeeper saved a shot, only for the referee to deem it to have crossed the line. Unable to exert any control over the match, Gimnasia opted for simple protest and the players all sat down. Play was waved on, while the Platenses sat and watched goal after goal being scored. The match ended 7–1, though it was abandoned before time. That season Gimnasia finished fifth, after a string of end-of-season losses.

Nevertheless, Hirschl's attacking style of play would take him to River Plate, where he secured the championship in 1936 and 1937. By the end of the decade, he had moved on to Rosario Central. When, in 1939, Hirschl returned to his former club, he witnessed carnage. River thrashed Rosario 6–0 in a one-sided encounter. Ever sanguine in footballing matters, Hirschl remarked, "I have come personally to gather the fruits of my teaching. Those six goals were scored by my boys."[20] Not that Carlos Peucelle—River's right-winger and the motivating force behind *La Máquina*—would have agreed. "Good football" depended not on managers but on how certain players influenced others. "No *director técnico* [manager] produced that [La Máquina]. The players made it happen. When Pedernera left River, he went to Atlanta. And there, at Atlanta, nothing happened . . . Atlanta was relegated. And there was no Máquina, nothing of the sort, in spite of Adolfo Pedernera being there. Millonarios in Colombia signed him and together with Di Stéfano, Néstor Rossi, Antonio Báez, Reyes, Mourin, produce a team that are known as 'Ballet Azul' [Blue Ballet], another 'Máquina.' Who produces it? The players. Not the managers."[21] Peucelle would joke that a 1–10 formation had been substituted for the more traditional 1–2–3–5.

Nicknamed "Barullo" (Disorder) because of the problems he caused his opponents, Peucelle had played in the 1930 World Cup, after which he moved from Sportivo Buenos Aires to River for 10,000 pesos. In 1932, the year after Peucelle signed, Bernabé Ferreyra was acquired for 35,000 pesos. The club's spending power would earn it the moniker "Los Millonarios" (The Millionaires). Peucelle would play for River until he retired in 1941. If there was ever a player who epitomized the spirit of the *potrero*, then it was Peucelle. The journalist Borocotó thought him "the personification of the *potrero*, the citizen of the *baldío* [vacant lot], he's the waste-ground in motion . . . He has the *baldío* in his heart."[22] Professionalism may have modernized the game, but the soul of Argentinian football remained rooted in the *potrero* and the barrio. The *pibe* (young working-class kid) and the *potrero* had become inextricably linked, ensuring the delivery of young players to the temples of football across the city. Borges, who became renowned for his dislike of the game, was once castigated by a sports journalist: "[Borges's childhood] must have been sad and boring, because not to remember a [pickup] game in the barrio with a *pelota de trapo* [rag ball] is not to have known or liked the sweetness of childhood."[23] This most Argentinian of writers, who prided himself on his *rioplatense* ancestry, had failed to grasp one of the fundamental tenets of modern *argentinidad*.

In its attitude to the game, the team incarnated, despite its partisan club colors, what it meant to be Argentinian. It was only after River's thrilling 6–2 victory against Chacarita Juniors in June 1942 that Borocotó christened the team "La Máquina." (Though the Uruguayan-born journalist tempered his praise with criticism, accusing the forward line of too much dribbling when victory was secure. Why had the players risked their legs with so little at stake?) The moniker stuck. It had, however, been used before. If one aspect of *argentinidad* was constant, it was its gift for inconsistency. In the late 1920s, *El Gráfico* had derisively used the word *máquina* to describe the repetitive and machinelike quality of English football.

Now the term was imbued with the beauty of orchestral timing: football played by artists. Fans would chant, *"Sale el sol, sale la luna, centro de Muñoz, gol de Labruna"* (The sun rises, the moon rises, center from Muñoz, goal from Labruna).

When Alfredo Di Stéfano, who would become Real Madrid's

most famous son, was asked who the five greatest players of all time were, he came up with La Máquina's five forwards: Muñoz, Moreno, Labruna, Pedernera and Loustau. Pedernera would often drop back into midfield, thereby taking bewildered defenders with him and allowing Labruna the space to score. (Labruna scored 293 goals in 515 appearances and remains Argentina's leading goal scorer alongside the Paraguayan Arsenio Erico.) La Máquina would eternally be identified with its celebrated forward line, though Peucelle always maintained that the success was due to the whole team. Perdernera denied that any one figure had invented La Máquina: it had been the combination of a favorable set of players. But if there was one architect of the team's success, then it was Peucelle, who would find his true vocation in management. He had Perdernera move position, from left wing to center-forward. When asked whether he was afraid of playing against Zizinho, Ademir and Jair in the 1950 FIFA World Cup final, the great Uruguayan captain Obdulio Varela responded tartly, "Scared, me? Have you forgotten that I played against Pedernera? I can assure you that no one plays like Pedernera."[24] Loustau had Deambrosio to thank for his career. According to Pipo Rossi, who would move from River to Millonarios in Bogotá, Deambrosio once told Peucelle, "'Carlos, send this kid, Loustau, on for a bit, who's been waiting [and] never plays, stick him on.' And when Peucelle sent Loustau on, *chau* [bye] to 'el mono' Deambrosio. He never played again."[25]

The stories of La Máquina would become legion. In Tucumán, River played a combined eleven to the delight of an expectant crowd. Security was high, and the mounted police were almost on the pitch. In one particular move, Félix Loustau received the pass, ran, went under the belly of a horse and squeezed the ball into the goal. Yet it was José Manuel Moreno who was not only La Maquina's best player but also its most charismatic. Varallo believed that Moreno might have even surpassed Maradona as a player had he taken better care of himself. Yet beautiful women and the tango hall would prove a necessary distraction. (He always thought doing the tango was the best way to train.) He was unabashed about his nocturnal activities: "Yes, I like the nightlife. So what? I never missed a training session. Don't come telling me to drink milk: the time I drank milk I played badly." Félix Loustau remembered his teammate's fondness for alcohol. "We were about to play Racing Club for the championship. 'Charro' Moreno had to be admitted to hospital for alcoholic intoxication. The doctor went to see him and said, 'If he so much as gets on the pitch, he'll die after twenty minutes.' Moreno got ready to play. Went on the pitch . . . and played the whole match . . . he was the best." Although loved by the fans, he was nevertheless chided by management. In 1939, River hosted Independiente in a crucial match for the championship. When River lost 3–2, Moreno was suspended for his lack of discipline. (He always maintained it was the one and only time he went to bed early.) His teammates, in an act of solidarity, decided to hang up their boots for the rest of the season. The remaining nine matches had to be played by a team of reserves, who played well enough to maintain the club's league position.

La Máquina may have loomed large in the popular imagination, but the quintet of Labruna, Loustau, Pedernera, Moreno and Muñoz only played together in eighteen matches over five years. The side was exceptional, but it wasn't invincible. Three matches from the end of the 1942 season, River secured its second title in succession at La Bombonera. Playing with only ten men—Norberto Yácono having had to leave the pitch when a projectile injured him—River equalized against Boca through two goals by Pedernera. But the following season Boca shaded River by one point to win the championship, and in 1944, that margin was doubled. River had to wait until 1945 to secure its third title of the decade; by now the team had become known as the "Knights of Anguish." "We didn't look for the goal," said Muñoz in an interview. "We never thought we couldn't score against our rivals. We went out on the pitch and played our way: take the ball, give it to me, a *gambeta*, this, that and the goal came by itself.

Generally it took a long time for the goal to come and the anguish was because games were not settled quickly. Inside the box, of course, we wanted to score, but in the midfield we had fun. There was no rush. It was instinctive."[26]

By the middle of the forties, the baton would be handed to one of the other five "big" clubs that had come to dominate the Argentinian game. According to Eduardo Archetti, the Argentinian anthropologist, "In 1936, the five largest clubs in Buenos Aires had 105,000 members and assets of 3,555,709 pesos, while the other ten clubs in the professional championship had only 55,895 members and assets of 1,351,845."[27]

In 1946, ten years since its last championship, San Lorenzo had managed to top the table by beating Boca by four points. And yet it was not the championship that would make legends of the 1946 team—which would be given the sobriquet "El Ciclón" (The Cyclone)—but the ensuing tour of Spain and Portugal. Although San Lorenzo lost 4–2 against Real Madrid, the team would demonstrate the superiority of Argentinian football. After the team beat a Spanish eleven 7–5 at Las Corts in Barcelona, *El Mundo Deportivo* exclaimed, "San Lorenzo de Almagro yesterday gave an excellent lesson in great football." The Argentines were praised for their positioning and skill on the ball: "They all play for each other, always to be found in the place where they need to be; they have such an excellent touch that they achieve with leather [ball] similar effects to a good billiards player."[28] When another Spanish eleven was dispatched 6–1 fifteen days later, the team's mission was complete: El Ciclón had passed into greatness. Before returning home, the squad put Portuguese football to sword in two matches. The Boedo-based club was hailed as legendary on both sides of the Atlantic and placed on a pedestal with La Máquina. The Iberian Peninsula had waited ten years for Argentinian football and was given a master class in the precision of the "mine-yours" short pass. Years later, Madrid's *El País* would remember "what occurred between 21 December and the end of January 1947 seemed unreal and inexpressible . . . The daily press and the magazines doubled their normal football coverage. San Lorenzo, despite playing with the cold, snow, and intense rainfall of that winter, caused a sensation."[29] Argentinian football would leave a lasting impression on the Spanish game. This was not lost on the imperialistic *El Gráfico*. The weekly believed that the tour had showed "the form, the quality, the science and the grace of Argentinian football."[30]

.   .   .

Another arena for the propagation of national identity was the cinema. Football, and its broad social appeal, would be employed to help reinforce a nationalist message. In 1948, the defining film on Argentinian football was released to widespread acclaim. *Pelota de trapo* (*Rag Ball*) charted the story of Eduardo Díaz, otherwise known as "Comeuñas" (Nail Biter), who dreams of becoming a *"crack"* footballer. Together with his friends, he learns to play the game with a ball made of rags on the vacant scrubland of his barrio. When Comeuñas finally becomes a hero to the terraces, he discovers he has a chronic heart defect and is told to retire or else he will die. In an international final against Brazil—who by this time had superseded Uruguay as Argentina's biggest rival in the popular imagination—the fans carry the player from the tribunes to the dressing room in order to make him play. Even with the specter of death hanging over him, and the appeals of his manager ringing in his ears, he cannot but accede to his country's calling.

In the film's defining moment, Comeuñas looks up at the Argentinian flag and says, "There are many ways to give your own life for the country. And this is one of them."[31] In heroic fashion, he dons the striped jersey of his country and scores the all-important goal. Though chest pains may still plague him, the film ends without the death of our hero. Unapologetically populist in tone, the film sought to mythologize the dirty-faced *pibe* and *la nuestra*. It comes as no surprise that the script was written by the Uruguayan journalist Borocotó, who effectively invented Argentinian football's identity in the pages of *El Gráfico*. The film also sought to create a bridge between the *potrero* and the national team, allowing working-class Argentinians to define themselves not just by their barrio but also by their national flag. The country, however, would maintain a complex relationship with *la selección* (the national team), which would in many ways allow the game to retain its barrio allegiances, sometimes at the expense of the national side. For all Argentinian football's swagger on the international stage, it would remain a parochial game.

It was also frequently a violent one. Argentina's golden era would be marred by regular outbreaks of aggression. In 1946, Newell's Old Boys hosted San Lorenzo in a match that would go down in history for the wrong reasons. With the game tied at 2–2, the referee disallowed the home side's goal five minutes from time, only for San Lorenzo to score in the eighty-eighth minute. The goal infuriated the Newell's *hinchas* (fans), who tried to lynch the referee with his own belt. Fortunately, two soldiers managed to save the referee, who, having fled the pitch, was about to be hanged from a nearby tree. Ever perverse in its rulings, the AFA had the remaining seventy seconds of the match played at the neutral ground of Ferro Carril Oeste. Newell's had to travel from Rosario to Buenos Aires to play two thirty-five-second halves. A year later, in a match between Atlanta and River Plate, *hinchas* of Atlanta stoned the River players whenever they approached goal. When River eventually scored, the referee, who was clearly terrified, disallowed the goal. When an Atlanta fan attacked the man, the game was called off.

The volatility of Argentine crowds, who tended to take out their frustrations on the referee, had been evident since the 1930s. Fourteen years earlier, in a match between Estudiantes and River Plate, the referee disallowed an Estudiantes goal and was swiftly encircled by both players and supporters. Having sought refuge in the dressing rooms, he emerged fifteen minutes later only to reverse his decision.

(It was rumored that the president of Estudiantes had held a revolver to his head.) This became known as "a goal scored in the dressing room"—*un gol de la casilla*.

The Land of the Two-Horse Race

For Uruguay, whose quixotic nature is at times tempered by an unhealthy strain of pessimism, her political history has been anything but straightforward. The overly complex electoral system, which employed the "double simultaneous ballot" as the agent of representative democracy, allowed for several candidates from the same party to accumulate votes; the candidate with the largest number of votes from the winning party secured the presidency. This system seemed excessively complicated for a country with such a small population (the size of Uruguay's armed forces in the latter half of the twentieth century was similarly excessive). Although the country did not have a Blanco president from 1865 until 1959, the hegemony of the two main parties (Colorados and Blancos, both of which contained factions from the right to the center-left wing) created a climate of perennial compromise. (Not until the twenty-first century would the left-wing coalition of the Frente Amplio [Broad Front] breathe life into the moribund political climate of the diminutive republic.)

In 1933, the country that had prided itself on its democratic traditions succumbed to the scourge of the continent: authoritarianism. President Gabriel Terra initiated a coup d'état, allowing him to implement the measures he argued were necessary to cope with the Great Depression—though the force of his own ambition was the more likely reason. The *dictablanda* (a soft dictatorship in which the semblance of civil liberty is maintained) revealed the frailty of Uruguay's institutions. On the day of the coup, the former president, Baltasar

Brum, accused those around him of being traitors and cowards, and in a moment of romantic self-sacrifice shot himself through the heart. Nine years later, Terra's brother-in-law and quondam chief of police, President Baldomir, carried out the *golpe bueno* (good coup) and restored democracy. The Second World War—that economic benefactor to many republics in the region—now ushered in an era of economic prosperity through increased export earnings and industrial growth. Uruguayans would suffer from a collective short memory as they entered what was perceived, even at the time, as a golden age.

No one could accuse Uruguayan football of having underachieved. The diminutive republic had surpassed all expectation, marshaling her resources to best effect on the international stage. Nevertheless, the domestic game would mirror the country's political duopoly. Since the mid-1910s, Peñarol and Nacional had settled into a comfortable routine of challenging each other for the Primera División (First Division) title, their dominance irregularly challenged by the other teams. The dawn of the professional era would cement the hegemony of both clubs. (It was not until 1976, when Defensor was crowned champions, that the stranglehold on Uruguayan football was broken.) But by 1933, the second season of professional football, Nacional had not won a championship since 1924, and the club would have to endure a protracted season in order to secure its first title of the new era.

With Peñarol and Nacional both even at forty-six points after twenty-seven games, a playoff was scheduled. The decider would become one of the most bizarre matches in the country's footballing history. In front of 42,000 spectators at the Estádio Centenario, the match remained goalless until the seventieth minute when a wooden case changed the course of the championship. The Peñarol winger, "Bahía," miscued his shot, which ended up flying past the post and hitting the case of Nacional's physio, Juan Kirschberg. The ball rebounded onto the pitch, where it was met by Braulio Castro. Not one to miss an opportunity, Peñarol's manager shouted, "Stick it in, just in case."[32] Castro duly obliged, and smashed the ball into the back of the net. In a moment of confusion, the referee signaled toward the goal with one hand while pointing at the center of the pitch. For a match that had lacked the usual hostility of River Plate derbies, the violent response to the conflicting hand signals was somewhat out of character. The referee, a bus driver called Telésforo Rodríguez, later recalled: "I saw Nasazzi [Nacional's captain] coming toward me, shouting something I couldn't understand. I thought he would make some observation, when he grabbed my shoulder with one hand, and started to punch me on the forehead with the other. Immediately, Chifflet started kicking me and at the same time other players attacked me."[33] Rodríguez managed to send off Nasazzi, Labraga and Chifflet, before retiring himself in order to seek medical attention. One of the linesmen took over as referee, though he kept his tenure to a minimum by suspending the match because of bad light. Nasazzi and Chifflet were detained overnight by the police, though the AUF had greater punishment in store. Nasazzi, who had led Uruguay to three world titles, was suspended for a year, while Labraga was handed fifteen months. The "goal" that had caused the furor was disallowed.

The decision was now taken that the remaining twenty minutes of the match would be played behind closed doors. Nacional was made to play with nine men. After playing extra time that stretched to an hour, there was still nothing to divide the rivals. Another play-off was scheduled, but the score remained 0–0. By this time, the new season had started and Montevideo's biggest fixture could not provide a single goal. In November 1934, Nacional was finally crowned 1933 champions after beating Peñarol 3–2. The one-handed Castro scored a hat trick.

Under the shrewd Hungarian Américo Szigeti, Nacional would repeat its success the following year, before Peñarol won the championship four years in succession. From 1939, it was the Tricolores' turn to dominate. For the first time in the history of Uruguayan football— something that Peñarol would replicate between 1958 and

1962—Nacional won five championships in a row (the Quinquenio de Oro). Even before securing the first of its five titles, Nacional had announced itself on the international stage. The best teams from Montevideo, Buenos Aires, Rosario and La Plata played a nocturnal tournament (Torneo Internacional Nocturno), hosted four times between 1936 and 1944. Independiente won the inaugural competition, with the Uruguayan entries Nacional and Peñarol managing only sixth and seventh place respectively. Two years later Nacional entered the competition under the Scottish coach William Reaside.

Nacional traveled to La Plata to face Estudiantes, which, thirty years later, was to become one of the most hated teams ever to play the game. The hostility of the home supporters was such that one of Uruguayan delegates asked Nacional's captain, Ricardo Faccio, to think about the team's safe passage. Might it not be better to let the hosts win? Faccio was adamant: "Whatever happens happens. We will win this match for our honor, for Nacional, our country and our family."[34] Nacional beat the Argentinians 2–1 with two goals from its own star Argentinian striker, Atilio García. The match would become known as *el partido de las camisetas ensangrentadas* (the match of the bloodstained shirts): several of the Nacional players had received cuts to the head.

Atilio García might never have been brought to Uruguay but for a moment of eccentricity on the part of the club's president. Atilio Narancio, who had been instrumental in furthering the Uruguayan game in the 1920s, had crossed the Río de la Plata to buy a striker. Unwilling to pay the asking price for the Boca forward he had hoped to buy, Narancio was given a list of suitable candidates. García only caught his eye because of their shared Christian name. (With that name, he must be good, thought Narancio.) With his film-star good looks—he possessed a passing resemblance to Clark Gable—García proved a revelation. He would go on to score 208 goals in 210 appearances.

Nacional had become invincible. In the 1941 season, twenty matches were played and twenty matches won. The ease with which the Tricolores brushed away all before them was a reminder of the great amateur teams of the Río de la Plata, such as Racing and Alumni. Not even the club's rival, Peñarol, could provide stiff competition, and succumbed 6–0 near the end of the season. Roberto Porta, who left the country to play for Independiente and Inter Milan before returning to his home club, stated: "I was lucky to play for many extraordinary teams, but the most notable of all was [Nacional] of 1941. This team had technical ability, speed, goals and strength. Or strength, goals, speed and skill; it doesn't matter which of these virtues was first or last . . . if it hadn't been for the Second World War, we could have gone round the world, winning and astonishing everywhere."[35] Unfortunately, this could not be said of the Uruguayan squad that Porta presided over in the 1974 World Cup. The country gave such an abysmal performance against Holland, succumbing to two goals by Rep, that Sergio Markarián decided to take up coaching. "I nearly cried because of the way they outclassed us. On that same day I decided to do something for Uruguayan football."[36]

By the end of the decade Peñarol turned to an Englishman for its coach. Randolph Galloway had played the game in the Midlands before ending his career at Tottenham Hotspur, though his managerial career would take him to Spain and Portugal. Dressed in a white tunic, the Sunderland-born manager cut a curious figure in Montevideo's Estádio Centenario. He was a disciple of the WM system, whose tactics produced flattering scores in the preseason. In the season that followed, the team produced a number of wins by large margins, but losses against Nacional would seal the Englishman's fate. The local press accused the coach of employing English tactics for a Uruguayan game.

In Brazil, a similar fate had befallen Izidor "Dori" Kürschner, who, after a peripatetic coaching career in Germany and Switzerland (he had coached, among others, Stuttgarter Kickers, Bayern Munich and Züricher Grasshoppers), had traveled to Rio in 1937. Here he would coach Flamengo and Botafogo. For Jonathan Wilson, the leading football tactician, "what Kürschner and the Brazilians call W-M . . . is actually rather closer to the *metodo*, more of a W-W shape, with the centre-half playing behind his half-backs, but in advance of the two full-backs."[37] In the 1937 Campeonato Carioca (Rio championship), Flamengo managed to score eighty-three goals in the season, but still were runners-up to Fluminense. Kürschner's European methods were now under scrutiny. When, in the following season, Flamengo lost its inaugural match to Vasco da Gama at the new Estádio da Gávea, Kürschner was dismissed. Flávio Costa, who had no small hand helping the Hungarian on his way, would now take over and Brazilianize the system. Kürschner moved on to Botafogo, but died three years later.

Peñarol would again seek out a foreigner; this time it was one with experience of *el fútbol rioplatense*. The club had already tried to lure the Hungarian émigré Emérico Hirschl across the Río de la Plata and in 1949 the club eventually managed to secure his services. Although he was another enthusiast of the WM, he also knew how the Uruguayans played. Moreover, he knew his own mind. Alcides Ghiggia, who would become the hero of Maracanã, later recalled, "[Hirschl] said, 'This one, on the right wing,' and pointed me out. Then the management stopped him and said, 'No. Now look, in that position we have Ortiz and Britos, who are internationals, players for Uruguay.' Brusque, the Hungarian did not take any notice. 'This one will play,' he said."[38] Ghiggia joined Hohberg, Míguez, Schiaffino and Vidal to create Uruguay's own *máquina*. When Peñarol romped to the championship that season, players such as Schiaffino and Ghiggia credited the coach. Obdulio Varela, however, believed that the success should be laid at the feet of the talented lineup. This belief would serve him well the following year.

Money and *la Violencia*

In June 1935, the whole of Latin America mourned the death of Carlos Gardel. The tango singer, whose smile and voice had beguiled the

Spanish-speaking world, had burned to death in an airplane disaster in Medellín. He had been Argentina's greatest cultural export. Now all that was left of Gardel—the charred remains—was returned to Buenos Aires. But the fervor endured—the tragedy only seeming to add to his greatness. Nowhere was this more pronounced than in the country of his death, Colombia.

The exodus of players from the River Plate had not abated. For the less adept, who stood little chance of making a career in Europe, the unsophisticated leagues of those republics with little footballing tradition would have to do. Such a one was Luis Timón, who had a successful career playing in Colombia in the 1930s. In an interview with an Argentine magazine, Timón explained: "[The Colombians] love everything that is Argentinian. There is no [high] wire fencing at the grounds and incidents hardly ever happen. But I have to say one thing. They don't just love the Argentinian as football player. They are sincerely fond of him, as of any fellow countryman. Their greatest idol was and is Carlitos Gardel."[39] By the end of the 1940s, what had been a footballing backwater had turned into the most sophisticated league on the continent. For that, Colombian football would have the Argentinians to thank.

Colombia had always been geographically compromised. Her contrasting topography—from Caribbean lowlands to Andean mountain ranges—may have given the republic an unusual diversity of resources, but it hindered her economic and political development. Transportation—or rather a poor railway network—had been a significant contributing factor. Whereas Argentina had extended her railway lines to 32,212 kilometers by 1912, the highest in Latin America, Colombia had only managed 1,061 kilometers of track. (The country had smaller networks than Cuba and Uruguay.) Even by the 1950s, the Caribbean coastline was not directly connected to the capital. Fortunately, air travel would solve some of these problems. No wonder football had taken its time to arrive.

Unlike the River Plate republics, whose football, even in its earliest years, can be discussed with some certainty, the early history of the Colombian game remains nebulous. Whether the first game was played in the early 1890s or ten years later continues to be a question for the country's historians to dispute. Only by the 1920s had the game become popular, though the Colombian version still practiced the code of "fair play" with which the southern republics had long since dispensed. The game, however, was played with a carnival spirit. When Deportivo Independiente Medellín was thrashed in Bogotá, its manager, Jesús María "El Cura" Burgos, cabled home, "because there are no defeats in sports, we drew 6–0."[40] This capacity for entertainment belied a more sinister strain in the nation's psyche.

The century had opened, as it would close: in terrible violence. Between 1899 and 1903, an estimated 100,000 Colombians lost their lives in the "War of the Thousand Days." Bloodletting on a grand scale was nothing new. In her short history, the country had suffered twenty-seven civil wars at a cost of 37 million gold pesos. Political stability would now follow, though it would only be a veneer over the perennial struggle between Conservatives and Liberals. By the 1940s, relative stability over four decades had given the country a reputation for democracy instead of anarchy. Memories in such matters were short. It took an act of wanton violence to plunge the country into yet another civil war.

On April 9, 1948, Jorge Eliécer Gaitán, the populist liberal leader, was shot four times on his way to lunch. As he lay dying, the assassin was set upon and beaten to death. Such was the frenzy of the attack that Gaitán's killer could only be identified by his documentation. The reasons for the assassination were never made clear: some thought it a communist conspiracy; others recognized the hand of the CIA. Gaitán had been a brilliant orator, whose own history of deprivation had proved attractive to the masses. Shortly before his death, he addressed an expectant crowd of 100,000 supporters: "Put a halt, Mr. President, to violence," he pleaded. "All we ask of you is the guarantee of human life, which is the least a country can ask."[41] The assassination ensured that the sentiments of Gaitán's well-intentioned speech were soon forgotten, and Bogotá erupted in rage. The *bogotazo*—as these riots would become known—killed five thousand people in the capital in a matter of hours, before escalating into a terrible civil war that lasted over a decade. *La violencia*, which would claim over 200,000 lives, became an exercise in sadistic vengeance. As Eduardo Galeano declared, "New ways of killing came into vogue: the *corte corbata* [cut tie], for example, left the tongue hanging from the neck. Rape, arson and plunder went on and on; people were quartered or burned alive, skinned or slowly cut into pieces; troops razed villages and plantations and rivers ran red with blood . . . the repressive forces expelled and pursued innumerable families."[42] And yet, in spite of this climate of terror, Colombian football enjoyed its golden age.

. . .

In 1932, the year after its River Plate neighbor, Uruguayan football turned professional. Professionalism may have solved one set of problems—especially the clubs' notion of players as chattel—but it would create another. Six years later, the Agrupación de Jugadores Uruguayos Profesionales (Association of Professional Uruguayan Players) was founded with José Nasazzi, the 1930 World Cup–winning captain, as its president. When the association failed to receive acknowledgment (and due recognition) from the Asociación Uruguaya de Fútbol (AUF), the first strike was staged. It would last for four weeks. In 1944, the first Argentine players' union, Fútbolistas Argentinos Agremiados, was established; Uruguay's Mutual Uruguaya de Futbóleres Profesionales would follow suit two years later. By 1948, both unions went on strike. In Argentina, the AFA finally recognized the union, but did not relent on requests for freedom of movement and a minimum wage.

Nearly two decades after the River Plate game had become professional, the relationship between club and player remained feudal.

When government intervention failed to resolve the issues at hand, clubs starting to cancel contracts and play amateurs. (The first players' strike in 1931 had been mediated by the Argentinian military dictator Uriburu.) In his autobiography, written once he had moved to Madrid, Alfredo Di Stéfano remained incensed. "It was a disgrace!" he wrote. "Basically we did it for two reasons: to defend our rights, trampled on by the clubs, and to obtain improvement for second division players . . . They exploited us in an intolerable way: low salaries . . . signing for a club meant submitting to its discretion for an unlimited time and, what was worse, to feel oneself undervalued by a few [people] without any class, with few scruples."[43]

In Uruguay, the strike had popular support. The Uruguayan players' union had deemed the AUF's statutes unconstitutional and sought assistance from the Ministry of Industry and Labor. By the end of the year, the striking unions from both countries, as an expression of solidarity and to collect funds, played an "international." The match took place outside Montevideo in Juan Lacaze, at the sports' ground of Campomar y Soulas, the country's largest textile company. Those that turned out that day included some of the best players on the continent. "Di Stéfano, 'Tucho' Méndez, Moreno, Loustau and Rossi on the Argentine side; Gambetta, Obdulio [Varela], Luis Ernesto, Schiaffino and Míguez on the Uruguayan," wrote Andrés Reyes. "The Argentinians won, but it mattered little."[44]

In Colombia, these labor disputes had not gone unnoticed. For Alfredo Senior, the president and founder of Millonarios FC, the idea was a simple one: "There was a strike in Argentina and as *El Gráfico* was already arriving by airplane, the idea occurred to me to bring players that were on strike and that were world-famous."[45] The plan may have been straightforward, but the fallout would be far-reaching.

Colombian football had long been a crisis waiting to happen. While the southern republics had organized the game in the late nineteenth century, it was not until 1924 that the Asociación

Colombiana de Fútbol (Adefútbol) had been founded. And even then the Barranquilla-based association had not provide the country with the sporting infrastructure it so desperately needed. Constant disputes between the regional leagues and the national association, and rather outdated attitudes to professionalism, hindered the game's development. By the mid-1940s, clubs in Bogotá, where football had come late, were playing semiprofessionally, to the distaste of other regional leagues. In 1948, Alfredo Senior and Humberto Salcedo founded Dimayor (División Mayor del Fútbol Profesional Colombiano) in the capital, though both men were of a different opinion as to what the nature of its organization should be. Salcedo hoped to establish a national championship, whereas Senior wanted a professional league, which would guarantee autonomy in setting up tours.

Two decades after the groundbreaking tours of Nacional and Boca, a team's identity could still be constructed by playing aboard. In 1946, the year the club was established, Millonarios toured Quito and Guayaquil. Two years later Millonarios undertook a five-match tour of Rio de Janeiro. The relative sophistication of the continent's other leagues threw the backwardness of Colombian football into sharp relief. In 1948, Bogotá hosted an international quadrangular tournament that would change Colombian football. Vélez Sarsfield and Montevideo's River Plate had made the journey from the Río de la Plata, while Millonarios and Independiente Santa Fe provided the domestic competition. When 12,000 spectators, a record attendance, turned up to watch Vélez take on Millonarios, the business community was quick to recognize the impact foreign players might make. While the Argentinians failed to win a match and came out last of the four-team table, *El Tiempo* lauded the Uruguayan winners: "The visit of a real team, like River Plate, is the only way that Colombian football might achieve true technical advancement."[46]

The untimely death of Jorge Eliécer Gaitán would prove the catalyzing force the league needed. With the country in extremis, the government of Luis Ospina Pérez looked to football to provide both a calming and controlling effect on an agitated population. The senate offered 10,000 pesos to the club that won the championship. Radio and newspapers, which had been banned from reporting on political topics, began to focus on footballing matters. Dimayor, now affiliated to Adefútbol, reached an agreement with the regional leagues to hand over 3 percent of gate receipts. Nevertheless, the fractious relationship between Dimayor in Bogotá and Barranquilla was reaching breaking point. When the clubs refused to release players for the Copa América, the federation finally had had enough. In March 1949, Adefútbol expelled Dimayor, with CONMEBOL following suit. The charges included an inability to adhere to FIFA regulations and a general lack of discipline, though Dimayor's overt professionalism was deemed inappropriate in the eyes of the Colombian federation. Late the year before, the president of Adefútbol, Bernardo Jaramillo García, had made his objections clear in *El Tiempo*. "I am a supporter of political parity, but not sporting parity . . . We live in an essentially democratic country and the majority should have more representation than the minority . . . Amateur football or nonprofessionals make up eighty percent of the football players in Colombia, and the paid or professional, only twenty percent."[47] In the 1948 season, which was won by Independiente Santa Fe, only three of the ten clubs comprised exclusively Colombian players (Atlético Junior, Atlético Municipal and América).

With the River Plate game in a state of stasis, and Dimayor free of any national and international restrictions, Senior made his move. He famously sent his Argentinian manager, "Cacho" Aldabe, to scout Buenos Aires for a world-famous player. Adolfo Pedernera was coming to the end of a successful career. After eleven years at River Plate, he was now playing for Huracán. His options had begun to narrow. Ever astute in his business dealings, Pedernera was bold in his request: a $5,000 bonus upon signing and a salary of $500 per month. The Millonarios president later recalled, "You're mad, said the board. How are we going to pay him? The takings are perhaps five or six thousand spectators."[48] When the Argentinian was presented to the fans at El Campín Stadium, 30,000 pesos were taken at the gate. "That was a *negociazo* [superdeal]," said Senior.[49] Pedernera arrived in Colombia after just five games. In the following match Millonarios thrashed Atlético Municipal 6–0. Though he may not have known it, Pedernera had opened the floodgates for foreign transfers. Short-lived though it was, this would be the golden age of Colombian football.

For all its sentimentality about barrio life, Argentinian football would have its head easily turned. That ineluctable bond between player and *potrero* would easily be broken where money was concerned. Strike action provided an excuse for a profitable spell of self-imposed exile. Moreover, free movement now meant just that. Players left their clubs without a second thought. There was no transfer documentation, and the clubs had no recourse to compensation. When Universidad Nacional de Bogotá offered Di Stéfano a better contract than Millonarios, he still opted to join his former River Plate teammates, Pedernera and "Pipo" Rossi, at Millonarios. Not that Universidad was the only club interested in the "Saeta Rubia" (Blond Arrow). Torino, which had lost its squad in the Superga air disaster, was interested in building a team around Di Stéfano, after watching him in a memorial match between River and Torino Simbolo.

Between 1949 and 1954—what must have seemed like a long summer—the Latin American game came together. "With *el Dorado* things went well for us: the dollar was about 1.75 pesos and at every match some ten thousand people stayed outside the stadium."[50] Of the first eleven players Millonarios fielded, seven had come from Argentina, one from Uruguay, Peru and Paraguay and a sole Colombian. Alfredo Di Stéfano would later remember: "It was strange how the players were distributed in towns according to nationality: the Uruguayans in Cucutá, Argentinians mostly in Bogotá, Brazilians in Barranquilla, Peruvians in Cali and the English in Santa Fé. At the University of Bogotá all the players were Ticos [natives of Costa

Rica] from Costa Rica who played beautifully on the ball."[51] There was even an entire team of Hungarians. While on tour of the country, and having been expelled by the Hungarian federation, Hungária FC disbanded, re-forming as Deportivo Samarios.

By 1951, over 60 percent of those playing for Dimayor's eighteen teams were foreigners. Unsurprisingly, this league of nations would be far from harmonious. Factionalism was rife—with the Argentinians the main offenders. When Neil Franklin, the Stoke City and England center-half who had broken with his club, moved to Independiente Santa Fe, he encountered resistance from his colleagues. "Most of our players came from Argentina, and they rather resented the intrusion of George Mountford and myself. Before we arrived, the Argentinians had held the monopoly, but when they realized that English, Scottish, Irish and Welsh stars were likely to invade Bogota they became insanely jealous, because they realized the British players would train and train hard. Training was not quite the strong point of the Argentinians. They were very good ball players, very good exhibitionists, but they were incredibly lazy in the training sessions."[52]

For the Argentinians, and other South American players, practicing ball skills was more important than flogging themselves around a training pitch. When Neil McBain left Leyton Orient to manage Estudiantes de la Plata for two years, the ex–Scotland halfback instigated a regime of ball practice and gymnastics. But the Argentinians would not tolerate running laps. In spite of the South Americans' superior technique, Franklin rated "Santa Fe and Millonarios as no better than the average Third Division side at home."[53] By the time Franklin returned home, English football would have been embarrassed by the unprepossessing play of the United States in her 1–0 defeat at the 1950 World Cup.

Millonarios was the club of the era, winning the title in 1949 and then three years consecutively from 1951. With its predominately *rioplatense* squad, the team was able to score at will. Known as the

"Ballet Azul" (Blue Ballet), it epitomized the attacking football of the era, having for the most part dispensed with defensive tactics. This meant that for all their extravagant talents, Millonarios was not invincible. In 1950, Deportivo Cali thrashed the Ballet Azul 6–1, with the Peruvian Valeriano López scoring a hat trick. López had joined Cali midway through the previous season, and had scored twenty-four goals. By the end of his career, he had averaged over a goal per match, having scored 207 goals in 199 games. Senior was proud of Millonarios, not just as a team but for what it represented for Colombian football. After Real Madrid and River Plate, the club was rated as one of the best in the world at the time.

For Di Stéfano, "football in Colombia was really in its beginnings . . . they had grand support but no one really knew much about the technical side of the game. It was all a ballet for players like myself but I repeat there was no mystery . . . just professionalism."[54] In 1952, while touring with Millonarios in Spain, the Argentinian's performance would attract the attention of Santiago Bernabéu, Real Madrid's patriarchal president, and a bid inevitably followed. With Barcelona also interested, a byzantine transfer tug-of-war ensued, ending with Di Stéfano heading to the Spanish capital in controversial circumstances.

Professional it may have been, but the Colombian game was nevertheless imbued with a carnival spirit. A dearth of tactics led to high-scoring matches. The league also attracted numerous players who displayed a less than professional attitude. In his memoir, Gabriel García Márquez recalled that while he was working as a journalist in Barranquilla, "the biggest journalistic event of the week . . . had been the arrival of the Brazilian soccer player Heleno de Freitas to play for Deportivo Junior . . . The stadium was crowded all the way up to the pennants. After six minutes of the first period, Heleno de Freitas scored his first goal in Colombia with a left rebound from the centre of the field. Although in the end Sporting won 3–2, the afternoon belonged to Heleno."[55]

By the time Heleno had arrived in Colombia at the end of decade, his best years were behind him. Gambling, drinking, drug taking (ether sniffed through a handkerchief) and womanizing had all started to take their toll. Ten years later, at the age of thirty-nine, one of Brazil's greatest talents would die half mad of syphilis in a sanatorium. And yet Heleno had promised so much. Born to an upper-middle-class family, the elegant Heleno was blessed with academic and sporting prowess. After completing his law degree, he turned to football and played for Botafogo, where he scored 209 goals in 235 matches. He was cultured and urbane, but his temperament belied his beauty: he may have resembled Rudolph Valentino but his temper could be appalling. His charm often gave way to cruelty, especially where less talented teammates were concerned. Ademir, who played with Heleno at Vasco da Gama, later remembered, "He'd never run to try and get the ball. He'd just stand there and tell me, 'Hey, you needn't bother playing me those horrible balls because I won't go after them. You'd better put some effort into it.'"[56] Although an idol on the Botafogo terraces, he was known as "Gilda"—after the Rita Hayworth vehicle that offered up a Hollywood fantasy of Latin America—to rival fans.

Ondino Viera, the Uruguayan-born manager who would spend a season at Botafogo before moving on to coach Fluminense, knew that the club would never win with Heleno playing. The year he was sold to Boca Juniors, Botafogo won the state championship. Though his stay in Buenos Aires, where he was rumored to have shared Eva Perón's bed, was a success, it was short. This was the beginning of the end. At Vasco, Flávio Costa found him too difficult, which put paid to extending his international career in 1950, and on he moved to Colombia. Here, García Márquez would write, "Heleno da [*sic*] Freitas, as a footballer, might be very good, very bad or simply a Brazilian dandy, but the truth is that the great gypsy, more than being the team's centre forward, was a kind of permanent opportunity to speak badly of someone."[57]

Although Colombian football had come a long way in a short space of time, the frenzied activity could not last. It was not long before FIFA became involved. Ivo Schricker had alerted Jules Rimet to the problem: "In Colombia the Bogotá DiMayor league, with the Millonarios club, have left the Colombian FA and are organising spectacular matches—almost all of the best players from Argentina and other countries have left their Associations to become well-paid performers in the Bogotá circus."[58] But it was after the 1950 World Cup, when some of the Uruguayan squad joined the rebel league, that FIFA thought to put an end to the problem. In September 1951, CONMEBOL convened a meeting in Lima, where the Colombian circus was effectively laid to rest. DiMayor was reaffiliated to the Colombian federation, while the freewheeling transfer agreements would now have to abide by FIFA's regulations. The league had bought itself some time, though: it would not be until 1954 that players would have to return to their original clubs. If this was the golden age of Colombian football, it was Colombian in name only. The best players had all been imported, ready to move on when the league ran out of steam. Though it was bankrolled by Colombian money, it cannot be said to have been in any way Colombian in character. Millonarios remained a foreign team that played its football in a foreign country. When the foreigners moved on—as they always would—Colombian football reverted to what it had been. *El fútbol rioplatense* had allowed the Colombian game to have aspirations. But it would have to wait to become truly competitive. The violence, however, would not.

PART TWO

THE BALL NEVER TIRES

1950–2014

CHAPTER SIX

WHOM THE GODS WISH TO DESTROY

1950–1960
The Defeat That Made Brazil

Other countries have their history. Uruguay has its football.

—Ondino Viera

Rio de Janeiro is the world's most beautiful city and the worst thing that has ever happened to Brazilians.

—Hernáne Taveres de Sá, *The Brazilians, People of Tomorrow* (1947)

Whom the gods wish to destroy they first call promising.

—Cyril Connolly, *Enemies of Promise* (1938)

If Brazil thought her triumph at the 1949 Campeonato Sudamericano was an indication that she had finally mastered the art of international competition, she was mistaken. Even though competitive football was no longer restricted to the Atlantic coastline, Argentina had been the best team of the 1940s. After the obligatory home triumph for Uruguay in 1942, Argentina had won the Campeonato Sudamericano three years running between 1945 and 1947 without losing a single match. The 1945 Copa Roca had, however, proved the exception.

In December 1945, Argentina traveled to Brazil to play the three-match rubber. Well organized and effective, the Argentinians managed to edge their opponents 4–3 in the first encounter in São Paulo. Brazil was not helped by the halfhearted reception from the Paulistas, who were not averse to booing their own if things were not going their way. Ever confident, the Porteño press asked for the *copa* for Christmas—a gift to the Argentinian fans. In Rio, it would be a different matter altogether. With three changes to her lineup, Argentina was ripped apart 6–2 by the attacking Brazilians. Zizinho played magnificently, while Heleno de Freitas, who was still in his prime, replacing Leônidas, proved decisive even with his first pass. Three days later, Brazil proved equally self-assured in front of goal, peppering the Argentinian goal with a series of headers and bicycle kicks. The first half may have ended goalless, but it was not without incident: Ademir fractured Battagliero's leg. By the end of the match, Argentina failed to deal with Brazilian aggression and succumbed 3–1.

Two months later, the rivals met again in the final match of the Campeonato Sudamericano. Although Battagliero's injury had not been the fault of Ademir, the Argentinian fans were bent on revenge. Street vendors sold unripe pears to throw at the Brazilian players. With the championship at stake, ill temper was always going to dog the match. Worse was to come when an injury to the Argentinian captain threw the game into chaos. After twenty-eight minutes, Jair clashed with José Salomón as he attempted a shot on goal. When the Argentinian went to ground, having suffered a break of the fibula and tibia, his teammates attacked the opposition. The fracas that ensued agitated the spectators, who now took to the pitch. Matters were made worse when the police entered the fray and were indiscriminate as to whom they dealt their blows. The match was only restarted after seventy-two minutes, by which time any momentum and goodwill had evaporated. With Chico and de la Mata off the pitch, both teams played out the rest of the match with ten men. Argentina may have won 2–0, but her captain would never play international football again. On seeing Jair after the match, Guillermo Stábile complained, "You have broken the leg of Argentina's best back." "You are mistaken. The best Argentinian backs are De Zorzi and Valussi," came the reply.[1]

In 1949, Argentina failed to participate in Brazil's Campeonato Sudamericano, while Uruguay, affected by a players' strike that lasted five months, sent a second-string squad. Brazil, in spite of scoring heavily (thirty-nine goals in seven matches), was beaten by 2–1 by a strong Paraguayan side. Paraguay was unlucky not to win the championship, losing unexpectedly against a mediocre Uruguay. In their previous match against Peru, the Paraguayans had been kicked off the pitch. With three important players absent through injury, Paraguay had faced the quondam World Cup winners on a wet evening and lost. Their surprise victory against Brazil would count for little, when three days later Paraguay conceded seven goals against Brazil in the rain-affected playoff. It was now obvious to all that the Paraguayans could not play in the rain.

The Brazilian desire to host the World Cup had been evident from the late 1930s, but the Second World War had put paid to any hope it had of hosting the 1942 tournament, which Argentina had also coveted. In 1947, FIFA handed the continent's largest republic the opportunity of fulfilling her footballing destiny. Rio de Janeiro, however, needed a stadium that would reflect the modern image Brazil wished to convey. Two years before, Mário Filho had asserted in *Jornal dos Sports* that a modern stadium would provide the population with a new soul that would awaken this slumbering giant of the country. Moreover, at a municipal level, there was a desire to build a temple to the game that would outdo São Paulo's 70,000-capacity Estádio do Pacaembu.

Maracanazo!

The construction of Maracanã, which took its name from the river that flowed near the site, was now a matter of national importance. The project was publicly funded and overseen by the prefect of the city, General Ângelo Mendes de Moraes. Stories recounting the different stages of construction were serialized in *Jornal dos Sports*. But this level of public scrutiny failed to ensure the stadium was built on time. Unaccustomed to completing a project of such magnitude under a time constraint—something that had also befallen the

Uruguayans twenty years before—the Cariocas had managed it with only a week to spare. The stadium may have looked like it had come from another galaxy, but its environs were definitely third world. Filho was prescient when he wrote: "Brazilian sport is not only great in terms of its tradition. Many years from now, when we write the history of this era, the miracle of the stadium will be noted as one of the most complete dreams ever brought to fruition in our country."[2] The tournament, however, would become the country's worst nightmare.

Unlike the 1934 and 1938 World Cup, both of which were knockout competitions, the organizers had reverted to the system of group matches used in the 1930. This would afford any team unfortunate enough to lose its first match the opportunity to play another two. Weak European teams would not have to bear the humiliation of playing one match and returning home. Nevertheless, India and France withdrew from the tournament—the latter citing the distance it would have to travel between matches—leaving one pool of three teams and one of two in addition to the two groups with a full complement of four.

Brazil opened the competition with consummate ease. The naive Mexicans were dispatched 4–0 by a team that mostly consisted of Vasco da Gama players. For their second match, the Brazilians traveled to São Paulo to face Switzerland. While the other squads would have to travel around the country, this was the only match Brazil would not play at the Maracanã. In an attempt at diplomacy, Flávio Costa called up three Paulista midfielders. When the French-born Fatton equalized two minutes from time, Brazil's aura of invincibility was exposed. The two-all draw was received by the host nation as a defeat. After the match, angry fans in Rio de Janeiro attacked the Swedish Embassy—a case of mistaken identity based on a tenuous grasp of European geography.

With Yugoslavia having beaten Switzerland and Mexico 3–0 and 4–1 respectively, Brazil needed to beat them in order to progress to the final pool. Fortunately for Brazil, the Red Star Belgrade striker, Rajko Mitić, cut his head on a steel beam in the as-yet-unfinished stadium and could not start the game. Yugoslavia had to make do with ten men for much of the first half, and conceded an early goal by Ademir. By the second half, Costa's WM formation was beginning to creak under pressure from Yugoslavia, and Brazil was lucky to sneak in another goal before seeing out the tie. By the time that Brazil made it into the final round, Uruguay had yet to play its first match. Uruguay, who had never lost a World Cup game because it had failed to defend its title, had been drawn against the absentee French and the Bolivians. Bolivia had not improved in the twenty years since its last appearance at the tournament and went down by eight goals to nil; Peñarol's brilliant striker Míguez thrilling the small Belo Horizonte crowd with a hat trick. But Uruguay's lack of playing time would tell in the final round.

The final round clearly favored Brazil, who stayed in Rio for all three matches, something that was not lost on Sweden's British-born manager, George Raynor, who complained openly about the fixture list. In Buenos Aires, *La Razón* questioned the validity of a tournament in which Argentina had failed to participate and from which Italy and England—who had suffered their infamous 1–0 defeat at the hands of the USA—had been eliminated. "Only four protagonists remain in the final round that do not represent—by any means—the best in world football," sniped the newspaper.[3] Uruguay made hard work of its match against Spain, but managed to secure a 2–2 draw because of a long-range shot from Obdulio Varela. Brazil, on the other hand, thrashed Sweden 7–1 in a perfect display of attacking football. *El Mundo Deportivo* lauded the performance: "The Brazilian team was outstanding . . . the central attacking trio played magnificently and, of them, the centre forward, Ademir, was the hero of the afternoon, since it was he who led the majority of attacks."[4] Pozzo, who was covering the tournament as a journalist, had not rated the Brazilians: now he changed his mind. In the next match Ademir failed to repeat his four-goal tally, even though Brazil waltzed to a 6–1 victory over Spain. When Chico scored the fourth goal, over 150,000 voices began to sing "Touradas em Madri" ("Bullfights of Madrid"). The score line flattered Brazil: the Uruguayans had clearly softened up the Europeans. The same could not be said of Sweden. Although not physically strong, the Swedes managed to resist the Uruguayan attack. With thirty-three shots on goal, Uruguay should have won by a greater margin than 3–2. After Míguez's goal in the eighty-fifth minute, Uruguay played out the match in Latin American fashion: strolling with the ball into a deciding match against Brazil.

As with many football matches, the buildup and the aftermath loom larger in the imagination than the game itself. And so it was with the 1950 final. Both countries had played each other regularly during the forced isolation of the 1940s, so there would be no tactical surprises. Moreover, ever since her inaugural 2–1 win at the 1916 Campeonato Sudamericano, Uruguay had had a good record against her larger neighbor. Flávio Costa was not employing prematch hyperbole when he stated: "The Uruguayan team has always disturbed the slumbers of Brazilian footballers. I'm afraid that my players will take the field on Sunday as though they already had the Championship shield sewn on their jerseys. It isn't an exhibition game. It is a match like any other, only harder than the others."[5] In May, Brazil had hosted Uruguay for the Copa Barón Río Branco, a three-match rubber between the two nations. Uruguay had won the first match 4–3 in São Paulo, with Míguez scoring a brace, but then lost the other two matches by a one-goal margin. In Montevideo, *El País* was quick to emphasize the squad's deficiencies: "All the players—with some exceptions—are completely lacking in *training*, fat, heavy. The tactical direction does not count for anything."[6]

The pressure on Brazil to win emanated more from without than from within: the country expected. This was not lost on the Hungarian journeyman coach Emérico Hirschl, who realized that the prematch fanfare was at times more impressive than the match itself (this was certainly the case against Yugoslavia). He was also skeptical about Brazil's prowess on the pitch. "I am convinced that the Brazilian team has various players that are already over the hill. A team with worn-out players . . . my impression is that Brazil won't go very far."[7] The Brazilians themselves, however, thought otherwise.

Now that Brazil had only to draw against Uruguay to top the pool, the World Cup seemed secure. *O Mundo* may have tempted fate with its sensationalist headline THESE ARE THE CHAMPIONS OF THE WORLD, under which were displayed the photographs of the players, but not all Brazilian newspapers were blinded by jingoism. In São Paulo, *O Estado* sought to rein in the overexcitement: "The excessive confidence is, from every point of view, damaging . . . the game is determined on the pitch and not in the stands."[8] While Rio's *O Globo* cautioned its readers not to misinterpret Uruguay's results against Spain and Sweden as heralding the demise of a footballing power.

The shock of Uruguay's eventual victory served to cloak the day in mystery. Something that was not dispelled by the myths that would later emerge as both Brazilians and Uruguayans somehow sought to make sense of the match. Even the film footage of the match took on the feel of fiction. For Uruguayans, it was Obdulio Varela, nicknamed "El Negro Jefe" (The Black Chief), who would emerge as the mythological hero. On seeing *O Mundo* in the hotel foyer, Varela was said to have bought every copy, laid them out on his bathroom floor and had the squad urinate on them. (Ironically Julio Pérez, who played on the wing, was said to have wet himself while the Uruguayan national anthem was playing.) The anecdote is so good it became truth. For many players, however, "it was a calm morning, the same as all the others [when] we were there."[9] What might have threatened their sense of calm was that Uruguay had to face Brazil in front of 173,850 spectators (though the unofficial figure was over 200,000).

"We arrived at the stadium around a quarter to one and the game started at three," Schiaffino later recalled. "When we arrived we saw that [the stadium] was full, but the attitude of the crowd was at all times very polite. Before the match, we rested a lot with our legs up because it was very hot, over thirty degrees [Celsius], which also didn't suit us."[10] The expectation was never to win but to lose with dignity. As one delegate from the Uruguayan camp cynically observed, "by losing by four goals and not making fools of yourselves, so that the ref sends someone off, you have done your duty."[11] Though Schiaffino claimed that Varela would not have allowed any management into the dressing room.

For Brazil the stage had been set, and it was now time for the Seleção to deliver the World Cup. While a draw may have sufficed to secure the title, there was an expectation that they would win in style. Barbosa felt nauseous when he entered the dressing room. Bigode was told to rein in his aggression and not to kick his opponents outside the area. Before the match, the president of Brazil stated: "You who I already consider champions . . . you take the field as authentic representatives of Brazil who will prove the worth of the Brazilian people to the entire world." Shortly thereafter, the mayor of Rio de Janeiro exerted more pressure: "The municipal government had done its part by building this stadium. Now, players of Brazil, you must complete your duty!"[12] Conscious of the size of the crowd and the effect it might have on his players, Varela issued the command, "Enter walking slowly, quietly confrontational. Don't look up at the stands but straight ahead, because the match is played on the ground and we are eleven *versus* eleven." Then came the measured cri de coeur: "They are rubbish out there! Let the show begin."

If Brazil thought that Uruguay would surrender in a similar fashion to the Europeans in the final round, it was mistaken. Luck, and tireless defending, seemed to favor the Uruguayans. Every time Uruguay cleared their lines, the ball seemed magnetically drawn back to her penalty area. Uruguay managed to break just before the halftime whistle, only for Barbosa to be equal to Varela's shot. By a miracle Uruguay had managed to keep the score goalless. Brazil, on the other hand, would rue their profligacy in not converting any of its seventeen chances.

When Brazil finally scored through a Friaca header in the forty-seventh minute, it seemed as if the floodgates might open. With the crowd celebrating an imminent victory, Varela now ran thirty meters with the ball and began to remonstrate with the referee. Years later

Varela admitted a certain gamesmanship: "I knew that if I didn't stall the match, they would have demolished us." Varela had been so adamant in his protestations that an interpreter had to be sent on to the pitch. With Uruguay now needing two goals to win, the World Cup was firmly within Brazil's grasp. Yet Brazil failed to capitalize on her position, and this failure seemed to strengthen Uruguay's resolve. The Uruguayans now became swift and assured in attack, much to the astonishment of a crowd, whose attention had been momentarily diverted by a corpse being taken out of the stadium. And there was an air of inevitability about Uruguay's equalizer when it came twenty minutes later. Varela, who was now marshaling his troops in attack as effectively as he had in defense, dispatched Alcides Ghiggia down the right wing. Not for the first, or last, time that afternoon, Ghiggia outwitted Bigode and found the unmarked Schiaffino, who put the ball in the top right-hand corner. It was the goal that destroyed Brazil. The Maracanã fell silent. And yet Brazil only had to keep the score level for another twenty-four minutes to be crowned champions. The Uruguayans now realized how terrified Brazil was of losing. Eleven minutes from the final whistle, the words of the Uruguayan radio commentator, Carlos Solé, passed into history: "Míguez stops the ball and assists Julio Pérez. Julio Pérez goes forward with the ball, waiting for Ghiggia to run in front. Julio Pérez continues to attack. Pérez to Ghiggia. Ghiggia to Pérez. Pérez goes forward, and crosses the ball to Ghiggia. Ghiggia gets away from Bigode. The fast Uruguayan right wing advances. He's going to shoot. He shoots. Goool, goool, goooool, gooooooool *uruguayo*."[13]

Once again, silence in the stadium. The goal, similar to Uruguay's first, had wrong-footed the Brazilian defense and goalkeeper. Instead of cutting the ball back, Ghiggia had drilled it home and had broken a nation's heart. Uruguay, against the odds and in the face of Brazilian audacity, had grasped victory from the jaws of defeat. "Down through its history, only three people have managed to silence Maracanã," Ghiggia was later quoted as saying. "The Pope, Frank Sinatra and me." Though whether he was as succinct as this has always remained in doubt.

When the final whistle was blown, silence reigned. (Rumor has it that two distraught fans leaped to their deaths when they realized their team had lost.) In his book on the history of the World Cup, Jules Rimet recalls handing the trophy over to Varela. The scene he paints is one filled with pathos. "There was no longer a guard of honour, nor national anthem, nor speech in front of the microphone, nor formal victory ceremony . . . I found myself alone in the crowd, shoved from all sides, with the cup in my arms, not knowing what to do. Finally I saw the Uruguay captain [Varela] and gave him the cup, almost surreptitiously, shaking his hand without being able to exchange even one word."[14] The gloom that descended on the Maracanã made it impossible for Uruguay to celebrate. The traditional lap of honor was witnessed by a near-empty stadium.

On their way back to the hotel, the Uruguayans realized they had not only silenced a stadium, they had silenced a city. Varela, wise beyond his years, reflected, "We ruined everything and won nothing. We had [won] the title but what was that in the face of such sadness? I thought about Uruguay. There the people would be happy."[15] That evening the players celebrated in their hotel. The Uruguayan management had advised the team not to leave for fear of Brazilian retribution. Varela flatly disobeyed and went out, taking the squad's physio, Matucho Fígoli, with him. They spent the night drinking beer with despondent Brazilians before returning in the early hours. Although Montevideo celebrated and awaited the new world champions, it remained a very Uruguayan victory: triumph shot through with an innate sadness.

If one game had ever caused a country to question its identity, it was what would become known as the "Maracanazo" (Maracanã Blow). Nelson Rodrigues would later remember the pain of the match. "Obdulio ripped the title from us. I said, 'ripped' as if I would say 'extracted' the title from us as if it were a tooth."[16] *Folha Carioca* likened the defeat to "Waterloo." The close scrutiny with which the match was examined would come to border on a national obsession. In *Anatomy of a Defeat*, Paulo Perdigão would write, "of all the historical examples of national crises, the World Cup of 1950 is the most beautiful and most glorified. It is a Waterloo of the tropics and its history our *Götter-dämmerung*. The defeat transformed a normal fact into an exceptional narrative: it is a fabulous myth that has been preserved and even grown in the public imagination." For Ghiggia, it was simple: "Barbosa did the logical thing, and I the illogical. But it turned out well for me."[17]

For three black players—Barbosa, Bigode and Juvenal—life would never be the same. Barbosa was never allowed to forget his mistake: "The Penal Code determines that twenty-eight years is the maximum sentence. In Brazil, I am condemned to perpetual imprisonment."[18] Roque Máspoli, the Uruguayan goalkeeper, doubted whether he would have done better than his opposite number. "Ghiggia's shots were hard to stop because he used to put swerve on them. From what I could see, Barbosa came off his line to cut out a cross because there were other players coming up in support. When you consider the way Ghiggia always hit the ball, the goal was more down to his skill than a mistake by the keeper."[19] "The scars never healed," Barbosa later would say. "They shouted 'Ghiggia,' 'Schiaffino' [at me], names that have pursued me all my life."[20] Bigode suffered taunts such as "lanky nigger" and would later admit, "I thought about dying. It would have been better for me."[21] And this from a player who in the early part of the campaign had been lauded for his strength and tenacity.

In the moment of truth, a racist strain, a baleful legacy of slavery, had revealed itself. And yet, how could Brazilians scapegoat their own black players as "weak" when their tormentor had himself been black? Bigode would be accused of cowardice, having been bullied by Uruguay's captain, something he would deny. It was said that Varela had punched Bigode. Though both players claimed it had been nothing more than a slight knock, Mário Américo, the Brazilian masseur, remembered it differently, "Obdulio ran over there, stuck his finger in Bigode's nose and barked, 'You son of a thousand bitches, if you hit the kid [Ghiggia] I'll kill you.'"[22] Uruguay may have had a black captain, but the country still suffered from manifest racial discrimination. As early as in the 1930s, the Afro-Uruguayan press sought to dissuade blacks from relying on a career in football for fear of exploitation. Like Andrade and Gradín before him, Varela would end his life in penurious circumstances.

But not everybody sought to blame the blacks in the losing team. David Nasser, the most prominent journalist writing in Brazil in the 1950s, was equitable in apportioning blame, pointing the finger at the whole team. In *O Cruzeiro*, he also criticized the media for portraying the relentless Uruguayans as tired, old men. Nasser was not wrong, though his journalistic ability would be called into question when he was later accused of fabrication. When Brazilians were not condemning each other, they would look to the tactics. In an interview with the writer Alex Bellos, Zizinho blamed defeat on the system. "The last four games of the World Cup were the first time in my life I played WM. Spain played WM, Sweden played WM, Yugoslavia played WM. The three that played WM we beat . . . [Uruguay's] system was crazy but it wasn't as bad as WM . . . That's why we lost the World Cup."[23] The Uruguayans had learned from the Swiss—not for the first time: in the early twentieth century the country had copied the Swiss collegial executive system—and employed the *libero* in a sweeper role behind the last line of defense.

For Brazil, it was not so much losing to Uruguay as the ignominy of defeat while the world watched that hurt so much. The defeat had revealed what Nelson Rodrigues would call the *complexo de vira-latas*, the "stray dog [who looks for scraps] complex." Obdulio had kicked Brazil around like a stray dog, and she had yielded. And yet this complex was not the result of one match. A sense of inferiority about its place in the world had marked the Brazilian psyche for decades. The country was, according to Paulo Perdigão, "without glory, giving up one dictatorship for the indifferent government of Dutra, before the return to power of the Vargas regime and the euphoric boom of the government of Juscelino Kubitschek."[24] It had been obvious to Argentina and Uruguay, now it was obvious to the rest of the world. The *vira-latas* complex not only manifested itself in physical weakness, but in mental fragility.

Even sixteen years after the event, Nelson Rodrigues was embittered. "Every people has its irremediable national catastrophe, something like a Hiroshima. Our catastrophe, our Hiroshima, was the defeat by Uruguay in 1950. The adversary [Uruguay] carried out a campaign of obvious mediocrity."[25] Rodrigues believed that Brazil had been afraid of Spain and yet had "massacred" them. Uruguay, however, posed no threat: "From Uruguay, nothing. No fear whatsoever."[26]

The Maracanazo exposed the brittleness of the country's spirit, but abject defeat would prove a catalyzing force. Grief would allow Brazil time to reflect and learn. For Uruguay, triumph in adversity would be her undoing: victory would render her lazy and forgetful of the very traits that had allowed her to succeed. Unlike her neighbor, she would not learn to become a tournament player. A belief became current that Uruguay could only win against the odds. *Uruguay contra mundum*. Uruguay's tragedy was to be suffocated not under the weight of expectation but by a misplaced faith that they could always rely on a miracle to rescue them—even in the most dire of straits. As Varela said in the aftermath of victory: "If we can do something that impossible, we can do anything."[27] Winning with both strength and style as they had in the twenties and thirties would be forgotten. Forty-six years after his country's greatest victory, the Uruguayan writer Mario Benedetti challenged the legacy of Maracana in his novel *Andamios* (*Scaffolds*). On returning to Uruguay, after years in exile, Benedetti's protagonist, Javier, considers the influence of the unlikely victory: "Forty-five years of the country's *maracanization* had left indelible marks of hypocrisy (indignant David who surprisingly defeats arrogant Goliath) in the sporting, sociological and political narrative of the day before yesterday, yesterday and today . . . We suddenly became the nouveaux riches of sport."[28] Unfortunately, the country never sought to emulate the humility and wisdom of Uruguay's captain and caudillo, Obdulio Varela. "Everything becomes smaller, everything changes. The past needs to be left in peace."

In his 1940 essay, *La cabeza de Goliat*, Martínez Estrada likened Buenos Aires to the head of Goliath on the country's body of David. Uruguayan football was in danger of becoming this very monster: overinflated and unable to sustain itself. In three decades, Uruguay had reached football's zenith four times. The fall from grace would be long and drawn out. The footballing gods would draw out the pain, offering the country glimpses of its great tradition before dashing its hopes. Club football in the 1960s, especially given its success at the continental level, would reinforce exceptionalism. But, at the international level, the game would get away from Uruguay. And it would become impossible for the country to catch up.

Uruguay may not have been such an underdog had she not entered the tournament without one of the greatest players Latin America would ever produce. Walter Gómez had been called up as a teenager to play against Argentina in the 1945 edition of the Copa Newton. His first match was auspicious: he consistently outwitted his marker and came off to clamorous applause from the Porteño crowd. And yet, in spite of his devastating talent, he would only play four games for his country. In 1949, a moment of madness would curtail a promising career. Not for the first or last time, the Copa Uruguaya had pitted Peñarol against Nacional. The match would be remembered as *el clásico de la fuga* ("the derby of the escape") for Nacional's unsporting behavior in an ill-tempered match. Trailing by a goal to nil, Peñarol was awarded a penalty, which it converted on the rebound. The usual protestations ensued, only for Gómez to lose his temper and punch the referee in the face. Gómez soon followed Tejera, who had been shown the red card earlier, off the pitch and Nacional was now down to nine men. During the halftime break, rumors began to circulate that Nacional might refuse to play the second half. When Peñarol took to the pitch, hoping to thrash its perennial rival, Nacional failed to show. After checking his watch, the referee awarded Peñarol the match. Gómez was handed a year's suspension from the game.

When Uruguay won the World Cup, Gómez was playing for

River Plate in Buenos Aires. His teammates "surrounded him and in his honour gave an affectionate 'hurrah' that they learned in Mexico during one of their tours."[29] His ability on the ball and to squeeze past two defenders made him excel in the last twenty meters of the pitch. Such was his fame that River fans would shout: *"La gente ya no come por ver a Walter Gómez"* (people no longer eat so that they can see Walter Gómez). The gap-toothed striker, Omar Sívori, who would leave River Plate for Juventus in 1957, said of Gómez, "I only knew of one player who could win a game when he wanted to, and that was Walter Gómez . . . he wandered around the pitch absent-mindedly, *returned* for five minutes and scored or made us score a few goals."[30] After leaving Buenos Aires for Sicily, Gómez returned to Montevideo briefly, before seeing out the last years of his career in the less arduous leagues of Colombia and Venezuela.

Dreaming of Albion

Unlike other countries in the region, which had long forgotten their British roots, Argentina remained fixated by the founders of the game. In 1951, the River Plate republic was handed the opportunity of playing a full international at Wembley, where England had never been defeated. In front of 100,000 England supporters, *la nuestra* would have to be on full show.

Though Argentina was restricted to only three chances in the first half, she made one count. In the eighteenth minute, Loustau ran into space and crossed for El Atómico Boyé to head home. "Boye [*sic*], a fast and dangerous player, flushed with the excitement of it, ran back towards the centre as if he had conquered the world," wrote *The Times*.[31] And in the Argentinian mind, conquering England would mean conquering the world. Argentina fought valiantly to maintain her slender lead against England's onslaught. Rugilo performed such miracles in the goal mouth that he would be christened "El León de

Wembley" (The Lion of Wembley). But with the partisan crowd roaring the home nation to victory, the breakthrough came in the seventy-ninth minute. Seven minutes later England added a second and buried the South Americans. Argentina had come so close to upsetting England, but had failed in the face of England's patent superiority. Nevertheless, Borocotó, in *El Gráfico*, felt obliged to reinforce his nebulous theory of *el fútbol rioplatense*:

> *The English are English and we are* criollo. *Neither can they play like us, nor us like them . . . But there exists a something that cannot be changed nor does it accept adaptation of any kind, and is bound up in the idiosyncrasy of each one. There is a way of thinking, feeling, performing and that is in the blood, [barbecued] meat and mate, or in oats with milk and ham with eggs.*[32]

Anglo-Saxon attitudes toward the Argentinians remained conflicted. Charles Buchan, editor of the famous *Football Monthly*, insisted that the Football Association send the England squad to the Commonwealth rather than to Argentina for international friendlies. He cited "Latin blood," which gave the Argentinians a predisposition to violent behavior and crowd unrest, as the factor. Although Buchan's approach, in comparing crowd etiquette, was rather high-handed, not to say xenophobic, he had a point: English referees were not renowned for brandishing pistols during matches.

Three years after her ignominious defeat against the United States in Belo Horizonte, England returned to South America. The end-of-season tour would take in trips to Argentina, Uruguay and Chile, the three countries of the Cono Sur (Southern Cone). In Buenos Aires, the English thought they were playing a "friendly" warm-up match when in fact the Argentinians had fielded a side comprising the complete forward line of Independiente (Rodolfo Micheli, Carlos Cecconato, Carlos Lacasia, Ernesto Grillo and Osvaldo Cruz). It was therefore not unexpected when England capitulated 3–1 to the Porteño eleven. Grillo scored the equalizer from an angle so audacious that it is remembered as an "impossible" goal. The Argentinian had left several English players in his wake, when he found himself near the touchline and shot between the post and the goalkeeper. Buchan now changed his mind: "[The Argentinians] were the artists, England the solid workmen, using the wrong tools."[33] Perón, who was no football fanatic but knew the political capital inherent in the game, declared the anniversary of the victory "Footballers' Day." For one Argentinian journalist, it was as if the country had gained her independence: "We beat them, like in the English Invasions of 1806 and 1807 . . . We recently nationalised the railways. Now we have nationalised football."[34] *The Times* of London, however, never recorded the match.

Three days later Argentina reselected the winning team for the official international. With the scores level at 0–0, the match had to be abandoned after twenty-three minutes because of a waterlogged pitch. The English officials proposed a rematch within three days, which the AFA declined on the grounds that the pitch needed five days to dry. The humiliation of the English, albeit in a disputed international, would persist.

After traveling to Santiago, where the Chileans were beaten 2–1, England was hosted by the World Cup winners. The score reflected well on the inventors of the game. Uruguay toyed with the English and, of course, played to the terraces with neat feints and dribbles. Billy Wright, the England captain, was made to look a fool by Oscar Míguez, the master of the *jopeada* (deft chip over the opposite player). Archie Ledbrooke, the *Daily Mirror* journalist who would tragically die in the Munich air disaster, reported: "Most of the members of the team thought the winners were the strongest combination they had ever met."[35]

. . .

Argentina, with its dominant Italian immigrant heritage, had provided many of the *oriundi* (those of Italian extraction born outside of Italy) who would ply their trade for the Italian national team, as had

Brazil and Uruguay, albeit in smaller numbers. And Spain would become a destination for many players of Iberian heritage after Franco extended dual nationality to immigrants in 1954. But the process was seldom reversed, an exception being the case of Jorge "George" Robledo Oliver. Born in the Chilean port city of Iquique to an English mother and a Chilean father, Robledo moved with his family to Yorkshire as a five-year-old. "Pancho" went on to have a successful career with Newcastle United, becoming the top scorer in the First Division in 1951–1952 and netting ninety-one goals in 164 matches. Despite speaking no Spanish, he was called up by his country of birth to play in the 1950 World Cup. In the opening match—as the gods would have it, he was pitted against his adopted country— Robledo hit the post, whereupon an England player wryly observed, "Steady on, George, you're not playing for Newcastle now, you know."

His brother Eduardo, "Ted," had followed "George" to Newcastle—the two were inseparable—where he played as a defender. When Ted was sold to Santiago's Colo-Colo for £15,000, it was George's turn to join him. "For us," said George in an interview, "Chile was always a magical word that contained a special charm . . . we already consider ourselves to be really Chilean."[36] The novelty of having an "Englishman" playing in the Chilean league was greeted with enthusiasm. *Estádio* ran an article entitled "Football Teacher," in which Robledo was lauded in rather hackneyed terms: "The pitch will be the school in which Jorge Robledo will teach this course . . . In each action of his, with or without the ball, Robledo is saying: 'this is how one plays football.'"[37] Moreover, Robledo's perceived perfect technique, acquired in England, would benefit the Chilean footballers. Not everyone was impressed. The same issue of *Estádio* ran a contradictory editorial entitled "El hara-kiri," which criticized the large number of imports that "are killing the excellent work of Chilean football."[38] Returning to Chile proved a success for the striker, who played for Colo-Colo until 1958 before transferring to O'Higgins. "Ted," however, met an untimely end in 1970 when he "fell off" a tanker in the Arabian Sea and was never found. It was generally accepted that he was murdered by the tanker's West German captain.

The Men from Another Planet

If the 1950 World Cup had reacquainted Europe with the multifaceted brilliance of South American football, the tournament four years later would reveal just what lurked behind the Iron Curtain. Uruguay may have never have lost a World Cup match—while Brazil was hoping to succeed where she had failed—but both countries would be undone by a brilliant Magyar team. Hungary had been undefeated for four years, and had secured gold at the 1952 Olympics. In May 1954, Hungary had shamed English football with a 7–1 defeat in Budapest. This rout had followed the 6–3 drubbing at Wembley the year before. The English had been gluttons for punishment. Ted Burgin, England's reserve goalkeeper, could only wonder from the touchline. "They are like men from another planet."[39]

The world champions looked a better prospect for the final than four years before. Though the Czechs did not believe so even after being outplayed in their opening group match. Their contention that "Whoever wins the World Cup, it won't be the Uruguayans" suggested a certain amount of bitterness. (Czechoslovakia surrendered five goals to Austria three days later.) Uruguay turned on the style against Scotland, who went down 7–0 in an abject performance. Borges, the Peñarol left-winger who would score the inaugural goal in the Copa Libertadores six year later, managed a hat trick, while Míguez and Abbadie netted a brace each. The Uruguayans had taught the creators of the passing game a painful lesson. England, the inventors of football, would be next.

On a hot afternoon, which suited Uruguay more than their opponents, Borges opened the score after five minutes with a deft flick on the turn. The England defenders looked as if they had been stranded.

England equalized, only for Varela to score from a long-range volley. Although England gave a spirited performance, the Uruguayans were too technically proficient. This served them well when they were beset by injury on the field. Abbadie could not run properly, having torn a ligament, while Andrade and Varela played with pulled muscles. The 4–2 score line may have flattered the Uruguayans, but this was Uruguay in her pomp. *The Times* of London was effusive in praising the sheer artistry of the Uruguayans. "They caress and stroke the ball with an expression of satisfaction. They love this ball, and they want to keep it, often withdrawing it from a tackle with the sole of the foot as if they were rolling a pat of butter. The jugglery and accuracy of their short passes at times is bewildering . . . in the moment of artistic achievement, are all the trimmings of the circus ring, and all the flamboyant by-play of the Latin toreador."[40] Arthur Ellis, the English referee, later wrote, "I haven't seen England play so well and yet lose."[41]

Brazil, like Uruguay, had topped its group, thrashing Mexico 5–0 but drawing with Yugoslavia. Brazil now had to face Hungary, a team that had scored seventeen goals in two matches.

The Brazilians had not had much luck with British referees. George Reader had overseen Brazil's defining defeat in 1950. Arthur Ellis, given the job of refereeing Brazil against Hungary, and who thought he might now officiate the best match he would see in his life, was sorely disappointed. From the outset, the Brazilians had sought to employ hostility instead of skill. Ever patient, the Hungarians finally gave in. The constant gamesmanship resulted in Santos and Bozsik being expelled for fighting. This was more in line with Uruguayan tactics. With Bauer the only player to have survived the post-Maracanã cull, Brazil was a shadow of its former self.

The final whistle did not bring an end to the violence. As the players tried to make their way off the pitch, fights broke out between the spectators and police on the field of play. The Brazilians, who had lost 4–2, seemed to have channeled *rioplatense* aggression when they took the fight to the Hungarian dressing room. *The Times* declared the match "one of the bitterest, fiercest and tensest matches probably ever fought—that is the correct word . . . Here were two of the greatest sides in the world finally destroying their own superb artistry by the barefaced and attempted annihilation of each other by unethical tactics. Never in my life have I seen such cruel tackling, the cutting down of opponents as if with a scythe, followed by threatening attitudes and sly jabs when officialdom was engaged elsewhere . . . History should accord this affair the title of The Battle of Berne."[42]

Ellis would later recount in his memoir, "I haven't been to Brazil for many years. I was told that if I dared to step into the country [Brazil] . . . I would be shot."[43] He had never sent a player off in an international match, and now had three to his name. He would later be reductive in his assessment of the match, arguing that it had been a "battle of politics and religion" (Hungarian communism *versus* Brazilian Catholicism).[44] After the match, a Brazilian woman made a thoroughly unladylike gesture when she spat on his car window.

After her defeat to arguably one of the most talented teams to ever play the game, Brazilians did what they do best: they turned on themselves. João Lyra Filho penned a scathing indictment of the Brazilian psyche. Race once again played its part in the judgment:

> *The Brazilian players lacked what is lacking for the Brazilian people in general . . . The causes . . . touch on the foundations of social science in the comparative study of races, environment, climate, eating habits, spirit, culture, and individual and common living processes . . . They go back to genetics itself. It is undeniable that Hungary has a better predisposition, like so many other countries, arming its respective all-star team with the best positive attributes. Our people's psychosocial state is still green . . . Given the state of the Brazilian people, only by chance or contingency might we become world football champions and establish hegemony in this sport . . . In Brazilian football, flashy trim lends artistic expression to the match, to the detriment of yield and results. Exhibition jeopardizes competition. It would be easy to compare the*

physiognomy of a Brazilian all-star team, made up mostly of blacks and
mulattos, with that of Argentine, German, Hungarian, or English
football . . . It does not meet up with the Olympic aristocracy, destined
to remark itself periodically.[45]

Uruguay, undefeated in World Cup games since 1930, had a new world order with which to contend. Hungary was probably the best team that the Uruguayans had ever played. Moreover, Uruguay would be without Varela and Abbadie through injury, while the mercurial Míguez had been left out because of an altercation with the squad's management. Hungary, still furious at Brazil's hostility, was wary of a Uruguayan side that was quick to anger. The match, played in the driving rain, would defy expectations: it would be one of the greatest matches ever played. Unfortunately it was only the semifinal.

Even without the injured Puskás, Hungary was formidable. After thirteen minutes, Czibor latched on to a header from Kocsis and put the Europeans in front. The Hungarians by no means controlled the game, though they kept possession. A minute into the second half, Budai crossed the ball, which was met with Hidegkuti's diving header. Uruguay, in spite of playing some excellent football, looked unlikely to rally. And yet, the two goals only seemed to galvanize the Uruguayans. Fifteen minutes from time, Schiaffino, who was playing beautifully in a deeper position, laid on the Argentine-born Juan Hohberg with a pass of perfection. Uruguay was still in the game at 2–1. Eleven minutes later, Schiaffino performed the same move and Hohberg equalized. Extra time, however, would be cruel to the world champions, when Schiaffino/Hohberg's shot hit the post. Two Hungarian defenders had sought to cut out the shot but instead had scythed down the man. Schiaffino could do little else for the rest of the match. The footballing gods would, however, smile on the Hungarians, who found the net twice through headers from Kocsis.

The Uruguayans may have been, according to the Hungarian manager Gyula Mándi, the best team the Hungarians had ever beaten, but their moment in the sun was now over. In the third-place match, a fixture at which Uruguayan football has never excelled, the *rioplatenses* lost heart and succumbed to Austria 3–1. The self-importance of not entering the World Cup would now be a luxury the country could ill afford. By the next World Cup, Uruguay would fail to qualify for the very tournament it had first hosted.

By 1956, a further competition was organized to establish footballing hegemony among the Atlantic republics. The Copa del Atlántico (or Taça do Atlântico) would be played on only three occasions in twenty years, with Brazil winning each time. For Uruguay, the tournament proved a disaster: La Celeste only managed to raise itself from the bottom of the table when landlocked Paraguay joined in 1960. In the opening match of the inaugural tournament, Uruguay returned to the scene of her most famous victory. The Maracanã would not be silenced again. This time it was Míguez—his penchant for trickery, such as the *mondonguillo* (flipping the ball over his opponent with the back of the heel), belied a bad temper—who cast himself as the pantomime villain. *Folha da Manhã* exclaimed, "Míguez (always him!) provoked riots in Maracanã." (The newspaper would publish a photograph of Míguez being held back from attacking the referee by his teammate Andrade.) After he was sent off for lashing out at Hélio, another four Uruguayans were expelled. Even one of the linesmen took to hitting Ramos with his flag. By the end of the match, there were only six Uruguayans on the pitch. The Uruguayan tendency to violence was not lost on *A Noite*: "The Uruguayans turned the [Maracanã] pitch into a boxing ring." The River Plate republic only lost 2–0.

While Latin America may have produced some of the best football in the world, it was also host to some of the worst. The Copa CCCF (Confederación Centroamericana y del Caribe de Fútbol) had been established in 1941 to offer the Central American and Caribbean republics competitive football. In 1957, Curaçao hosted the tournament, which was attended by Haiti, Honduras, Panama and Cuba. Although the stadium had a capacity of 11,000 spectators, the pitch was nothing more than a dirt track. The football may have been insubstantial, but the fervor of the players would not have been amiss in the stadiums of the Río de la Plata. The English referee Arthur Ellis recorded a comic scene at a match between Honduras and Cuba, in which the referee abandoned play fifteen minutes from time: "Suddenly, all the Honduras reserves, sitting on a bench near the incident, sprang up when the Cuban retaliated with a kick, and, literally, the fight was on. The Honduras reserves started to fight the Cubans . . . Throughout this five-minute farce I didn't see a blow land accurately, and it was almost like watching two heavy-weights attempting to fight blindfold."[46] The animus did not last long; two hours later the spirit of Latin fraternalism was restored.

International football had not been kind to Mexico. Even though the Central American republic had participated in the inaugural World Cup in Montevideo, it was not until 1958 that it secured its first tournament point against Wales. In the intervening years, there were numerous victories, though many of these came against weak opposition in the form of the Central American republics, Cuba, Haiti and the United States. In 1950, Mexico hosted two friendlies against Spain, the second of which provided the home nation with its first draw against a European side. The following month, it was business as usual: three World Cup ties ended in three defeats.

Mexico did not travel well. Not only did the national team find it difficult to compete against the traditional footballing republics, but also it was prone to homesickness abroad. This was epitomized by one of Mexican football's most famous anecdotes. On their way to the 1958 World Cup, the Mexican squad found themselves in Lisbon. One evening, José Villegas, the "Chivas" (Club Deportivo Guadalajara) defender, went missing. He was finally found sitting under a tree on the hotel grounds. When asked by his manager why he was not in the dining room, Villegas answered: "How can I have dinner, when they have prepared such terrible food. What I want are my *chalupas* [stuffed tostadas], some good *sopes* [thick tortilla with toppings] or a *pozole* [stew] and not this filth that's not even Mexican."[47] The Mexicans had form in these matters. Four years before, in Switzerland, according to the journalist Manuel Seyde, a player exclaimed, "'I've had it up to here with only escalopes, milk and butter. I'd love some pork meatballs, like those my mum makes.' And his eyes lit up."[48]

José "Jamaicón" Villegas epitomized what Mexicans would term "Síndrome del Jamaicón" (Jamaicón Syndrome): the inability of Mexican football to perform abroad. This condition, in many ways, would isolate the game. And yet it was not a neurosis that pertained solely to Mexican football. Other Latin Americans republics would find playing abroad difficult. It was not a question of a different style of play, rather a question of culture. The insecurities of the third world when facing developed nations would not be easily shed.

The Death of *La Nuestra*

For ten years Latin American's two strongest footballing republics had avoided each other. From 1946 until 1956, Brazil had not played Argentina in a competitive match. The last time both teams had met was at River Plate's Estádio Monumental, in the deciding game of the 1946 Campeonato Sudamericano. "Tucho" Méndez had scored a brace to put the match beyond the Brazilians. Tucho, who together with Zizinho remain the competition's record goal scorers, would be immortalized in the 1953 film *Con los mismos colores* (*With the Same Colors*). The film charts the careers of three players—"Tucho," Mario "El Atómico" Boyé and Alfredo Di Stéfano—from the barrio to the First Division. Before a match Boyé utters the unifying phrase, "They may be different, but they're the same colors."[49] For Argentinians the barrio continued to be the country writ large. Later Tucho would tellingly state, "Huracán was my girlfriend; Racing, my wife; and the [*seleccción*] national team, my lover."

The plucky Uruguayans may have outmaneuvered Brazil in 1950, but Argentina remained the team to beat. When Brazil defeated Argentina by a single goal in the 1956 Campeonato Sudamericano, it was the first time they had beaten their rivals in the tournament since 1922. Argentina had come to seem almost unbeatable in the championship, at a time when the kind of continental matches against weak opposition, in which forwards were lining up to score, were becoming less common. Even the Argentinian goal-scoring machine, Ángel Labruna, found that "the South American tournaments are becoming more and more difficult."[50] Five months after Argentina's defeat, both teams met at Avellaneda in front of 80,000 spectators. Vittorio Pozzo said of the Atlantic Cup (Taça do Atlântico) match, "The beauty of the game was outstanding. Very seldom can one see two teams with such skill in controlling the ball. I have seen few matches with such technical skill. You will never see this in Europe."

The 1957 Campeonato Sudamericano confirmed that Argentina was a cut above her fellow South Americans. In Lima, the team was scoring at will: 8–2 against Colombia, Ecuador and Uruguay put to the sword 3–0 and 4–0 respectively, and Chile succumbed 6–2. Brazil may have beaten Colombia 9–0—Evaristo managed a hat trick in four minutes just before halftime and added a brace in the second half—but the team capitulated against Argentina. After the 3–0 defeat, Nelson Rodrigues was acerbic in his evaluation: "The team [Brazil] did not do anything, absolutely nothing. Terrible technically, tactically and psychologically, we escaped, without doubt, an astronomical thrashing."[51] Even by Latin American standards, the Argentinian forwards were exceptional. No wonder Pedro Escartín, the Spanish referee and journalist, believed that Argentina would be the star attraction at the World Cup in Stockholm.

The young triumvirate of Sívori, Angelillo and Maschio—otherwise known as the "Trio de la Muerte" (Death Trio)—had been clinical in front of goal: in six matches they had scored twenty goals among them. They would not, however, play for Argentina again. By the end of the year, all three players had moved to Italy, where they were granted Italian citizenship. The departure of "the Angels with Dirty Faces" would render Argentina toothless in attack. Juventus paid £91,000 for Sívori, a brilliant dribbler, while Angelillo and Maschio headed to Inter and Bologna respectively. "El Cabezón" (The Huge Head) Sívori, would score 135 goals for Juventus, despite gaining a reputation for indolence and a slack attitude to training. Continental allegiances counted for nothing when the Paraguayan Heriberto Herrera was appointed manager of Juventus. Sívori fell out with the "iron sergeant" and moved to Naples, where, on one occasion, he slowly tied his laces in front of his former manager to the laughter of the Neapolitans. Angelillo would also fall foul of his employers including Helenio Herrera and the Inter board. He not only had looks (a 1940s' film-star mustache and swept-back hair) but also an exquisite first touch. In his second season he managed to score thirty-three goals in thirty-three matches, though even this was not enough to win Inter the title. Angelo Moratti once said of him, "Angelillo is an actor, when he wants, he is the best actor of all, when he doesn't, he hides."[52] His cause was not helped by a public affair with an Italian singer, for whom he seemed to save his best performances. The promise he showed on the international stage would never be fulfilled: he only played twice for Italy, and because he had failed to see out his military service, he was not allowed back to Argentina for twenty years.

For all the high-profile successes abroad of the Angels with Dirty Faces, the goal of the year—if not the decade—would come from another Argentinian. Overshadowed by his teammates, Omar Corbatta, who played for Racing and Boca Juniors, had only scored two goals in the 1957 championship. Later that year, in the World Cup qualifier against Chile, he would score a goal of such magnitude that *El Gráfico* labeled it "the most impossible move ever." A right wing of sublime quality, Corbatta was undisputed master of the *caño* or nutmeg. (Maradona once likened him to an Argentinian Garrincha.) Against Chile he would use his skills to best effect. In the fortieth minute of the match, "El Loco" (The Crazy One) received the ball, dribbled his marker and with only the goalkeeper to beat waited for another Chilean to tackle him. With the Chilean committed, Corbatta took the ball around him and was clear on goal. Once again Corbatta stalled, while the spectators pleaded with him to score, and waited to be surrounded by opposing players. He now pretended to shoot, tricked the Chilean goalkeeper and defenders, and gently stroked the ball into the net. The year before, Corbatta had shown off in a similar fashion against Uruguay and made a fool of Pepe Sasía. Intolerant at the best of times of such sorcery, a Uruguayan player had enough and scythed El Loco down. With the Argentinian on the ground, Sasía sought to give him solace by kicking him in the mouth. For all his genius on the field, Corbatta descended into alcoholism and penury. Unable to read or write, he would always have a newspaper at hand when interviewed by the press. He would later give a sad indictment of life after the game, "There are no friends in football . . . Especially when one is in a bad way. They all disappear."[53] For years the Latin American game had failed to look after its own.

.   .   .

Shortsightedness, not to mention vanity, would be Argentina's undoing at the 1958 World Cup. The golden age of Argentinian football had already come to an end—only many Argentinians had failed to notice. Victory at the 1957 Campeonato Sudamericano had only reinforced the country's belief in her own superiority. So much so that the AFA made the mistake of not calling up its European-based players, and arrogantly assumed that the local leagues produced enough players of quality to triumph in Sweden. *El Gráfico* was prescient when it stated, "it is less improbable that [the team] becomes world champions than plays well."[54]

The West German manager Herberger employed logic rather than emotion and refused to be intimidated before his opening match against Argentina. Absence from international competition had not made Argentinian football stronger. Moreover, he questioned the Argentinians' tenuous grasp of European tactics. Herberger was proved correct in his thesis when West Germany beat the Argentinians 3–1. Guillermo Stábile, who had played against the Uruguayans in 1930, stated without a hint of irony, "We are not used to such violent football."[55] Northern Ireland did not prove difficult opposition in the following match. Argentina would bewilder Northern Ireland with her deft play, though the Ulstermen did not help themselves. "I had to call all the players together on the field and tell them to shut up as they were only causing confusion for one another," said the former captain Danny Blanchflower.[56] While his midfielder, Jimmy McIlroy, may have deemed the Argentines overweight and frivolous, they were nonetheless able to break at dizzying speed. Czechoslovakia would ultimately be Argentine football's undoing. In ninety minutes, the Czechs put paid to a golden age that had exhibited some of the most tantalizing football in the game's short history. Czechoslovakia, which had already held the reigning world champions, West Germany, to a 2–2 draw, was by no means an exceptional side. But she ripped apart the torpid Argentinians, who were mere spectators as one goal followed another. *El Gráfico* published a photograph of Guillermo Stábile, with his head bowed and arms folded defensively, a few minutes before the end of the match. The score line was a national catastrophe: 6–1. On their return to Argentina, the squad was pelted with coins as they arrived at Ezeiza International Airport.

Before the match, the inventor of *la nuestra*, Borocotó, had been supercilious: "The truth is that all [the teams] are dangerous rivals. There are no mediocre [teams] and football has spread to such an extent that it is amazing to find good standards in countries without much of a footballing tradition."[57] The opinion a week later was less than sanguine: "The Argentinian team is poor. This is nothing new."[58] And, in spite of the loss, Borocotó yet again defended River Plate football: "On the Atlantic, one knows how to play football better than in many places in the Old World."[59] He may have grasped that speed had changed the game, and that the Argentinian rhythm of play was slow, yet in the same article asserted that "the Uruguayans, the slowest of the Atlantic, have been able to crush many European teams."[60] That Uruguay had failed to make it through Latin American qualification was, for him, beside the point.

El Gráfico became obsessed with the physical prowess of the Germans and how, the day after the match, they would start training as they would on any other day at 9 a.m. Meanwhile, the Argentinians slept. Pedro Dellacha, who had captained Argentina to victory in the 1957 Campeonato Sudamericano, realized that for many of the players the World Cup lacked any importance. It was as if they were playing another match in Buenos Aires. José "El Nene" Sanfilippo typified the prevailing attitude: "I don't run at San Lorenzo; I don't see why I have to do it for *la selección*."[61]

"No Longer a Mongrel Among Nations"

Unlike the Argentinians, Brazil would leave nothing to chance. Dr. Hilton Gosling, the team's psychologist, traveled to Sweden a year before the 1958 World Cup in order to prepare. He recorded the weather, inspected the grounds, and assessed the food and entertainment. Twenty-five towns were visited so that the perfect accommodation might be found. When Gosling returned to Brazil, he would file a forty-page report.

This methodical approach to the game had begun to mirror the country's politics. By 1956, the incumbent president, Juscelino Kubitschek, sought to implement his "Plano de Metas" (Goal Plan) in which fifty years of progress were to be achieved in five. Brasília was created with 30,000 laborers in forty-one months, after work had commenced in February 1957. These would be Brazil's golden years.

But for all her talent on and off the ball, Brazil failed to trust her instincts. A deep-rooted complex still remained in the Brazilian psyche. In the face of difficult competition, Brazil could not muster itself. In 1956, Nelson Rodrigues was still attempting to explain what amounted to a deep flaw in the Brazilian character. "I even think that we are brilliant technically, mental agility we are unbeatable. It is also true that before the match against Hungary, we were defeated emotionally. I repeat: we were defeated by one of those terrors, obtuse, irrational and pointless. Why this animal fear, this wild panic, why? No one knows how to explain it."[62] Unlike Uruguay, who had flourished early and knew how to win, Brazil did not.

For the writer Betty Milan, Brazilians remained the masters of invention, more so than their River Plate rivals. "The Brazilian player invents in every possible way, for . . . he has been schooled in invention. If we have no money, then we'll make a tambourine out of an old tin can. We haven't got a hat for fancy dress? An old cheese box will serve the purpose."[63] No one epitomized this style more than Manuel dos Santos—known as "Garrincha" for, as a child, he had been as small as a wren—from Pau Grande.

Garrincha should never have played the game. His legs were not straight; one curved in and the other curved out. This deformity had its compensations, giving him the dexterity to twist and turn. He became renowned for his ability to dribble past players at will, though his searing pace is now often overlooked. When interviewed, he would say, "I dribble a lot only because I think it the best way to win matches. Never do I do it to make an opponent look foolish, or humiliate him."[64] This attitude was at odds with the Argentinian approach, which enjoyed the very act of humiliation. For Garrincha, however, tactics were impractical to his style of play. Before traveling to Sweden, Brazil played two matches in Italy. Fiorentina and Inter were both beaten by the same 4–0 score line. In one match, Garrincha dribbled around four opposing players, including the goalkeeper, only to roll the ball over the line. "But when the match was over I was warned never to play like that again!"[65]

Conscious of their reputation for panicking when it mattered most, the Brazilians had employed psychological tests at São Paulo four years earlier, and with the nations still chastened after the last World Cup, the tests were being used again. Garrincha only managed a lowly thirty-eight points out of 123, which did not even qualify him to drive a bus. His lack of aggression on the field was deemed to be a further indication of his inability to perform at the international level. Pelé was also damned by the tests: "[He] is obviously infantile. He lacks the necessary fighting spirit. He is too young to feel aggression and respond with the appropriate force . . . he does not possess the sense of responsibility necessary for a team game."[66]

So, for the opening two group matches, Garrincha and Pelé were left out of the side. Austria may have been swept aside 3–0, but the Brazilian commentators felt the team had failed to live up to its promise. Brazil had played badly, but she had won well. Against England, the Brazilians were by far the better team, though were fortunate not to have had a penalty awarded against them with the match goalless. When they had met nine years before, the teams managed to cancel each other out. Tomás Mazzoni gave a telling assessment of both styles: "The Englishman considers a player that dribbles three times successively a nuisance; the Brazilian considers him a virtuoso. English football requires that the ball [move] faster than the player; Brazilian football requires that the player be faster than the ball. In English football, discipline comes first and the players last; in Brazil the players come first and discipline last. The Englishman goes on to the field disposed either to win or lose; the Brazilian either to win . . . or to blame the referee."[67]

The final group match against the Soviet Union proved to be the supreme justification of the Latin American game. Garrincha had made the starting eleven, though it remains unclear whether this was the decision of the team's portly coach, Vicente Feola, or the result of player power in the form of Nilton Santos. While watching Kurt Hamrin, the talented winger who would score 150 goals for Fiorentina, play for Sweden, Feola had exclaimed, "It's going to be very difficult to stop him, he's like a South American." Offended, Nilton

Santos replied, "Pelé and Garrincha do this shit better than that gringo, and you call them individualists and ill-disciplined."[68]

In the opening minutes, Brazil surprised their opponents with their force of attack. Garrincha evaded his marker to hit the left post, while Pelé then hit the right post. Finally Vavá scored, with the match only three minutes old. For many observers, it was the finest three minutes in the history of the game.

Without the injured John Charles, the odds were stacked against Wales, Brazil's opponents in the quarterfinals. The indomitable Welsh defense made up for its somewhat toothless attack. However, although Brazil had thirty-one shots on goal to Wales's five, only one goal would separate the teams. Pelé's second-half right-footed volley would prove one of the most important of his career, for both him and his country. Had Brazil not won the match, it might have changed the course of the Brazilian game. The semifinals against the French would prove easier than the contest with the more resolute Welsh. Though the free-scoring French were better technically, Pelé believed Wales had been Brazil's most dangerous opponent in the competition. France may have scored eleven goals in her three matches, but she had also conceded seven. This would be Pelé's match: after Just Fontaine equalized Vavá's opener, he astounded his teammates with his audacity: "Let's stop wasting time, let's get started." He would score a second-half hat trick. The seventeen-year-old had made his mark. Not prone to modesty in these matters, João Havelange, president of the Confederação Brasileira de Desportos (CBD) said, "Pelé owes me a great deal, and his debt to me began in the 1950s when I gave him the chance of going to Sweden."

The World Cup final would finally lay to rest the ghosts of Maracanã. Sweden may have opened the scoring after four minutes, but George Raynor's belief that Brazil would panic was misguided. Bellini may have collected the ball from the back of the net, but it was Didi who employed Obdulio Varela's tactic of slowing the game down. He took his time in walking back for the restart. When Vavá scored five minutes later, the Brazilians began to play their natural game. Garrincha hit the left-hand post with a beautifully floated chip that left the Swedish goalkeeper sprawling. It was Pelé, however, who sealed the win in the ninetieth minute by outjumping the Swedish defense to head the ball home. For the English commentator Brian Glanville, "The Brazilians, in 1958, were as impressive in their way as the Hungarians, five years earlier."[69] Though not everyone agreed. There were European commentators who thought that Brazil had been flattered by the lack of opposition—that Uruguay and Hungary in 1954 had been better sides.

Pedro Escartín, the Spanish referee and journalist, realized that football might have changed forever: "When Europe takes up the many South American virtues without losing its own, and the players on the other side of the Atlantic accept the good from Europe, football will reach the pinnacle of perfection that Brazil today symbolizes with its practical and dazzling style."[70]

For Nelson Rodrigues, the final whistle and the lifting of the trophy symbolized something more profound. "With the 1958 victory, Brazilians changed even physically. I remember that after the game between Brazil and Sweden ended, I saw a small black woman. She was the typical slum dweller. But the Brazilian triumph transformed her. She walked down the sidewalk with the charm of a Joan of Arc. The same was true for black men, who—attractive, brilliant, luxurious—seemed like fabulous Ethiopian princes. Yes, after 1958, the Brazilian was no longer a mongrel [vira-lata] among men and Brazil was no longer a mongrel among nations."[71]

In the aftermath of Argentina's disastrous showing, Di Stéfano and Maschio, Argentinians who played for Spain and Italy respectively, would come to question the more indulgent and ostentatious tenets of lo criollo. Dribbling, for its own sake, was now seen as a dangerous luxury. Eleven years later, in response to Argentina's dismal failure to qualify for the 1970 World Cup, El Gráfico summoned the ghosts of the Helsingborg disaster:

We do not have the time to search for those guilty of this frustration. We do not wish to do it, because we are convinced of its uselessness, or, to put it another way, of its negativity. When the disaster in Sweden hit us with tremendous impact, we chose to search for and point to the guilty parties. We searched them all out: those who lead, those who keep football going with popular support, those of us who cover football, and those who play. And through that witch hunt we discovered a few guilty parties and one important victim: the school of Argentine football. As of that crucial moment, we began to lose our most significant characteristic: the personality of players born to attempt what they know and feel best. The need to erase the memory of those six goals in Czechoslovakia pushed us towards a defensive game, towards the eternal fear of losing that made us forget the necessity and the happiness of making more goals than our adversary in order to win. The need to overcome our deficit of speed and physical prowess over the Europeans led us to indiscriminate imitation, to scorn ability and intelligence. And thus we fell a little farther, year after year. Let's not fool ourselves with the honorary classification of the World Cup in England: with a mental scheme of fear, we have arrived where we are today . . .[72]

Following the country's disastrous showing, short-term solutions, a local specialty, were employed to reinvigorate the domestic game. For Pablo Alabarces, the Argentinian sociologist, "the appearance of the football-spectacle, a term coined by the then-president of River Plate, Antonio Liberti, consisted in a purely economic gesture. This was the incorporation of foreign players, especially Brazilians, following the success of Brazil in the World Cups of 1958 and 1962. This experience neither increased profits [nor] sporting victories— Argentine football continued to be defeated both nationally and at club level."[73] Although this was for the most part true, the 1959 Campeonato Sudamericano proved to be the exception. Argentina would not win the championship again until 1991, by which time the event had long been rechristened the Copa América.

On home soil, Argentina opened her account with a 6–1

thrashing of an emergent Chile, a country in preparation for the 1962 World Cup. The following day, Uruguay dispatched Bolivia 7–0, though this would have more to do with the frailties of the Bolivian game than Uruguayan prowess. For Uruguay, it would be an abysmal tournament, not helped by internal wrangling that had the squad broken up and re-formed in a twenty-four-hour period. The low point was against Brazil, when the pitch turned into a battleground for the opposing players. The Brazilian Almir, who would later be murdered in a Rio bar, had not helped matters by provoking the Uruguayans. The Chilean referee sent off four players, two from each side, though this did little to abate the animus, which erupted at the end of the match. In the final ten minutes, Brazil had managed two goals to make it 3–1. With four defeats in six matches, only Bolivia fared worse at the bottom of the table. Uruguayan football had sunk to a new low. Captain Humberto Mendívil, the national team's physical trainer, sought to reverse the decline by profiling the squad psychologically on and off the pitch. And yet the abject performance at the Campeonato Sudamericano could not compare with the country's utter humiliation in the 1958 World Cup qualifier against Paraguay. At the Estádio de Puerto Sajonia—which had been renamed "Uruguay" in 1924 after the Uruguayans' Olympic triumph—Paraguay put five goals past Uruguay without reply. After the match, Pedro Cea called the defeat the worst moment in Uruguayan football. For Montevideo's *El País*, the country could no longer be counted as a footballing power.

For Brazil, however, eight goals from Pelé, in his first Latin American tournament, could not stop Argentina from being crowned champions by one point. After her glorious win in Sweden, this was a competition in which the Brazilians could afford to come in second. The balance of power in the South American game had already shifted. And the River Plate republics well knew it.

Latin America's first great football team. Alumni of Buenos Aires
won ten championships between 1900 and 1911.

Rio de Janeiro, 1914. Brazil vs. Exeter City. Brazil wins
her inaugural international 2–0.

Above: Uruguay shows the world how
the game should be played. The 1924
Olympic Games, Paris. Action from
Uruguay, 3 vs. USA, 0.

Right: Violence on the pitch. Alianza vs.
Universitario derby, Lima, 1928.

Champions of the world. World Cup Final, 1930. Uruguay, 4 vs. Argentina, 2.
The neighbors will not meet in the competition for another fifty-six years.

POPPERFOTO/GETTY IMAGES

River Plate's *La Máquina* ("The Machine"), one of most magnificent
teams to have ever graced a football pitch.

World Cup Final, 1950. Maracanã. The referee blows the final whistle and
Uruguay beats Brazil 2–1. The tragedy will define the Brazilian game.
POPPERFOTO/GETTY IMAGES

The death of *la nuestra*.
Czechoslovakia, 6 vs. Argentina, 1. Sweden, 1958.
POPPERFOTO/GETTY IMAGES

Atlantic vs. Pacific, 1970. Brazil, 4 vs. Peru, 2. Pelé in his pomp.
POPPERFOTO/GETTY IMAGES

Santiago de Chile, 1973. Prisoners on the terraces.
The stadium as concentration camp.
FLICKR VISION

Buenos Aires, June 1978. Argentina finally wins what she feels is rightfully hers. Daniel Passarella, the captain, with the World Cup trophy.
VI-IMAGES VIA GETTY IMAGES

June 1986. Argentina's avenging angel. Maradona vs. England.
AFP/GETTY IMAGES

1998 World Cup Final. Whom the gods wish to destroy . . . Ronaldo, the world's best player stands dejected as Brazil loses in bizarre circumstances.

Hugo Sánchez, Mexico's greatest export.

Above: The lunatics take over
the asylum. Boca Juniors' fans
at La Bombonera.

Right: The future of Latin
American football: Lionel Messi,
born in Argentina; made in
Europe.

CHAPTER SEVEN

THE LIGHT AND THE DARK

1960–1970
Futebol Arte Versus *Anti-Fútbol*

Because we have nothing, we want to do it all.

—Carlos Dittborn (1956)

The champions of South America (Interclub) tournament, [Libertadores] was unappreciated in its first outing. It did not stir up the masses; it got no one excited.

—*El Gráfico* (1960)

Our best football will come against the team who come out to play football and not act as animals.

—Alf Ramsey (1966)

Three years after her team's abject performance at the 1958 World Cup, Argentina had still not learned her lesson. Even Pelé, normally diplomatic in such matters, was uninhibited in his assessment of the Argentinian game. When asked by *El Gráfico* whether the Argentinians looked Brazilian in their recent outing in Rio, the answer was unequivocal: "Not at all: they play differently. There is much slowness, an excess of lateral passes, and they don't have any depth."[1] He also questioned whether some of the Argentines could play the full ninety minutes at a fast pace. "Can you imagine them on heavy ground? It would be a disaster." Nor were Argentinian tactics off-limits: "To use a slow centre midfielder and to play 'lateral' is already a tactical error; and especially when he is expected to mark a quick player."[2]

Not that Latin America's leading sports magazine was any less complimentary about Argentinian football. One of the country's leading writers on the game, Dante Panzeri, was unforgiving. "For the moment, it's worth stating that WE STILL DON'T KNOW HOW TO PLAY FOOTBALL. We know how to play very well *with the ball*. Or, more precisely, we know to play very well 'A LA PELOTA.'"[3] The cult of the individual—the very characteristic of the Porteño game that had distinguished it yet made it fallible—had once again become problematic. "We have no team," continued Panzeri. "We have inspired individuals. Some ALWAYS inspired."[4]

The game, which had always had a penchant for the sentimental, had failed to modernize. Much like the country itself, Argentinian football had remained isolated, secure in the knowledge of its own greatness. Yet, any success at the 1962 World Cup would necessitate change. *El Gráfico* had the measure of the domestic game, believing it to be backward tactically and in need of organization. "For a long time it is said that we're playing with a different ball, and we need to adapt to 'that which is used there.' Like so many things here we say we should do but we never do. And because of them we then cry."[5] Culturally indisposed to the middle ground, Argentinian football would take professionalism to the extreme by the end of the decade.

In 1961, Argentina's tour of Europe had promised well with a 2–0 win over Portugal in Lisbon. This was the high point, as defeats to Spain and Italy quickly followed. Di Stéfano scored against the country of his birth in the 2–0 Spanish victory, while the Italians handed the national team a 4–1 thrashing. At club level, however, Argentinian football could compete with the best. In the same year, River Plate beat the European champions, Real Madrid, 3–2 in front of 100,000 spectators, while Juventus was easily dispatched 5–2. Only the year before, representatives from Boca and River had traveled to Europe to lure expatriate players back.

The decade, however, would belong to the artistry of Santos (known as *ballet blanco*: "white ballet"), and to one player in particular, before the Argentinians took the game to a far darker place. For many impartial observers, Santos epitomized the way the game should be played. "To see Santos," said one, "is an indescribable experience, and one comes away convinced that they have no equals. Each of the players is an artist . . . the Santos brand of soccer is more an exhibition of craft and skill: a soccer circus with ringmaster Zito cracking his whip now and again to insist that they score goals."[6]

In September 1956, a month short of his sixteenth birthday, Pelé scored his first goal for Santos against Corinthians. The goal, which was poached on the rebound, may have been of little consequence in the 7–1 thrashing of the Paulistas, but it augured well for the precocious footballing talent from Três Corações in Minas Gerais. Three years later, Edson Arantes do Nascimento was scoring 125 goals in a season. Though impressive even by his own high standards—from 1957 to 1965, Pelé was the top scorer in the Campeonato Paulista—the number of goals had a direct correlation with the number of games Santos had begun to play. In an interview, Pelé said, "In 1960 . . . I remember counting that I had played 109 times for Santos alone . . . There is no break in the year's football, as with as many as three games a week to play, there is not much time for training."[7]

With Zito, Pepe and Pelé, Santos played the kind of attacking football that attracted audiences. Moreover, the Brazilian triumph at the 1958 World Cup had only whetted the appetite of foreign clubs who found an opportunity to fill their stadiums. The club could not oblige all invitations to play. In early 1959, Santos toured Peru, Ecuador, Costa Rica, Guatemala, Mexico and Venezuela, though by the middle of year the club would embark for Europe. The schedule was punishing, even by Brazilian standards. "We were scheduled to play almost daily, and in different countries. We played Bulgaria two days in a row, had a day for travel, and then played in three Belgium cities on three successive days . . . We would play, eat, sleep, catch a train."[8]

The tour took in nine countries, where fifteen games were played in twenty-two days. By the time Santos faced Real Madrid, two days after beating Enschede eleven 5–0, the squad was exhausted. Not only did the players not have time to recuperate between matches, but many were playing with injuries and stomach upsets. It was no surprise when Real Madrid beat the Brazilians 5–3, thus maintaining its reputation as the greatest club in the world. The two teams would not meet again in Pelé's playing career.

There was a considerable financial imperative to play certain players, especially Pelé. It was those very skills that Waldemar de Brito, the scout who discovered the young Pelé, had imparted that provided the excitement. Pelé listed them: "The skills were about the *tavelinha* [give and go], shooting through the tunnel of legs, feints, counter feints, dribbling, controlling on our chests, back heels over the opponents' heads, but all with humility." Néstor Rossi, one of the greatest defensive midfielders that Argentina would ever produce, thought Pelé the inventor of the wall pass, which entailed rebounding the ball against an opponent's leg. He was also credited with being master of the "sombrero," a skill that allows the player to lift the ball over an opponent's head only to run around him and control it on the volley. This he had done effortlessly against Sweden in the 1958 World Cup final.

By 1963, the praise was starting to wear thin. In an interview with the young Eduardo Galeano (both were born within a month of each other), Pelé spoke with honesty. "I'm never pitied. On Brazilian fields, the other is always right. The referee or the adversary . . . It wasn't me who started people saying that I'm the best player in the world. I've got nothing to do with it . . . I believe the greatest player hasn't been born yet. He'd have to be the best in every position: goalie, defence, forward."[9] Pelé had become a target for every defender who came up against him. There was no respite for the Brazilian; such was the physical treatment handed to him that being on the pitch for ninety minutes was akin to playing 120 minutes. For a player who had become a marked man from the opening whistle of every match in which he played, Pelé's disciplinary record was commendable. In 1959, he had for the first time been sent off during a national service match, which pitted a Brazilian army eleven against its Argentinian counterpart. Two years later, he was sent off again. "When a hard player hits Pelé, he's twice as hard . . . In friendly matches, Santos play to play, and the opponents play to win. That's what happens. I don't take risks in friendly matches." The innocence of the game had long passed for the number 10. "When I think something might happen to me, I don't take risks."[10] By the end of the decade, Santos was fast gaining a not altogether favorable reputation as "the Harlem Globetrotters of world football."[11] The exhausting schedule of exhibition matches played by Santos, partly to pay Pelé's wages, had taken on a fantastical quality. In 1969, Santos played against Congo-Brazzaville and Congo-Kinshasa: both games brought a respite to the civil war in the African nation. Not even Nigeria, who was engaged in a civil war of her own, was off-limits.

· · ·

After they had taught touring European sides a lesson in how to play the game, it was now the Latin Americans' turn. Late in 1961, the Soviet Union took on Argentina, Chile and Uruguay and won all of its matches. The Chileans, however, took the game to the Russians and were unlucky to lose 1–0. "The Uruguayans, like the Argentinians but unlike the Chileans, relied far too much upon individual bursts of brilliance . . . The triumph of the Soviet Union party in Latin America was the triumph of team play over individualism." For Argentina, the 1–2 home defeat had come as a shock—the first defeat by a European team on home soil. Other European teams had not fared as well. In 1953 England failed to overcome the Uruguayans, though managed to draw against Argentina. Three years later, Italy went down to Argentina and Brazil. When England returned to the Americas in 1959, the team lost to Brazil, Peru and Mexico in quick succession, though pride was restored with an 8–1 win over the USA.

The international tour continued to be an important part of the Latin American game. Whereas in the past, touring Europe was a way of establishing identity for both club and country, many tours were now undertaken purely for financial reasons. As one British sports journalist sought to point out in 1960: "Unofficial tournaments are arranged on the slightest pretext—often just to raise the cost of rebuilding the national stadium in one of the smaller countries like Paraguay, Peru or Bolivia."[12] But for the weaker Latin American teams the exposure to European football could prove a baptism of fire.

In 1961, Mexico began a short European tour with a victory in Amsterdam. Following a narrow defeat against a talented Czechoslovakia, the Mexicans faced England at Wembley. Two years before, England had suffered a 2–1 defeat at seven thousand feet in Mexico City. After Mexico had scored the winning goal, a twenty-second earth tremor, which shook the grandstand, interrupted the match. It was now Mexico's turn to be given a primer in how to play by, according to *The Times*, "the full masters of the basic grammar of the game."[13] The Mexicans had no reply to the eight goals that England put past them that day as "they floated about on pointed tread, tip tapping the ball in pretty circles that got them nowhere in attack."[14] After the match, the Mexican coach, Ignacio Trelles, remarked without irony, "We come here to learn and the lesson has been good."[15] The following year, in Chile, a British journalist praised the attacking play of Mexican football. "In the most miserable, depressing, negative and stereotyped of all post-war World Cups, there was at least one improvement of Mexico."[16] Pelé also admired the way the Mexicans were able to take the ball into the area, though he was quick to acknowledge that they lacked effectiveness in front of goal.

The state of the Mexican game had not been helped by the late arrival of professionalism, which had only taken place in the early 1940s, and the dearth of competitive football in the region. In 1950, the Mexicans traveled to Rio de Janeiro only to be beaten by Botafogo in a warm-up match. *El Nacional* was incensed: "Our national team lost and should not go to Brazil. Like this they'll make the name of Mexico ridiculous."[17]

It was only against the weaker opposition of their nearest neighbors, such as the Central American republics and the Caribbean islands, that Mexico could succeed. At the Juegos Centroamericanos y del Caribe (Central American and Caribbean Games) in 1935 and 1938, the country had secured two gold medals for football. For the Mexican writer Juan Villoro, defeat would become "a national calling."[18]

In *Mañana Forever?*, his discursive portrait of Mexico, Jorge Castañeda sought to determine why Mexicans were deemed "lousy" at football. He argued that the cult of the individual inherent in the culture had manifested itself in sporting heroes rather than famous teams. "If one goes back to the pre-Columbian era, there is confirmation of this individualistic trend, as well as evidence of how weakness in collective sports was aggravated but not invented by the later Spanish conquest of other peoples in what today is known as Mexico."[19]

Mexico would have to wait until the 1958 World Cup to secure her first point. (Its team fared little better in the Olympics, only securing its first draw in 1964.) But a late goal against Wales, scored a minute from time, proved to be the turning point in the country's undistinguished footballing tradition.

At the 1966 World Cup, Mexico would manage two draws, this time against France and Uruguay. After years of coming bottom of her group, Mexico had begun to elevate herself. In England, "La Tota" Carbajal, the country's goalkeeper, would celebrate his fifth World Cup. His record, however, was less cause for celebration: twenty-five goals conceded in eleven appearances. (Though it was better than the hapless Antonio Mota, the diminutive goalkeeper who had conceded eight at Wembley five years earlier.)

In 1964, the thirty-fourth FIFA Congress was held in Tokyo. For the third time since 1936, Argentina failed to garner enough votes to secure the privilege of hosting a World Cup. The delegates had decided to favor Mexico instead. For a country that prided itself on being the most European on the continent to lose against another Latin American nation was galling. Even more so since it was not the first time that Argentina's bid for an international tournament been usurped by Mexico.

In 1949, Buenos Aires lost out to Melbourne by one vote for the right to hold the 1956 Olympics. This had been a disappointment to Perón, who was determined to have his "New Argentina" host the games. For the historian Raanan Rein, "no Argentine government prior to Perón . . . invested as much effort and as many resources in both the development and encouragement of sport and in the effort to earn political dividends from this policy."[20] Even Eva "Evita" Perón used football to further her interest in the young. In 1949, the Argentine Children's Football Championship was established to allow children to play a knockout competition dressed in the strips of professional teams. *El Gráfico* swooned: "The Campeonato Argentino Infantil de fútbol 'Evita' is nothing more or less than the realization . . . of wonderful dream that always seemed unrealizable."[21] (Evita seemed to embody an aspect of *argentinidad* that was not lost on the British ambassador to Buenos Aires in the late 1940s: "In many ways Evita Perón was an ambitious, self-willed, self-seeking schoolgirl who had never grown up. Argentina . . . was still an adolescent country. The youth, glamour, and uninhibited eloquence of Eva Perón were the embodiment of this adolescence and as such made a strong popular appeal."[22])

For Perón, who did not actively dislike football but preferred boxing, the game was not deemed Argentinian enough. Even so, his government had sought to help channel funds to certain clubs. Racing was one such beneficiary. Ramón Cereijo, Perón's minister of finance and a Racing fanatic, secured a soft government loan to build a new stadium. (In 1951, the Estádio Juan Domingo Perón was inaugurated in front of Cereijo and his president.) And yet, was there any sport that more adhered to the country's sense of self than *la nuestra*? By the end of the decade, Perón sought to create sports that were Argentine in nature: "We have an Argentine cuisine, and we cannot accustom ourselves to other food; we have a music of our own. By the same token, we must have physical training and sports that are adapted to our people."

But in 1963 the Argentines would only manage two votes to Mexico's thirty as they battled for the 1968 Olympics nomination. Any hope Argentina might have had of hosting the Olympics evaporated in light of the dire political situation. With Perón in exile and the Peronists excluded from political life, Arturo Frondizi had wooed his supporters with his brand of *peronismo sin Perón* (peronism without Perón). His election to the presidency in 1958 had ushered in optimism, especially among the middle classes. It would not last. The following year, Frondizi was accused of betrayal when he was seen to have reneged on his election promises. Having inherited dwindling foreign exchange reserves, Frondizi sought to address the balance-of-payments crisis with austerity measures. Frondizi's economic policies led him to become politically compromised. The legalization of Peronist politics did not endear him to the military, especially the significant gains made by the peronists in the 1962 elections. The military had had enough: Frondizi was ousted in a coup d'état.

Not that the choice of Mexico City was wholeheartedly endorsed. There remained a degree of cynicism as to whether the Mexicans could host one international event, not to mention two in short succession. Mexican sport would be transformed forever. This was not lost on *El Nacional* the year before the event. "The Olympiad will confirm to us that we are now young adults; that it is now time to abandon our short-trousers mentality. This is not only because the world is not as terrible as we thought, but also because we have matured, and that it is good to make ourselves aware of this and the responsibilities that it brings."[23]

According to President Díaz Ordaz, Mexico could now put her sense of inferiority and "timid provincialism" behind her. Ten days before the opening ceremony on October 12, 1968, Díaz Ordaz would, according to Carlos Fuentes, commit "the most terrible crime in modern Mexican history."[24] With the international press corps in the capital for the Olympics, troops opened fire on a student demonstration in the Plaza de las Tres Culturas. The government had misconstrued the left-leaning protests for social revolution. Heavy-handedness, which had become the trademark of the Díaz Ordaz administration and against which the students were protesting, would result in over three hundred deaths and thousands of injuries. The customary arrests and disappearances followed. Díaz Ordaz would later state, "I do not have my hands stained with blood." (On the anniversary of the massacre, the ex-president's statue would be vandalized with red paint.) When Díaz Ordaz inaugurated the World Cup nearly two years later, he was greeted by a stadium full of whistles.

Earthquakes in Chile

For a country that had adopted the game so early, Chile's record in international competition had been poor. The Andean republic had been the second country on the continent to establish an association, two years after Argentina. In 1913, the Asociación de Football de Chile (FAC) had affiliated itself to FIFA, ten years even before Uruguay. And yet in the opening three decades of the Campeonato Sudamericano, Chile never finished higher than the third place they achieved in 1926. The team was similarly unsuccessful in the other competitions the country entered. Although by the 1940s Chile had managed consecutive runner-up spots and had hosted the South American championships five times, the likelihood of its securing the World Cup nomination seemed remote.

In many ways Chile remained an isolated and despondent nation, in spite of her democratic traditions and belief in her exceptionalism. In a speech given at the Ateneo Club at the turn of the century, the politician Enrique Mac Iver brought this unease to the fore: "It seems to me that we are not happy. We note a malaise that is not confined to one class of people nor to particular regions . . . The present is not satisfactory, and the future is cast in shadow."[25] Chileans may have styled themselves as *los ingleses de Sudamérica* (the English of South America), but for much of the twentieth century the country had been cast in the shadow of its eastern neighbor Argentina.

The 1952 Summer Olympics, held in Helsinki, had given a group of Chilean football executives the idea that the country might have a chance of hosting the World Cup. If the small Scandinavian country of Finland could successfully host the world's foremost athletic event, then why could Chile not host the most important football tournament? At the thirtieth FIFA Congress in Lisbon in 1956, Argentina seemed to be the insurmountable obstacle to this dream. The Argentines had a far more developed infrastructure—with some of the largest stadiums on the continent—and there was a feeling that, after Uruguay and Brazil had successfully hosted the competition, it was surely their turn. Moreover, few delegates could even place Chile on the map. After a persuasive seventy-minute speech by the president of the AFA, the confident Argentinian delegation abandoned all pretense of humility and made it clear that "we can have the World Cup tomorrow. We have it all."

With the Chilean delegation's chances fading, the press in Santiago favored honorable withdrawal rather than the disappointment of failure. If the Argentinians' presentation was somewhat overblown, the Chileans took the opposite tack. Carlos Dittborn, the eloquent former director of the Universidad Católica, took just fifteen minutes to make his speech. Humility and strength in weakness would prove decisive as Dittborn invoked the amateur spirit upon which FIFA had been founded. Dittborn came out with a phrase that would pass into history: *Porque no tenemos nada, queremos hacerlo todo* (Because we have nothing, we want to do it all). It was a very Chilean remark. Nearly half a century before, the president of Chile Ramón Barros Luco had famously said: "In politics there are two types of problems: those that resolve themselves on their own and those that have no solution." Moreover, he presented Chile as a tolerant, politically stable republic. This could not be said of Argentina, where, in June 1955, in an attempted coup d'état, the military bombed the Plaza de Mayo, causing 364 casualties. Perón furiously demanded five bodies for every dead Peronist, but within a matter of weeks the military finally ousted the president. Nor had the anticommunist stance of the Peronist government endeared Argentina to the Eastern Bloc delegates. With thirty-two votes in favor of Chile—as opposed to Argentina's ten—the destination of the 1962 World Cup was decided. Dittborn, however, would never see the fruits of his rearguard action: he would die of a heart attack thirty-two days before the tournament.

In the literature that followed her nomination, Chile portrayed herself as a proto-European nation, without the mestizo and black social problems of some of her fellow republics. The fact that Chile had an indigenous Amerindian population, of whom she was simultaneously proud and ashamed, was conveniently forgotten. As with all the South American republics, the establishment of the right reputation abroad verged on the obsessive. Not only did Chile wish to be perceived as a "white" nation, she also wanted to be seen as stable. On both accounts the effort was misleading.

In 1958, Jorge Alessandri secured the presidency without a majority, having gained marginally more votes than the socialist Salvador Allende. Alessandri sought to stabilize the country's struggling economy through curbing inflation. The Chilean peso was replaced by the escudo, which in turn was pegged to the dollar. Chileans were invited to bring monies back into the country, as Alessandri sought to create a stable economy that might attract foreign investment. When imports continued to grow, Chile's export economy failed to keep up. In May 1960, the country was thrown into chaos when the most powerful earthquake ever recorded took place in southern Chile. The earthquake killed between three and five thousand Chileans, leaving two million homeless. The damage was estimated at half a billion dollars.

By 1960, the migration from the provinces to the capital had only exacerbated the growth of slums, so much so that a *cinturón de la miseria* (poverty belt) surrounded the city. Santiago had become a third-world capital. This was not lost on the Italian journalists who visited the country before the tournament. *Corriere della Sera* dispensed without any tact, "This capital [Santiago] is the sad symbol of one of the least developed countries in the world, and one afflicted by all possible evils: undernourishment, prostitution, illiteracy, alcoholism, poverty . . . Chile is terrible and Santiago her most sick expression."[26] Another journalist took a more sardonic tone: "The atmosphere is so depressing that some federations have sent psychiatrists to prevent their players from becoming depressed."[27] This was not the idea Chile had of herself, though the discrepancy between the reality and her idealized self-image was clear for all to see. Chile may have been isolated on the wrong side of the southern Andes, but she saw herself as the most powerful of the Andean republics. This was something the Italians would learn to their cost.

The 1962 World Cup was Chile's greatest sporting triumph, but for many European commentators the tournament was something of a disappointment. In *World Soccer*, that arbiter of international football, Roger Macdonald, voiced his distaste: "I for one am utterly sick of the World Cup. This feeling of disgust arises not from the quadrennial failure of England, but from the renewed burst of thuggery and sadistic brutality throughout the length and breadth of Chile."[28] This kind of high-handedness, so often the default position of the British, was not without reason. The first three days of play had, according to the Chilean press, resulted in over thirty injuries.

For three years, Chile played regular international matches in preparation for her tournament. In 1959, the Andean republic suffered humiliating defeats against Argentina and Brazil, which thrashed her 6–1 and 7–0 respectively. Nevertheless, before the year was out, Chile managed to beat Argentina for the first time in forty-three years. On that November night, Chile's most famous son and goalkeeper, "El Sapo" Livingstone, played his last match. When Livingstone walked off the pitch, after being substituted, the Estádio Nacional fell silent. After a few minutes soft voices began to sing "La Canción del Adiós" ("The Farewell Song").

At the World Cup itself, Chile was favored by playing her group matches at the Estádio Nacional in Santiago. Uruguay, however, was handed a less-than-favorable venue. Arica was Chile's most northern city, which was tantamount to playing in Peru (which the city, in fact, had been until the late nineteenth century). While Chile played to a full stadium of over 65,000 fans, the Uruguayans and Colombians were attracting seven thousand spectators, many of whom had crossed the border from Peru and Bolivia. Uruguay had never lost a FIFA World Cup match in the Americas, but if the diminutive republic was hoping to win its third trophy, their pretournament preparations did not augur well. The qualification round, which had entailed a two-leg match against Bolivia, proved heavy going. For all Bolivia's improvement, a 1–1 draw and a 2–1 win at home would have been unthinkable a decade before. In order to expose its players to European competition, the AUF (Asociación Uruguaya de Fútbol) organized a tour against the wishes of Nacional and Danubio. West Germany and Czechoslovakia managed to put three goals past the Uruguayans, while Hungary edged a 1–1 draw. But it was the Soviet Union that revealed Uruguay's weakness for individual play and an inability to deal with her wingers. Uruguay had no reply to the Soviet Union's five well-taken goals. Scotland provided a consolation victory in a physical match, but the Uruguayans were already psychologically damaged. After defeating World Cup debutants Colombia in their first game, in the second group match Uruguay was unable to outclass Yugoslavia as she had done in 1930. The 3–1 defeat would break the heart of Uruguay's mascot. Manuel Molina González was an eighty-year-old Chilean who had been taken up by the Uruguayan players. After the defeat, Molina's anguish was such that he died of a heart attack. The squad, which went on to fall to another defeat against the Soviet Union that ensured they wouldn't make it out of the group, attended the funeral.

The Colombians' loss at Uruguay's hands was followed by a disastrous first half against the USSR that left them looking out of their depth and losing 3–1. But to everyone's surprise, Colombia managed a comeback of epic proportions in the next forty-five minutes. Marcos Coll scored from a corner kick, which visibly emboldened the Latin Americans, who went on to score two more, though not before the Soviets added another goal of their own. For Colombia, who nevertheless came bottom of the group, the 4–4 draw proved tantamount to victory.

Unlike Brazil, Argentina had failed to learn from her mistakes. Antonio Rattín, who would captain Argentina in 1966, was unimpressed with the setup: "I am convinced that we were not ready to take part in that championship . . . Everything was improvised!"[29] He would later maintain that it was the worst team for which he played in his career. In her first match against Bulgaria, the Argentinians scored after only four minutes, only to shut the game down physically. England, however, exposed Argentina's frailties—which were exacerbated by the number of injuries she had picked up in her opening match—with a 3–1 victory. Argentina went home early.

Chilean hospitality lacked consistency, especially where Italy was concerned. The comments made by the Italian journalists had not been forgotten. This was not lost on the Azzurri, who, having been stoned by the public, sought to win over the partisan crowd who had come to see them play Chile by handing out bouquets of flowers before the match. Not that this emotional bribery would change anyone's opinion: the Italians were met with loud jeers. The English referee should have better gauged the atmosphere. One of the worst displays of sportsmanship in the history of the game would ensue. After six minutes, Leonel Sánchez, who would be Chile's leading goal scorer in the tournament, clashed with Ferrini. A few minutes later Ferrini was sent off for having retaliated against Fouillioux, who had kicked him. Sánchez, the son of a boxer, should have been sent off for knocking out David with an uppercut after the latter had fouled him. Untroubled by the violence occurring right in front of him, the English referee only cautioned the players. Shortly before halftime, David was finally ordered off the pitch for executing a high kick against Sánchez. Two Chilean goals followed in the second half, the second from the pugilistic Toro, who had a reputation for shooting from any angle and dribbling without purpose.

Brazil, so adept four years earlier, was not as sprightly as they had been, especially at the back. Certain players treated tackling as if it were a luxury. Dr. Gosling had done his homework, having visited Chile three times before the tournament, where he realized that many visiting teams tended to wilt in the second half of matches. He attributed this to low oxygen levels rather than any lack of fitness. Thus the players had their red corpuscle count increased. Mexico, so often quick but inherently weak in front of goal, was eventually undone by Zagalo's header. Pelé added a second, dribbling past four players before beating the Mexican goalkeeper. Against Czechoslovakia, however, his body would give up. Anxious about having to sit out the match because of injury, Pelé had not disclosed his concerns. After beating several players, he had hit a thunderous shot, which rebounded off the post. As he made a second attempt to score, Pelé had suffered a muscle strain. Brazil would have to continue without her star player. Their next game was against Spain, who, even without Luis Suárez or her River Plate imports, Di Stéfano (who had switched national allegiance in 1957) and José Santamaría, would prove tricky opposition. But Amarildo scored two adept goals to secure their progress.

Victories for Chile against the Soviet Union and for Brazil against England pitted the Latin American republics against each other in the semifinals. After a slow start to the tournament, England had brought the best out of Garrincha, who "once pulled down a high ball as smoothly as drooping an egg into a cup."[30] To his brace against England, Garrincha added another two against the Chileans, despite their attempts to intimidate the Brazilian. When Zito was fouled by a Chilean, his response was pitying: "This will not help you. We are Brazil, the World Champions . . . and prepared even for this."[31] Perhaps inevitably, Garrincha eventually could not stop himself reacting to the Chilean assault and was sent off seven minutes from time; he would justify his actions by arguing that "I had been provoked beyond endurance for most of the game. Near the end, I felt I had to have my own back. Somehow my knee finished in a Chilean player's stomach."[32] Nevertheless, *El Mercurio* lauded the Brazilian star with the rhetorical question "From which planet does Garrincha come?"[33]

While the Chilean Landa, who had been sent off a few minutes before the Brazilian, would miss the third-place match, Garrincha's transgression was overlooked by FIFA. In the final against Czechoslovakia, Brazil reverted to a 4-2-4 formation, which dulled the Czechs' 3-3-4 tactics. But it would be an error on the part of Viliam Schrojf, who had been voted the best goalkeeper, that put the match past the Czechs. Only fifteen minutes into the match, Brazil would concede her only goal, through Masopust's well-judged run. Two minutes later Amarildo took the ball into the left-hand side of the penalty area and scored from the unlikeliest of angles. Zito's header then put the Brazilians a goal ahead; but it was Schrojf's inability to grasp a high ball that allowed Vavá to seal the match. Brazil had secured her second World Cup title: she was now level with her diminutive neighbor. For Chile, who had scored in the ninetieth minute against Yugoslavia after a goalless match, third place was as good as victory. As one folk song declared,

> *we were third in the world,*
> *and that for our land*
> *is worldwide glory.*[34]

The Strongest Among the Weak

On a continent long dominated by the Atlantic triumvirate of Argentina, Brazil and Uruguay, Bolivia had come to terms with her humble footballing tradition. Even when professionalism was ushered in by the Asociación de Fútbol La Paz (AFLP) in 1950, it retained a hybrid amateur status. Most clubs were not commercially equipped to embrace professionalism, and those that were would need to look abroad for better players. That same year, Uruguay hammered the plucky Bolivians 8–0, scoring four goals in each half.

Failure on the pitch was reflected in the sociopolitical landscape. By the middle of the twentieth century, Bolivia remained a semifeudal society with over 70 percent of the country's workforce employed in agriculture. Absentee landlords, who were for the most part of European extraction and belonged to the professional classes, owned the largest estates, on which the Indian tenants toiled. The mining industry was effectively in the hands of three companies. Despite such a huge proportion of its population being engaged in farming the land, the country was unable to sustain itself and had to rely on imported foodstuffs. Until the national revolution of 1952, Indian tenants could be used for the personal service of their landlords, a pre-independence edict that had somehow survived into the twentieth century. No wonder attitudes to the Indian population remained high-handed. In 1956, Bolivia's minister of education sought to explain the indigenous population thusly: "The Indian is a sphinx. He inhabits a hermetic world, inaccessible to the white and the mestizo. We don't understand his forms of life, nor his mental mechanism . . . Retiring, silent, immutable, he inhabits a closed world. The Indian is an enigma."[35]

The national revolution, which brought Víctor Paz Estenssoro back from a six-year exile in Argentina, sought to build on some of the reforming initiatives of President Gualberto Villarroel's administration in the 1940s. Villarroel, however, had come to an unfortunate end, when he was hanged from a lamppost by antigovernment protesters in the Plaza Murillo in 1946. An execution thought to have been inspired by newsreels of Mussolini's very public death. Under Paz Estenssoro, the Movimiento Nacionalista Revolucionario (MNR) expropriated the larger estates for redistribution, encouraged agrarian reform, nationalized the mining industry and implemented universal suffrage. Bolivia had broken with its semifeudal past. In the 1960 elections, Paz Estenssoro chose the labor-union leader Juan Lechín as his vice-presidential running mate. The son of a Lebanese father and Bolivian mother, Lechín had supposedly been employed by the Patiño Mines for his excellent prowess as a footballer.

As late as the mid-1950s, Bolivian football remained for the most part in the hands of the AFLP, though clubs from other regions had been integrated into the La Paz league. San José from Oruro had joined in 1954 and had won the league—which now included Cochabamba's Jorge Wilstermann and Aurora—a year later with a team nicknamed "Los Húngaros Bolivianos" (The Hungarian Bolivians). Wilstermann, which had been founded by Lloyd Aéreo Boliviano employees in 1949, would win its first titles nine years later. By 1960, the team, which played with a five-forward lineup, had won three championships in a row. But their participation in international club competition that year would expose the naïveté of the Bolivian game.

The inaugural Copa de Campeones de América (later Copa Libertadores) had drawn the Bolivian club against Peñarol. In Montevideo, Wilstermann was put to the sword 7–1 by the Uruguayans, in a not dissimilar fashion to the national team ten years before. The brilliant Alberto Spencer, an Ecuadorian who played six times for Uruguay but was never naturalized, scored four goals. *El Diario* lamented Wilstermann's woeful performance and called for a restructure of Bolivian football, adapted to its own racial advantages, so that the country would not have to endure such disparity of technique. The return leg spared the country's blushes with a 1–1 draw, though the effects of high altitude undoubtedly played its part. The following year Wilstermann was fortunate to not be drawn against the reigning champions, Peñarol, or a strong Palmeiras side. Santa Fé provided the opposition, and a 3–2 win in Cochabamba gave the Bolivians a chance of progressing. In Bogotá, Santa Fé only managed a single goal. With the clubs level on goal difference, the president of the Asociación de Fútbol Cochabamba (AFC) tried to have a deciding game played in "neutral" Bogotá, pleading Pan-American solidarity: "We consider Colombia like our own country."[36] But when it came to drawing lots, instead of playing a decider, Bolivia was prone to bad luck.

In 1963, Bolivia hosted the Campeonato Sudamericano for the first time. In order to improve the country's poor record on the international stage, the Bolivian federation looked to a Brazilian coach. Although Danilo Alvim had played for the great Vasco da Gama side, the "Expresso da Vitória" (Victory Express), in the 1940s and early 1950s, he had also been part of Brazil's greatest disaster in the 1950 World Cup final. The Bolivian press thought Alvim another bird of ill omen when the national side succumbed 3–0 and 5–1 to Paraguay in the Copa Paz del Chaco (Chaco Peace Cup) a month before the tournament. Ondino Viera, the former Vasco da Gama coach, had outwitted Alvim. The Brazilian was now accused of ignorance and setting back the national sport, though in truth there was not very far for it to go.

The 1963 tournament, however, would prove the high point in the country's otherwise unremarkable sporting history. In her first match against a mediocre Ecuador, Bolivia salvaged a respectable 4–4 draw. Yet in the next four matches she managed wins against Colombia, Peru, Paraguay and Argentina. In her final match against Brazil, Bolivia would need to better Paraguay's result to secure the championship. On the last day of the tournament, the Bolivians beat Brazil 5–4, while Paraguay could only manage a draw against Argentina. At the end of the match, Alvim was hoisted on to the shoulders of the defeated Brazilians, who accompanied the victorious Bolivians on a lap of honor. The president of the landlocked republic, Víctor Paz Estenssoro, said, "Bolivia was able to organize the tournament, and her players able to win it."[37] The following year, Paz Estenssoro was himself a victim of revolt. The army commander General Ovando had drily stated, "I am taking you either to the airport or to the cemetery. Which do you choose?"[38] No stranger to exile, Paz left the country yet again.

Although Bolivia had played the better football and had deserved her victory, the tournament had not been of the highest standard. Uruguay and Chile had decided not to enter; the latter because of strained diplomatic relations with the host nation over what the Bolivians termed "imminent geographic aggression." Argentina, on the other hand, had sent a reserve team, without players from Boca Juniors and River Plate. Nevertheless, after Bolivia's 3–2 victory over the *rioplatenses*, *El Diario* lauded the Argentinian performance as better than anything the AFA had offered in the 1958 and 1962 World Cup. That said, although Argentina played to a high standard, her violent match against Peru had made the Chile-Italy encounter of the previous year seem mild by comparison. Brazil, whose record in the competition had been underwhelming, chose to field a squad from Minas Gerais as a reward for good performance.

In 1967, the Campeonato Sudamericano returned to Montevideo, where Uruguay had never lost a championship. In the opening game, Uruguay beat the Bolivians 4–0, though worse was to come. After putting up a valiant fight against Argentina and Paraguay, against both of whom she lost by one goal, Bolivia was thrashed 3–0 by Venezuela. The magnitude of the loss was not lost on the Bolivian historian Peñaloza: "Venezuela, the only South American country that allowed us to separate ourselves from the idea that we were not the last wheel of the cart, thrashed us 3–0, which probably hurt more than if we had been beaten 6–0 by Argentina."[39] After five matches, Bolivia had only managed one point and no goals. Four years after her greatest triumph, she was now officially the worst team in South America.

By the end of the decade, ignominy had been replaced by tragedy. The Strongest, a stalwart of the Paceño league since 1908, had been invited by the Asociación Cruceña de Fútbol (Santa Cruz Football Association) to take part in the commemorative friendlies at the end of the season. The team never returned to La Paz. On September 26, 1969, the Lloyd Aéreo Boliviano DC-6, carrying seventy-four passengers, lost all radio contact. It took twenty-four hours to establish that the plane had crashed into the mountains because of fog and bad visibility. On board were sixteen players from the Strongest. The tragedy engendered a sense of Pan-American solidarity. Alberto Armando, president of Boca Juniors, offered four of his players to the La Paz club and La Bombonera for a testimonial match.

Death on Terraces

While violence had always been an expression of fierce rivalry on the pitch, it would begin to take its toll on the terraces. In 1955, Chile hosted its first Campeonato Sudamericano in ten years. With Brazil having declined to participate and Uruguay flattering to deceive after its heroics in Switzerland, it was Chile's best chance of securing the championship. The Uruguayans secured a draw with the hosts before being dismantled 6–1 by a rampant Argentina. Such was Uruguay's bad luck on the day that the brilliant Labruna had to return to the field after being substituted, when his replacement was knocked out. Chile only needed a win against the Argentinians in the Estádio Nacional to get their hands on the trophy, but the tournament ended in tragedy even before the match began. The anticipation for the final was such that some 30,000 spectators had turned up early. When the doors opened the crowd rushed into the stadium, and in the ensuing scrum, six lost their lives. According to the magazine *Vea*: "The crowd trampled, crushed, flattened, surged and pushed. Balance of fatalities: five dead on the ground."[40] The stadium, which had been designed to hold 50,000 spectators, had exceeded its capacity by 20,000. It would not be the last time that blood would be spilled in Santiago's main stadium.

In May 1964, Lima played host to one of the worst riots ever to take place inside a football stadium. The qualifier for the Tokyo Olympics between Peru and Argentina in a packed Estádio Nacional was always going to be a fraught affair. Ever since the disputed quarterfinal in 1936, the Olympics had overwhelmed the Peruvian imagination. In the intervening years her record had been undistinguished, with the country failing to reach any World Cups between the inaugural tournament in Montevideo and Mexico in 1970, and only managing a solitary win against India at the Rome Olympics of 1960. Now Peru needed a draw against Argentina in order to qualify for the Tokyo games.

Argentina went 1–0 up through Néstor Manfredi, and it was not until two minutes from time that Peru managed to equalize with a fortuitous goal that rebounded off one of their players. The euphoria was short-lived when the Uruguayan referee disallowed the goal, penalizing Peruvian rough. The decision prompted jeering from the excitable crowd. In the meantime, two fans had scaled the perimeter fencing only to be dealt with by the local police. (One of troublemakers was brutally assaulted.) The spectators were now irate. Bonfires were lit and bricks thrown onto the pitch. In order to quell the ensuing riot, the police commander issued the order to launch tear gas into the terraces. This act of gross stupidity led to panicked fans rushing the gates, which had been locked. In the confusion, 312 fans were killed (90 percent of them by asphyxia) and over five hundred injured. The riot, in spite of the tragic loss of life, moved on to the surrounded streets, where cars and buildings were set alight. Three policemen died: one was lynched with his own tie, while another was tossed from the terraces onto the pitch below. For Jorge Basadre, the Peruvian historian, the riot was an expression of the underlying discord in an unequal society: "Our people, especially our lower classes, are full of tensions and frustrations, dark, pent-up passions and angers. This situation is becoming acute under the impact of the population explosion and the poverty of the masses . . . These people have lost some of their faith and hope. When this happens, then sometimes people will behave more like brutes than men."[41]

Peruvian football was no stranger to tragedy. In 1930 and 1931, Montevideo's Bella Vista undertook an extensive tour of the Americas, under the leadership of Uruguay's Olympic captain, José Nasazzi. The match against Arequipa, which had been watched by an unruly contingent of Peruvian soldiers, descended into chaos during the presentation of a cup to the victorious Uruguayans. A disgruntled soldier had made for the pitch, only to be beaten by the flat of the policemen's swords. When the soldier's comrades tried to come to his aid, the police started firing into the crowd. The riot would leave five dead, though demonstrators after the event were still asking that the result be overturned.

In June 1968, the Superclásico (Superderby) between River Plate and Boca Juniors failed to live up to its name, when it ended in a tiresome goalless draw. The match, however, would become infamous as Argentina's greatest football disaster. Over 90,000 spectators had watched the game peter out before the visiting Boca fans made for the exit. Access to Puerta 12 (Gate 12) was dimly lit, and in the avalanche of bodies seventy-one fans were crushed to death and 150 injured, many of them teenagers. "The atmosphere was dangerous. Some fans had burned River flags. Others were throwing firecrackers, coins and glasses of urine at those in the lower terraces," recalled an eyewitness at the time.[42] In the time-honored tradition of Argentinian justice, the investigation into the tragedy failed to apportion any blame. This was not helped by a number of conflicting accounts as to why the exit was blocked. Some eyewitnesses remembered seeing the gate locked, while others said the turnstiles were still in place and had not been removed for the end of the match. (Gates to stadiums were usually opened fifteen minutes into the second half.) The Boca *barra brava*, *la doce* (the twelfth man), committed fans with a tendency for hooliganism, believe that the gate had been left half open in order for the police to apprehend the troublemakers.

The mounted police were accused of using batons against the exiting fans, who were forced to retreat. The quondam president of River Plate, William Kent, believed "the fans answered the call of nature in coffee cups and threw urine and excrement at the mounted police, who were in the street. That provoked police repression and then, the tragedy."[43] By the end of the year, AFA and the clubs of the league had managed to collect 32 million pesos for the victims' families.

British Bulldogs and Other Animals

On June 1, 1964, *The Times* of London ran the headline ENGLAND BEWITCHED BY BLACK DIAMOND.[44] The football correspondent, filing from Rio de Janeiro, had been seduced by the city, and it showed in his prose. Early on in the second half, Tottenham Hotspur's Jimmy Greaves managed to equalize an early Brazilian goal, only for Pelé to contribute to the four Brazilian goals that followed. "This was fiesta: this was a reflection of the moving colour film, *Black Orpheus*; this was life: this was the night of Pele . . . It was worth being alive to see, even in defeat . . . In this mood he can beat the world. He was sheer poetry," swooned the journalist.[45] Greaves was more prosaic: "Pelé is on another bloody planet."

The intention of the 1964 Taça das Nações (Nations Cup) had been to celebrate the fiftieth anniversary of the Confederação Brasileira de Futebol. This "Little World Cup" had become even smaller when Brazil rescinded her invitation to the Soviet Union on political grounds. Italy, on the other hand, had chosen to stay away. In the end, a neat foursome, comprising the hosts, Argentina, England and Portugal, would celebrate the landmark. The flair that had been on show against England would desert Brazil in her next match. Argentina may have beaten Portugal in her opening match, but she remained an inconsistent force in the region. This had not been helped by the disorder of the Argentinian league, which was at the mercy of the larger clubs. (When hosting a River or Boca, the smaller clubs had been asked to hand over 60 percent of their receipts.) On a bad pitch at the Pacaembu, Messiano man-marked Pelé out of the game. Increasing frustration at being stalked led the Brazilian genius to head-butt his marker. Messiano had to be taken to hospital for a broken nose. With Pelé unsettled, Rattín took over. Brazil capitulated by three goals to nil, evidence once again of her ability to panic. There were rumors that, after routing England, the CBF had had watches engraved for its prospective cup-winning players. Thirteen years after Maracanã, Brazilian football had yet again fallen victim to the perils of premature self-congratulation.

Ever forward thinking, unlike some of her neighbors, Brazil had started to engage in a sophisticated analytic process before every match they played. This strategy was intended to give the coach a clearer idea of who would be best suited to play. When Argentina beat Brazil 3–0 in June 1964, Dr. Hilton Gosling stated, "I said Brazil would probably lose—which is better than being wise after the event."[46] His psychological tests would leave little to chance: "I carry out tests to check how well a man can remember what he has been told. Then I tell the coach how many times he will have to repeat his orders before they are obeyed."[47]

Feola, by contrast, sought to damn Argentina with the faintest of praise: "Well, to us, Argentina, however bad, are still Argentina, and they have now developed a very good defence, almost adopting a 1-9-1 formation." In Argentina, Boca Juniors had won the 1964 season with a miserly defense. The Xeneizes had conceded fifteen goals in thirty matches, though had only managed an average of just over one goal per game. In the land of polarities, the free-flowing, attacking football of the 1940s and 1950s had turned into a stalemate. Even after the AFA had dispensed with the system of relegation, and the fears associated with it, goals remained at a premium. For Argentina, there seemed to be an inability to take the middle ground. When Renato Cesarini returned to River Plate from managing UNAM (Pumas) in Mexico, he still complained that Argentinian football was twenty years behind the times. "In the modern game, only one thing counts—to win."[48]

Not that aspects of the Brazilian game were any better. With thirteen clubs in the Campeonato Carioca (Rio championship), there was always one club that would have to sit out each round of fixtures. Moreover, there was a telling difference in quality between the top and bottom of the league. The solution was extreme: five clubs were relegated to create an eight-club league. Brazilian football also had to contend with what João Havelange termed an "exodus" of players to foreign clubs. Nevertheless, Brazil continued to trial young players— between 1958 and 1964, the team had played 661 players.

This abundance of players would not serve Brazil well at the 1966 World Cup. Meticulous though its plans had been, the CBD had left the squad selection until too late. Brazil would remain a squad rather than a team, individuals *à l'argentine*. In a warm-up match against Scotland, Servílio scored in a one-all draw but was sent home for no obvious reason. Even those in the Brazilian camp realized a third world championship in a row was increasingly unlikely.

In their opening match, Pelé and Garrincha once again faced Bulgaria, as they had done eight years earlier. Unable to match Brazil's virtuosity, the Bulgarians opted for a more physical approach. Pelé was singled out for severe treatment, especially to his ankles, and he was offered little in the way of protection. Two goals, coming from set pieces, put the match beyond Bulgaria. The second from Garrincha's free kick—with which he deftly gave the ball power and movement in the air—offered a glimpse of his fading skills. Against Hungary and Portugal, Brazil's light would be snuffed out. Without Pelé, who had been rested, and with Garrincha, who should have been rested, the Brazilians were defeated by Hungary. Brazil now needed to win against Portugal, and to win well. The selectors panicked and made nine changes, one of which was Orlando, who had not played in the World Cup since Brazil's first win. Moreover, Manga, the goalkeeper, feeling the weight of expectation placed on him, was nervous. Pelé noticed the number of times the goalkeeper crossed himself before the match. Two Portuguese goals inside the first thirty minutes put paid to any notion of progressing ahead of the Portugese on goal difference. A late goal rallied the Brazilians, but Eusébio soon put them out of the match. Once again Pelé was kicked and punched—the poor man had been marked for extinction in the tournament—this time by Morais. He cut a forlorn figure at the end of the match, walking off the field, a raincoat draped across his shoulders. Infamous for scapegoating their goalkeepers, Brazil did so again, this time with Manga, who had had a terrible game. (A few years later, Manga would leave Botafogo for Montevideo, where he would win the Copa Libertadores in 1971.) The world champions were out of the competition. Tactically, Brazil's 4-2-4 formation had failed her compared to *futebol força*, the more disciplined European power game; though preparation for the tournament had fallen short even by the CBD's high standards.

. . .

The kind of game *el fútbol rioplatense* played should have come with a health warning. Before the tournament began, Sir Stanley Rous, the president of FIFA, had asked that the conduct and quality of the football befit this august competition. The *rioplatenses* failed to heed the Englishman, or any other official for that matter. Both republics, Argentina and Uruguay, would face the host nation, whose supporters were more than ready to adopt double standards when it suited them. Throughout the tournament, the FIFA Disciplinary Committee would have its work cut out for it.

The England-Argentina match, with Rattín's expulsion as its centerpiece, was in many ways tame compared to the aggression meted out by the Uruguayans upon West Germany. In the opening match of the tournament Uruguay had held England to a goalless draw. The exquisite play of Pedro Rocha was only seen in glimpses, while Julio "El Pocho" Cortés took to shooting from long range. The England striker, Jimmy Greaves, would later recall, "Uruguay's negative tactics soon choked the life out of the game. Uruguay became a clinging cobweb of shifting pale blue shirts, hell-bent on suffocation." The Uruguayans were not in England to entertain. As the English forward John Connelly remembered, "If you got the ball past them they just stood in front of you."[49] Not that England played much better.

In their next game, although Uruguay was without some of her best players, who were playing in Buenos Aires and had not been called up, she took the match to the West Germans. "El Pocho" hit the crossbar with a long-range shot, though Silva kicked the West German goalkeeper once the latter had scrambled to hold the ball. The West Germans proved they were not above a dash of Teutonic cunning themselves when Schnellinger, the AC Milan defender, kept Rocha's header out of the net with some handiwork of his own. Trailing by a single goal, the Uruguayans lost their heads in the second half. With the ball at the other end of the field, the Uruguayan captain, Horacio Troche, kicked Emmerich in the stomach and was duly sent off. To add insult to the West Germany's injury, the Uruguayan slapped his opposing captain in the face as he left the field. Five minutes later Silva followed his captain, having scythed down an opponent. The Uruguayans hung on, but the floodgates eventually opened and the West Germans scored three goals in quick succession. In a moment of *machista* bravura, Cortés kicked the English referee as he left the field; he was suspended for six international matches. This ill-tempered affair did not stop Troche, who had been born in Nueva Helvecia (a small River Plate town colonized by the Swiss and Germans in the nineteenth century), from transferring to Alemannia Aachen the following year. He stayed a year before moving on to Bonn, finishing his career in West Germany.

Argentina had drawn the reigning European champions in her opening match. A tactically astute performance in her 2–1 defeat of Spain revised expert opinion: Argentina was now among the favorites. Against West Germany, however, the tide would run against her. The West German sweeper, Franz Beckenbauer, may have opened the account for dangerous play, but it was the Argentinian with the German surname, José Rafael Albrecht, who was sent off, for kicking Weber in the stomach. The usual melee ensued—that River Plate tradition of crowding the referee into submission—for which FIFA would warn the whole team for unsportsmanlike play. The loss of a player seemed to galvanize Argentina, who played the better football in the last twenty minutes of the goalless match. Argentina now only needed a draw against Switzerland. The reception for the Argentinians was less than welcoming. (West German supporters had turned out to support the Swiss in Sheffield, while the English cheered on the underdog.) For once, the Argentinians behaved themselves. Defending a slender one-goal lead, Onega latched on to a long pass, before employing the subtlest of flicks to send the ball over the head of the Swiss goalkeeper. In the next match, against England, the Argentinians would revert to type.

. . .

Neither team deserved to win, though after Rattín's expulsion, Argentina played the better football. The eight-minute interlude and the ensuing loss of a player seemed to suit the Argentinians. If the match wasn't as violent as the ensuing controversy would make it out to be, neither was it a free-flowing example of the beautiful game. According to Ray Wilson, the England left-back, the Argentines had let themselves down: "They seemed to get more satisfaction out of niggling, shirt pulling, nasty stuff, than playing. If they'd played, they could have been a massive side, they were wonderful."[50] England didn't play with much more flair, and for all the nation's roseate memories of their single World Cup triumph, wouldn't do so for much of the competition. Karl Rappan, the Austrian inventor of the *Schweizer Riegel*, the "locking system" football strategy (known as the *verrou* in Switzerland), said of the final, England's footballing zenith: "If this match had been played before 2,000 spectators with a regional title at stake, the players would have been whistled."

The standard of refereeing throughout the tournament had been similarly unimpressive. And that of Rudolf Kreitlein was no exception. Brian Glanville's telling portrait of Kreitlein for the *Sunday Times* of London summed up the fussiness of the West German referee: "a small man, strutting portentously about the field, bald, brown head gleaming in the sunshine, put name after Argentinian name into his notebook. One was reminded of a schoolboy collecting railway engine numbers."[51] He had seen the Argentinians at close quarters the year before, when he refereed Inter's 3–0 victory over Independiente in the Intercontinental Cup. Nevertheless, he was the wrong choice for the volatile match. England and Argentina had form, and not just on the pitch.

In 1933, the Roca-Runciman Treaty had sought to strengthen

Anglo-Argentine trade relations, especially those that concerned the meat market. For Vice President Roca, Argentina had become, from an economic standpoint, "an integral part of the British empire." After the war, however, the price of meat would strain relations between the two countries. Opportunism on the part of Perón—part of his drive for economic independence—did not amuse the British ambassador, the Australian-born Sir Rex Leeper, who felt that the Argentinians should learn their place. On a continent where Britain had had to vie with the United States for hegemony, the Argentinian elites had for the most part proved amenable to London's influence. Under Perón, this would all change. The Argentinian railway companies—that symbol of British imperialism, though three were French-owned—were nationalized by Perón in 1948 amid great national celebration. Perón's speech was bathed in sentiment: "I consider the act that we are celebrating today so important that I firmly believe that if my political career, or even my physical life, were to end today I would die with the intimate satisfaction that I had paid off my debt to Argentina. Men perish. The *patria* [fatherland] remains and its well-being is what matters."[52]

Perón also sought to revive the question of Argentina's "lost" territories. Maps were redrawn and schoolbooks rewritten to include what were deemed to be the country's possessions. (The Antarctic Peninsula added over a million square kilometers to Argentina.) The slogan *Las Malvinas son argentinas* (The Malvinas belong to Argentina) had become part of the national curriculum. Anglo-Argentine relations would never truly recover. The dispute over the sovereignty of the Falklands made sure of that.

In the first minute of the match, Artime, Solari and their towering captain Rattín were cautioned. Thirty-four minutes later Rattín was off the pitch.

Rattín, whom Perfumo would later call "a *caudillo* [chief] like Obdulio Varela," had baited Kreitlein from the first whistle.[53] In the end, Rattín's constant attempts to countermand the referee's decisions had led the West German to lose his temper and expel the

Argentinian captain. The punishment did not fit the crime: Rattín had hardly perpetrated some foul offense, and his behavior would have been considered entirely acceptable in the Latin American game. The situation was not helped by the language barrier: the referee failed to understand the captain's request for an interpreter. Kreitlein may not have understood Spanish or the expletives that would no doubt have accompanied the pleading, but he had seen something in Rattín's face. Rattín would later partly blame his manager, Juan Carlos "Toto" Lorenzo, for advising him to ask the referee for an explanation on any questionable decision. Said Rattín, "It was clear that the referee played [the match] with an England shirt on."[54] On his way to the changing room the Argentinian was pelted with chocolates, which in retrospect would amuse him. As he passed the corner flag, however, he crumpled the small Union Jack in his hand—a sign of *machista* disrespect.

Dropping deep, Argentina managed to keep England in check. After halftime, the Argentinians started to regain their confidence in the belief that they might just sneak a goal. But a header by Geoff Hurst twelve minutes from time put the game beyond them. The goal was very much against the run of play, though it would probably be England's most significant of the tournament. For once England had managed to hold her nerve. While the match was over, the ill feeling between the sides persisted. This time one Englishman in particular was at fault.

Alf Ramsey now took a somewhat schoolmasterly approach to the affair, in spite of having seen his side progress to the semifinals. There would be no postmatch rapprochement. Ramsey physically intervened when Oscar Más, the prolific River Plate forward, tried to swap shirts with George Cohen. José Pastoriza, unable to control his temper, as he had failed to do with Rattín before the tournament, went for the West German referee. The England players would accuse the Argentines of attempting to storm their dressing room, something that the South Americans would later deny. They would also have to deny that they had urinated in the passage between the changing rooms.

In a moment of ill-concealed irritation, Ramsey let his guard down and said, "Our best football will come against the team who come out to play football and not act as animals." The remark was not untainted with xenophobia, especially where South Americans were concerned. Ramsey had revealed himself as the "little Englander" that he was. Though not completely unjustified, the saloon-bar remark would wound Argentinian pride. It would never be forgotten. Had it come from another Latin American republic, the slur might have passed unnoticed into history. Delivered by the British, a country the Argentinians admired, the comment took on an imperialist aspect. Is this what the British secretly thought? More than any other country in the region, the fear of being perceived as uncivilized was part of the Argentina's psychological makeup. (This complex had its roots in the nineteenth century.) On the one hand culturally racist, on the other quick to accuse others of neocolonialism, Argentina could not have it both ways.

The British could abide many eccentricities, but a lack of "respect for authority on the field of play"[55] was not one of them. Paradoxically, a "persistent flaunting of authority" had its roots in the tough, physical game that the British had brought to the continent. For all their skill and elegance on the ball, the *rioplatenses* had resorted to aggression where guile might have served better. *The Times* was thoroughly disapproving of the Latin American performance: "Brazil apart . . . the South American effort as a whole has been dismal . . . Two Argentinians and two Uruguayans sent off; and a spate of defensive play, which, for all its fiendish cleverness and masterly technical control, proved utterly suffocating for the game itself and soporific for the spectators. Their whole attitude—Brazil again excluded—has been negative . . . They deserve to be out, since they are killing the game in more ways than one, not least in certain instances by undisciplined, cynical behaviour and flaunting of authority."[56] Would the River Plate republics have gained more respect had they played like Brazil?

Not all Englishmen were as appalled. In a letter to *The Times*, penned from the Guards Club, Lord Lovat castigated Ramsey's outburst, reminding him that "his own side were penalized no less than

33 times against 19 fouls perpetrated by Argentina." He found Argentina to have been "quite definitely the best footballers," though he was of the opinion that the image of "Argentines jerking in agony like shot rabbits on the ground" should best be forgotten.[57]

FIFA's Disciplinary Committee now fined the AFA one thousand Swiss francs, while Rattín, Ferreiro and Onega were suspended for ten international fixtures between them. (Onega had famously spat into the face of a FIFA commissaire in the melee after the match.) What seemed to hurt the Argentinians the most was the proposal to the World Cup Organizing Committee that the country be barred from the 1970 World Cup. The response from the head of the Argentinian delegation, Juan Santiago, was to call Sir Stanley Rous "a moron." FIFA's actions established a principle: that players and officials behave in sportsmanlike fashion or else face the consequences. In an attempt to be evenhanded in what had become an international incident, the Disciplinary Committee stated that Ramsey's saloon-bar remarks—an example of a latent British xenophobia—"do not foster good international relations in football."[58]

Ever intent on finding conspiracies where none existed, the *rioplatenses* pointed to the nationality of the referees. This was unsurprising: conspiracy theories had become a fundamental part of the Latin American game. Interviewed years later, Rattín sarcastically recalled, "And just by chance the referee for our game against England was a German, who sent me off. The referee for the Uruguay v Germany match was an Englishman . . . Everything was set up."[59] Ryszard Kapuściński was not wrong when he observed that "Latins are obsessed with spies, intelligence conspiracies and plots."[60] Here was *la viveza criolla* (creole cunning) at work.

Although the press in Buenos Aires felt some degree of vindication now that they could blame the scandal on FIFA's choice of referee, this did little to temper the ire of the headlines and editorials. *Clarín* took a more racially abusive approach: "Ramsey is a gypsy dressed as an Englishman."[61] Across the Río de la Plata in

Montevideo, the usual repercussions were exacted on the Anglo community. The British Embassy's information officer sent an alarming report back to London, which only reinforced Anglo-Saxon attitudes to the Latin American game:

The Residence, Chancery and Consulate were now bombarded by anonymous telephone calls, often of an extremely abusive nature, asking, among other things, how much we had paid the German referee. There have been about 300 calls in all. Groups gathered outside the residence (empty except for the servants), pulled the street-bell out of its socket and threatened the servants ... It would be comforting to say that the only moral of the story is, never let a South American team lose a football game. But unfortunately the net result has been to raise doubts in the minds of many normally friendly people as to whether the traditional British "fair play" really exists now, and whether Association Football in Europe has sunk to the meretricious level of professional boxing in the United States.[62]

Rattín had been willing to take his chances against Uruguay. "If we played Uruguay, I think the story would have been different and we would have been in the final."[63] Whether Argentina could have won the tournament remains uncertain. The squad that Argentina took to England was unlike those that had gone before. "This team," wrote Juan Sasturain, "unlike those before it—hung on, like a pilot hangs on in the rain, as Uruguay had played to hang on for decades: halting the rhythm [of the game], 'concealing' the ball."[64]

On their return, the Argentinian players were hailed as "moral victors." Ezeiza Airport, that Janus-like symbol of Argentinian welcome and exile, was distinguished by a different mood from the one that greeted the 1958 World Cup squad. On its front page, *The Times* ran the story "Argentines Are Home Like Heroes":

Thousands of Argentines stood in torrential rain chanting "Argentina champion," to give their defeated World Cup players a hero's welcome at

*the international airport here today. The fans surged through a cordon
thrown round the airport buildings by security police and troops.
Women rushed up to the team captain Antonio Rattin . . . kissed him
ecstatically on both cheeks and tried to wrap him up in an Argentine
flag. Several people carried home-made posters depicting as donkeys the
leaders of the international football federation (F.I.F.A.), who put penalties on some Argentine players and officials and said that the country
will be barred from the next World Cup in 1970 unless assurances of
good conduct are given . . . Topical slogans set to the tune of popular
Peronist marches were roared deafeningly. After getting clear of the
crowds the players boarded buses taking them to the presidential residence, where the President, General Juan Carlos Ongania, was waiting
to thank them officially on behalf of the nation.*[65]

While the squad had been in Europe, President Illia had been
deposed in a military coup. The junta lasted a day before General
Onganía took office. It would not be the first or last time that a dictatorship would use football for its own ends. In its Acta de la Revolución Argentina (Argentinian Revolution Act) the military junta put
an end to civilian rule, dissolved congress and the Supreme Court and
banned political parties. "A bunch of cynics [military government] is
converted into national pride," Dante Panzeri would later write.[66]

"La Copa, La Copa, Se Mira Y No Se Toca" (The Cup, the Cup, Is Seen and Not Touched)

From its earliest days, Latin American football had sought glory
abroad through sporting victory. The British had seen to that by
instilling in the *criollos* a penchant for cup competition. The problem
in organizing a continent-wide tournament in such a vast and various stretch of territory had always been logistical. Nevertheless

Argentina and Uruguay's geographical proximity positively encouraged the proliferation of *copas* between them. In 1913, the Copa Ricardo Aldao was founded to determine the strongest team on the River Plate. Rain stopped play that year, and the match was never replayed. In rather eccentric fashion the cup would not be held for another three years, when Nacional beat Racing.

In 1929, Roberto Espil and José Usera Bermúdez, two board members of Nacional, sought to organize a continental tournament. But the complexity of the travel arrangements proved insurmountable. The continent was not yet ready to host the competition. Nineteen years later South America finally held her first club championship, the Campeonato Sudamericano de Campeones (South American Championship of Champions). Though this time the idea had come from Chile. In 1948, Santiago hosted River Plate (Argentina), Litoral (Bolivia), Vasco da Gama (Brazil), Colo-Colo (hosts), Emelec (Ecuador), Deportivo Municipal (Peru) and Nacional (Uruguay). The results were eccentric. Vasco thrashed Nacional 4–1, only for the Uruguayans to then beat River by three goals to nil. With only a point separating each team, Vasco da Gama emerged victorious from the round robin, while the Argentinians and Uruguayans took second and third place respectively. The competition was slow to take hold.

A decade later, it was once again the Chileans who sought to establish a continental cup. (Though Chile's entry, Universidad de Chile, would be humiliated 6–0 by Millonarios in its first match.) The response from the traditional footballing powers was less than enthusiastic. The Chilean journalist Julio Martínez remembered, "We struggled for the idea to take shape, especially because the Atlantic leaders [Brazil, Argentina and Uruguay] did not consider this tournament attractive from an economic viewpoint; they gave much more importance to their league tournaments."[67] Uruguay, which had excelled at the Copa América, felt that the new *copa* would have an adverse effect on the South America championship. But for the Pacific republics, whose football continued to be played in the shadow of their eastern neighbors, visiting clubs from the Atlantic seaboard would provide a huge boost to gate receipts. After much wrangling, and the proposal and rejection of a number of variations on a tournament, the Copa Libertadores de América was finally born. The cult of the *caudillo* was manifest in the Pan-American club tournament, which was named in honor of the Latin American *libertadores* (liberators) who had fought for independence in the nineteenth century.

For a continent that had always craved an international club competition, Latin America's response to the first Copa Libertadores in 1960 was surprisingly indifferent. Peñarol only needed to beat Bolivia's Jorge Wilstermann to reach the semifinal against San Lorenzo. In Montevideo, Alberto Spencer, Peñarol's magnificent Ecuadorian, scored four in a seven-goal thrashing. The team would be given a surprise welcome in La Paz when they arrived for the return leg. The Wilstermann players were waiting at the airport with their wives and girlfriends so that they could be photographed with the Uruguayans. (The cordiality between clubs would soon been extinguished.)

In Buenos Aires, however, the welcome for the Uruguayans was muted. Roberto Scarone, the club's manager, would remember, "We arrive in Buenos Aires on a Wednesday, and the taxi driver didn't even know there was a match between San Lorenzo and Peñarol."[68] There were only 15,000 spectators to witness the goalless draw. But for the Great Chilean Earthquake of that year, the playoff would have been held in Santiago de Chile. Humid Asunción was dismissed by the Uruguayans as a viable venue, so the match was moved to Montevideo. The Argentinians, either underestimating the advantage that playing on home soil would bring Peñarol, or swayed by the sizable gate receipts that were on offer, traveled across the Río and lost to two goals by Spencer.

In the final, Peñarol beat Asunción's Olimpia over two legs. The Paraguayans had reached the semifinal against Millonarios, having secured a bye when Lima's Universitario failed to take part. Not that

Peru was the only country to stay away. Ecuador had failed to host a football championship for two years, so could not provide a champion. *El Gráfico* did not exaggerate its assessment of the 1960 tournament: "The champions of South America (Interclub) tournament [Libertadores] was unappreciated in its first outing. It did not stir up the masses; it got no one excited."

Peñarol, unlike other teams from the Río de la Plata, recognized the significance of the tournament early. Its faith was rewarded with a two-legged fixture against the European Cup winners, Real Madrid. In 1958, the president of CONMEBOL, José Ramos de Freitas, corresponded with the secretary-general of UEFA on the subject of an intercontinental playoff. "It is difficult if not impossible, to organize a match among the national teams of Europe and South America . . . the World Champion resulting from these matches."[69] The Intercontinental Cup became a monster of UEFA and CONMEBOL's making: a violent and ill-tempered affair that would have commentators, especially in Europe, clamoring for its termination.

The first leg at the Estádio Centenario was a bruising and defensive affair, a goalless draw played in the rain and mud. The conditions favored the Uruguayans, who would be taken apart at the Estádio Santiago Bernabéu. After fifty-four minutes Real had scored five without reply. The Spanish daily newspaper *ABC* was merciless: "If there was 'k. o.' [knockout] in football, like in boxing, the first final of the intercontinental tournament, genuine club world championship, it ended after nine minutes because of Peñarol being *hors de combat*."[70] The mortal blows had come from Puskás and Di Stéfano. Spencer snatched a consolation goal before the final whistle. The *garra uruguaya* (Uruguayan fighting spirit) was nowhere to be seen. Humiliation in Madrid had an immediate effect on the Peñarol board. On the flight back to Montevideo, the club's president, Washington Cataldi, decided "to do what Real [Madrid] does: to have a powerful and spectacular team in order to give great performances and at the same time raise great sums [of money]."[71] The following year, Peñarol faced Palmeiras in the final. In the first leg, the Brazilians "owned" the ball, though Spencer managed to score in the last minute. São Paulo in the return fixture was less than welcoming, especially after Sasía's volley broke the goal net. The Brazilians harangued the referee, insisting that the ball had failed to enter the goal. It was enough to secure the draw that Peñarol needed to be crowned champions for a second time. The Uruguayans would have to play three matches against Béla Guttman's Benfica—who had come from behind to beat Real Madrid 5–3 in the European Cup final. The Portuguese carried a one-goal victory to Montevideo, where they were routed 5–0. After Peñarol's 2–1 win in the play-off, *L'Équipe* lauded the Montevidean club: "No one could beat Peñarol . . . At this moment there is not one European team, you understand, not one that can aspire to beat the champion here in Montevideo."[72] Guttmann had asked the Benfica's board of directors for a pay raise, to which the response was in the negative. He now moved on to Peñarol, having left behind the curse that Benfica would not win the European Cup again. He would not last the season. After losing to Santos in the final of the Copa Libertadores, Guttmann stayed for Peñarol's *clásico* (derby) against Nacional before leaving.

The following year, having beaten its great rival Nacional in the semifinal, Peñarol fell to the exquisite play of Santos and Pelé in Buenos Aires. The second leg, played in Vila Belmiro, ended in farce when a bottle hit the Chilean referee in the neck. When the referee decided to abandon the match, he was threatened with police detention by the president of the Federação Paulista. When that failed to move the Chilean, he was called a coward and a thief. The playoff was scheduled for the Monumental in Buenos Aires, and this time a Dutch referee was employed. Pelé scored twice as one of the greatest Latin American teams strolled to a three–nil victory.

Now Washington Cataldi, president of Peñarol, sought to have the tournament expanded to the runners-up of each league. Many on the continent thought this a political move in order to ensure that the duopoly of Nacional and Peñarol could both enter. In an interview, published in *El Gráfico*, Cataldi justified his position: "The history of the *Copa Libertadores* is well known by many. We were pioneers, together with other managers in South America, to start it first [1960], and much later to add the runners up [1966]. They then said that this was a trick in order to assure the presence of the two big Uruguayan teams. Something of this is true. But not the only reason. I personally took charge of travelling to all the South American countries to demonstrate to everyone that, for a greater *Copa* experience, it was better to play with twenty teams instead of ten. History has proved me right."[73]

The larger format proved the making of the competition, though it undermined the element of surprise that had been such a large part of the golden age of Latin America's appeal. As Pelé observed: "It is harder to beat Boca, Peñarol or other teams like Botafogo than a national team in the World Cup. We knew one another well."[74]

The sixties were Peñarol's years of international glory. But even amid their triumph, there was a sense of melancholy and regret, and a longing for an idealized past. Buenos Aires' *La Nación* recognized a footballing culture mired in nostalgia. "Probably nobody lives on memories as much as Uruguay. Their Olympic and world titles, instead of giving them a spirit of improvement, proved to be a burden. Everybody is trying to emulate those great masters who won the laurels ... few realize that football has changed and that one needs something more than zeal and skill. There was the attempts of one team, Peñarol, to give up the classic moulds, and they contracted the top technician Béla Guttmann; but the intolerance and narrow-mindedness of directors, journalists and players wrecked the enterprise."[75]

By the mid-1960s, time had caught up with the country. Uruguay had begun to stagnate economically. After the boom of the Korean War, domestic production had steadily declined. With the rise of inflation, the purchasing power of the middle and lower classes had diminished. It would only be a matter of time before leftist groups took matters into their own hands. Wrote one Tupamaro (urban guerrilla), "The crisis gets worse from day to day. It is our best ally."[76] The British historian George Pendle gave a rather poignant account of Montevideo: "Walking along the streets . . . I could feel—or imagined that I felt—that there had been a decline in prosperity. It seemed that many of the people were not quite so well dressed as before. Buildings looked rather shabby."[77] This image, of a capital timeless in its decline, would haunt the country into the twenty-first century. Parochial and unkempt, the city seemed destined never to recapture its former glory; it was increasingly hard to imagine a golden age had ever existed.

The Uruguayans saw themselves for what they were. Carlos Maggi made no apologies in the left-leaning weekly *Marcha*: "Here is a country whose people do not aspire to greatness, or to anything absolute, but who desire that things shall be kept in good, human proportion . . . With such people one does not build empires or alter the course of history. Here, nothing is very rigorous. Everything is improvised, haphazard and rather ineffectual."[78] The Uruguayan writer was not mistaken, though one thing the country had altered was the course of world football.

Consecutive Libertadores championships for Independiente in 1964 and 1965—though the club would fail against Inter at intercontinental level—had whetted Argentinian appetite for the regional competition. In 1966, the two great teams from either side of the Río de la Plata, Peñarol and River Plate, faced each other in the final. With honors even, the Estádio Nacional in Santiago hosted the playoff. For the Uruguayan players, the match would become the greatest of their lives. River Plate's two goals before halftime had seemingly put the game beyond Peñarol, who fought back to equalize in a second-half six-minute spell. In extra time, Spencer and Rocha both headed the winners. Against Real Madrid, whom the Uruguayans beat 2–0 in both legs, Spencer scored three out of the four goals. A consummate header of the ball, so much so that Pelé rated him better than himself, the Ecuadorian would become the all-time-greatest goal scorer in the Copa Libertadores.

Anti-Fútbol and the Dark Side of the Latin American Game

For the major clubs in the region, the Intercontinental Cup came to be seen as *the* glittering prize. Vanity, that most Latin of personality traits, was demonstrated by the need to be crowned "World Club Champion." The Copa Libertadores no longer sufficed. But sometimes this will to win blurred into something less savory. In 1967, European Cup winners Celtic played Avellaneda's Racing Club (La Academia) over two legs for the Intercontinental Cup. The Hampden Park tie was a tight affair, with Celtic edging the game 1–0. The return leg in Buenos Aires was marred even before the match had started. The Celtic goalkeeper had to be taken from the field and substituted when a missile hit him on the head. He thought it must have been a bottle, though witnesses said that a stone had come from a catapult. The violence did not stop there: the Scots were hacked throughout the game, having received no protection from the Uruguayan referee. With the scores level at 1–1, Juan Carlos "El Chango" Cárdenas secured a replay for the Argentines in the dying minutes of the game.

The playoff, which Uruguay hosted at the Estádio Centenario in Montevideo, would be one of the most ill-tempered matches of all time. Five players—three from Celtic and two from Racing—were sent off by the Paraguayan referee, and a fourth Celtic player was dismissed but managed to stay on the pitch during the chaos that ensued. (The Uruguayan police had to separate the brawling players with batons.) It took a moment of magic from Cárdenas to rescue the game: a searing left-foot drive from thirty-five yards curled into the top right-hand corner of Celtic's net. Racing held out to be crowned world champions, only to be pelted with litter by the predominantly Uruguayan crowd during its lap of honor. *La Mañana* wrote: "This was no football, it was a disgrace."

While La Academia was celebrating its victory both in Montevideo and Buenos Aires, fans of sworn rivals, Independiente, broke into El Cilindro de Avellaneda in order to place a curse on the team. Seven black cats were buried around the stadium. For thirty-four years Racing failed to win another title. The club tried everything to locate all seven feline skeletons, including digging up the pitch, but only six were found. With the club on the verge of bankruptcy and its fortunes in free fall, an exorcism was performed in front of 100,000 fans. The seventh cat was eventually found in 2001 when the stadium was rebuilt. That season Racing finally won the Apertura championship.

After the match, at a British Embassy reception, Jock Stein said, "I would not bring the team back here for all the money in the world."[79] *The Times* of London was equally outraged, running the headline VICTORY WITHOUT HONOUR FOR THE ARGENTINES.[80] Sir Stanley Rous proposed that the self-styled tournament now be regulated by FIFA, which would also appoint the referees. "What is needed mostly is greater courage by referees to deal with the sinners," he said. And yet Rous could not be drawn to condemn what had become an overreliance on violence by *rioplatense* football. "As for physical styles and matters of temperament and climate, those, I'm afraid, are beyond our control."[81] *The Times* was evenhanded in its assessment of the state of the international game. "At Montevideo the Celtic players apparently were provoked and by retaliation shamefully surrendered their own standards. But before casting stones at others Britain had best remember her own glass house. At the root of all the evil is money, greed for power, the size of the rewards and the penalty for failure. No one can afford to lose any more."[82] For Racing's half, Juan Carlos Rulli, the problem lay elsewhere: "Celtic were not the same team as at Glasgow. When European teams cross the Atlantic they always seem to lose something."[83]

By the end of the decade, European commentators had lost their enthusiasm for the two-legged playoff. *World Soccer* sought to itemize the transgressions: "In 1963 Santos beat AC Milan in a playoff which made Celtic's match look like a garden tea-party; the winning goal was a disputed penalty, while Maldini and Ismael were sent off; in 1965 Inter drew no-score in Buenos Aires against Independiente to take the title: Herrera and several players were struck by stones, and they did not dare, as Herrera recalled afterwards, to score from a penalty."[84]

Ten years after the infamous Montevideo encounter, Celtic's former manager, Jimmy McGrory, was unrepentant in his views on the bruising game: "The record will say that Celtic lost the football match, but I am not sure there was a great deal of football played in any of the meetings between the two sides. The Argentinians did not want to play a game; they wanted to fight a battle . . . if the club plays the game it should do its best to win by the rules. If the other side do not want that, the club should simply not play."[85]

.   .   .

For all its modern sophistication, Latin American football had now become prone to nineteenth-century barbarities. Failure to understand that it was only a game, and not a matter of life and death, continued to haunt the region. In one match, a fan took matters into his own hands when he shot the opposing goalkeeper as the latter attempted to make a save. The game had always been predisposed to overexcitement on the part of player and fan, but cold calculation had never been the region's strong suit. Verbal abuse or mind games have become common to most sports—cricket with its "sledging"; basketball employs "trash talk"—but in the late 1960s, Estudiantes de La Plata took the game to a far darker place.

In 1967, during the presidency of Valentín Suárez, the AFA

changed the structure of the championship that had served Argentina since 1931. Under the new system, which established a season of two tournaments, the smaller clubs, especially those from the provinces, would now be able to compete with the "big five." The Campeonato Metropolitano in effect split the existing league in two (eleven teams in each) and allowed the top two teams from each to progress to the semifinals of the championship. In the second half of the season, the first six highest-placed teams from each group would join the provincial clubs to contest the Campeonato Nacional. The new format would change the Argentinian game forever. After thirty-five years, the hegemony of Boca, River Plate, San Lorenzo, Independiente and Racing was now over. For some provincial clubs, however, the introduction to the national game was brutal. Club Atlético Chaco For Ever, a club from the subtropical climes of Chaco, conceded forty-four goals in fifteen matches in the inaugural tournament.

Even in Latin America, Estudiantes remains one of the most reviled teams ever to play the game. *The Times* went so far as to call "Los Pincharratas" (The Rat Stabbers)—the sobriquet stems from the medical students who supported the club—"one of the most despicable teams ever to emerge from South America." And yet, from 1968 to 1970, Estudiantes would win the Copa Libertadores three years in succession. Under Osvaldo Zubeldía, who unsuccessfully and briefly managed the national team, the *conjunto de laboratorio* (laboratory group) had attempted to win at all costs. At the end of the 1967 season, *El Gráfico* sought to explain the club's success. "This triumph has been the triumph of a *new mentality*, often proclaimed since Sweden, but rarely manifested concretely in *actions*. A *new mentality* served by men who are young, strong, disciplined, dynamic, vigorous, whole in body and in spirit. . . . It is clear that Estudiantes *did not invent anything*. They simply followed the example set by Racing last year . . . the most laudable of their attributes at their hour of triumph: their *humility*."[86]

The 1961 home defeat to the European champions had proved as traumatic as the disaster in Sweden. The Soviet Union had been well disciplined and team-spirited, characteristics in short supply in Argentina. Estudiantes had forsaken *la nuestra*, with its ritual humiliation through skill and guile, for a more direct approach. The squad had evolved from an under-nineteen team nicknamed "La Tercera Que Mata" (The Killer Juveniles). When Zubeldía arrived at the club he quickly realized that the third string played better than the first team, and only kept four of the senior players. Preparation and practice, activities with which Argentinian football had hitherto had an uneasy relationship, became the tenets of the clubs. Former referees were hired to lecture the players on every loophole of the game; man-to-man marking included the use of pins to stab opposing players; character flaws were exposed through verbal incitement; brutality was mandatory.

Said Juan Ramón Verón:

> We tried to find out everything possible about our rivals individually, not just the way they play, but their habits, their characters, their weaknesses and even about their private lives, so that we could goad them on the field, get them to react and risk being sent off. For example, we knew that "Cococho" Álvarez continually protested to the referee and frequently he would gain advantage from this for his team [Nacional] in the end. When we played against the Uruguayan team in the 1969 final and we saw him move towards the referee, four or five of us used to get in his way and would not let him get near, so he could only shut up, push us out of the way or shout at the referee and in the two latter cases he risked a warning or sending off.[87]

"Bocha" Flores, who played for the club between 1962 and 1971, recalled the team never having lost a match in the final ten minutes, such was the calculation of the game.

Estudiantes had become synonymous with *anti-fútbol*—the game taken to extremes—during the Copa Libertadores in 1968. The label may have suited the club from La Plata, but it seemed to have been given in a spirit of hyperbole. Uncompromising though Estudiantes's style of play may have been, it only reflected the more physical English roots of the game. For too long Argentinian football had suppressed its heritage, unable to come to terms with what it actually was. It had more in common with English football than it would have liked to think.

In the 1968 Intercontinental Cup, Estudiantes played Manchester United over two legs. At the Estádio Alberto J. Armando, the European champions played so badly that Oscar Malbernat thought the British must be hiding something. (He could not understand the club's fame otherwise.) Manchester United had failed both in attack, having fallen for the offside trap all too often, and defense. George Best remembered the matches as "sword fights," with "firecrackers landing on [his] boots" in Buenos Aires.[88] When Alex Stepney handed the referee a bottle that had landed near him, the Argentinians thought that the Englishman was bribing him with whiskey. The *Daily Mirror* was outraged by the gamesmanship: "Savage and stupid . . . that was provocative Estudiantes . . . We now know Sir Alf wasn't far out."[89] Sir Stanley Rous even praised the "remarkable tolerance" of the Manchester United players.

Best was wrong to think that anything would change when the Argentinians played at Old Trafford. Had the referee watched the players, rather than the ball, the match might have been abandoned for not having the requisite number of men. With tempers running high, and his frustration growing, Best was red-carded after "chinning" an opponent, who was being booked. "It was the most satisfying red card I've ever had," wrote Best in his autobiography.[90] Carlos Bilardo was not being obtuse when he said, "English football is too much. So hard it amazes me that players survive for more than three years."[91]

This time it was the Argentinians' turn to remonstrate. "On 'Animals' and 'Gentlemen'" ran *El Gráfico*'s editorial. Photographs of Argentinian players being pelted by an English crowd dominated the match report. The magazine's reporter Osvaldo Ardizzone maintained a rather eccentric position, indignation mixed with disappointment: "Fair play is a lie. Yes, I am positive that it is a lie . . . The well-dressed man that was next to me, who stared at me coldly, did not applaud the winners . . . It's the same in my Mataderos, in my Avellaneda . . . No, here they cannot admit defeat, just as they can't at home . . ."[92] Constancio C. Vigil ended his editorial by ridiculing the British: "In order to be *gentlemen* like them, we prefer to be *animals* in our simple, open, humane and sincere Argentinian way."[93]

Not everyone agreed. The year before, Gordon Meyer, an English writer who had taken up residence in Punta del Este, had defined the Argentinian mind-set. "The Argentines are not tractable like their neighbours (Chileans, Uruguayans, Paraguayans), on whom they look down. They live in the nominative case and optative mood, a nation of individualists, which at times one cannot but conclude— and some of them do too—needs a steelfisted [*sic*] dictator, gloved or otherwise. Nothing is argued objectively, dispassionately. In fact, the moment it becomes clear that, to pursue a given topic, a certain amount of *knowledge* will be required, the disputant is likely to fall back on the classical formula: Well, that is how it appears to me. The view is that the self is the only object of real knowledge, the only thing that really exists. Solipsism par excellence."

In 1969, Estudiantes took part in one of the most violent games in history. La Vergüenza de La Plata (The Embarrassment of La Plata) pitted Estudiantes against the new European champions, AC Milan. Such was the extent of the violence that the home team, who had to overturn a three-goal first-leg deficit, finished the game with nine players. Aguirre Suárez broke Néstor Combin's cheekbone with his elbow; the goalkeeper Alberto Poletti struck Rivera, who was then hacked down by Manera. President Onganía—not a stranger to violence, having suppressed university reform in La Noche de los Bastones Largos (The Night of the Long Batons) three years earlier— was dismayed: "Such shameful behaviour has compromised and sullied Argentina's international standing and provoked the revulsion of a nation." All three offenders were sent to prison for thirty days, and Poletti was banned from the game for life. Combin, a naturalized Frenchman who had been born in Argentina, was arrested after leaving the field to attend to his broken cheekbone. The charge: not having completed his national service.

That same year *la guerra del fútbol* (the football war) reflected what Latin America had become: both politically and morally bankrupt. The war was never about football: it was about hunger, markets and foreign and domestic interests. If commentators outside the region thought this one-hundred-day war between Honduras and El Salvador was a tragic state of affairs, worse was yet to come. The 1970s would see Latin America and its football descend into turmoil. An insignificant Mexican league match, in the final year of the decade, epitomized just what the game had become. When Carlos Villegas Zomba scored four goals for Atlante, the club's supporters hailed him a hero. His finest hour would, however, end his career. After the match a disgruntled fan pulled out a revolver and shot the striker in his legs. Villegas Zomba was shot four times: one for each goal scored. He would never play again.

CHAPTER EIGHT

PRISONERS ON THE TERRACES

1970–1980
Football in the Shadow of Death

When the Argentinian player runs he doesn't think, and when he thinks he doesn't run.

—César Luis Menotti (1974)

How can you play soccer a thousand meters from a torture centre?

—Johan Cruyff (1978)

Not a leaf stirs in Chile without me moving it.

—Augusto Pinochet (1981)

I t is a paradox that Latin America's darkest decade, politically, opened with a sporting display of dazzling luminosity. In the Brazilian eleven (Félix, Carlos Alberto, Brito, Wilson Piazza, Everaldo, Clodoaldo, Gérson, Jairzinho, Tostão, Pelé and Rivelino) that lined up against Italy for the World Cup Final on June 21, 1970, the "beautiful game" had found its embodiment. Even if this team was arguably not the best side the continent had ever produced—for some, more consummate football had been played on the River Plate in the 1930s and 1940s—the fact that its glorious football was played in front of a global television audience, for the first time in living color, helped enshrine its position as the most celebrated team in history. Brazil's play was distinguished not only by her technique and skill, but also by a certain swagger. This was football as entertainment. In the

New Yorker, the Scottish poet and Hispanist Alastair Reid wrote, "The Brazilians are miserable in defeat—I remembered how crushed they had looked in England—but they are jubilant and jaunty when a game goes their way, and their play becomes nothing short of celebration."[1]

Before the World Cup, Brazil had had her detractors. There were those who, having witnessed the South Americans' 1968 European tour, believed a rigid adherence to a 4-2-4 formation—without the specialists in midfield or strength going forward—would be her undoing. Defeats in July and October 1968 to Mexico, both by a 2–1 margin, did little to assuage the critics. Losing at the Maracanã had been Brazil's second home defeat in twelve years. Moreover, predictions of a defensive tournament, based on the region's preoccupation with *anti-fútbol* of the previous decade, would be proved wrong. Said an astute Brazilian commentator, "Zagallo was the one who showed the world 4-3-3, who made it clear to all of us that a footballer must have two shirts—a defender's and an attacker's."[2]

The final Brazilian goal, for which the tournament would be remembered, summed up the ease with which the South Americans had taken the game away from the Europeans. Uncharacteristically, Clodoaldo dribbled past four Italian players before pushing the ball on to Rivelino, who sent a long pass to Jairzinho. The Botafogo winger then found Pelé in front of goal. Ever nonchalant in his precision, Pelé rolled the ball into the path of the oncoming Carlos Alberto, who, seeming to have harnessed a tailwind, drilled the ball past the hapless Italian goalkeeper, Albertosi.

When Carlos Alberto lifted the Jules Rimet Trophy, it was the last act of a golden age of Latin American football. Not that anyone knew it at the time. The continent's teams would continue to enjoy success on the international stage: Brazil would be crowned world champions in 1994 and 2002, while Argentina would win the trophy she had always regarded as rightfully hers in 1978 and 1986. And yet, an intrinsic part of the continental game would be missing. Glimpses of former glories would resurface—especially Brazil's performance at the 1982 World Cup—but somehow the assurance of the prewar game had gone. For Brazil, whose reputation had come to rest on playing the game for fun, winning would become a suffocating priority, one that eclipsed *jogo bonito*.

The manner in which Brazil had won three World Cups in quick succession had made her loved. No matter how admirable her football, the River Plate would never enjoy such adulation. Argentinian victories, in spite of their brilliance, would always be viewed with suspicion by the rest of the world. Triumph was at times hollow. Perhaps the country's greatest flaw—and at times her greatest asset—was arrogance. As early as 1933, the writer Ezequiel Martínez Estrada recognized this: "Vastness is not greatness: it is merely the idea of greatness."[3] Displaying more humility might have gained the country greater affection, but this strategy remained unexplored. Off the pitch, the 1970s was a decade of untold cruelty, one in which Latin America had all but lost her way in the world. The game in Latin America may have always possessed a vicious streak, but the continent now developed a penchant for more violent pastimes. Nowhere was this more evident than in qualification for the 1970 World Cup.

Qualification for football's greatest tournament had become an inexact science. In 1970, all five World Cup champions may have made the finals, but the tournament would be poorer for the absence of Hungary, Argentina and Chile. The inclusion of El Salvador, Israel and Morocco—countries that, despite a certain amount of pluck, displayed precious little quality—failed to add luster to the competition. El Salvador had arrived in Mexico with a reputation, though not for her football.

Unlike the terrible birth pains suffered by her South American neighbors, independence for the Central American republics in the nineteenth century had for the most part been peaceful. Nevertheless, the creation of the United Provinces of Central America, which sought to unify Costa Rica, El Salvador, Guatemala, Honduras and Nicaragua, was doomed to failure. A shared history did not make for a common political union, and the United Provinces failed to stay united for long. The hegemony of Guatemala, the largest of the provinces, engendered bitterness among the other states, while the factionalism of liberals and conservatives across the region invariably led to bloodshed. Subsequent attempts at reunification tended to be short-lived and violent. As General Fidel Sánchez Hernández, El Salvador's president during the infamous "Football War," would say, "All wars in Central America are essentially Civil Wars."[4]

On a continent where land was otherwise abundant, El Salvador suffered from being trapped between Honduras, Guatemala and the Pacific Ocean. Space was at a premium. Property remained in the hands of the few. The disparity between rich and poor was evident for all to see. In the 1930s, the U.S. military attaché to El Salvador noted in his report that "about the first thing one observes when he goes to San Salvador is the number of expensive automobiles on the streets . . . There appears to be nothing between these high-priced cars and the ox cart with its bare-footed attendant. There is practically no middle class . . . A socialistic or communistic revolution in El Salvador may be delayed for several years, ten or even twenty, but when it comes it will be a bloody one."[5] In the late nineteenth century, poor Salvadorians began to cross into neighboring Honduras to find workable land.

By the 1960s, over 300,000 Salvadorians had settled in Honduras. Many of these immigrants, who made up 20 percent of the agrarian population, had settled illegally without citizenship or title. Not that the immigrants were all well received. In 1959, three hundred Salvadorian families returned home after being harassed by Hondurans. The border between both republics had become a demimonde where police and groups of vigilantes would illegally dispense "justice." Worse was to come; with the introduction of land reforms in the 1960s, the Honduran government found it more expedient to seize land from Salvadorian immigrants than rich landowners and international banana companies. By the end of the decade, only those born in Honduras could hold title to land. If the language in which the new laws was couched was formal, their execution was not. The process of removal was given brutal impetus by the work of the clandestine governmental organization, the Mancha Brava. Sublieutenant Víctor Manuel Méndez y Reyes would later recall, "The victims of the 'mancha brava' suffered unbelievably when the mobs enraged by hate started to loot, torch and [commit] all manner of outrage, in an orgy of blood and abuse ordered by the foreigners of the United Fruit Company, so that all over the world it would be known that owing to a football match of two undeveloped people, in a half-savage state, they launched themselves into mutual destruction."[6] Even the radio broadcast the slogan "Honduran, grab a stick and kill a Salvadorian." When in 1969 the two countries faced each other in the semifinal round of World Cup qualification, it would be in a climate of overt animosity.

The first leg, played in Tegucigalpa, Honduras, was relatively uneventful, with the home side edging the game by a single goal to nil. The hosts had shown their guests the usual footballing courtesies by "celebrating" outside their hotel for much of the night before kickoff. The day of the match, sixty-three expelled Salvadorians arrived at the border, which did little to quell the tension. Across the border in El Salvador, an eighteen-year-old by the name of Amelia Bolanios, who had been left traumatized by the defeat, shot herself through the heart with her father's pistol. Her funeral became a national affair. The following week, the teams met in San Salvador. In spite of the political tensions, Honduran supporters traveled to the capital, though many would not leave their hotels. The El Salvadorian newspaper *El Mundo* published a doctored photograph of the visiting Honduran players with bones through their noses.

The usual courtesies were extended to the visiting squad: a racket was made outside the Hondurans' hotel, though this time the windows were pelted with firecrackers, eggs and dead rats. In the Estádio Nacional Flor Blanca, which was surrounded by soldiers, Salvadorians armed with water bombs filled with urine hunted Hondurans. The Honduran national anthem could not be heard over the jeers of the crowd. Moreover, the country's flag was burned and replaced by a rag, which was hoisted high above the stadium. El Salvador scored three goals without reply, prompting a playoff. The Honduran manager, Mario Griffin, who had seen the scale of the ferocity directed against his players and his nation, was not joking when he said, "We were terribly lucky to lose."[7]

The Honduran press employed hyperbole in place of any attempt at impartial reporting. Salvadorians were accused of assaulting Honduran women and serving the visiting supporters excrement-filled sandwiches. It was now impossible to play the deciding match in either country, and it would instead be hosted by Mexico City. Although Honduras took the game into extra time with a goal in the last minute, El Salvador went on to win 3–2. Nearly three weeks later the countries were engaged in the somewhat misnamed "Football War." On July 14, the Salvadorian air force violated Honduran airspace with a preemptive strike. El Salvador now sought to take the Honduran capital, Tegucigalpa, in seventy-two hours. In the event, the war only lasted one hundred hours, with both sides running low on ammunition. Moreover, the Salvadorians were desperately short of oil, having had their energy resources targeted. Not without difficulty, the Organization of American States (OAS) managed to broker a cease-fire, though sanctions were later imposed on El Salvador as the aggressor. President Fidel Sánchez Hernández asked the country, "How is it that a man can walk with safety on the moon and cannot do so, because of his nationality, on the prairies of Honduras?"[8] The touch paper had been lit decades before; football provided the excuse. The two countries would not play each other for another ten years.

"Mountains of My Peru, Peru of the World"

In José Carlos Mariátegui, Peru had produced one of the most influential Latin American intellectuals of the twentieth century. An autodidact who had traveled to Europe in the early 1920s, Mariátegui returned to his native Peru and founded the Socialist Party. In 1928, two years before his untimely death at thirty-five, he published the seminal *Siete ensayos de interpretación de la realidad peruana* (*Seven Interpretive Essays on Peruvian Reality*), which attempted to analyze the state of the Peruvian nation. Mariátegui argued that revolution in Peru would come from the peasantry rather than the industrial working class. He believed that the creole had impoverished Peruvian culture by his rejection of the indigenous and the dismissal of popular tradition. Mariátegui's idealized Peru was one in which the traditions of the Spanish, Indian and African could coexist. Three decades after his death, Mariátegui's idiosyncratic brand of Marxism continued to shape left-wing political thought across Central and Latin America, nowhere more so than in Cuba, where he influenced Fidel Castro and Che Guevara.

The 1968 coup d'état that put an end to Fernando Belaúnde Terry's presidency—which had failed to deal with the economic crisis while allowing U.S. petroleum interests into the country—would be a turning point in Peruvian history. Unlike the right-wing dictatorships that would bring many other countries on the continent to their knees in the following decade, the self-styled "Revolutionary Government of Armed Forces" ushered in a wave of socioeconomic reform. Neither communist nor capitalist, the dictatorship sought to bring social justice to a country that had hitherto remained the domain of its upper classes. On June 24, 1969, the country's new leader, General Juan Velasco Alvarado, a short man of working-class, *cholo* (mestizo) origin, gave a famous speech in which he outlined the Agrarian Reform Law: "Today, for the Day of the Indian, the Day of the Peasant, the Revolutionary Government honours them with the best of tributes by giving to the nation a law that will end forever the unjust social order that impoverished and oppressed the millions of landless peasants who have always been forced to work the land of others . . . To the men of the land, we can now say in the immortal and liberating voice of Túpac Amaru [Peru's eighteenth-century rebel leader]: 'Peasant: the Master will no longer feed off your poverty!'"[9] Other reforms would include the educational system and the selective nationalization of foreign-owned enterprises, though the government sought to incorporate ideas from the political spectrum both at home and abroad. The country's newly acquired pragmatism would prove an inspiration to her football; while the dictatorship would keep a close watch on that reflection of national identity, the national team.

. . .

If Argentinian football thought it could mete out violence without punishment, it was wrong. The Furies were on its tracks. The reckoning would take the form of two Andean republics, Peru and Bolivia.

In her first qualifier for the 1970 World Cup, Argentina traveled to La Paz to acclimatize to the altitude fifteen days early. Nevertheless the extra preparation made little or no difference. After the third goal, the Argentinians lost their composure and the traditional insults, punches and hacking ensued. Estudiantes's midfielder, Carlos Pachamé, punched Bolivia's Ramiro Blacut to the ground. As far as the Bolivians were concerned, Alf Ramsey had not been wrong in his assessment of the Argentinians. General Onganía, whose own evaporating authority had left him a broken man, warned the squad to conduct themselves with more decorum. Two months before, he had sent in the troops to quash student and worker riots—which had started out as labor strikes—in Córdoba. His attempts at modernizing the country's economy had met with resistance. The Cordobazo, as the riots would become known, only highlighted the impotence of

Onganía's fading regime. His presidency would only last another year, hastened to its end by the nascent guerrilla movement Los Montoneros.

Peru would not fare any better at high altitude, losing 2–1 in La Paz. Nevertheless, the Peruvians managed three goals without reply at home, improving on Argentina's single-goal defeat of the Bolivians in Buenos Aires. After the match, while waiting at a set of traffic lights, the Bolivian bus came under attack from Argentinian fans. By the final round of qualifying, only a win would suffice for the Argentinians against Peru. In the cauldronlike atmosphere of Boca Juniors' La Bombonera, Peru caused one of the greatest upsets in the history of the Latin American game. The fleet-footed Sport Boys striker Oswaldo "Cachito" Ramírez opened the scoring, only for Albrecht to equalize from the penalty spot. Two minutes later Ramírez intercepted an Argentinian pass on the halfway line and made for goal. A deft chip left Cejas, the Argentinian goalkeeper, stranded. With Peru 2–1 up, Alberto Rendo equalized by dribbling past five Peruvians, hitting the post, only for the ball to fall auspiciously for him to score. It was, however, too late. For the first time Argentina had failed to qualify for the World Cup. Not that her record at this tournament was in any way illustrious: in nearly forty years, Argentina had only once made it past the quarterfinals. The enraged Argentinian fans hurled objects at the Peruvian players.

Osvaldo Ardizzone was scathing in *El Gráfico* about the amount of time the Argentine players had spent together before the match: "There is no team just because the majority of the best Argentinian players have been brought together and nothing more. With four [team] talks, three kick-abouts and a couple of essays on the offside rule, you can't win anything."[10] The English, who had assumed a position of energetic prejudice where Argentina was concerned, enjoyed the country's comeuppance: "It's over . . . for Argentina. The country for whom brutality has always gone hand-in-hand with brilliant tactical football, failed by one point to scrape a play-off in their qualifying group."[11] Roberto Perfumo, Racing's stalwart defender, was more reflective: "The Argentinian player had lost all joy in playing football. Moreover, those who join the national team know their fate to be only one thing: to be made a fool of."[12]

Peru would play some of her best football under the Brazilian Didi, who had won the World Cup in 1958 and 1962. After coaching Lima's Sporting Cristal to the 1968 championship, Didi had been offered the job as national coach and employed a 4-2-4 formation, which had the Peruvians play free-flowing football. Not that this was the first time a foreigner had made a difference to the Peruvian game. Ten years before, the Hungarian György [Jorge] Orth had coached Peru to a 4–1 thrashing of England in Lima. England had been forewarned that the left-winger Juan Seminario might prove problematic, though this advice availed little; nor did it reckon with the strength of the rest of the team. Seminario, who would later play for Barcelona, toyed with the English, scoring a hat trick and hitting the post. This kind of triumph was difficult to repeat, and the bad results that followed Peru's historic win did not endear Orth to the press, even though the national side had been weakened by many of the country's stars moving abroad. (The inability of the domestic Peruvian game to retain its best players would continue to hamper it for years to come.) In order to appease Lima's journalists, he was forced to select a team of which they might approve, picking players they had been clamoring for him to call up. But even this was not enough. A 5–2 defeat to archrival Chile, whom Orth had coached at the 1930 World Cup, paved the way for the Hungarian's resignation. Orth would leave Lima for Portugal to manage FC Porto a disillusioned and embittered man. By 1962, he was dead.

The 2–2 draw against Argentina proved one of the greatest moments in Peru's sporting history. "La Blanquirroja" (The White and Red) had not played in a World Cup final since the inaugural tournament. Brian Glanville, the doyen of English football journalists, wrote that "[Peru] has let new light and hope into the darkening world of professional football. At a moment when negativity seems paramount, violence condoned and encouraged, along come Peru and, against every expectation, qualify for Mexico by playing *attacking* football."[13] Having seen the Argentinian game at close quarters, the Englishman felt the elimination of Argentina "a cause for celebration."

Peru's revolutionary government had engendered a newfound sense of nationalist pride. The regime did not adhere to the traditional authoritarianism of other Latin American regimes, but had found its own distinctly "Peruvian" path. General Velasco saw the national team as a potential means of furthering his political agenda. Ahead of the qualifying rounds, he had stated, "We need goals, many goals, and real triumphs."[14] Before Peru's 3–0 win over Bolivia, Velasco took to the field to welcome both teams and was showered with applause by the spectators. As had been the case in Argentina and Brazil, politics had tethered itself to the country's favorite sport. After qualifying for the World Cup, Velasco articulated what this had meant for the country: "From the capital to the borders, Peru is pulsating. We are now making a real impact; a noble and sovereign Peru, everything is possible, and these eleven Peruvian hearts have obtained a triumph outside our borders and *we will continue getting them*."[15] Velasco had demanded that Peru rid herself of the tag of moral champions and underachievers. Peru now had aspirations to win the World Cup. And yet the country failed to recognize that her draw against Argentina was just a one-off, a moral victory at best.

On May 31, 1970, two days before Peru's opening match in the tournament against Bulgaria, the country suffered her greatest natural disaster. An earthquake registering 7.9 on the Richter scale devastated the Ancash region, taking 70,000 lives and leaving over 500,000 homeless. Although the tremors were felt as far away as Lima, for certain Limeños (inhabitants of Lima) it may as well have taken place in another country. The Peruvian social historian Carlos Aguirre found that for all the country's newfound nationalism, there existed a lack of integration between the capital and the provinces. In spite of the earthquake, football fever still gripped Lima.

Nevertheless, the tragedy unsettled the Peruvian squad. Bulgaria raced into a two-goal lead before Peru managed to score three in the second half to win the match. Hugo "El Cholo" Sotil, a brilliant dribbler and exquisite passer of the ball, galvanized Peru's resurgence. "El Cholo" (The Mestizo), with his Indian background, epitomized the new Peru. Victory against Morocco, which had unnerved the usually steadfast West Germans by taking the lead against them in their match before eventually succumbing to a late Müller winner, gave Peru the chance to top her group. Nevertheless, three German goals before halftime against a solitary strike from Cubillas sent Peru into the quarterfinals as group runner-up. Didi was left with the unwelcome prospect of facing the country of his birth.

In the prizefight of the opening rounds, Brazil had beaten the reigning world champions. By no means as talented as Brazil, England had proved to be masters of endurance in the searing heat of Guadalajara, holding their gifted opponents at bay until Pelé's exquisite layoff allowed Jairzinho to seal the match. The brilliance of England's goalkeeper, Gordon Banks, though, would be the enduring memory of this epic confrontation. England, however, had not been made to feel welcome in Mexico. Local fans booed the visitors and threw bottle tops at their first practice session. Moreover, Uruguay, still smarting from what the country perceived as the injustice of 1966, continued to hold on to its belief that the World Cup had been fixed and thus the world champions were mere "imposters." *The Times* of London summed up the anti-British sentiment: "The Uruguayans regard [Sir Stanley] Rous as a European enemy of Latin America."[16]

Peru was no match for a resplendent Brazil. The 4–2 score line flattered the Peruvians, whose attacking vivacity could not make up for defensive frailties. Defeat was no disgrace, but unlike the euphoria that had followed the draw against Argentina, the reception for the returning Peruvians was indifferent. At Lima's Jorge Chávez Airport, certain players now had their suitcases confiscated for being overweight. The politicians had begun to lose interest in the game that had, albeit briefly, served them so well.

. . .

Unsurprisingly, Brazil was another country where football could be successfully exploited for political ends. The 1964 coup d'état that had ousted the left-wing reformist João Goulart ushered in a succession of military dictators: Brazil would not return to democracy for another twenty-one years. In 1969, Emílio Médici, a conservative general from Rio Grande do Sul, ascended to the presidency. His regime would become infamous not only for its repression but also for its manipulation of popular culture. The propaganda machine Assessoria Especial de Relações Públicas (AERP, Special Assessor of Public Relations) was especially skilled at promoting the authoritarian government as the driving force behind the upturn in the economy. Television was utilized to push the message to the millions, who in turn received generous terms for the purchase of new sets. According to the historian Thomas Skidmore, "One of AERP's most effective techniques . . . was to link soccer, popular music, President Médici, and Brazilian progress."[17] Médici also nurtured a reputation as the country's number one football fan. Unlike Perón, whose attitude to the game was ambivalent at best, Médici genuinely loved football. He even took to watching Flamengo from the terraces, and had Dario, his favorite player, transferred to the club. With Brazil hoping to secure her third World Cup, it was more than could be hoped for to expect that the president would be able to resist interfering in the affairs of the national coach, João Saldanha.

Médici and Saldanha possessed nothing in common politically—the latter had been a member of the PCB (Brazilian Communist Party)—though both were *gaúchos*, hailing from Brazil's southernmost state, Rio Grande do Sul. Saldanha had played for Rio-based

Botafogo before coaching them to the state title in his first year as manager. He believed that the temperate year-round climate, competitiveness attained at an early age, Afro-Brazilian ethnicity and the passion of the supporters came together to produce a national style. As an outspoken journalist and television commentator, Saldanha was unlikely to tow any party line. Moreover, the fact that he had been a journalist, something that he hoped would appease the fellow members of his profession, was now quickly forgotten. Paulo Machado de Carvalho, a media businessman who had been appointed the head of the national team by João Havelange in 1958, thought the appointment the most bizarre choice. He even used his radio station to say so, though Saldanha went on television at the same time to say that he would now be choosing the squad.

Saldanha, according to Pelé, was an entertaining character. Nevertheless, his "plain-speaking, hard-man approach . . . started to be a problem. He couldn't take criticism and the relationship between him and his former colleagues in the press deteriorated . . . One fight he did have, and was bound to lose, was with João Havelange. When he was removed from the job as coach, he told the press the team was in trouble."[18] Saldanha had diagnosed Pelé with shortsightedness, which would keep him off the team, while Gerson was accused of being psychologically unstable. The high-strung Saldanha's moniker, "João Sem Medo" (Fearless João), said it all. When criticized by Yustrich, an ex-goalkeeper and Flamengo's coach, Saldanha went to the club's training ground, brandishing a pistol. (Yustrich had coached the national team for one match.)

In early 1970, Saldanha's Brazil may have defeated Argentina on the way to securing qualification, but that was not enough for his critics. It was, finally, an off-the-cuff remark—said more in jest than with any intention to provoke—that led to the end of the manager's international career. When it was suggested that the president might like to see Dario on the team, he responded with the infamous line "I don't choose the president's ministry, and he can't choose my front line."[19] Not that Médici's selection of Dario was an idiosyncratic choice: many Brazilians had wanted his inclusion. In the event, Saldanha did not go quietly. "I am not an ice cube to be dissolved," he said. "If you are firing me you had better say so. Don't hide behind words."[20] Saldanha was fortunate to lose only his post; he would later criticize Médici as the worst murderer in the country's history. The Brazilian squad was now delivered into the safe, and conservative, hands of Mário Zagallo.

The World Cup was played in the searing heat of the Mexican midday sun to allow for European television scheduling. The temperatures favored the four Latin American teams (Brazil, Uruguay, Peru and Mexico), adept as they were at playing at a slower tempo, and they all reached the quarterfinals. Against Uruguay in the semifinals, Pelé had not forgotten the promise he had made his father: that he would deliver the World Cup. Though he had first secured the world championship twelve years earlier, the ghosts of Maracanã still lingered. The Uruguayans had made his father, Dondinho, cry, and Pelé would exact his revenge. He would later write, "Even if we ended up losing the World Cup, what mattered most was that we beat Uruguay."[21] This time, unlike 1950, had Uruguay won, it would have been a travesty. The Uruguayans played defensively and with pronounced aggression. Uruguay's players knew their only chance was to rely on their knowledge that the technically gifted Brazilians were easier to dominate physically than the Argentinians, fellow skilled practitioners of the sport's dark arts. Uruguay played, according to Pelé, "a game of brutal containment."[22]

And yet it was a moment of majesty that came to define the match, a flourish of play that showed up the pedestrian nature of the Uruguayans. Tostão played a divinely weighted diagonal pass into the path of an oncoming Pelé, who deliberately failed to touch the ball and in so doing tricked the Uruguayan goalkeeper, Mazurkiewicz, into coming out of the penalty area. Pelé glided past Mazurkiewicz and ran to the ball on the Uruguayan's left side. The fact that an off-balance Pelé missed the chance to score seemed irrelevant. The Brazilians were playing football that felt as if it had been set to music. Pelé would later say, "We were a better team than the Uruguayans, just as we had been in 1950; the difference now was that, twenty years on, it was the better team that won."[23]

Victory against a disappointing Italy would secure the World Cup for the third time in twelve years. Said one unbiased British journalist of the final, "a velvet performance against cynical spoilers."[24] But then Italy had played her football in the quarterfinals against the hosts and the semifinals against the West Germans. The team managed eight goals in two matches compared with the paltry return of a single goal after three group-stage games (and it still won the group). If Italy thought she could soak up the pressure while allowing the Brazilians to play their game, she was mistaken. Had the Italians taken the game to Brazil, the South Americans might have panicked. In the event, Pelé scored the opening goal with a powerful header. It was as important as any he had scored, and in many ways as symbolic as the penalty kick against Vasco da Gama at Maracanã the previous year for his thousandth goal. A Brazilian mistake allowed Italy back into the game shortly before halftime, but two goals in five minutes in the second half put the match beyond the Europeans. The final goal, when it mattered least, was extravagance on the part of Brazil. Even the Argentinians must have been impressed.

For President Médici's government, not winning a tournament broadcast to the world was unthinkable. The *Jornal do Brasil* asserted that "Brazil's victory with the ball compares with the conquest of the moon by the Americans." The country would no longer be recognized just for her Carnival. *O Estado de São Paulo* pointed out the obvious: "We are a country of football, which is surely an improvement."[25] Médici was quick to make the victory his own: "I identify the success of our [national team] with . . . intelligence and bravery, perseverance and serenity in our technical ability, in physical preparation and moral being. Above all, our players won because they know how to . . . play for the collective good."[26] When he lifted the trophy with both hands, it was as if he had won it himself. Brazil had found its place in the world. Slogans, which linked the country's footballing prowess with its economic prosperity, began to be touted: "Brasil Potência" (Brazil Power), *Brasil: o gigante adormecido acordando* (Brazil: the sleeping giant awakens), *Ninguém segura este país* (No one can hold back this country) and *Brasil: ame-o ou deixe-o* (Brazil: love it or leave it).[27]

. . .

Success with Peru took Didi to Argentina. The master of the dead ball, of whom Nelson Rodrigues wrote that he had the dignity of a Paul Robeson or an Ethiopian prince, would manage Di Stéfano's former club, River Plate. His time at Real Madrid had been an unhappy experience for Didi, not helped by the Argentinians' animus toward him. Didi had been ignored on and off the pitch, and even stated that he had been pushed away when about to take a free kick. He was not a player to "sweat his shirt" or tackle, which failed to endear him to the Madridistas. Di Stéfano felt that the Brazilian did not fit in, though the latter's fame may have not helped Didi's cause with the cantankerous Argentinian.

At River Plate, Didi sought to restore *la nuestra* to the Argentinian game. In 1971, the AFA (Argentine Football Association) introduced goal difference as a means of distinguishing between sides that had reached the same point total. As far as Didi was concerned, the equation was a simple (and Brazilian) one: if the other team scored goals, his team had to score more. He wanted players who were happy and wanted to play. While coaching Peru, the Brazilian had threatened to resign because of abusive language from one of his players. But while Didi attempted, with some success, to impart the *jogo bonito* to his players at River Plate, other clubs continued to play a darker game.

The Copa Libertadores continued to bring out the worst

characteristics in South American football, which seemed to have forgotten the opprobrium heaped on it in the aftermath of the infamous 1969 Intercontinental Cup match between Milan and Estudiantes. In 1971, Boca Juniors found itself in the same group as Rosario Central, whom it had defeated the year before to clinch the Campeonato Nacional, together with Lima's Universitario and Sporting Cristal. With Boca's match against Sporting Cristal finely balanced at 2–2, nothing could have prepared the Uruguayan referee for what would ensue. Frustrated by having surrendered its two–nil advantage, Boca screamed for a penalty in the dying minute of the game when Boca's Roberto Rogel went to ground in Cristal's area. The referee remained unmoved. In the ensuing passage of play, the captain of Boca, Rubén Suñé knocked a Peruvian player to the ground. The game now turned into the "Stalingrad of football." Suñé attacked the Cristal defender Gallardo with a corner flag, only for the Peruvian to defend himself by employing a flying kick to the Argentinian's head. This did not stop the pugilistic Suñé, who would need seven stitches after the police eventually managed to bring him under control. Cristal's Campos had his nose broken as he lay on the ground, while Mellán was kicked in the face and had to be stretchered off with a fractured skull. De la Torre managed to take on two or three Argentinians at once. Tragically his mother died of a heart attack while watching her son on television. The only three players not to be sent off were both goalkeepers and Boca's Meléndez.

Alberto J. Armando, president of Boca Juniors, was incensed. He maintained that he would not protect the guilty, and felt shame in being an Argentinian. The federal police sentenced those arrested to thirty days in jail, a sanction that was never imposed. Boca's remaining fixtures remained unplayed, registered as goalless losses. Teófilo Salinas, the Peruvian president of CONMEBOL, was unimpressed: "If Argentina cannot, or will not, put their own house in order, the South American Federation will be compelled to recommend that the 1978 World Cup be transferred to a country of greater integrity.

Argentina should realise that the European members of FIFA already regard this venue for the finals with the greatest misgivings."[28] Ever prone to retaliation when it believed itself slighted, the Argentinian press insulted the Peruvians as only it knew how. "Peru lives from football, famine and ignorance. The Peruvian fans are savages and the aggression is motivated by multiple inferiority complexes." They could have been referring to themselves.

The following year nothing had changed: Argentinian football remained in a parlous state both on and off the pitch. After one particular match, a Colón de Santa Fe fan was lynched by opposing supporters. European commentators, who had disapproved of the country's uncompromising approach to the game, needed little encouragement in their criticism. Brian Glanville, the master of English football writing, began to call Argentina's ability to host the 1978 World Cup into question (a theme to which he would return with frequency). "Things, in Buenos Aires and Argentinian football at large, seem to be as bad as they have been for a long time . . . the violence of the Buenos Aires crowds was a byword; one was forever seeing photographs of steel helmeted police shooting tear gas into impassioned crowds. If the World Cup were to be played there this year, can you imagine what would happen?"

.   .   .

On the other side of the Río de la Plata, the situation was no better. By the early 1970s, the Uruguayan political system, unable to cope with the country's economic decline, suffered exhaustion. The era of *las vacas gordas* (the fat cows), which had been artificially prolonged by the economic boom from the Korean War, was now a memory. In the words of the historian José de Torres Wilson, "Uruguay, a country without problems, suddenly becomes a problematic country." Economic comfort had made the country lazy. The Uruguayan caricaturist "Menchi" Sábat, who moved to Buenos Aires in the mid-1960s, could see clearly across the River Plate: "Our provincialism was backed up by our football—a proof of greatness that had no relation with reality . . . And we thought: If we are world champions in football, then we must be world champions in everything."[29] The great Uruguayan novelist Juan Carlos Onetti had realized this in the late 1930s. In his first novel, *El pozo* (*The Pit*), he had his protagonist ask of the country: "What can you do in this country? Nothing, not even deceive yourself . . . And here? Behind us there is nothing. One gaucho, two gauchos, thirty-three gauchos."[30] Obsession with the country's lack of history had allowed football to fill the void. The game had given Uruguay meaning, but it couldn't solve all its problems. With rampant inflation, high unemployment and expanding foreign debt, Uruguay's sense of entitlement evaporated. The coup d'etat of 1973 was essentially an extension of the authoritarian civilian presidency of Jorge Pacheco. The rise of left-wing protest and terrorist cells would be quashed with a harshness unprecedented even in a region where human rights had been historically overlooked. Between 1973 and 1984, 10 percent of Uruguay's three million inhabitants would be incarcerated.

Fidel Castro had always believed that Uruguay, given her stability, was the one Latin American republic where violent revolution was improbable. The Tupamaros, or the Movement for National Liberation (MLN), though no strangers to acts of violence, were more concerned with staging stunts that would capture the public's imagination and embarrass and shame the establishment. The 1969 Copa Libertadores had produced an all-Uruguayan semifinal of Nacional and Peñarol. Nacional won 2–1 on aggregate, which pitted the club against the infamous gamesmanship of Estudiantes in the final. While the first leg of the final was being played at the Estádio Centenario, the guerrillas hijacked Radio Sarandí and interrupted the football commentary of the famous Carlos Solé. A five-minute tape was now broadcast to the country: "Uruguayans, today a worthless government restricts and deprives you. Do not lose hope. There has always been injustice in this country, but we have never seen the like of what has happened during this past year."[31] Having been warned that the radio station was mined with explosives, the police had to destroy a pylon in order to stop the tape. Nacional lost by one goal to nil, and the club would fare no better in La Plata, losing by two goals. In the meantime, the Tupamaros had sent a letter of apology for interrupting the commentary.

In August 1970, two months after the end of the World Cup, the dead body of a CIA operative was found in a stolen car in Montevideo. Dan Mitrione, whose cover was working for the Agency of International Development (AID), had been shot four times; there were no signs of torture. The Tupamaros,* usually so politically erudite in their guerrilla tactics, had crossed a line from which they would not return.

Uruguayan football's fortunes began to mirror the country's ailing economy. Attacks on referees, unpaid wages and low attendance figures became staples of the season. Such was the general air of financial instability that Nacional and Peñarol had to embark on that redeemer of Latin American football: the foreign tour. Earlier in the century, identity had been sought abroad; now all they sought was just money. The desperation for gate receipts was such that the tours were undertaken midseason. Not that they were financially successful. The politics of failure had now soaked into all aspects of Uruguayan life and the country was fast falling to her knees.

After the team had won three Copa Libertadores in succession, Estudiantes's brutal run finally came to an end in 1971. As expected, the Argentinians did not relinquish the continent's most prestigious trophy without a fight. The final was a repeat of 1969. The teams would be evenly matched both in ability and temperament. Estudiantes may have been universally loathed for employing *anti-fútbol*,

---

* The movement had been conceived by Raúl Sendic, a Marxist lawyer who had sought to support the country's sugarcane workers.

but Nacional was wasn't averse to its own brand of violent games-manship. La Plata hosted the first leg, in which Estudiantes played such a good game that Nacional's president accused the players of having taken drugs. Nacional won the playoff in Lima 2–0 to secure its first trophy.

Nacional expected to meet the European Cup winners, Ajax, in the non-FIFA-recognized Intercontinental Cup at the beginning of the following year. Ever wary of the physical side of the Latin American game, the Dutch declined to take part. The Uruguayans, who were now terrified of losing potential revenue for the two-legged affair, looked to the beaten finalists, Panathinaikos, to provide the opposition. The *rioplatense* reputation for violent conduct was not enhanced when Julio Morales broke the leg of Yiannis Tomaras, and both players had to leave the pitch. The great Puskás, who was now managing the Athenian club, was able to maintain his composure: "It may be rough but we go to South America because it is part of our soccer education. We did not like much of what went on today, but there is no point in putting up an umbrella after the rain has fallen."[32]

It was, however, to remain Argentina's decade, with a brilliant Independiente that won the Pan-American title four years in succession between 1972 and 1975. (No other team has managed the *tetra-campeonato*.) When in September 1972, against its better judgment, Ajax traveled to Argentina to play Independiente, the match, which the Romanian-born manager Ştefan Kovács likened to war, was a variation on the usual violent theme. Johan Cruyff scored the first goal after six minutes, but he was kicked off the pitch after twenty-five. At halftime, the Dutch threatened to walk off the pitch if another professional foul was committed. Having seen Cruyff off, the Argentinians felt emboldened to attack and equalized through Sá eight minutes before time. In the return leg, Independiente was soundly beaten 3–0. The Avellaneda club had first won the Copa Libertadores in 1964 and 1965 under the guidance of the hardwork-ing Manuel Giúdice, who had turned out for River Plate in the

1940s. Not the most flamboyant of sides, Independiente showed that an intelligent approach to the game could overcome skill. By the 1970s, the club had consolidated a strong back line and midfield. If any team came close to playing an Argentinian version of "total football" it was "El Rey de Copas" (The King of Cups).

The Copa Libertadores may have become the leading club competition on the continent, but its expanded structure was not welcomed by all, including the Brazilians. Ignacio Klein, president of Bogotá's Millonarios, complained when his club had to play Portuguesa and Valencia in neighboring Venezuela. "There is no proper football association in Venezuela . . . and as a result it's complete chaos. In one of the matches the referee and one of our players were threatened with firearms . . . Four of the players we faced were not registered with the professional board nor with the South American federation." Millonarios may have lost and drawn in the neighboring republic, but a lack of respect may have been the cause of the outburst. There had been no one to meet the squad at the airport, and the accommodations had been less than acceptable.

The Ragamuffin War: Part I

Throughout the sixties and early seventies, successive Latin American governments actively tried to present football as a unifying force, one that would heal their factious, torn societies. It was a pretense that would be savagely exposed. Since 1964, the Brazilian military had worked to accelerate the national integration that had started in the 1930s through political and economic centralization. Television had helped with the process of instilling cultural unity, so too had the country's triumph at the 1970 World Cup. But in 1972, a "friendly" took place at Internacional's Estádio Beira-Rio in Porto Alegre that revealed just how prone Brazil was to superficial gestures of collective spirit.

Rio Grande do Sul, Brazil's southernmost state, had always been different from the rest of the country. Bordering Uruguay, it shared a similar topography and culture to its Spanish-speaking neighbor. In 1835, displeased with high taxes imposed by central government on its commodities in spite of the region's economic power, Rio Grande do Sul sought its independence. The ten-year war—known as the "Guerra dos Farrapos" (Ragamuffin War)—that ensued would end with the state's reintegration into the Brazilian empire and an amnesty for the *gaúcho* (inhabitants of Rio Grande do Sul) rebels. Nevertheless the separatist cause, which never wished to secede completely, simply to retain a certain degree of autonomy, would remain strong in the *gaúcho* mentality.

In 1972, Brazil celebrated her 150th anniversary of independence with the very sport that had made her famous. Conceived by the Confederação Brasileira de Desportos, the Taça Independência (Independence Cup or Mini Copa) brought together a disparate group of footballing nations. There was symmetry to the final, in which Brazil faced her former colonizer, Portugal. One hundred and fifty years before, on the banks of the Ipiranga, Dom Pedro had declared the nation's liberty from her Portuguese masters with the cry, *"Independência ou Morte!"* (Independence or Death!). In a close and uneasy match in July, Jairzinho's headed goal in the last minute proved the difference between the two sides. Zagallo thought that Brazil's victory displayed *garra* (tenacity) and persistence.[33] These were traits closely associated with Rio Grande do Sul, yet he had failed to choose a single *gaúcho* player for his tournament squad. The absence of Grêmio's Everaldo, who had acquitted himself in Mexico so well two years before and would die in an automobile accident two years later, was especially galling for the state. Brazilian football had always favored players from Rio and São Paulo, but this time the omission implied outright bias. In order that honor might be restored, the Federação Gaúcha de Futebol (Rio Grande do Sul Football Federation) organized a match between the national team and a combined *gaúcho* eleven, drawn from the state's club sides, which included an Argentinian, Chilean and a Uruguayan. Unfortunately, the match was not played in the spirit of cordiality that was intended. Zagallo openly criticized the ex-referee and journalist Aparício Viana e Silva, who had been invited to coach the *gaúcho* selection, before a ball had even been kicked. The match, which took place in front of 110,000 spectators, was played in a climate of hostility. The national anthem was booed, and local fans took to burning the national flag. Whenever the "Brazilians" had the ball, they were greeted with jeers and abuse; they responded by celebrating their goals by pulling on their shirts and kissing the badge in front of irate *rio-grandenses*. To the relief of the Seleção, the match ended 3–3. Conspiracy theories that the result had been fixed to spare the Seleçãos embarrassment would begin to circulate almost as soon as the final whistle was blown.

Caravans of Death

The 1974 World Cup was a disaster for the Latin American republics. Brazil may have come in fourth—losing 1–0 to Grzegorz Lato's Poland in that redundant match for third place—but she had failed to capture the imagination of the public in the way she had four years before. In the warm-up matches before the tournament, the Brazilians were accused of acting like scared sheep and playing without purpose. The preparations were not helped by the hope that Pelé might make a last-minute appearance and join the squad. For many, the April Fools' joke played by one radio station—that Pelé had changed his mind and would make himself available—was deemed to have been in bad taste. This desperation exposed the country's lack of belief in their ability to retain the trophy. And yet it was understandable. Twenty years had passed since the country last played a World Cup without Pelé in the squad, twenty years in which Brazil had won the title three times.

The CONMEBOL qualification rounds were an indication of the meager Latin American fare that might follow. Uruguay only managed to top her group on goal difference, after a 4–0 home win against Ecuador in the final match. With the Uruguayan Football Association (AUF) now in a state of penury, there was not enough money to bring back some of the foreign-based players. The government was now asked for a loan to help finance the national team. Such was the level of desperation that yet another moneymaking tour was organized. Argentina, on the other hand, was intent on not repeating the mistakes of her 1970 World Cup campaign.

By 1972, the rebel angel Omar Sívori, whose demonic dribbling had made him one of Argentina's greatest players, had grown up. He now took over the management of the national team from Juan José Pizzuti. One of the main obstacles to Argentinian qualification lay in La Paz, that footballing graveyard for the Atlantic republics. Faced with having to play at high altitude, the Argentinians conceived of an ingenious solution. With the qualifying matches being played in September 1973, the AFA would put together a second-string B squad that would acclimatize itself the month before. The players, which included the young Mario Kempes and Ricardo Bochini, were first sent 2,500 meters above sea level to Tilcara in the northern province of Jujuy, before playing friendlies in Peru and Bolivia. Nevertheless, the squad could have been forgiven for thinking that their very existence had slipped the minds of those in Buenos Aires. Kempes would later recall: "It was terrible. The AFA forgot about us and we had a seriously bad time. We were in a third-rate hotel and there was nothing to eat. We had two friendlies scheduled and in the end we played seven in exchange for some money. That's how we bought things in the supermarket . . . I returned home eight or nine kilos lighter."[34] The squad became known as "La Selección Fantasma" (The Phantom National Team). Sívori's first team dismantled Bolivia 4–0 in Buenos Aires; the Argentinians managed a narrow one–nil victory in La Paz.

Chile faced their own challenge when they were drawn against the Soviet Union in a two-legged playoff. It would not be FIFA's finest hour.

On the morning of September 11, 1973, Salvador Allende delivered a farewell speech to the people of Chile. "These are my last words, and I am certain that my sacrifice will not be in vain, I am certain that, at the very least, it will be a moral lesson that will punish felony, cowardice, and treason." Within hours, he would be dead, though whether it was suicide or assassination would be shrouded in controversy. Henry Kissinger had stated three years before, "I don't see why we need to stand by and watch a country go communist because of the irresponsibility of its own people." And a CIA cable of the same year demonstrated just what Washington had in mind: "It is firm and continuing policy that Allende be overthrown by a coup . . . We are to continue to generate maximum pressure toward this end utilizing every appropriate resource."[35] Allende's election to the presidency had been a close run. He had edged the former president, Jorge Alessandri, by 40,000 votes. While the country waited on congress to endorse Allende, General Roberto Viaux attempted to kidnap General René Schneider, the commander-in-chief of the army, and thereby provoke the army into a coup d'état. Schneider, ever the constitutionalist, was shot as he tried to defend himself. The country was scandalized; congress now confirmed Allende's election. The new president's "Chilean Road to Socialism," however, would be a dead end. The realities of governing the country would differ from the theory. When Fidel Castro paid an extended visit to the country in late 1971, housewives marched down the street banging pots and pans in protest against inflation and an ailing economy. By late 1972, fearing nationalization of the transportation industry and their livelihood, the country's truck drivers went on strike. This industrial action, which would garner the support of other disenfranchised groups in Chilean society, only exacerbated the country's economic troubles. The coup d'état that the United States had craved would be but a matter of time.

Fifteen days after the overthrow of Allende, the first leg of the match ended in a goalless draw in Moscow. The teams now had nearly two months to prepare for the return match. The Soviet Union, however, would never make it to Santiago. By mid-October, the Football Federation of the USSR requested that FIFA have the second leg of the playoff moved to a neutral venue. FIFA, in spite of having already voted in favor of playing the match in Santiago, sent a small delegation to investigate the situation. The report reached "the conclusion that, based on what [the delegates] saw and heard in Santiago, life is back to normal . . . the safety of the visiting delegation was guaranteed and there is no increase in danger to them."[36]

The delegation was mistaken. In the weeks after his accession to power, General Pinochet had unleashed the Caravana de la Muerte (Caravan of Death), a death squad that sought to impose a hard-line uniformity and encourage loyalty among the provincial garrisons. Under General Arellano Stark, the deputation flew the length of the country by helicopter, meting out summary executions to the fortunate and sadistic torture to the less so. Among the thousands who would lose their lives during Pinochet's reign, the brutality with which these seventy-five detainees were murdered stands out for its savage cruelty.

The Soviets made their position remain clear in a cable from early November: "Fascist upheaval overthrow legal government national unity now in Chile prevails atmosphere bloody terrorism and repressions . . . National stadium supposed be venue hold football match turned by military junta into concentration camp place of tortures and executions of Chilean patriots. At stands also stadium building are kept under arrest thousands innocent people among them many foreigners including Cuban trainers."[37] With the USSR Football Federation unwilling to change its stance, FIFA asked the Chilean federation whether another city might hold the match. The Chilean response refuted the "offensive and slanderous imputations of Soviet football which has disqualified itself morally."[38] The USSR Football

Federation remained resolute in its telegram to FIFA: "Match in Chile impossible."[39] FIFA finally managed to agree on Spain as a neutral venue, only for the USSR Federation to pull out a few days later. On November 21, 1973, Chile lined up without opposition. The players waved to the sparse crowd, and after a dozen touches, the ball was in the back of the net. The match only took thirty seconds.

Two months before, the Estádio Nacional had been turned into a detention camp for over six thousand prisoners. Music boomed across the stadium to deafen the cries of those prisoners who were being tortured or killed. Mock firing squads were set up, with prisoners receiving "last rites" before being bludgeoned. No communication was allowed between prisoners or with those families that waited outside the stadium. "Chile's new military leaders," wrote Ariel Dorfman, who had been Allende's cultural adviser, "finding themselves with an excess of political prisoners on their hands, hit upon what they must have considered an ingenious idea: Turn the National Stadium, our largest sports arena, into a gigantic concentration camp. Then, a few months later, after thousands of dissidents had been arrested and tortured, after hundreds had been interrogated and executed, the authorities scrubbed the floors and painted the benches, and reopened the coliseum to the public."[40] Not that the use of stadiums as concentration camps was a novel idea. The Paraguayans had employed them in the 1947 civil war.

By 1975, Santiago's Estádio Nacional was, for the most part, empty. According to one observer, "It is a rare occasion when more than 3,000 people show up, this in a stadium of 80,000 seats. In a recent B-League match, a world record was no doubt established when only seventeen fans bought tickets to watch twenty-two men on the field contest a game. Nobody had any money to do anything, except maybe feed themselves."[41]

Chile was one of the stronger Latin American teams. Nevertheless, the country seemed to have capitulated even before a ball had been kicked. Australia might provide an easy victory, but the two

German sides seemed insurmountable. The president of the Chilean federation, Francisco Fluxá, said, "It's a good job Germany isn't split into three parts or we'd still have to play them all." Against the eventual winners of the tournament, West Germany, Carlos Caszely became the first player in the history of the tournament to be sent off the pitch with a red card.

Pinochet's regime worked with ghoulish energy to stamp out any kind of dissent. One person who was difficult to silence was the Colo-Colo striker Carlos Caszely, who was as outspoken politically as he was audacious on the pitch. Caszely refused to wear shin pads because he thought they slowed him down, and was difficult to mark, being fleet of foot both on and off the ball. He had refused to be sold to Santos for $130,000 because Colo-Colo had not discussed the matter with him first. While Real Madrid had made overtures, Caszely ended up at Second Division Levante in Spain. Although he had professed in *El Clarín* not to want to leave the country, he would leave anyway. In a region where economic mismanagement and penury had become the norm, the opportunity of financial security proved attractive. Miguel Ángel Brindisi, Huracán's attacking midfielder, revealed: "The chance of world fame is the main reason why so many of our players go abroad."[42]

While many Chilean professional players were apolitical, Caszely had aligned himself with the left in the in the 1960s. He had been a keen supporter of the Unidad Popular (Popular Unity) Party, a coalition of left-wing parties head by Salvador Allende. He had also backed Gladys Marín, who would later become president of the Communist Party and the first person to file a lawsuit against Augusto Pinochet.

Before leaving for the World Cup in West Germany, the Chilean squad had been granted an audience with the president. Caszely famously failed to return Pinochet's greeting, ignoring his salutation. In 1985, the two met again and the now-famous, and oft-quoted, exchange ensued:

PINOCHET: You, always with your red tie. You're never separated
   from it.

CASZELY: So it is, Mr. President. I wear it close to my heart.

PINOCHET: (using his fingers like a pair of scissors) Here I would
   cut that red tie.

CASZELY (quick to respond) You may do it, but my heart will for
   ever remain red.

Three years after this encounter, the country prepared to vote to
extend Pinochet's presidency. Pinochet maintained that he would
need another eight-year term to rid Chile of Marxism. Victory for the
junta had seemed secure, in spite of the demonstrations, but the tide
was about to turn. The regime would underestimate the power of
television when it granted the opposition, La Concertación de Parti-
dos por el No (Cooperation of Parties for No), a number of fifteen-
minute television broadcasts. In one broadcast, an elderly woman
recounted having been kidnapped, interrogated and tortured after
the coup d'état, but never telling her family what had happened.
Caszely now entered the frame and said that he would also be voting
against the regime with a resounding no "because her sentiments are
my sentiments . . . because this beautiful woman is my mother."[43] By
October 1988, 54 percent of the registered population voted no to 43
percent who had voted yes. The general who, seven years before, had
stated that "not a leaf stirs in Chile without me moving it" was furious. He remained defiant, reminding everyone that in another pleb-
iscite the people had chosen Barabas over Christ.

   If Chile under Pinochet had sunk to a new low, then her football
was no better. The country that had pleaded to host the 1962 World
Cup now no longer wished to participate. Over ten clubs petitioned
the Federación de Fútbol de Chile to pull out of the tournament in
West Germany. Without their leading players, who would be called
up for the national selection, clubs feared financial ruin. After a
twelve-year hiatus, the Copa Chile was resurrected to increase gate

receipts. Not that the tournament provided a high standard of play. The last team to have won the cup was a Second Division club from the small town of Curicó in 1962. Only the year before, Luis Cruz Martínez had turned professional. A year later it would end its fairy-tale run by defeating Universidad Católica 2–1. With gate receipts dwindling, rumors began to circulate that Chilean football would revert to amateurism.

Chile's best player had already left the country before Pinochet's coup. Elías Figueroa was arguably the greatest footballer in the history of the Chilean game. Unlike the flashier republics, whose leading *cracks* sought glory by finding the net, Figueroa was dominant in his own area. Said Nelson Rodrigues, the Brazilian writer, of Don Elías: "Elegant like a count in black tie, dangerous like a Bengal tiger. [He] was the perfect defender."[44] Figueroa was less ornate in his opinion: "The area is my home. Only those I want enter there." Even as a young player, he was assured, playing with great technical ability and poise. After winning a number of trophies with Montevideo's Peñarol, he moved on to Internacional of Porto Alegre in southern Brazil. While playing for Internacional he was voted Futbolista del Año en Sudamérica (South American Footballer of the Year)—a prize conceived by the press in the least adept country, Venezuela.

An example of Don Elías's authority came in the 1978 World Cup qualification that had yet again pitted Chile against her archrival Peru. In the final match, the two republics met in Lima. Chile was a point better off than Peru and only needed a draw to send their team through. But two goals in the second half, the first by Barcelona's brilliant "El Cholo" Sotil, crushed their hopes. After the match the Chilean dressing room was disconsolate. When a Peruvian player was heard to shout *"¡Viva Chile mierda! ¡Viva Chile mierda!,"* Figueroa, outside, calmly got up and asked him: "Sorry, my friend, 'Viva Chile,' is that with or without a comma before the 'mierda' [shit]?" Intimidated by Don Elías's steely politeness, the Peruvian said that it was definitely with the comma. "Ah, I had thought so. Now you'd better go and celebrate on the other side," came the reply.[45]

Latin American Sturm Und Drang

The 1974 World Cup was a tournament for Uruguay to forget. It was yet more evidence of country's slow but sure fall from grace. Unrest in the camp, where a group of senior players were rumored to make the important decisions, showed on the pitch. The Dutch eased through her match against the combative Uruguayans, who were fortunate to have only one player sent off. The guilty party, Julio Montero Castillo, would pass this "gift" on to his son, Paolo Montero, who seemed to collect red cards as if they were badges of bravery. (The younger Montero would later hold the record of receiving the greatest number of red cards in the history of Serie A.) Pablo Forlán, a tall defender who played for São Paulo, should have been sent off for kicking Neeskens. After a one-all draw against Bulgaria, Uruguay was still in with a chance of progressing through to the next round. Faster than the languid Uruguayans, who sought to keep possession of the ball in midfield before attempting an attack, Sweden exploited the gaps in the Latin Americans' defense to score three goals in the second half. Uruguay had been snuffed out.

Argentina did manage to progress to the second round before reverting to dismal type. It had been very different the year before when the self-proclaimed "moral" champions of 1966 had beaten West Germany in style. After four minutes, River Plate's Jorge Luis Ghiso scored an extraordinary volley with the outside of his left boot. Ten minutes later the Argentinians doubled their count, before Brindisi added a penalty in the second half. Two late goals from West Germany failed to mask Argentinian supremacy. *Kicker*, the West German sports weekly, was unequivocal in its assessment of the

European champions: "A Massive Disgrace . . . This defeat ruined all our dreams."

So expectations of a fine performance were high when Vladislao "El Polaco" (The Pole) Cap, Argentina's new manager, sat down to watch Argentina's first match, against the country of his forebears. What spectators received was a primer in incompetence. Early on, the teenage Kempes was clear on goal, only to scuff his shot and send the ball rolling past the right-hand post. Soon after, two Argentinian mistakes in as many minutes gave Poland a two-goal advantage. Another goalkeeping error by Carnevali—who had earlier mishandled the ball only to have Lato pounce—put the match beyond the South Americans, whose two second-half goals were of no avail. Bad luck would dog the Argentinians, who should have won their next match against Italy. The one-all draw flattered Italy, who was saved by Perfumo's own goal. Although in their final game against Haiti, Argentina was not able to replicate Poland's 7–0 thrashing of the tiny island republic, their 4-1 victory was enough to see them through on goal difference. The Dutch, however, were waiting.

Any momentum Argentina might have gained was destroyed, in the most humiliating fashion. If Argentinian football needed reminding of what *la nuestra* could be, they would find it on that night in Gelsenkirchen. The Dutch toyed with the South Americans as the *rioplatenses* had done with the Europeans before the war. Had rain not affected the match, the 4–0 score line might have been turned into the country's greatest defeat. Not that the Argentinians had learned their lesson. Víctor Rodríguez, one of Cap's assistants, refused to believe what was plain for everyone to see. "The result is deceptive. I want the rematch," came the call. No one listened.

The rout was hardly suitable preparation for facing Brazil. After forty-four years of World Cup tournaments, Argentina finally played her greatest rival for the first time on the planet's biggest stage. Brazil would offer some respite by adhering to a South American tempo that Argentina could keep up with. But with the score tied at one-all,

Jairzinho scored early in the second half to put the Argentinians out of the tournament. The day after his country's team lost to her neighbor, the man who had shaped postwar Argentinian politics finally died. Juan Domingo Perón's third term in office had barely lasted a year. His legacy, however, would blight the country's politics into the twenty-first century. The country's final match of the tournament, against the German Democratic Republic, was not televised. Not that there was anything to miss in the meaningless one-all draw. In the aftermath of the World Cup, Menotti highlighted an Argentinian vice: "When the Argentinian player runs he doesn't think and when he thinks he doesn't run. I'm not interested in winning 1–0 with a goal from a free kick. I want us to win because we are capable of overcoming our rival footballistically."[46]

Argentina's performance had flattered Brazil. By eschewing the tight marking favored by the European teams, the Argentinians had allowed Brazil to play her natural game. Holland, however, would not extend the same courtesy to the reigning world champions. Expectation ahead of the match—especially given the technical ability of both teams—was high. Brazil had started the tournament slowly, drawing consecutive games without scoring for the first time in a World Cup. A three–nil victory against a poor Zaire team, which had been crushed 9–0 by Yugoslavia, sent Brazil into the second round on goal difference. But the prospect of facing the *carrossel holandês* (Dutch carousel) troubled Brazil's manager, Zagallo.

Zagallo had kept the services of fourteen players from the previous tournament, filling the rest of his squad with young players. Pelé had resisted the temptation to return to the national side. More significantly, he had resisted the government's repeated attempts to persuade him to play in West Germany. Looking back at the 1974 World Cup and the coercion he had to endure at the hands of the General Geisel regime, Pelé recalled, "They pressured me, they cajoled me, they did everything they could. But at that time, I had begun to become aware of the barbarities practiced by the dictatorship, the tortures, the people who disappeared. I learned that while we were winning championships many injustices had taken place, and I stayed firm; I didn't give in. I think it was my way of protesting . . . they made veiled threats that I'd better be careful with my income tax returns, these things. I ignored them."[47] But Pelé's obstinacy over this matter didn't preclude a more pragmatic personal assessment of the political situation: "During the period that the army was taking care of things, things weren't so bad. It wasn't what the people wanted, and there was a good deal of barbarity, but we made great advances . . . When the civilians got back into government, things got worse."[48]

Pelé's reluctance to play in the tournament contrasted sharply with the enthusiasm of another Brazilian legend to make his own dramatic return to the game. Garrincha, *o anjo das pernas tortas* (the angel with bent legs), in spite of his lack of fitness, had attempted another comeback, this time with Olaria, a small team from Rio. Nilson Santos wanted to hold back the passing of the years: "I don't want to see him playing now because I want to maintain the picture of the man who played with me for 10 years and was the best player I saw in the world."[49] In December 1973, a FIFA eleven, comprising mainly Argentinians and Uruguayans, played Garrincha's Brazil as a farewell gesture to this most idiosyncratic of players. Ten years later, he would be dead. He had given up on life: "I drink and you put me in hospital. I get out and I drink again and you put me in hospital again. Why do you want me to keep returning to this shitty life?"[50]

If the spectators were expecting a primer in the beautiful game, they would be disappointed. Both teams were guilty of aggressive physical play: their body checks, flying tackles and professional fouls marring the game. Ze Maria tripped and effectively rugby-tackled Cruyff to the ground, while Marinho Peres hit the tournament's marked man Neeskens in the face. Both Dutch players scored in the second half to put the game past the Brazilians. When Luis Pereira scythed down Neeskens six minutes from time, the cause was lost.

Pereira entered into a heated altercation with the Dutch fans as he left the pitch, an appropriate end to a bad-tempered tournament performance.

1978: *La Fiesta De Todos* (The Feast for Everybody)

In 1871, two decades after its author, Esteban Echeverría, had died in self-imposed exile, "El matadero" ("The Slaughterhouse") was first published in Argentina. Brutal and vicious, the short story drew a parallel between the slaughterhouse and Buenos Aires under the dictator Juan Manuel de Rosas. When an elegant, young opponent of Rosas is attacked and stripped—so that the butchers can rape him—blood spurts from his mouth and nose as he bursts with rage and then dies. By the twentieth century, bloodletting and violence had become part of the Argentinian psyche. V. S. Naipaul recognized this in his travels: the country's wealth, together with its ensuing greed, "had destroyed the idea of the pioneer, the idea of self-fulfilment coming through work; it ennobled instead the idea of sharpness, *la viveza criolla* [creole cunning]. It had encouraged the idea of blood and revolution, in unending sequence: just one more fresh start, the finding out and killing of just one more enemy, and the wealth of the country was going to cascade down."[51]

The 1976 coup d'état that ousted Perón's widow, Isabel Martínez de Perón ("Isabelita"), after her inept twenty-month reign was without fanfare. "On that first, deceptively peaceful, day of the military takeover," wrote the British journalist John Simpson, "several hundred lower-ranking union officials had been arrested and taken to vessels moored out in the River Plate."[52] They were all shot. The killing—which Isabelita had sanctioned by decree the year before, as a war against subversion—would not stop. Under the new junta, the Proceso de Reorganización Nacional (National Reorganization

Process) sought to eliminate subversion and further economic development. Congress was shut down, so too was the federal and provincial judiciary, while all political parties were suspended. The press was now silenced by a memo that stated: "As from today, 22/4/76, it is forbidden to inform, comment or make reference to subjects related to subversive incidents, the appearance of bodies and the death of subversive elements and/or of members of the armed and security forces in these incidents, unless they are reported by a responsible official source. This includes victims of kidnappings and missing persons."[53] Argentina had, along with Chile and Uruguay, become part of the "holy" trinity of dictatorships in the Cono Sur (Southern Cone). If state terrorism in Uruguay had been bad, in Chile it was worse, but for Argentina, her dictatorship would be the cruelest of the entire continent—a hideous lesson in repression.

On the anniversary of the coup in 1977, the Argentinian investigative journalist Rodolfo Walsh sent his *Carta abierta de un escritor a la Junta Militar* (*Open Letter from a Writer to the Military Junta*), in which he assembled an inventory of atrocity, to the local and international press. "Fifteen thousand missing, ten thousand prisoners, four thousand dead, tens of thousands in exile are the naked numbers of such terror . . . With ordinary prisons filled, you [the dictatorship] have created in the main garrisons of the country virtual concentration camps, where not one judge, lawyer, journalist, international observer can enter." The following day, Walsh was murdered in a hail of bullets. They had been waiting for him. The year before his daughter had shared a similar fate, though she had shot herself rather than be taken.

In his letter Walsh had stated that "at least 25 corpses floated on to Uruguayan beaches between March and October 1976."[54] These bodies had been thrown off a boat. The Río de la Plata and the forests of Tucumán had become dumping grounds for the disappeared. The air force and navy had now taken to drugging their prisoners and throwing them out of planes alive. When the bodies washed ashore, the official explanation was at times fanciful at best: that these were not *rioplatenses* but in fact Chinese—the faces of the dead, bloated by death and exposure, having taken on Asiatic features. The army preferred to bury its victims in unmarked graves.

The junta appointed General Jorge Videla as president, of whom Christopher Hitchens would later write, "I possess a picture of the encounter [interview in December 1977] that still makes me want to spew: there stands the killer and torturer and rape-profiteer, as if to illustrate some seminar on the banality of evil. Bony-thin and mediocre in appearance, with a scrubby moustache, he looks for all the world like a cretin impersonating a toothbrush."[55] Like Perón, Videla was a man not given to the charms of the beautiful game. Nevertheless, he had the imminent hosting of the World Cup with which to contend.

Even when awarded a long-term project, Argentina could not help but conceive it in the short term. The country had wanted to hold the World Cup since 1938. When Argentina was finally chosen in 1966, she had twelve years in which to prepare, but even after the 1974 World Cup, doubts remained as to whether the country might be able to host the competition. The joke that circulated among journalists was at the expense of the AFA. As one Argentinian official would say to another, "When we've shown the FIFA delegates the stadia and hotels, what do we do for the rest of the day?" Ever practical in such matters, Sir Stanley Rous thought Montevideo and Porto Alegre in southern Brazil might help provide their stadiums; otherwise Spain should be made the 1978 hosts.

The fears extended to the very state of the country and its finances. As early as 1972, João Havelange was driven to pronounce, "The only thing that can prevent the World Cup from being held in the Argentine in 1978 is the country's falling economy, which is continually being put in danger through internal disturbances."[56]

Under the presidencies of Perón and his widow, the hosting of the World Cup seemed an unnecessary luxury. Not only was the social fabric of the country disintegrating, the economy was out of control. By 1975, inflation had soared to 335 percent, and was being projected to reach 566.3 percent. With GNP in free fall, hosting an expensive international tournament was the last thing on the minds of the country's succession of ministers of finance. Moreover, if Argentina were unable to keep herself out of economic crisis, what chance would there be of keeping the international tournament within budget? At times, the country's most perceptive sports commentator, Dante Panzeri, seemed the sole voice of reason: "The 1978 World Cup should not take place for the same reasons that a guy who doesn't have enough cash to put petrol into a Ford T should not buy himself a 'Torino.' If he does it that's because he's stealing from somebody."[57] His untimely death in April 1976 would mean that he would not cover the tournament that would cost the Argentinian people so dear.

The president of CBD (Confederação Brasileira de Desportos), Admiral Heleno Nuñes believed "the change of government in the Argentine will perhaps be the best guarantee for the realization of the World Cup," and that the "Argentinian revolution will have such success as the Brazilian."[58] In order to expedite preparations, the government entity Ente Autárquico Mundial '78 (Autarkical 1978 World Cup Organization) was created in June 1976 under General Omar Actis. The following month, a decree was passed that made the tournament a matter of national interest. By August, Actis, who had played for River Plate's third string in the 1940s, had been assassinated. It was expedient to blame the guerrillas, though the order was rumored to have come from within the government. (The junta was given to internal wrangling.) New stadiums were built in Mar del Plata, Mendoza and Córdoba, while River's Estádio Monumental was modernized. Ten percent of the country's national budget, more than $700 million, was needed to host the tournament. The official figure was $521,494. The secretary of the treasury, Juan Alemann, would describe it as "the most visible and indefensible case of non-priority spending in Argentina today."

For Jorge Luis Borges, this national obsession with the game gave him the opportunity—not that one was ever needed—to be contrary. He took to quoting Kent's line from *King Lear*, "Nor tripped neither, you base football player." In conversation with Alastair Reid, he said, "I have written many stories about my military ancestors and about the knife-fighters of this city [Buenos Aires]. I still feel that, although killing was involved, there was a certain nobility about it, which I cannot find in men kicking a ball."[59]

Fearful of creating any sympathy for the military regime, Amnesty International had sought to educate rather than dissuade the press from covering the World Cup. Journalists were encouraged to be vigilant, not in case of violence, but as regards what the country might betray in a moment of weakness. The regime propagated a slogan that read, *Los argentinos somos derechos y humanos* (We Argentinians are honest and humane), a play on the phrase *derechos humanos* (human rights). From the welcoming banner at Ezeiza International Airport—where, awaiting Perón's arrival in June 1973, his left-wing supporters succumbed to sniper fire from rival Peronist factions—to stickers on cars and lapels.

Attitudes to the dictatorship, and its misdeeds, remained polarized even within the same national squad. The terrierlike German defender "Berti" Vogts concluded that "Argentina is a country in which order obtains. I did not see a single political prisoner." Sepp Maier, Vogts' teammate, wanted to show his solidarity for those mothers whose children had been disappeared, Las Madres de Plaza de Mayo (The Mothers of the Plaza de Mayo), by joining a demonstration. The threat of expulsion from the competition, however, proved a sufficient deterrent for the politically literate goalkeeper.

With the freedom of the press severely curtailed—and many journalists persecuted for merely working in the profession—the junta had been able to create a climate of collusion. *El Gráfico* asserted that

"for those on the outside, for all those insidious and malicious journalists who for months pursued a campaign of lies about Argentina,
this competition is showing the world the reality of our country and
its ability to do important things responsibly and well. As for those
on the inside, for the unbelievers whom we had in our own house, we
are certain that the World Cup has managed to shake them up, thrill
them, and make them proud."[60] The first issue after the World Cup
victory carried an interview with Argentina's leader, Videla. *El Gráfico*'s golden age of sports journalism had come to an end.

. . .

The fate of the country's football team had been put into the hands
of César Luis Menotti. Born in 1938, "El Flaco" (The Thin One) had
played his football for Rosario Central, Racing and Boca, before seeing out the rest of his career in the United States and Brazil. He had
been brought up in the golden age of the Argentinian game, and his
footballing philosophy reflected this. Tall, elegant, and addicted to
the cigarette, Menotti had stated his beliefs in *El Gráfico* in 1975, a
year after his appointment.

1. Talent and technical ability should predominate over physicality
    and power.
2. A dialectical articulation between bodily and mental speed was
    needed: he did not want players running without thinking or
    thinking without running.
3. A flexible system of zonal and man-to-man marking was the best
    defensive strategy.
4. Attacking with two wings and one center-forward was the best
    response to the system 4–4–2 imposed by the Brazilians and
    followed by so many teams.
5. A sense of belonging to a footballing tradition with great heroes
    was important for the players.[61]

But Menotti would not have it easy. Two years before the tournament, there were rumors that he might be dismissed, though the AFA did not have the money for his severance pay. Juan Carlos "Toto" Lorenzo, the national team's former manager, lurked in the shadows, adamant that Menotti's style of play would not succeed against the Europeans. El Flaco remained true to the spectacle of the game. It was not a case of just winning the World Cup, but winning it in the finer traditions of the Argentinian game. "My country's football needs total reorganization. If we could win the World Cup the way I would like us to, it would inspire others to reassess the way we play the game—our basic philosophy. Perhaps it would stop us placing such reliance on violence and cynicism, which are the tools of fear. Argentinian football possesses too much skill to need to be afraid."[62]

The length of the Argentinian season had not allowed Menotti enough time to develop a cohesive squad. At the international level, the Argentinian game had long suffered a lack of consistency not only in terms of results but also in personnel. The diminutive midfielder Osvaldo Ardiles would remember Menotti asking, "Why is it that hardly anyone plays thirty times for Argentina when Europe is full of footballers with fifty caps or more?"[63] This lack of stability was also evident at club level. When Ricardo "Ricky" Villa arrived at Tottenham Hotspur in the late 1970s, he could not believe that English players (in this case Steve Perryman) could be with one club for ten years. "In Argentina . . . this sort of extended stay with the same team is a notably rare occurrence. Virtually unthinkable. The only example that springs to mind is Ricardo Bochini, a marvellous player whom Diego Maradona cites as his idol. 'El Bocha' spent his entire career with Independiente . . . Staying at one club for a number of years is generally regarded as lacking prestige in a way. Boring almost."[64] Despite being one of the country's leading playmakers, "El Bocha" would not be chosen by Menotti. He would later maintain that had he played for Boca, he would have been twice as popular. Maradona, with whom he would later enjoy an uneasy relationship, would overshadow the later stages of his career.

. . .

The restoration of the Copa América in 1975, after an eight-year hiatus, had allowed Peru to secure her second continental championship. The importance of the Copa Libertadores had cast a shadow over this once-august competition. Not that certain republics sent their best players. Argentina had a young squad, which included Ardiles, Kempes, Luque and a nineteen-year-old Valdano, for the most part hailing from Rosario and Sante Fe. Brazil had opted for clubs from Belo Horizonte rather than the powerhouses of Rio and São Paulo. The highlight of the competition was Argentina's 11–0 thrashing of Venezuela in Rosario; seven players would find the net. For Peru, it would be beating Brazil 3–1 in Belo Horizonte in the semifinal. The final, against Colombia, would need an underwhelming playoff before thirty thousand Venezuelan spectators to separate the sides.

Peruvian football, however, continued to suffer from its perennial crisis of confidence. The World Cup would clearly demonstrate the two sides of the Peruvian game: the brilliant and the abject. Not that qualification for the tournament had augured well. The Peruvians were slow and seemed to play without any tactical judgment, yet still managed to top a group that comprised Chile and Ecuador. Peru, however, was now without a manager and a World Cup committee, the latter having resigned.

In a negation of responsibility, the Federación Peruana de Fútbol (Peruvian Football Federation) asked the First Division clubs to select a squad and a manager. The squad, in spite of the collegiate selection process, mainly comprised players from Alianza Lima and Sporting Cristal. The new manager, Marcos Calderón, who would die with the Alianza squad in the 1987 air crash, was optimistic. His critics pointed to his lack of international experience—and that of many of his players—as an indication of imminent failure. The stars in the squad were aging: Chumpitaz had slowed at thirty-four, and Cubillas and "El Cholo" Sotil looked ready for retirement. Peru's best player was the Argentinian-born Ramón "El Loco" Quiroga, a goalkeeper not known for his orthodox play. Moreover, a group that comprised Holland, Iran and Scotland would be difficult to navigate.

Even though this was her golden decade, few gave Peru any chance. In fact the Peruvians would be one of the better teams of the tournament. Scotland may have beaten Holland—exemplified by Gemmill's exquisite *gambeta a la escocésa* (Scottish dribble)—in the last match of the group, but the Scots had been slain by a rampant Cubillas in their opening game. Peru's wingers, Oblitas and Munante, had cut Scotland's defense to shreds. Unlike their fellow Europeans, Holland did not allow Peru to play her natural game. "El Loco" Quiroga, who would be lambasted for his performance against the country of his birth, was equal to the Dutch attacks on goal and kept a clean sheet. Iran had provided little resistance and the great Cubillas, despite having been deemed too old at twenty-nine, scored a hat trick. The prize for coming top of her group would be to share the second-round Group B with Argentina, Brazil and Poland. (The round-robin format—FIFA having dispensed with a knockout quarter- and semifinal—would only allow the group winner to contest the final.) The light that shone brightly at the group stage was now extinguished in the second round.

The host nation, who played all her first-round matches at River's Estádio Monumental, might have gone out in the first round. After an opening victory against the Hungarians, Argentina now faced France. In the dying minutes of the first half, Argentina was the beneficiary of a lucky penalty when Tresor inadvertently palmed the ball as he fell. When one Argentinian journalist was asked who handled the ball, he replied, "The Hand of God."[65] Argentina could thank the Swiss referee for another favorable decision, which saw her through into the next round. Now playing for first or second place, Italy won the last match 1–0, which sent the hosts to Rosario. There, Argentina would meet Brazil, whom she had not beaten for eight years.

The Brazilians had had an uninspiring tournament. Two low-score draws and a final victory against group leader, Austria, albeit by a single goal, had failed to inspire. The West German tabloid press accused the Austrians of having thrown the match. Spain might have even taken Brazil's place had she been more clinical in front of goal. The Brazilians were not helped by having to play on the recently laid surface at Mar del Plata—not that the Estádio Monumental was any better for having been "watered" with seawater—and by a partisan crowd shouting for Sweden. The Welsh referee blew his whistle while a Brazilian corner was in flight. Controversially, Zico's goal did not stand. By the time Brazil met Peru in the second round, injury and exhaustion had taken their toll on the Andeans. Moreover, Brazil had started to find her form. Peru succumbed to Brazil (0–3) and Poland (0–1), leaving her at the bottom of the group with little to play for except pride.

The fear of failure loomed over Argentina's match with Brazil, with both teams unable to find a breakthrough. Predictably the match, which would become known as the "Batalha de Rosário" (Battle of Rosario), was ill-tempered, as these encounters had become. Brazil would come to think of herself as moral champions, but based on this performance, there was nothing to show she had earned it.

The final group matches took place at different times. Brazil would play two and a half hours before Argentina. The Brazilians were outraged by the decision, though the Argentinians failed to do anything. After Poland was well beaten 3–1, its coach, Jacek Gmoch, refused to acknowledge the South Americans' superiority: the Poles had lost the match. For Roberto Dinamite's goal there was a thirty-second period during which the ball hit the post, then the crossbar, then post before being converted. The Brazilian coach, Claudio

Couthinho, would later say, "When I saw Menoza I *knew* we could win the World Cup because there we could play our real game. We had a better defence than the other teams in our group—including Argentina—though up front we weren't as good as we would like to have been."[66] It was all for Argentina to do. To win by four clear goals—otherwise Brazil was heading to Buenos Aries. In the event, Argentina scored six without reply.

While conspiracy theories abound as to why Peru capitulated in such a craven manner when they came to play Argentina, it is essential to bear in mind that it had been impossible for her to progress any further in the competition. Ardiles believed that "Peru gave up in the second half . . . They showed no desire to exert themselves when the result was of no importance."[67] Even if there had been some kind of subterfuge, the Argentinian team knew nothing of it. In the era of the conspiracy theory, the incongruity of the presence of Videla and his guest Henry Kissinger in the Peruvian dressing room ahead of the match gave credence to the belief that the game had been fixed. And the 35,000 tons of grain and credit agreements extended to Peru by Argentina would do little to allay these suspicions. Menotti believed that it was not a case of a poor performance by the Peruvians, but a brilliant one by the Argentinians. He had gambled on all-out victory. Moreover, if Brazil could score three goals with two forwards, then Argentina could double that tally with five strikers. The mathematics was off, but the sentiment stood. Cubillas blamed injury and tiredness, and exceptional football played by the hosts. In his groundbreaking study of the world game, *Soccer Against the Enemy*, Simon Kuper interviewed a source who believed that "Mario Kempes and Alberto Tarantini were still so 'high' after the Peru match that they had to keep running for another hour before they came down again, and that Ocampo, the team's water boy, came up with most of the post-match urine samples; though there must have been other suppliers too, for after the final, one sample showed a player to be pregnant."[68]

Argentina was about to fulfill her destiny. Her passage to the final had been even more gratifying by having beaten Brazil. The racist chant—*Ya todos saben que Brasil esta de luto / Son todos negros, son todos putos* (Everyone knows that Brazil is in mourning / They're all niggers, they're all queers)—now rang out.[69] Holland, whose "Total Football" Menotti had dismissed out of hand three years before, was waiting in the final. "People talk of speed and strength," said El Flaco, "but this is just silly. Football is a question of space on the pitch, of creation and restriction of space. I do not believe in so-called 'Total' football."[70] He believed that the theory sought to mask the failings of the European game.

Argentina's shortcomings had always included a certain gamesmanship. In the final, Holland was made to wait for the hosts in front of an inhospitable crowd. Not before Daniel Passarella, Argentina's *caudillo* captain, made a complaint about René van de Kerkhof's plaster cast, which had been worn throughout most of the competition. All this to unsettle the most sophisticated side in world football. Kempes put Argentina ahead after thirty-eight minutes by sidestepping a Dutch defender. Holland would have to until eight minutes from time to equalize through substitute Nanninga's header. Just before the final, Krol flighted a long ball through to Resenbrink, who managed to evade Fillol but hit the post. Argentina would have been runner-up. In extra time, the excellent Kempes—who would win the Golden Boot for his six goals in the competition—would score the pivotal goal, before Bertoni sealed the victory after an exquisite one-two with "El Matador."

Victory for Argentina had come late in her footballing history: forty-eight years after Uruguay's inaugural triumph and two decades after Brazil's. Still smarting from France's defeat at the hands of the hosts, *Le Figaro* castigated the Italian referee: "What Gonella did was worse than awarding a penalty which was unjust. Little by little he allowed Argentina to prevent Holland from playing."[71]

Argentina had secured what she felt had always been rightfully hers, in spite of her inconsistent showings at the international level. The celebrations would last for days. Political prisoners and free men and women shared the victory. Though for those incarcerated in the country's prisons—Argentinian waiting rooms between this world and the next—being made to shout "gooooooool!" was a bitter exclamation of victory for the very people who were on the verge of defeat. Argentinians would conceal their pain beneath the national flag. The victory, however, showed the frailty of Argentinian culture: that a society so terrorized could be anesthetized by the ephemerality of a single sporting triumph. This was football as sedation.

In the days after the final, Videla rode the wave of euphoria for his own political ends. "This unanimous cry of 'Argentina!' that rose up from our hearts, this singular flag of sky-blue and white that fluttered in our hands, are signs of a deep reality that exceed the limits of a sporting event. They are the voice and insignia of a Nation that is reunited in the plenitude of its dignity . . . All the Nation had triumphed. We are one people who today assume the challenge we put to ourselves: that of creativity, of fruitful work, and shared effort."[72]

The Argentinian journalist Alberto Ferrari felt there was another way of looking at Argentina's victory. "There are two ways of remembering the 1978 World Cup. One is to repeat the goals of Kempes or the final against Holland. The radio and television stations did it endlessly. The other is through the list of those who disappeared while in the stadia and the streets we were celebrating the attainment of victory."[73] Twenty-nine people disappeared during that time. For Brian Glanville, after having covered six World Cup tournaments, "[Argentina] was the worst. Won by the worst of the six teams in the worst and most unsatisfactory circumstances. Disfigured by negative football, ill temper, dreadful refereeing, spiteful players, and the wanton surrender of Peru."[74]

In 1979, the Ente Autárquico Mundial '78 produced the propagandist film *La fiesta de todos* (*The Feast for Everybody*), which interspersed footage from the tournament with at times comic scenes played by famous actors. The film sought to present the national cohesion that Videla had championed. But it was having bettered Brazil—in spite of only being able to scrape a goalless draw against a team that remained unbeaten in the tournament—that mattered most. As the film's narrator says, "It was inevitable. Our happiness meant the sadness of the Brazilians. That's the way it is. In other times, they celebrated their victories as if they were Carnivals, while we comforted ourselves with the fact that we were moral champions."[75]

The *Clarín* journalist Oscar Barnade believed the 1978 World Cup had been the most important sporting event in the country's history:

> It has all the seasoning of a country full of contradictions and injustices, just like ours. On the one hand, it was experienced like a true popular festival, of a people whose favourite sport is football. And it was capped by securing the title, the first in the country's history. On the other hand, the shame. The military dictatorship utilising, in the worst way possible, the goodwill of the sporting triumph; creating an illicit economic debt, with the management and military lining their pockets; and compromising the economic future of the country. And finally, the tragedy. The terrorism of the state, of a bloody military dictatorship. With a concentration camp only metres away from the main stadium, that of River, and the perverse idea of taking prisoners out in the mist of the celebrations, as they did with Graciela Daleo. This is the tragi-comic history of Argentina.[76]

CHAPTER NINE

DEUS EX MACHINA

1980–1994

The Rise and Fall of El Diego

There are two types of football, prose and poetry. European teams are prose, tough, premeditated, systematic, collective. Latin American ones are poetry, ductile, spontaneous, individual, erotic.

—Pier Paolo Pasolini

Shilton! All goalkeepers are useless. You're no exception. Relax. You were had—but don't worry. Shilton! You think you're the hero, the phenomenon. The honest Shilton! Tell me, if the ball crossed just over the line, and you swept it away without the referee seeing it had gone over, would you go and tell him it was a goal?

—Maradona

I no longer like Maradona; he's like a small doll.

—Argentinian fan after the 1982 World Cup

Carlos Martínez Moreno had witnessed the decline firsthand:* "[The saying 'There's no place like Uruguay'] started out as the pride of the country's vision and ended up as the 'slogan' on a brand

---

* Two years before the 1973 coup d'état.

of cooking oil. *Sic transit gloria mundi.*"* By 1980, seven years of military rule and an ailing economy had taken their toll on the country. Unable to give voice to the disquiet for fear of being detained, tortured or disappeared, Uruguayans had long sought the relative anonymity of the football stadium for self-expression. In 1973, 40,000 spectators had watched the country lose by one goal to nil against Colombia. During the singing of the national anthem, the crowd raised its collective voice for the line *tiranos temblad!* (tyrants tremble!). Not that the attending military contingent could punish the whole stadium. The tradition, usually with rest of the anthem sung *sotto voce*, would endure during these dark years.

The eighties opened with the *Copa de Oro de Campeones Mundiales* or *Mundialito* (Little World Cup), a short-form tournament to celebrate the fiftieth anniversary of the 1930 World Cup. Only those countries that had previously won the tournament were invited. For fear of disturbing her winter season, England declined to participate, so the Netherlands, twice-beaten finalists, took her place. With the endorsement of João Havelange, the tournament had been organized by FIFA; though Silvio Berlusconi provided much-needed income by buying the television rights. At the outset, the Uruguayan dictatorship had been ambivalent about participating for financial reasons, but now saw the tournament as an opportunity to improve its rather dubious reputation abroad. Gamesmanship and some less than impartial refereeing would help the Uruguayans throughout the tournament.

Failure to qualify for the 1978 World Cup had left Uruguayan football deflated. In 1980, the national squad endured a string of mediocre results before scoring at will in December of that year. Roque Máspoli, who had kept goal for Uruguay at the 1950 World Cup final and was now head coach, stated, "Nothing has harmed my

---

* In 1986, exiled in Mexico, the Uruguayan writer and lawyer died while waiting in line at the Mexican State Migration Office. He was preparing his documentation to return to Uruguay.

country's football more than living from memories."[1] Impressive victories ahead of the *Mundialito* against Finland (6–0), Bolivia (5–0) and Switzerland (4–0) catalyzed the team, who were drawn against Holland and Italy in Group A. After beating Holland by two goals to nil, Uruguay played a bruising match against Italy. Three expulsions in the second half did not dampen the Uruguayan will to win. Italy's manager, Vincenzo "Enzo" Bearzot, could not believe what he had witnessed. "It was an affront to the game. I've never seen so many bad things on a football field . . . I never suspected [Uruguay] would resort to such violence to win a game."[2] Bearzot was being either disingenuous or extremely naive. He had surely seen it all before.

In Group B, West Germany, which had been crowned European Champions in Rome the previous year, had to play Brazil and Argentina. Both South American republics brushed the Germans aside, Brazil scoring four second-half goals in under thirty minutes. But in a match played in more than ninety-degree heat, Argentina failed to overcome Brazil. The draw sent Argentina home on goal difference. Not that they were unhappy to leave, given their shabby treatment at the hands of their hosts. A twenty-year-old Maradona was indignant: "I think we treat them [the Uruguayans] so much better than they treated us. They think we are monsters. They throw stones at us in the streets . . . always saying nasty things about us. We have to do something about it. We should never play in Uruguay again."[3] Complaints such as this failed to stir the Uruguayans, who were now focused on seeing their countrymen play out "El Maracanãzo" yet again. Brazil, in spite of her three World Cup trophies and its thrashing of Uruguay 5–1 at the Maracanã the year before, was still intent on exacting revenge. In the intervening thirty years, the numerous Brazilian victories had done little to dull the pain.

Before the final, Uruguay had had a week's rest, whereas her opponent had only been given two days off after her second-half demolition of West Germany. The final 2–1 score line was the same as that in 1950, though this time Uruguay scored first. Waldemar Victorino, Uruguay's journeyman forward, had scored in every match. *Guerin Sportivo*, Italy's oldest sporting monthly, commented, "The Uruguayan victory was unexpected after the beautiful performances of Brazil, which makes it even more valid. Máspoli's team was tactically perfect."[4]

The *Copa de Oro* had been played against a changing political landscape. In November 1980, the Uruguayan electorate had voted against a new constitution, one in which the military had attempted to secure its long-term tenure in the country's political system. The authoritarian dictatorship might have followed Pinochet's lead, but it had underestimated its own population, which, in spite of the prevailing censorship, had been rallied by the country's political parties. Fifty-seven percent had voted against the new constitution. But it would take another four years before the country returned to democracy.

Victory may have made Uruguay feel like world champions again, albeit briefly, but the tournament had been tainted. Uruguayans liked to think of their greatest victories during periods of political democracy and economic well-being. This victory had come under one of the continent's most repressive regimes. Not that there would be much choice over the next three decades. International honors would be few, which would not sit well with the country's august history. Uruguay had now perfected that common trait of the underdog: winning when it mattered least and losing when it mattered most. Nevertheless, little notice was paid to the country's footballing woes as the world turned its attention to a single player, one who would dominate the game for nearly two decades. He came from the other side of the Río de la Plata.

"El Sueño del Pibe" ("The Kid's Dream")

Renown had come to Maradona at an early age. In a match between Argentinos Juniors and Independiente, the ten-year-old player had impressed the home crowd with his ball-juggling skills at halftime.

Clarín saw something in the young prodigy that recalled the golden age of Argentinian football. The reporter may have been mistaken about his name—calling him "Caradona"—but he was not mistaken about what he saw: "His shirt is too big for him, and his fringe hardly allows him to see properly. He looks as if he's escaped from a piece of wasteland . . . He holds himself like a born football player. He doesn't seem to belong to today."[5] When asked in a television interview what his dreams were, he answered humbly that the first was to play in a World Cup and the second was to win it. This was what the country had been waiting for—the appearance of *"El Pibe"* (The Kid) incarnate: *"El Pibe de Oro"* (The Golden Kid).

Years later, as an adult and in surprisingly good voice, Maradona would reinforce the nostalgic image of *El Pibe* on Argentinian television by singing *"El sueño del pibe"* ("The Kid's Dream"). Written in 1943 by Reinaldo Yiso and Juan Puey, the tango tells the story of a kid who is called up to play for his football club.

> *Mamita querida,*
> *ganaré dinero,*
> *seré un Baldonedo,*
> *un Martino, un Boyé.*
> *Dicen los muchachos*
> *del Oeste Argentino*
> *que tengo más tiro*
> *que el gran Bernabé.*
> (Dearest Mommy,
> I will make money,
> I will become a Baldonedo,
> a Martino, a Boyé.
> Say the boys
> of the west of Argentina
> that I have stronger shot
> than the great Bernabé.)

The kid dreams of a crowded stadium on a glorious Sunday afternoon. With one minute to play in a goalless draw, he takes the ball and "dribbling past everyone he faced the goalkeeper / and with a strong shot broke the stalemate." Maradona reinterpreted the tango, inserting his name and that of Kempes for Baldonedo and Martino. Eduardo Archetti, one of the country's leading sociologists, maintained that the existence of the tango had allowed Argentinians to believe that the life of Maradona had either been fated or adhered to a script already written. When Maradona came to write his autobiography, he opened it thus: "Sometimes I think that my whole life is on film, that my whole life is in print."[6] Even at the Oxford Union, where he spoke in 1995, he still referred to himself as a *pibe*.

Born in 1960 into the working-class slum of Villa Fiorito, Diego Armando Maradona took to the round ball as a young child. "The first ball I had was the best present I've ever received in my life; my cousin Beto gave it me. It was a leather number one; I was three years old and I slept with it hugged to my chest all night."[7] His parents, Chitoro and La Tota, had come to Buenos Aires from the humid northern province of Corrientes to seek a better life. La Tota had already left the small town of Esquina for the capital in 1950, but returned. Between 1935 and 1947, internal migration to the capital, encouraged by Perón, had increased from 400,000 to 1.5 million. Chitoro and La Tota were what had become known as *cabecitas negras* (little blackheads), a demographic strongly aligned with Peronism. The capital may have offered more opportunities than Esquina, but it was a city in which the safety net for the poor had all but disappeared. Chitoro would have to build his three-room shack from scrap and bricks that he had found. In slums like Villa Fiorito where criminality, which took many forms, was rampant, families had to be "clever" to survive. Fortunately for Chitoro and La Tota, in Diego they had a prodigious talent.

The young Maradona learned to play on the waste grounds not far from his home. "There was no grass, synthetic or otherwise, but to us it was wonderful. The pitches were made of earth, really hard earth."[8] Rather than the docks, where the myth of the English sailors and their knock-about games had originated, this was *the* birthplace of the Argentinian game, the *potrero*. From here, Maradona graduated to Cebollitas (Little Onions), the youth team of Argentinos Juniors, where, in spite of his small, stocky physique, he outshone his peers. Even at that age, he could do things with a ball that were beyond the older players. As Cebollitas's star player, he guided the team to the championship in 1974. His rise up football's unpredictable career ladder became vertiginous. In spite of interest from River Plate, Maradona signed with Argentinos Juniors. Two years later, days short of his sixteenth birthday, he came on as a second-half substitute against Talleres de Córdoba, only to demand a penalty from a supposed handball incident. His first match ended in defeat. Although there were only 20,000 spectators in the stadium, the myth of Maradona's debut would play havoc with people's memory. Every football fan had been there. Four months later, the *wunderkind* was playing for Argentina against Hungary. Menotti had hardly gambled in sending on his young charge; Argentina had already scored five goals to the Hungarians' single-goal reply. In La Bombonera, the *porteños*, who had long awaited their savior, chorused "Maradooona!"

But the very man who had put Maradona on the international stage would leave the young player heartbroken. Maradona's relationship with Menotti would be defined by rejection when he was not picked for the 1978 World Cup. The young star's exclusion was a brave decision by *El Flaco*. Other managers might have succumbed to the country's demands for their young hero to be selected, but Menotti remained faithful to his footballing philosophy. Moreover, he had enough players, including Mario Kempes, on whom he felt he could rely to deliver the trophy. Maradona would later state, "I've already said a thousand times and I don't mind saying it again: just as Passarella was Menotti's pet, I am Bilardo's pet."[9] The relationship between the two men would always be complicated. There were those who believed that the Argentinian squad only had space for one star: the architect of the 1978 World Cup victory.

The following year Menotti proved that the World Cup had been no stroke of luck, when he coached the country's youth squad to victory at the 1979 FIFA World Youth Championship in Japan. The 3–1 triumph over the Soviet Union in the final reinforced Argentinian hegemony. With his six goals and captain's armband, Maradona proved a commanding presence in international football. (*"El Pelado"* Díaz was the tournament's top scorer with eight goals.) His self-styled role as *caudillo* (leader) was manifest early on. Rubén Favret, Maradona's teammate at Argentinos Juniors, remembered, "In 1979 we went to play in Brazil. It was the era of colour television and all of us wanted to bring one back. But they hadn't paid us prize money. Diego stuck up for all of us and said to Consoli [president of Argentinos Juniors] that if they didn't pay us he wouldn't play. They paid us and we all brought back a television. Even as a young boy, he was already a leader."[10]

It would only be a matter of time before Argentinos Juniors could no longer afford to keep the player it had reared. The question was whether Maradona would stay in the country or leave Argentina, like generations of the best players before him. In May 1980, an editorial in *El Gráfico* pleaded: "In something we nearly all agree: WE WANT MARADONA TO STAY IN THE COUNTRY. It does not matter which colour strip [he wears], but that he stays."[11] Two months later, the cover of the country's foremost sporting weekly had Maradona standing next to the national flag, draped in the colors of Argentinos Juniors. In the same issue, Daniel Passarella published a letter, addressed to his teammate, in which he expressed his happiness that Maradona was staying. Argentinos Juniors had received a subsidy of $400,000 from the AFA so that Maradona would remain. It would not be enough. By 1981, he had been loaned out to Boca Juniors for a fee of $4 million as well as $1.1 million to help pay off his former club's debt. He was not allowed to play against his former club and his contract would expire during the 1982 World Cup. Such was the fervor for the player that *El Gráfico* published the contents of the contract. Boca Juniors, with its working-class immigrant roots, would become Maradona's spiritual home.

In his first match for Boca, against Talleres, Maradona scored from a penalty in a 4–1 win. Such was the reaction to this momentous occasion that the earth seemed to move. Despite the exceptional start he made, questions would begin to be asked by the middle of the year. After he went four games without scoring a goal, *El Gráfico* inquired, "Maradona and Boca: does he have feelings for the shirt? Does he train well? Do the fans love him?"[12] Any doubts were soon dismissed as he galvanized the club to win its first championship since 1976. With only a draw needed against Racing, Maradona slotted home a calmly taken penalty to set Boca on their way to a 4–1 victory. After he had been runner-up with Argentinos Juniors the year before, this would be the high point of his domestic career. But Maradona's odyssey had only just started. His next stop, Spain, would not be a happy one.

"Las Malvinas Son Argentinas"

In his diary entry for March 10, 1834, the year after the Falkland Islands had been forcibly taken by the British, Charles Darwin wrote: "Arrived in the middle of the day at Berkeley Sound [northeastern East Falkland] . . . Mr Smith, who is acting as Governor, came on board, & has related such complicated scenes of cold-blooded murder, robbery, plunder, suffering, such infamous conduct in almost every person who has breathed this atmosphere, as would take two or three sheets to describe."[13] What Darwin would come to call "these miserable lands" in *The Voyage of the Beagle* had been contested by Britain, France and Spain for centuries. Britain, without any particular care and attention on her part, would manage to hold on to the Islands until her hand was forced by a belligerent Argentina dictatorship.

As Argentinian national identity began to assert itself in the early twentieth century, the sovereignty of the Islands became a thorny subject for the British. In 1934, a decade before he returned as ambassador to Argentina, Sir David Kelly observed, "Our policy in regard to the Falklands must be to maintain our rights while avoiding all incidents calculated to fan the always smouldering embers of Argentine resentment. There is absolutely no hope of our reaching any agreement on the question of principle involved, and our guiding principle must be to avoid dragging this century old controversy into the limelight."[14] In Perón, Argentina's territorial claims on the Falklands would find their champion. And with the temperature of the debate over their ownership rising, the British did little to further their self-professed policy of avoiding the limelight when they issued stamps depicting the Falkland Island Dependencies. Even anti-Peronists were outraged. The Argentinian press now began to devote more attention to what they saw as Argentinian possessions in the South Atlantic.

In the early 1970s, Argentinian workers had helped the British build an airport on the Islands. Football proved a bond between the cultures when a mini-tournament was established between the workers and the military. In front of five hundred spectators, a record turnout, the Argentinians were beaten 2–1, but the fraternal sentiments on show here would not last. In 1981, shortly before he ascended to the presidency through the now time-honored coup, General Leopoldo Galtieri set out his position in a *Día del Ejército Argentino* (Army Day) speech: "Nobody can or will be able to say that we have not been extremely calm and patient in our handling of international problems, which in no way stem from any appetite for territory on our part. However, after a century and a half they are becoming more and more unbearable."

It was not only the British-controlled territories that were singled out. Chile had endured a fractious relationship with Argentina over border disputes in the Patagonia since the nineteenth century. In 1978, the sovereignty of another set of islands, this time in Tierra del Fuego—Picton, Lennox and Nueva in the Beagle Channel—had both republics on the verge of war. After the ownership of the Falklands had been secured, Argentina would resolve the question of the Beagle Channel. Galtieri told General Basilio Lami Dozo, "[The Chileans] need to heed what we are doing now, because they will be next."[15] Hostilities with Chile were not without their own set of risks, which might involve the other republics in the region. Argentina could afford to confront Brazil on the football pitch, but military aggression was another matter. The British would have to do for now. Patrick Watts, who was in charge of the Falkland Islands Broadcasting Station, later recalled, "In late March 1982 I was playing for the Islands against HMS *Endurance*—we lost 5–3—on the afternoon that she was called away unexpectedly to sail for the island of South Georgia where some Argentine workers had landed illegally. The rest is history."[16] On April 2, 1982, Argentinian forces invaded the islands that very few British could even place on the map.

. . .

For twenty years the opening match of the World Cup had invariably been a sterile affair. Since 1962, four tournaments had begun with goalless draws. Before the tournament, Menotti was still maintaining his theory about *la nuestra* (our game). "A German team can't play like a Spanish team, or vice versa. Every nation's football has different characteristics. If I have achieved anything, it is in giving Argentine football faith in itself, in our own style of play . . . You can't ask players to do something they're not born to. You couldn't ask Sinatra to sing a tango better than Gardel, any more than you would have asked Gardel to sing 'Strangers in the Night' better than Sinatra."[17]

At the Camp Nou in Barcelona, the reigning world champions faced Belgium, who had never made it past the first round. The

Argentinians had been unsettled by the European coverage of the Falklands War. In the aftermath of the invasion, patriotism had swept the nation. The Argentinians had celebrated as if they had won a second World Cup, but now they were presented with a very different story than that which they'd been told. When the Argentinian squad traveled to Europe in late May, it was under the impression that the war would be won. In a gesture of politically naive solidarity that would become something of a trademark for him, Maradona said that the team would play the best they could in order to cheer up the troops. "All I want is for my country to be the best in the world."[18] With the country suffering one of her regular bouts of economic crisis, these seemed hollow words from a player who now had a $7 million price tag on his head after his record-breaking transfer to Barcelona.

For Maradona, the reality of the situation was a shock. "We were convinced we were winning the war, and like any patriot my allegiance was to the national flag. But then we got to Spain and discovered the truth. It was a huge blow to everyone on the team."[19]

Maradona hit the bar from a free kick. This near miss was the shape of things to come in Spain. Argentina lost by a single Belgian goal. His petulance had made Maradona refuse the shirt of Belgium's captain, Eric Gerets. The following night the country would lose a war. *Clarín* had given its front page two headlines—BOMBARDMENT OF BRITISH TROOPS and FAILED DEBUT IN THE WORLD CUP—one of which was accurate.[20] *El Gráfico* accused the squad of having "stayed in Buenos Aires." Menotti became an apologist for his star player: "In 1970, in a brilliant Brazilian team, Pelé was just one piece more, without being forced to pull rabbits out of hats like we now expect of Maradona."[21]

Against Hungary, Maradona scored twice in an emphatic 4–1 victory. Among the crowds watching were banners that sought to remind those who might have forgotten that British imperialism not only extended to the South Atlantic but also to Gibraltar. Now

Maradona complained of an Argentinian propensity either to praise or vilify. As with Argentina, there was never any middle ground.

Argentina's next match was against El Salvador, who had deprived the Spanish tournament of the acrobatic goal-scoring skills of Hugo Sánchez. Mexico's greatest footballing export may have been the leading scorer in the 1981 CONCACAF championship—whose champions and runners-up qualified for the World Cup—but his feats were enough by themselves to prevent El Salvador from qualifying ahead of his country. Although El Salvador had made it through qualification, the country was in the midst of a bloody civil war, which would last another ten years, and in no position to send a squad to Spain. And yet in Jorge "El Mágico" González, they possessed one of the world's great players. Footballing comparisons being given to hyperbole, El Mágico was said to be technically superior to Maradona, though he never kept the company to prove it. Nevertheless, his teammates failed to provide this erratic genius— who liked to stay out late and needed to be woken up by a club official, such was his bad timekeeping—with the service he required.

In their first match, against Hungary, the El Salvadorians immediately had to confront the Latin American fear of making a fool of oneself (*hacer papelones*). By halftime Hungary had scored three goals; she would score a further seven in the following forty-five minutes. (In the fifty-sixth minute László Kiss came on to score a hat trick.) San Salvador's *Prensa Gráfica* sought to lay the blame at the feet of the country, not the players. "We are all involved in this, but the public forces them to play to win. If the coaches had taught them defensive tactics, our spectators would have booed the players."[22] After this humiliation, El Salvador managed to concede only three goals in her remaining matches. Against Argentina Maradona marked out of the match. Jaime Rodríguez, the Central American defender, rugby-tackled him around the waist. With tactics such as these, the score was kept down to two goals to nil.

In the second round, Argentina shared a group with Brazil, her eternal rival, and Italy, her cultural colonizer. Italy, who had started sluggishly in her group with three draws and only two goals, now hit a rich vein of form that continued through the championship. Claudio Gentile, Juventus's Libyan-born fullback, may not have scored a goal, but he made sure of Maradona's impotence by marking him out of the game. The Romanian referee, like many other officials, did little to protect the young genius. In the second half, the Italians were far quicker, cleverer on the counterattack, with Cabrini's winning goal coming on the break after Paolo Rossi had missed an easy chance.

With defeat, the possibility of progression receded. Brazil was unlikely to give the wounded Argentinians any quarter. After eleven minutes, Eder's beautifully swerved free kick rebounded off the post and fell for Zico, who put the ball over the line. In the second half, Brazil found her rhythm, and put the game past the Argentinians with two goals, the last created by an exquisite pass from Zico that put Junior through to score. Five minutes from time, Maradona's fate in Spain was sealed with a red card when he kicked out at Batista. He cut a lonely figure as the stadium booed him. Before he left the pitch, he crossed himself: a god among men, but a man among gods.

It had been an unhappy tournament for the young Argentinian, who, in an interview in *Clarín*, was now singled out for criticism by his hero, Pelé: "My main doubt is whether he has the sufficient greatness as a person to justify being honoured by a worldwide audience."[23] The Argentinian may only have been twenty-one, but by his age Pelé had already won the World Cup twice. It was the beginning of an uneasy relationship that, even more than twenty-five years later, had the Brazilian casting aspersions on Maradona's ability to manage his country. Pelé accused him of only taking the job for the money and blamed those in charge of the Argentinian game for allowing it to happen. Maradona's riposte was succinct: that Pelé "should go back to the museum."

Reporting on the 1982 World Cup, the Peruvian novelist Mario

Vargas Llosa sought to crown *El Pibe de Oro* thus: "Maradona is the Pelé of the 1980s. More than that: he is one of the living deities that men create in order to worship themselves through these deities."[24] Vargas Llosa predicted that he would enjoy a brief reign—as was the tradition in the sport—as "the personification of football."[25] Yet Maradona's dominion lasted longer than most, especially in the country of his birth. The worship of this false god endured into the twenty-first century. Maradona epitomized a sense of Argentinian-ness that many Argentinians found it difficult to express themselves. He would continue to epitomize the *Pibe de Oro*, even when his best playing days were behind him. Moreover, his more objectionable traits, which came in the guise of those twins, hubris and self-pity, were a reflection of Argentina. In many ways, hatred of Maradona was simply a form of Argentinian self-loathing.

Unable to offer praise where it was due, Menotti stated that he did not think Brazil the better team. The clash of two very different footballing cultures was as evident in this game as it had been in nearly every match played between these teams over the previous century. In early 1946, after Argentina beat Brazil 2–0 in Buenos Aires, *El Gráfico* compared their different approaches to the game. "The different styles of play could be perfectly observed. That of the Argentinians: self-possessed, positive . . . and cerebral. That of the Brazilians: light, fluent, elegant, conferring more importance on individual ability . . . The Argentinians, calculating, without risking one line; the Brazilians, more given to improvisation and lacking, in short, in potentiality."[26]

Ten days before the tournament, *La Nación* had published an article entitled "Saber Perder" ("Knowing How to Lose"): "The progressive disintegration of Argentine optimism, causing a real national neurosis observable in certain social phenomena, such as compulsive attention to the 1978 World Soccer championship, where the triumph against the best teams of other countries gave back the public the lost certitude that they could be the best of the world. Such glory, achieved in a gladiator circus . . . gave an ersatz consolation for national soul wounds, lacking more significant triumphs in other meaningful areas of international competition."[27]

Had Argentina failed to become world champions in 1978, the military dictatorship might not have lasted until 1983. Football may not have had the power to inspire change, but its effects were potent enough to suspend disbelief. As Mario Vargas Llosa would write at the 1982 World Cup: "What characterizes an entertainment, however intense and absorbing, and a good game of football is enormously intense and absorbing, is that it is ephemeral, non-transcendent, innocuous. An experience where the effect disappears at the same time as the cause."[28] The euphoria that came with victory anesthetized the population, but it soon wore off. Failure in Spain was of little use to the ailing regime, but it took dead bodies—of the conscripts who returned from the Falklands rather than those that the military had disappeared—to bring down the junta. Whereas in the rest of the continent the military negotiated its exit, in Argentina the junta collapsed.

The workings of the regime had by now become so byzantine that they had begun to take on a Borgesian aspect. A special report run by the *Economist* on the country was as perceptive as it was chilling:

The use of official terrorism to counter ordinary terrorism made Argentina a more dangerous place than Chile after its coup because the rules of the game, for the government's critics, were so ill-defined. A journalist, for example, might be given a wink by a minister to go ahead and publish an article criticizing an aspect of government policy. But he would not know whether a security service belonging to the army, or to the air force, or to the navy, or to the local military governor, or to the provincial governor, or independent of any of these, would or would not take umbrage. And even a top minister might be unable to help him if he was whisked off by a group of unknown men one night.[29]

With the resignation of Galtieri after the Falklands debacle, the navy and the air force abandoned the junta, leaving a political vacuum. General Reynaldo Bignone filled the void, though he was quick to promise democratic elections for the following year. With inflation rising to over 200 percent—it would soar to 900 percent—and the economy shrinking at 10 percent per annum, Argentina was *in extremis*. The country had no choice but to turn to the IMF and negotiate a standby arrangement for $1.4 billion. The dire economic situation was reflected in the football stadium. Crowd violence increased shortly after the Falklands War, though there was little in the way of police protection. The military government was said to have turned a blind eye to yet another problem. Football violence might have provided a release for the republic's pent-up frustrations.

Tragédia do Sarriá (Sarriá Stadium Tragedy)

Even before the Italians had been crowned world champions in Madrid, Marcelo Rezende wrote in *Placar*: "I believe that the Hungarians in '54, Holland of '74 and now Brazil can set three decisive stages for the beauty of this sport of millions."[30] It was a belief shared by the players themselves. In his 1982 World Cup diary, also published in Brazil's sporting monthly, Sócrates stated, "I had one obvious thing in my mind. Our team was the best in the world . . . the team that played the best."[31] The Brazilian side of 1982 had played the game beautifully, but there was something ethereal about the team. For many it would be a romantic vision of a bygone age. Alastair Reid in the *New Yorker* wrote, "Brazil's whole play seemed more instinct than design, and it was clear the Brazilians relished playing . . . an impression that came all too rarely in the Mundial."[32]

Telê Santana had taken over from the much-maligned Captain

Cláudio Coutinho as coach of the Seleção. His predecessor's appointment had been met with consternation in certain quarters. Coutinho had been a physical training instructor with a penchant for basketball. As with his army career, he had risen through the footballing ranks before taking the Olympic squad to fourth place at the 1976 Olympics in Montreal. When he returned to Brazil, he went to Flamengo, before being asked to guide Brazil through the qualifying rounds of the 1978 World Cup after Osvaldo Brandão resigned. Imbued with a modernizing instinct that he shared with the dictatorship, Coutinho sought to improve, or Europeanize, Brazil's style of play. He likened a football team to a platoon. Tactics and fitness took precedence over creativity. He even regarded that Brazilian specialism, dribbling, as a sign of weakness.

His tenure with the squad during the World Cup in Argentina was fraught with rumors: Coutinho was said to have fallen out with both Zico and Rivelino, and was reported to have been sacked during the first-round matches. After Argentina's match against Peru, Saldanha criticized his fellow *gaúcho* for not having had the team score more goals against Poland. (But who would have predicted that Argentina could score six goals?) Coutinho insisted that Brazil had been moral champions of Argentina's compromised tournament. Three years later, he would die in a scuba-diving accident in Rio de Janeiro.

Like Menotti, Santana was allowed the freedom to put a team together that reflected his idea of the how the game should be played. Ademir, the great Vasco and Fluminense striker of the 1940s, thought Santana in the tradition of great managers such as Flávio Costa and Zezé Moreira. In *Placar*, Santana insisted he did not have a plan in his head. For him, the game was straightforward: "My football is simple, there's nothing revolutionary. I want a team that plays the ball quickly, that knows to return and mark, who take the field away from the opponent and who, when attacking, complete the moves quickly. I want [the team] well prepared so that it plays the kind of football that everybody wants to see."[33]

Santana's early results were auspicious. In 1980, Brazil only lost one match, a 2–1 friendly against the Soviet Union. The following year the squad undertook a short European tour and dispatched England, France and West Germany in quick succession. Zico believed that while tactics were needed at the club level, international players were just too good for them to be necessary. The squad's last match before the World Cup was a seven–nil thrashing of the Republic of Ireland. With a 4-2-2-2 formation, Brazil cut a fine figure in her group. The team reversed its 1980 defeat against the Soviet Union and put four goals past both Scotland and New Zealand. The magical midfield of Falcão, Zico, Sócrates and Cerezo proved so dazzling that many observers were blinded to the side's vulnerability. Flamboyant though they were, the team was not invincible.

Bearzot, who had played for Internazionale and Torino, could see what was obvious to any ex-defender. Brazil's great surges up the pitch left gaps in defense. These he would exploit. Italy had come to the match with renewed confidence after having dispatched Argentina. Nevertheless, Paolo Rossi, who had just completed a two-year ban for match fixing, seemed to have to come to the tournament as a tourist rather than a striker. Against Brazil, his selection would be vindicated. After five minutes, Rossi headed Carbrini's cross for the opening goal. It would give the team, hitherto lacking in confidence, the psychological cushion it needed. Seven minutes later Sócrates combined elegantly with Zico to score the equalizer. Moments before, Serginho had shot wide, a miss that seemed to epitomize the incongruity of the graceless targetman's selection. Cerezo's inaccurate pass turned the game. Rossi latched on to the opportunity offered by the hideously misplaced ball and took it. When Falcão equalized in the sixty-eighth minute, it seemed that order would be restored: the Brazilians only needed a draw to see her through to the next round. But the footballing gods would kill off Brazil for their sport when Rossi flicked the ball past Waldir.

For Brazilians, it was the day on which *futebol-arte* was usurped by *futebol-força* (power football). Rossi and Zoff—who had also been resurrected after an indifferent tournament in Argentina—would evoke the specter of Ghiggia and Varela in the Brazilian mind. The defeat, however, was more prosaic: Brazil's midfield, magnificent as it was, could not mask its frailties in defense and up front. Lyra Filho's words, written in 1954, would come back to haunt Brazil. "In Brazilian football, flashy trim lends artistic expression to the match, to the detriment of yield and results. *Exhibition* jeopardises *competition*."[34] *A Gazeta Esportiva* put it metaphorically: "Brazil was a light team, a dancing team that played in pumps. Italy was a dour, robust, killer team that played in spurs. Brazil played beautifully and mistakenly. Italy played unattractively and assuredly."[35] Zico, however, now condemned Italy for not allowing Brazil to play her natural game. He had not expected to lose. The year before he had captained Flamengo against Liverpool in the Intercontinental Cup. Flamengo had been far too good for the English, faster-paced and more aggressive. After the three–nil defeat, Liverpool's ever-perspicacious manager, Bob Paisley, commented, "They [Liverpool] were dead, physically and mentally, I have never seen the team so dull, so lacking in ideas and aggression. I simply cannot understand it."[36] The victory was dedicated to Cláudio Coutinho.

In the final of the 1981 Copa Libertadores, Flamengo had faced a Chilean team with no history. Club de Deportes Cobreloa had been founded in 1977, though within three years the club had won the country's First Division. The title challenge had come down to the penultimate match of the season. With Cobreloa and Universidad de Chile level on points, the latter, having led by one goal to nil against Lota Schwager, conceded a penalty in the ninetieth minute. (Universidad de Chile, which had won five titles in the 1960s, would not be crowned champions until 1994.) The small club from Calama, a mining town in the Atacama desert, would win its last two matches.

Cobreloa enjoyed the financial backing of División Chuquicamata de Codelco, a state-owned copper-mining concern. Moreover, a flourishing club kept the miners and local population content. In the Copa Libertadores, Cobreloa proved equally at home, especially with its Uruguayan strike force. In Calama, the team had thrashed Peru's Sporting Cristal and Atlético Torino by 6–1. No wonder Flamengo protested that it had to play the Chilean leg of the final in the club's "dustbowl." The Brazilians now threatened to play their leg at Flamengo's training ground in Gávea. Cobreloa even offered the Brazilians a $40,000 payment to drop the complaint. After winning at the Maracanã, Flamengo would lose in Santiago, where the match had been moved. The playoff, at a poorly attended Estádio Centenario in Montevideo, was won with a brace of goals from Zico.

Nothing in Latin America lasts. The year after Italy's triumph in Spain, the Jules Rimet trophy was stolen from the headquarters of the *Confederação Brasileira de Futebol* (CBF) in Rio de Janeiro. Brazil had been allowed to keep the original trophy, after winning the tournament for the third time in 1970. The president of the CBF, Giulite Coutinho, was despondent that part of the country's national heritage—a trophy it had worked so hard to secure—had been taken. Pelé made a public call for its return, but it would never be seen again. Numerous theories circulated as to its whereabouts, though the trophy was most probably melted for its gold.

· · ·

At the club level, the South Americans were making a habit of beating the European champions in the Intercontinental Cup. Nevertheless, the competition was considered by many to be a "dog without a master." In 1979, *El Mundo Deportivo* predicted a slow death for the peripatetic competition. "What is certain is that the Intercontinental

Cup is an accidental competition without any foundation. It has no known master, depends on a strange consensus; and the clubs concerned are not tempted to risk so much for so little money, as witnessed by the attendance at the game in Malmö, played, of course, in the absence of this year's champion, Nottingham Forest."[37]

In 1979, Paraguay had enjoyed a golden year, which had been long overdue. Whereas other republics in the region had sought to imitate a Brazilian or Argentinian style, Paraguayan football married the obduracy of the Uruguayans with the speed of the English. Its eternal problem was to find a distinct identity. And yet, of all the republics that had been overshadowed by the sporting prowess of the continent's triumvirate—Argentina, Uruguay and Brazil—Paraguay would have the best footballing record. The game had had to find its place in a country that, before General Stroessner's rise to power in 1954, had been a martyr to the coup d'état. Under Stroessner, who would be overthrown in 1989 by the military, the country enjoyed a semblance of economic prosperity. During the 1970s, investment in agriculture and the construction of the $19 billion Itaipú Dam produced a boom, during which GDP grew to nearly 9 percent annually. Trade in contraband also contributed to prosperity, as the country benefited from the protectionist policies of her neighbors. The imaginatively named Ciudad del Este (City of the East), which had been founded in the late 1950s, would come to epitomize the lawless frontier town. Located on the Brazilian border and close to Argentina, the town acquired a reputation for being able to supply everything from arms and narcotics to electronic goods.

The country's most successful club, Olímpia, had secured not only the 1979 Copa Libertadores, but also the Copa Intercontinental and the Copa Interamericana. In the same year, Paraguay won the *Copa América* for only the second time in her history. In the Copa Libertadores, the Paraguayan clubs Olímpia and Sol de América were drawn against Bolívar and Jorge Wilstermann of Bolivia in the group stage. With the team's passage to the semifinals at stake, it was rumored that that Olímpia paid Sol de América $50,000 not to lose against Bolívar in Asunción. In the event, Olímpia beat the Bolivar squad by three goals in the final group match. The two-legged final against Boca Juniors, who were expecting to be crowned champions of the continent for the third year in a row, was something of a disappointment. In front of their home crowd, Olímpia opened the scoring after two minutes, which forced Boca to attack rather than settle for the traditional away draw. By halftime, Boca had conceded a second goal, from which there would be no way back. Both teams had employed the pressing game, which effectively ended in stalemate. Juan Carlos Lorenzo, Boca's manager, could not help but resort to a dash of racism: "We were beaten by a team that was starving to death."* In Buenos Aires, both teams canceled each other out in a goalless draw. The rotund Uruguayan coach Luis "El Negro" Cubilla who had won the first edition of the tournament with Peñarol, had engineered the victory—something he would repeat for Olímpia in 1990.

The *Copa América*, however, proved better fare. Paraguay may have beaten Chile over a three-legged final, but it was against Brazil in the semifinals that she had made her mark. At Defensores del Chaco in Asunción, Eugenio Morel, who had gained a reputation for his speed at Libertad, scored one of the goals of the decade. With his back to the goal, Morel controlled the ball on his chest, before executing a *chilena* (overhead kick), which hit the crossbar and dropped over the goal line. Although Paraguay had prevailed by two goals to one, Saldanha thought that the team had missed the opportunity to thrash the Brazilians. At the Maracanã, he said, Brazil would win by a healthy margin, so no matter. The match ended in a two-all draw. But then foresight had never been a Brazilian forte. The Paraguayan Manuel "El Brujo" (The Wizard) Fleitas Solich, who coached Flamengo to

---

* For Argentinians, Paraguay remains a poor country.

three consecutive titles in the 1950s using a 4-2-4 formation, would have been proud. Thirty years before, he had coached Paraguay in a 7–0 defeat by Brazil.

. . .

Before his country had been stunned by Italy, Brazil's former minister of justice told the Spanish daily *El País*, "If Brazil wins the Mundial, it will be much easier to govern. To win the World Cup in football is much more important than winning general elections."[38] The offhand remark was especially glib given that Brazil had not enjoyed democratic elections since 1964. The *abertura* (opening), which followed ten years later, sought to relax the constraints that had been imposed on the country. The dictatorship had already succeeded in taming the guerrillas and expanding the economy. The country had enjoyed some of the highest growth rates in the world. Nevertheless, the path to democratization would not be uncomplicated. The oil crisis of 1973 and 1979 demonstrated just how reliant the country was on oil imports. By 1981, the "Brazilian miracle" revealed itself not to have supernatural powers. The country was about to endure the worst recession in its history. The following year Brazil's foreign debt spiraled to $87 billion, the largest in the world.

In this climate of economic uncertainty, Corinthians won the Campeonato Paulista two years in succession (1982 and 1983). The São Paulo club had gained a reputation not only for its football but for the idiosyncratic way in which it ran its affairs. In 1982, the election of the club's president pitted Waldemar Pires against Vicente Matheus. The former, running on the Democracia Corinthiana (Corinthian Democracy) ticket, represented the *abertura* and liberal reform, whereas the latter stood for authoritarianism and the establishment. Sócrates, who said he would retire from the game if Matheus won, backed Pires. The elections, albeit for the president of a football club, symbolized what the people had been denied for nearly twenty years. In the event

Corinthian Democracy won the presidency; the name had been printed on the back of the players' shirts. This was football as an act of political defiance.

Sócrates had been instrumental in changing the tenor of the club. Consensus politics made its way into the dressing room. From deciding when to have lunch to the drinking of alcohol and whether to dispense with the *concentração*,* the players would take a vote. Sócrates had also sought to educate players who had come from less privileged backgrounds. He would later say, "There was no consciousness; there was no knowledge. People had no critical skills . . . I used to buy the newspaper and bring it in for the 'concentration.' I kept aside the sports pages, put it out on the table and the other pages on this side. This side no one ever picked up. No one has ever wanted to know about the economy, about politics or about culture or anything . . . I would like to promote a constitutional change so that the football player might be obligated to have an educational background because he plays a very important role in the development of future generations in a country like mine. Because he is the one that is heard the most, he is a reference for a lot of people."[39]

Corinthians was not the first club to have exercised its autonomy. Brazilian football had a tradition of self-reliance that could be traced back to the late 1950s. Democracia Corinthiana was in many ways the culmination of that tradition. At the 1958 World Cup, Didi, Nilton Santos and Zito had ensured the selection of Garrincha and Pelé. During the 1960s, Santos and Palmeiras had also employed democratic self-governance. The legendary 1970 World Cup winners had been subversive in managing to extract freedom and liberty from discipline and order. These were Sócrates's role models. As with many

---

* The isolation of players, usually in a hotel, days before a match. This is meant to reduce the risk of distraction.

of his generation, Sócrates was defined by the dictatorship. "I am the child of a dictatorial system. When I started college at sixteen, I started to live through the repression—there were colleagues who had to hide, who had to run away."[40]

By 1984, the campaign for direct presidential elections (*Diretas Já*) was gaining momentum. At mass rallies, which now featured artists and show-business personalities, there was a sense of social cohesion. The national anthem would be sung at the end of the demonstrations, an indication of patriotism should the military forget. In April 1984, in front of one and a half million *paulistanos*, Sócrates promised that he would not go to Italy, where Fiorentina had offered him a contract, if the constitutional amendment were passed. True to his word, the next season he left for Europe.

The Power and the Glory

In November 1982, Colombia withdrew from hosting the 1986 World Cup. For once, common sense had prevailed. Shortly after taking office, President Belisario Betancur had decided against what would undoubtedly have been a luxury in straitened circumstances. "After a democratic appraisal and consultation on what our needs are, to preserve the public good, as we know that waste is unpardonable, I announce that the 1986 World Cup finals will not be held in Colombia. The golden rule whereby the championship would serve Colombia and not a group of multi-national companies, was not observed. Here we have many other things to do and there is no time to attend to the extravagances of F.I.F.A."[41]

Nine years before, President Misael Pastrana Borrero had sought to follow in the footsteps of Uruguay, Brazil, Chile, Mexico and Argentina. "It is in everyone's mutual interest to demonstrate to the world that a country such as ours is perfectly competent to put this challenge to our sports administrators, thus conveying to all other nations just how capable it is of organizing an event of this magnitude in 1986."[42] FIFA's executive committee would unanimously agree on the republic at a meeting in Frankfurt in 1974.

The costs of the competition were not feasible, especially given the disparity between the respective forecasts of the government and the Federación Colombiana de Fútbol. Eager to host the tournament, the Colombian federation had estimated costs at a mere $60 million, whereas the government believed it would cost three times that amount. Colombians seemed indifferent to the decision, especially once it became clear that Mexico had already been lined up to host the competition. In 1980, Horst Dassler, the president of Adidas, admitted in *Sport Intern*, "The 1986 Football World Championship will probably be given to Mexico if Colombia returns its mandate, a possibility which, in the meantime, is almost being counted on by the International Football Federation (FIFA)."[43] And so it transpired at a meeting in Stockholm, whereby Mexico's bid was approved. Henry Kissinger had tried to secure the tournament for the United States, but his experience of dealing with FIFA, and Havelange especially, made him nostalgic for the Middle East.

Mexico nearly gave up her newly acquired mandate when an earthquake struck Mexico City in September 1985. The natural disaster, registering 8.1 on the Richter scale, was responsible for 10,000 deaths and leaving 250,000 homeless. Álvaro Mutis, the Colombian poet and longtime Mexican resident, realized the seriousness of the situation while watching the country's patrician president, Miguel de la Madrid, on television. "I think it dawned on everyone who saw him that he had *no idea* what to do. You could tell from his face . . . I think everybody saw then that this huge mechanism called Mexico had no driver, that it was shuffling along with nobody in control."[44] Nevertheless, the tournament went ahead.

Televisa, the Mexican media conglomerate, had too much to lose if it didn't. Mexico's organizing committee gave assurances that the capital's stadiums were fit for purpose.

. . .

Ahead of the 1986 World Cup, it was expected that Argentina would repeat the dismal pattern of underperformance that had typified the majority of their tournament displays over the years, and few gave the squad any chance of victory in Mexico. The results of the warm-up matches were uninspiring. A 7–2 thrashing of Israel did little to assuage the concerns raised by defeats against France and Norway.

Similarly, the Uruguayans had not qualified for a World Cup since 1974 and seemed to have learned little in the intervening twelve years. Uruguay was the only Latin nation in a group of Northern Europeans. In the opening minutes against West Germany, the Uruguayans started as they meant to go on. The fouls on Völler and Brehme had both Germans writhing on the ground. After four minutes, however, Antonio Alzamendi poached an ill-judged back pass and scored. Uruguay held out until six minutes from time when West Germany equalized.

Before the tournament, *El Gráfico* ran an interview—which would inadvertently take a comic turn—with two Uruguayan defenders, José Batista and Nelson Gutiérrez, who were both playing in the Argentina's Primera División.

> *Batista: . . . the bogeyman might be Denmark.*
>
> *Gutiérrez: Hang on! Let's talk about Denmark after the World Cup. I've got a Uruguayan friend here in Mexico who has recorded Denmark's last ten international games: he thinks they're inflated by the hype.*[45]

Denmark opened their tournament—the first World Cup in which the Scandinavian kingdom had played—with a single-goal victory over Scotland. Nevertheless, in their next match they gave Uruguay a master class in counterattacking football.

The Danes were not only quick—something that was most certainly not part of Uruguay's repertoire—but they seemed able to dribble past their opponents at will. After nineteen minutes, the inevitable happened: Uruguay had her first player, Bossio, expelled from the pitch. Playing with ten men, the Uruguayans were powerless against the Danish onslaught. At halftime the score line was 2–1, but by the end of the match the Danes had scored another four goals. Michael Laudrup was not wrong when he called the team "Europe's answer to Brazil." (After beating West Germany, Denmark ran out of steam against Spain, whose Emilio Butragueño would score four in a 5–1 thrashing.) The Uruguayans were stunned by the manner of their defeat. Northern European football would now prove insurmountable in the Uruguayan mind. (Psychologically it would be easier to play Brazil or Argentina than the fleet-footed Northern Europeans.) Apart from the death threats that were customary after such defeats, the coach Borrás had his library destroyed by intruders. In a highly literate country, this was a very Uruguayan *housebreak*. He would later say that these men had known where to hurt him.

In her final match, against Scotland, Uruguay only needed to draw to progress to the next stage (the Round of 16), whereas the Scots had to win. After fifty-six seconds, José Batista was sent off for a terrible foul on Gordon Strachan. The match failed to improve and did not deserve any better than a goalless draw. The Scotland manager, Alex Ferguson, criticized Uruguayan gamesmanship, complaining that the Uruguayan players had bullied the French referee into calling time early. This appreciation for stoppage time would become even more evident at Manchester United. When Borras blithely stated, "I don't know what all the fuss is about . . . We played a fair game," Ferguson saw this as "a statement of historic hypocrisy": "I lost my temper and refused to shake hands with him."[46] Even FIFA threatened to send Uruguay home early if her standards of fair play did not improve. Despite finishing third in its group with a goal difference of minus-five, Uruguay was still able to take the last berth of third-placed teams. *La garra charrúa* no longer entailed winning against the odds; it now entailed progressing by stealth. (Uruguay had ceased to be the master of her own fate. An unhealthy reliance on the misfortune of others would now be required.)

It was hard to believe that this was the same country that had brought the beautiful game to Europe in the 1920s. The label *garra charrúa* had stuck after the 1935 Campeonato Sudamericano Extraordinario, at the end of which Uruguay had beaten Argentina three–nil. With an aging squad of players, many of whom were in their thirties, Uruguay was crowned champions in Lima. The golden years had come to an end. Uruguayan football had now become defined by the *garra charrúa*, a pugnacious national trait that could be traced back to the nineteenth century. It would sit uneasily with the finesse that many of the country's players possessed. In 1967, at the funeral of his teammate Héctor Scarone, José Nasazzi gave the address. "We were young, we were winners, we were united, we believed that we were indestructible." It might as well have been a eulogy for an entire era of Uruguayan football. A year later Nasazzi was dead. Twenty years later in Mexico, while the rest of his team was busy adhering to the *rioplatense* trait of playing like "animals," there was only one player who remained faithful to Uruguay's more elevated sporting heritage. Enzo Francescoli, whose exquisite touch would earn him the sobriquet "El Príncipe" (The Prince) and a move to Olympique Marseille, where he became an idol to the young Zinedine Zidane, tormented the Scottish defense and shone above the rest of the squad. But he could not rescue his country by himself.

With her reputation in tatters, it was only a matter of time before Uruguay was eliminated. Argentina, who had ridden her luck in the opening phase, would prove more testing opposition. The two neighbors had not faced each other in a World Cup match since the final of the inaugural tournament. Against Argentina, however, Uruguay refused to be psychologically cowed—after all, history was on her side—though she seemed contrite after FIFA's warning. Nevertheless, the better team won. A single goal in the match belied Argentinian dominance. Maradona was at his best, demonstrating the grittier side of his game alongside the flamboyance. He was as unimpressed by his neighbors as he had been six years earlier. "That wasn't just another victory: the Uruguayans' paranoia really pissed me off in those days, and also we hadn't beaten them in a World Cup for fifty-six years."[47]

. . .

As with most world championships, the tournament was defined by one match. In 1986, however, it was not the final. For ninety minutes, history was played out within the confines of the Estádio Azteca. The Falklands War may have given the encounter added tension, but the match symbolized an Anglo-Argentinian conflict that had its origins in the early nineteenth century. Not that the British had ever paid much attention. Her history had not happened in Latin America. Argentinian history, however, had become defined by the unsuccessful British invasions of 1806 and 1807. For the British, these had amounted to little more than skirmishes: a footnote in the annals of British history. For the Argentinians, they represented resistance to a colonizing force. Attitudes toward the English* would continue to remain ambivalent. This was never anything but provincialism writ large. Unable to come to terms with their own brittle identity, Argentinians felt a sense of unease when confronted with older and richer

---

* For which read British. There remains a sweeping interchangeability inherent in Latin American Spanish: *chinos* (Chinese) is shorthand for the inhabitants of the Far East; *turcos* (Turks) for anyone from the Levant and the Arabian peninsula; *hindús* (Hindus), pertaining to those from the Indian subcontinent.

traditions. The relationship with Britain would remain fraught with difficulties: on the one hand, father of the nation's greatest pastime; on the other, a neocolonial power.

. . .

In 1984, England had undertaken a three-match South American tour. There would be no friendlies against Argentina. When the tourists landed in Brazil, the local journalists immediately questioned the England manager's tactics. "Four-two-four?" they echoed, shaking their heads in disbelief. "Impossible. Everyone plays four or at least three in midfield against Brazil. We don't believe you. It is impossible. We will wait and see."[48] The anticipated massacre was never to be. Bobby Robson was vindicated when England won by two goals to nil. John Barnes, one of the few English players of sufficient ability, dribbled the Brazilian midfield and defense to score a goal that graced the Maracanã. Uruguay proved stiffer competition, beating the English by two goals in Montevideo. On the other side of the Andes, Chile, ever diplomatic in these matters, offered the visitors a goalless draw.

The Falklands War made the quarterfinal between England and Argentina a tense affair. Before the match, Maradona maintained a tactful stance that, on later evidence, belied his true feelings. "Look, the Argentina team doesn't carry rifles, nor arms, nor ammunition. We came here only to play football. How can I talk about war when only last month 30,000 Tottenham [Hotspur] fans cheered me in Ossie Ardiles's testimonial? I'm tired of always being asked the same question. Look, we are in the World Cup, we have come here to play football not politics."[49] (Tottenham fans were apt to chant "AR-GEN-TI-NA" during matches.) Victory would give Maradona the chance to reinterpret the significance of the match. Jorge Valdano, the most literate of footballers, held that only fools would confuse the game with politics. He believed that the prospect of sporting glory was sufficient reason for the players to motivate themselves, there was no need to bring politics onto the pitch. This did not stop the British press, who were always ready to allude to their country's martial past, from referring to the conflict. In 1982, the *Sun* had run the infamous headline GOTCHA . . . OUR LADS SINK GUNBOAT AND HOLE CRUISER after the controversial sinking of the *Belgrano*. Four years later the suggestion of British military superiority was evident: IT'S WAR, SEÑOR! In Argentina, the response was more balanced. *La Razón* declared, "Las Malvinas are Argentinian, football is of the people."[50]

In spite of Maradona's intimidating presence, the English did not fear the Argentinians. England believed itself to be a team, whereas Argentina seemed overly reliant on one player. The clinical Carlos Bilardo realized that Pedro Pasculli, who had scored the only goal of the match against Uruguay in the previous round, would have to be sacrificed for the midfielder Héctor Enrique. "You can't play against the English with a pure centre-forward. They'd devour him, and the extra man in midfield will give Maradona more room."[51]

Argentina was the only Latin American team left in the competition. The day before, Brazil and Mexico had both been knocked out in penalty shoot-outs. Against West Germany, Mexico played out an unappetizing goalless draw, which had gone into extra time. The West Germans had had to play most of the second half without Thomas Berthold, who had been sent off. Harald "Toni" Schumacher proved as adept with his feet as he had with his fists in 1982. The Mexicans could only score one penalty, through Manuel "Manolo" Negrete. The year before, he had scored an extraordinary *chilena* (bicycle kick) for UNAM against Puebla, having deftly controlled the ball on his chest from a whipped-in cross. West Germany took four penalties and scored them all.

Brazil's position as the pretournament favorite had been based more on sentiment than empirical evidence of her current strength. Yet, after the team won all her group matches and then thrashing Poland by four goals to nil in the last sixteen, it looked as if Brazil might have learned lessons from her chastening experience in 1982.

Even Sócrates sought to reassure: "In Spain, we offered spectacle and did not manage to win the title. Now we play in a less showy fashion and are winning."[52] The Brazilians had not conceded a single goal in four games. Against France, Careca scored after seventeen minutes; it now looked as if more goals would follow. But Platini's goal shortly before halftime changed the psychological complexion of the game, before Zico's missed penalty definitively shifted the advantage toward the French. After replacing Müller in the seventy-first minute, Zico threaded a perfect pass to Branco, who was brought down by the French goalkeeper. Nevertheless, his weakly taken penalty was easily gathered by the French goalkeeper, Joel Bats. The shoot-out started badly when Sócrates's coolly taken penalty was parried. Worse was to come when the French winger Bellone hit the post, only for the ball to rebound off the head of the Brazilian keeper, Carlos, and into the net. Platini's miss kept Brazil in the game until Júlio César hit the post. The Spanish-born Luis Fernández would make no mistake from the spot. Once again, Telê Santana's squad failed to live up to expectation.

England did not accord the world's best player any respect. Terry Fenwick picked up a yellow card for a foul on Maradona after nine minutes. Another nine minutes passed before the Englishman, seemingly having forgotten the caution he had already received, sent an elbow into the Argentinian's face. He escaped punishment. Heightened expectation had led to stalemate: the first half ended goalless.

Six minutes into the second half the match came to life. The England midfielder, Steve Hodge, witnessed the drama at close quarters. "[Maradona] flicked the ball, I think he miss-hit the pass, and it bobbled off to my left side. The ball was spinning behind me and Valdano was leaning on me probably hoping he'd make me put it out for a corner but the ball spun just perfectly for me and I wanted to knock it back to Shilton. I caught it perfectly . . . I turned around thinking, 'That will be Shilton's.' I hadn't seen Maradona run into the box and when I saw them both going up for the ball I just thought,

'Why is he there?'... I hadn't seen a hand of God."[53] His assessment of Maradona's crime was remarkably evenhanded: "He took a chance, he cheated, and he got away with it."[54]

The watching Tunisian referee gave the goal, and was immediately surrounded by the remonstrating English defenders. For Bobby Robson, the England manager, it was the way in which Maradona had celebrated his goal—without any guilt—that disturbed him the most. (The British would rail against Luis Suárez for his off-the-pitch celebration at the 2010 World Cup after Ghana's Asamoah Gyan missed the last-minute penalty that had been awarded after Suárez stopped a certain goal with his hands.) Four minutes later, with England in disorder, Maradona administered the *coup de grâce*. He scored a goal of sublime beauty, one that, just as much as his disputed opener, summed up the Latin American game. Víctor Hugo Morales, a Uruguayan journalist who'd taken residence in Argentina, gave one of the greatest commentaries in the history of the game:

> *The ball to Diego. Maradona has it now. Two are marking him. Maradona controls the ball, breaks down the right, the genius of world football! And he abandons the third [player], and he's going to give it to Burruchaga . . . still Maradona. Genius! Genius! Genius! Ta, ta, ta, ta, ta . . . and Goooooool! Goooooool! I want to cry! Dear God! Long live football! Golaaaaazoooo! Diegooool! Maradona! Sorry I want to cry. Maradona, on a memorable run, in the best move of all time. Cosmic comet, from which planet have you come to leave so many English [players] in your wake? Turning the country into a clenched fist, screaming for Argentina . . . Argentina 2—England 0. Diego! Diegol! Diego Armando Maradona. Thank you, God, for football, for Maradona, for these tears, for this . . . Argentina 2 England 0.*

Enrique, who had given his teammate the ball, would later say that his pass was so perfect that it would have been impossible for Maradona not to score. The uneven pitch seemed not to affect the

Argentinian, who, in his own half, turned two players inside out, before setting off for goal, leaving several English defenders floundering in his wake before bamboozling Shilton and rolling the ball into the net. *El Pibe de Oro* was back in the *baldío*: that patch of wasteland glorified by Borocotó in the opening chapter—"Fue Así" ("It Was Like This")—of his memoir of a life spent in sport.

For Brian Glanville, Maradona's goal also harkened back to a better time. The goal was "so unusual, almost romantic, that it might have been scored by some schoolboy hero, or some remote Corinthian, from the days when dribbling was the vogue. It hardly belonged to so apparently rational and rationalized an era as ours . . . to a period in football when the dribbler seemed almost as extinct as the pterodactyl."[55] And yet it was the most Argentinian of goals: the cult of the individual at work. England came back into the game, after Lineker scored a trademark goal from a cross, but would be unable to equalize.

Maradona would initially deny his handiwork in the first goal, before admitting that it had been in part due to the "Hand of God." The English took this as an insult, a contravention of the spirit of the game. The goal should not have stood, which would have meant a one-all draw, went the erroneous argument. Though those who sought to castigate Fenwick's heavy-handedness were few. Maradona had seen his chance and took it. This was *la viveza criolla* writ large. The English expatriate writer Gordon Meyer had written the most succinct description of this mode in the late 1960s. "More important to [the Argentine] the lightning riposte, however illogical, than reasoned argument. If to overthrow his logical absurdity takes *time*, the validity is considered unimpaired. The thing is to be is rapid. There could not but exist a word for such a widespread phenomenon: *viveza*, the well-known *viveza criolla* . . . which is that of being smart at the expense of another, a quality of smart-aleckness, circumscribed by the saying: *El vivo vive del zonzo y el zonzo de su trabajo*, the smart one lives off the fool, and the fool off his job."[56]

In later years, the sleight of hand would be recast as an act of defiance. "I felt—and I feel, I do not deny it—that with this [victory] we won something more than a soccer game. We defeated a country. It was our contribution, in our way. We all declared before the game that soccer had nothing to do with the Malvinas War . . . A lie! . . . *In our skin was the pain of all those kids who had died there, so close and yet so far.* Emotionally, I blamed every one of the English players— our rivals—for what had happened. And my goals—both of them— had special significance: the first was like sticking my hand in the pocket of an Englishman and removing the money that did not belong to them; the second . . . topped everything."[57]

Maradona would also become less than gracious. After years of being hounded and vilified, his reaction would verge on the feverish in its glee. In the documentary *The History of Football*, Maradona delivers his piece to the camera. "Shilton! All goalkeepers are useless. You're no exception . . . Tell me, if the ball crossed just over the line, and you swept it away without the referee seeing it had gone over, would you go and tell him it was a goal?" The Argentinian had always reveled in being provoked. When interviewed by his former team-mate Jorge Valdano before the 1990 World Cup, he admitted, "The more they fuck me off the bigger I get; it's just another incentive."[58]

Following on from his display of genius against England, Mara-dona turned the semifinal against Belgium into a two-goal master class. (Before the match, Bilardo had told his squad, "Boys, kill your-selves [out there] because if there's something I can't stand it's to watch the finals on television."[59]) In the final, Maradona's finely threaded pass sent Burruchaga through to score the winning goal. Argentina had won her second World Cup in eight years, though few had foretold her success. Daniel Passarella, who was kept out of the squad by injury, stated openly that there was "no chance in Mexico" unless Argentina improved.[60] Oscar Ruggeri would later recall, "Before the World Cup, no one could stand us. Neither the people, nor the press, nor the politicians. Except for our families, everyone was against us."[61]

Before the tournament, Raúl Alfonsín, Argentina's president, had asked his minister of sport, Rodolfo O'Reilly, "When are you going to sack Bilardo?" The question was now best forgotten. After the final, Alfonsín employed the kind of bombast to which the continent's politicians are given: "This is not only an Argentinian victory. It is also a victory for all of Latin America, which, at last, has understood the need to come together."[62] Not that Maradona would agree. "To champion Latin Americanism . . . to champion Latin Americanism, complete balls! When the [West] Germans equalized we really looked like the visiting team at the Azteca [stadium]. That made me furious."[63] Many Mexicans, reacting to Argentinian arrogance, had overtly supported the Europeans. Even some of the local coverage subtly implied an anti-Argentinian tendency: Argentina's triumph had been reported as West Germany's defeat.

Eight years later, in the USA World Cup, a demoralized Argentina staggered into the last 16 as the best-placed third team from the group phase. They would not be missed. In Asunción, there was no sense of South American solidarity. Banners, asking for a Romanian win, went up across the city. In Gheorghe Hagi, Romania had her own "Maradona of the Carpathians," who would inspire his team to send the Argentinians home early. The following day the banners were replaced with others that read THANK YOU, ROMANIA!

Twenty years after the match, Jorge Valdano had had time to reflect on Maradona's two goals:

With the second goal I realized immediately what it meant. Not only for Argentina. I have seen many goals but this one had everything. It had significance. In a match of the greatest importance symbolically, Maradona showed two characteristics of the Argentinian. In the first goal it shows the trick [cheat], that which is known in Argentina as picardía criolla [creole craftiness] or viveza [cunning]. Argentina is a country in which deceit [deception] is held in more esteem than honesty. But it also has another face. It is that of virtuosity and skill. With the second goal

Maradona crowns the match with a work of art. It is skill, dribbling,
la nuestra *[our game]. Another esteemed factor in Argentinian football*
is that it is more important to known how to dribble than to know how
to pass.[64]

Death in the Andes

Ill health and an equally ailing economy had helped depose the Peruvian president General Velasco in 1975. Under the new president,
General Francisco Bermúdez, fiscal cost cutting under the guidance
of the International Monetary Fund had averted economic free fall.
Though not before the military had decided it had had enough and
sought a return to civilian rule. In 1980, Fernando Belaúnde Terry
was elected president for a second term. It would not be a happy one.
Hampered by a moribund economy, Belaúnde Terry's presidency
would coincide not only with the global recession but also with the
fallout of El Niño, which cost the government over $600 million in
lost exchange earnings. Moreover, to coincide with the general elections, the Sendero Luminoso (Shining Path)—which had taken its
name from Mariátegui's words *"El Marxismo-Leninismo abrirá el sendero luminoso hacia la revolución"* (Marxism-Leninism will open up a
shining path to the revolution)—had declared a war of insurrection.
Not only would the terrorist activities of the Maoist guerrilla organization cause thousands of fatalities, it would also become a drain on
the government's fiscal resources. When Belaúnde Terry left office,
the country was $14 billion in debt. Under the subsequent presidency
of Alan García, who pursued a policy of economic and administrative
decentralization, Peru would ignore the IMF and negotiate directly
with her creditors. By 1990, hyperinflation had reached an annual rate
of 12,378 percent.

The 1980s became known as the *década perdida* (lost decade) for
the economies of Peru and other countries in Latin America, but it

was also a decade to forget for the country's football. It started brightly with qualification for the 1982 World Cup at the expense of Uruguay, who had failed to capitalize on her success at the *Mundialito* earlier in the year. But the performances the Brazilian-born coach "Tim" (Elba de Pádua Lima) had managed to coax from his charges in the 2–1 win in Montevideo that clinched qualification would not be repeated in Spain. Cameroon, playing in her first World Cup in a naive style that reminded some of Brazil in the 1930s, held the Peruvians to a goalless draw. In a wearyingly close group where five out of the six matches ended in stalemates, Peru's matchup with Italy ended in a one-all draw; though Peru was unfortunate not to be awarded a penalty after a piece of Gentile's usual overzealous defending. Poland, however, put Peru's unstable defense to the sword with a 5–1 thrashing. The Peruvians had made it easy for Poland with a primer in inept possession. For some of the older players, it had been a tournament too far.

Club performances at continental level were little better. Since 1972, when Universitario succumbed to Independiente, no Peruvian club had contested a Copa Libertadores final. Even progression to the competition's second phase seemed beyond their clubs. When Universitario finally made it through the first round in 1988, it had been ten years since a Peruvian club had achieved this distinction. (In the event, the club was knocked out by América de Cali.) Whereas the Primera División (First Division) had belonged to Limeño (Lima) football, the game now extended itself to the country's provinces. What had been a manageable division of fewer than twenty teams had by the 1986 become forty-four clubs. Paradoxically, as football went to the country, the regional population—fleeing violence and poverty—had started to flock to the capital.

In this climate of economic uncertainty and decentralization, football clubs now had to take on extra travel expenses, which, depending on the distances involved, at times exceeded gate receipts. Thus a cheaper means of transportation than the country's expensive, and for the most part unreliable, commercial aviation was needed. The military, seeking additional revenue, undercut the competition and chartered out its own aircraft. With the country *in extremis*, even the government was unlikely to object.

In December 1987, tragedy, which had long stalked the Latin American game, took center stage in Peru. For its match against Deportivo Pucallpa in the Amazon rain forest, Alianza Lima had chartered an aircraft from the navy. After securing a 1–0 win over their opponents, the Limeños seemed eager to return to the capital. At 6:30 p.m., the Fokker F27 A-560 took off. Unable to ascertain whether his landing gear had been deployed, the pilot contacted the air traffic controller to check and was told it was safe to land. No more was heard from the plane after 8:15 p.m., when air traffic control lost contact with the pilot. Piecing together what little could be confidently said afterward, it seemed that, having lost too much height, the pilot misjudged his landing and was unable to stop the aircraft from crashing into the sea. Of the forty-three on board— including players, staff, fans and officials—only the pilot, Ediberto Villar, survived.

Aldo Panfichi and Víctor Vich, in their excellent study of the impact of tragedy on Peruvians, stated that: "According to the [Villar's] testimony, [he and the Alianza striker, Alfredo Tomasini] had both survived the accident and had been swimming for hours, holding on to parts of the plane as they waited for someone to come to their rescue. These accounts stress Tomasini's courageous struggle to keep afloat, with a broken leg, while he confessed his undying love for his mother to the pilot. The navy pilot had encouraged this conversation to prevent the soccer player from surrendering to fatigue. However, just when a rescue helicopter was preparing to save him, Tomasini could hang on no longer and disappeared into the Ocean of Ventanilla."[65]

The country was now plunged into mourning. Masses and football matches were held for the victims, who now ascended into the pantheon of the great, even though many had yet to prove themselves. Politicians, cognizant of the power that the game held over a grieving population, revealed their lifelong obsession with the club, and vendors of sporting memorabilia cashed in on the loss of this "golden generation." The Peruvian navy's own communications were tempered by a feeling of embarrassment that they would be accused of not being able to keep their aircraft in good working order. Relatives of the victims went to Lima's naval base in a futile quest for answers. It was rumored that shots were fired to warn off these distraught relations. Evasion was the now the mother of conspiracy. In traditional Latin American fashion, the theories started to circulate. It was said that the players had discovered a cocaine trafficking operation, which they threatened to expose, only for the navy to have the aircraft shot down; that the pilot was not qualified to fly at night. Understandably it was widely held that the responsibility lay with the navy, which had failed in its responsibility to protect its charges.

Tragedy would, however, unite the region. Colo-Colo sent four players from Santiago, while the evergreen Cubillas came out of retirement in the United States to play for his former club. Alianza had been at the top of the league when disaster struck, but at the end of the season it would be the club's great rival, Universitario, who was crowned champion. The championship match, which was won by a single goal, may have ended in the same result as the first contest between the two, but it was played in a far better spirit. The two clubs had first played each other in 1928, in a match that would be remembered more for class conflict than for football. With Universitario, whose roots lay in the University of San Marcos, winning by a goal to nil, the Alianza players lost their nerve and resorted to the more physical side of the game. The Uruguayan referee had no choice but to expel five Alianza players, and therefore end the match early. When the middle-class supporters of "La U" started to heckle Alianza in no uncertain racist and classist terms, the players launched themselves at the fans, who, according to legend, saw them off with their canes.

The Flight of the Condor

Shortly after Salvador Allende's ascension to the presidency of Chile, the employees of Editorial Zig-Zag, the publishers of the sporting weekly *Estádio*, went on strike. Their aim was to be nationalized; so the government duly obliged and took the company over. Renamed the Editorial Nacional Quimantú, the publishing house made books accessible to the average Chilean by pricing them in line with a pack of cigarettes. *Estádio* now fell under the spell of the new socialist regime, with journalists making the link between sport, exercise and politics. The journalist Edgardo Marín attempted to contextualize his country's sporting prowess while understanding its shortcomings. "We lose, but cleanly; we show who we are, poor still, but dignified without artificially inflating ourselves. This purity of ours (though we lack other virtues) is an excellent foundation to begin to construct better sports on."[66]

Though the Chileans were not averse to *la viveza criolla* (creole cunning), it was never a part of their repertoire in the same way as it was for the Argentinian or Uruguayan. Maradona's "Hand of God" goal epitomized a lack of scruple that would continue to pervade the game. Nevertheless, the rule in the region has been simple—do not get caught. Escaping punishment is in many ways equal to the very act of deceit. While Maradona was applauded for having picked the pockets of the English, the Chilean goalkeeper Roberto "El Cóndor" Rojas would be reviled for feigning injury.

The emergence of Cobreloa, a small club with great expectations, had boded well for the Chilean game. Flamengo and Peñarol may have beaten the Cobreloa in successive finals of the Copa Libertadores, but both victories were close-run efforts. In 1991, Colo-Colo became the first—and last—Chilean team to secure the trophy that every club on the continent coveted. The intervening years, however, were ones that Chilean football would choose to forget.

Chile had not won a single match at a World Cup since she hosted the tournament in 1962. After failing to qualify for the Argentinian edition, the country sought to prove herself in Spain. Luis Santibáñez, the manager of the national team, was optimistic; so much so that he stated that Chile should not be frightened of any other team. The football association only asked that the country not disgrace herself. Chile would lose all three of her matches. Five years later, in the 1987 Copa América, honor was restored when Chile trounced Brazil 4–0 in Córdoba on her way to reaching the final against Uruguay. In a closely fought match—there were four red cards—Pablo Bengoechea's goal was the difference between the two teams. It seemed that Chile would never win the tournament in which she had first competed in 1916.

Chile's fall from grace, which took place two years later, would shame the country in a way that no defeat, however humiliating, ever could. Qualification for the 1990 World Cup had pitted Chile against the hardest team to defeat on the continent, Brazil, and the easiest, Venezuela. Only the group winner would qualify. In Santiago, the Chileans let Brazil wait for them in a hostile stadium—the electronic scoreboard read CHILE 3 BRAZIL 0—before coming on. Two red cards ensued in an ill-tempered affair: Romário punched an opponent and Ormeño committed a career-threatening foul on Branco. The match ended one-all, though both goals were scored in peculiar fashion: Brazil benefited from a Chilean clearance that rebounded into the goal, while Chile equalized from a quickly taken free kick in the penalty area. As punishment for nonsporting behavior, FIFA made Chile play her "home" tie against Venezuela in neighboring Argentina. For the final match, the Chileans flew to Rio to play in front of 140,000 spectators. They had to win.

With Chile one–nil down through a well-taken goal by Careca, drastic action was needed to stop Brazil. In the seventieth minute, a firecracker was thrown from the terraces onto the pitch near the Chilean goal. Rojas took the opportunity to dive into the smoke. While he was on the ground, his coconspirator, the defender Fernando Astengo, took the razor blade Rojas had secreted in his glove and cut him.

In protest, the Chileans carried their bloodied goalkeeper into the dressing room, though not before Patricio "Pato" Yáñez had grabbed his own genitals as an insult to the Brazilian crowd. The game was now abandoned.

Only the Chileans believed what to every other Latin American had obviously been a ruse. The country was furious. Admiral Merino, one of the instigators of the 1973 coup, ranted that "the Brazilians have only recently come down from the tree."[67] Sergio Stoppel, president of the Chilean Soccer Federation, stated that "Chile has filed a protest asking FIFA to annul the game and to apply sanctions against Brazil and the Maracanã Stadium. It was physically impossible for us to compete."[68] More than 10,000 fans greeted the returning squad.

Tests were now carried out by experts, which proved that a firecracker could not have caused the injury. The photographic evidence showed conclusively that the flare had missed the player. Pinochet sent two envoys to speak to the Argentinian referee in Buenos Aires; he had wanted to understand the circumstances better. When the deception was discovered (including the submission of a falsified medical certificate by the team doctor), Chile was disqualified from participating in the following two World Cups and Rojas banned for life. He felt he had risked his career for the good of the country but received little credit for doing so. Rojas stayed in Brazil, where he had played for São Paulo. Later he said, "Had I been Argentinian, Uruguayan or Brazilian I would not have been suspended . . . but since I am Chilean they did not give me the opportunity of vindicating

myself." In 2001, FIFA lifted Rojas's ban, to which he said: "At forty-three, I'm unlikely to play again, but at least this pardon will
cleanse my soul." The woman who threw the firecracker ended up
modeling for *Playboy*.

Forza del Destino

Víctor Hugo Morales's *barrilete cósmico* (cosmic comet) was always
likely to burn out. That Maradona managed to continue as long as he
did showed extraordinary resources of self-belief and self-delusion,
not to mention exceptional ability. The difficulties he experienced in
the first half of the decade had now given way to sporting glory and
its attendant fanfare. At Napoli, Maradona would transform a club
that, before his arrival, had beaten relegation only by a single point,
though success came slowly. In his first season in Italy, Verona, whose
fans had a reputation for overt racism,* won the Scudetto, while Napoli had to endure midtable anonymity. Two seasons later, in 1986–
1987, the club won its first title, together with the Coppa Italia.

The extravagance of the club, which had signed Maradona for a
world record £7 million, a fact that did not sit well with the population of a city that lacked proper infrastructure and sanitation, seemed
to goad the smart clubs of Piedmont and Lombardy. Naples would
suit Maradona in a way that Barcelona never could. Not only did the
club represent the underdog, but the city's culture was not dissimilar
to that of Villa Fiorito, where he had grown up. Here Maradona was
no longer an outsider; or worse, in the eyes of the Catalans, a *sudaca*
(a pejorative term for a South American).

These were El Pibe's golden years, though they were also a time
when he was subject to temptation, especially the pleasures of the

---

* They once hanged a black doll with the message, "Give him the stadium to clean."

rich. His lifestyle took on all the attributes of the flashy demimonde, with its drinking and drugs, prostitutes and mobsters. The drug of choice, cocaine, which he had first tried in Barcelona, took hold. The city had an intoxicating effect, as Goethe had discovered two centuries before. "Naples is a Paradise; everyone lives in a kind of intoxicated obliviousness of self. It is the same for me; I scarcely recognize myself; I seem to be a quite different person. Yesterday I thought: 'Either you used to be mad before or you are so now.'"[69]

And yet this brash, young Argentinian had given southern Italy a voice, one that stated, "Naples champion, screw the nation."[70] The following year Napoli lost the Scudetto to AC Milan by three points. With five games of the season remaining, the Partenopei were four points ahead of their rivals. The uncharacteristic way in which the club failed to maintain its momentum was viewed with some suspicion, especially given the company that Maradona now kept. His relationship with the Neapolitan *tifosi* suffered as his performances became more erratic. Jeering and whistling from the fans was one thing, criticism in the press for his on- and off-the-pitch antics was another. Paranoia and conspiracy now enjoyed a symbiotic relationship. Nevertheless in the 1989–1990 season, with the prospect of leading Argentina in the World Cup in his sights, Maradona scored sixteen goals to help Napoli defeat the challenge from Internazionale and AC Milan. There was still affection in southern Italy, but the rest of the country had grown to hate the diminutive Argentinian. When Italy hosted her second World Cup in 1990, Maradona would find out just how much.

Although England and Germany have, for different reasons, come to sentimentalize that "one night in Turin," the tournament turned out to be a mediocre one. Its real highlight was a stroke of marketing genius, which brought classical music to the masses in the form of "The Three Tenors," Luciano Pavarotti, Plácido Domingo and José Carreras. (Pavarotti's rendition of "Nessun dorma" would become the tournament's signature tune.) For once, Uruguay looked as if she might relive former glories and move on from the disgraceful performance of four years before. In her opening match, the Uruguayans played with confidence, knowing it was only a matter of time before Spain surrendered. When Villarroya handled the ball on the line, Rubén Sosa stepped up to take the penalty. He would later admit to having studied Zubizarreta's penalty saves beforehand, but in the event his careful preparation was of little use. With the miss—he launched the ball high above the crossbar—went Uruguay's dreams. The country's confidence, never that resolute to begin with, was easily shaken. The former world champions would only make it out of the group in third place, while Spain found herself the group winner. In the next round, the Italians showed just how impotent the Uruguayans were. The *rioplatenses* reverted to defensive type, and were undone by two second-half goals. It was as if the players were still ruing Sosa's missed penalty.

An unlikely candidate for the Azzurro shirt, let alone the competition's "Golden Boot," was Salvatore Schillaci, who scored the first goal in the two–nil win against Uruguay. For the month of the tournament, in spite of his Sicilian, working-class origins, Schillaci became a national hero. As with most summer romances, this love affair would be brief. Maradona, on the other hand, was vilified from the outset. In the opening match of the tournament, Argentina lined up against Cameroon, a team whose exuberant performances added luster to the otherwise disappointing competition. Maradona was booed as his name was announced. His detractors must have been equally pleased when the world champions fell to a one–nil defeat. Nevertheless, Argentina beat the Soviet Union and drew with Romania to make it to the next round as the best third-place team. Brazil—yet again—awaited the Argentinians. In the eightieth minute, Maradona's finely threaded pass, through the legs of a Brazilian, set up Claudio Caniggia to score what Juan Sasturain called "the greatest and most unfair counterattack in the world."[71] Against Brazil's attacking play—it had been relentless—Bilardo had opted for defense and counterattack. Underhand tactics had also played their part. The Argentinians were said to have given Brazil's left back, Branco, water laced with a sedative, which had made him feel faint and unable to concentrate. A decade and a half later, Bilardo refused to admit or deny that the subterfuge had taken place. The goal would send the Brazilians home, and not undeservedly. For a country that had showed the world how the game should be played, Lazaroni's introduction of a *libero*, especially against Sweden and Costa Rica, was inviting punishment. Brazil was still struggling to achieve the right balance between attack and defense.

Argentina's route to the finals would be facilitated by two penalty shoot-outs, though a questionable German penalty defeated her in the end. Despite missing two penalties in its shoot-out against Yugoslavia, Argentina scraped into the semifinals. Sergio Goycochea, the reserve goalkeeper, had replaced Nery Pumpido, who had broken his leg against the Soviet Union, and was Argentina's savior. Maradona and his team now returned home to Naples, where Argentina had been drawn against Italy.

When Antonio Matarrese, president of the Italian Football Federation (FIGC), called for national unity and asked that Neapolitans support their country, Maradona was quick to reply, "For 364 days out of the year you are considered to be foreigners in your own country; today you must do what they want by supporting the Italian team. Instead, I am a Neapolitan for 365 days out of the year." But not even Napoli's greatest player could overcome national loyalties. One banner read MARADONA, NAPOLI LOVES YOU, BUT ITALY IS OUR COUNTRY. And yet when Schillaci opened the scoring, as he done in the previous match against Ireland, not all the Italians celebrated. In the second half, Argentina created more space and movement, which allowed Olarticoechea to flight a pass onto the back of Caniggia's head that was past the flailing Walter Zenga. It was the first goal, for which he was unlucky but ultimately at fault, that Zenga had conceded in the tournament. Extra time, which never seemed to end, failed to divide the teams. In the penalty shoot-out, Maradona, having failed against Yugoslavia, made no mistake with his attempt. As the Argentinian ran back to his teammates, the stadium went quiet. Goycochea's second save earned Argentina a place in the final. The celebrations, however, would be short-lived.

In Rome, against a newly unified Germany, Argentina experienced one of the low points in her sporting history. During the singing of the Argentinian national anthem—which Bilardo had thought of shortening so that the team would not have endure the jeering— Maradona looked to his left before mouthing *"hijos de puta"* once, and then again for emphasis. For Bilardo, who had a reputation for toughness, it would be hardest defeat of his life. The blame was leveled at his fellow *rioplatense* medical professional, Edgardo Codesal. Born and brought up in Uruguay, the recently naturalized Mexican referee took his life into his own hands when he awarded Germany a penalty five minutes from time for an unlucky challenge on Rudi Völler. His calls had already incurred the wrath of the Argentinians when he sent Monzón off for a foul on Klinsmann, who performed the most theatrical of dives. Argentina would end the match playing with nine men.

If Argentina had deserved her victory in 1986, four years later she did not even merit a place in the final. Football's finest showpiece allowed the Germans to exact her revenge. The game itself was poor, and would set a tradition for uninspiring World Cup finals. In the modern game, there was too much to lose. Pablo Alabarces captured Argentina's poor showing: "At Italy 1990, with an appalling team, supported by what little a Maradona, blighted by injury, could do, Bilardo arrived at the final against Germany, riding on a double continuity: that of illegitimate practice—violence [on the pitch], and some other tricks—and that of the paranoid discourse—in the global conspiracy theory pronounced by Maradona."[72]

In October 1990, Maradona announced his retirement from international football. "It was like ripping out my own heart," he would say.[73] The following year, the game exiled, albeit briefly, a tarnished El Pibe de Oro when he was banned for fifteen months for cocaine use. His life now became a cycle of criticism, conspiracies and comebacks. The Mexican writer Juan Villoro believed "[Maradona's] well-aimed criticisms [to be] of a restricted scope: João Havelange does not deserve a place on the [football] pitch because he is a water polo player turned politician; FIFA should not allow eleven men with diarrhoea to play at midday in Mexico, at 2,200 metres above sea-level, and at 'the hour of the ravioli.' Maradona is correct in relation to the abuses suffered by the players, but fails to stand as a Túpac Amaru in short trousers."[74] By 1994, he had taken the law into his own hands when he starting firing an air rifle at journalists outside his home in Buenos Aires. Looking back at the Argentinian's career, one psychologist believed the "grandiose and delusional beliefs exact a heavy price on the psyche and Maradona paid in full. Flip over a messianic delusion and you'll find doubt, insecurity and often self-loathing. Maradona has talked about the unsettling impact of falling literally into a ditch of human shit as a young boy. He never lost the smell in his nostrils, he never forgot what he rose up out of. And perhaps too a small corner of him never escaped the feeling of being 'shit.'"[75]

Driven on by an unshakable sense of destiny, Maradona would lead his country onto the field once more, making a superhuman effort to get into shape for USA 1994. His former teammate at Barcelona Bernd Schuster was unequivocal in his assessment: "If Diego were German, he would not have played in this World Cup. Only someone with the mentality of an Argentinian and the genius of Maradona is capable of trying this folly at his age, especially after so many battles." The physical transformation—he had lost twenty-six pounds—and the crazed celebration after his left-footed strike against Greece said it all. So too would the drug test that found ephedrine, phenylpropanolamine, pseudoephedrine, non-pseudoephedrine and methylephedrine in his body. Michel d'Hooghe, a medical official on FIFA's executive committee stated, "Maradona must have taken a cocktail of drugs because the five identified substances are not found in one medicine."[76] Having played only two matches, Maradona was suspended for the rest of the competition. FIFA needed the Argentinian to ensure a commercially successful tournament; now it had to deal with the situation as quickly as it could. The ban would have to come later. The shock, however, would continue to resonate, even after Argentina's early exit.

As he sat in a chair in a messy hotel room, Maradona had the look of a man who had just grasped the magnitude of his actions. Stunned, he stated, *"Me cortaron las piernas"* (They have cut off my legs). He knew his career was now over. Had he read *Rayuela* by his fellow countryman Julio Cortázar, he would have been reminded of Jacques Vaché's maxim:* *"Rien ne tue un homme comme d'être obligé de représenter un pays"* (Nothing kills a man as much as having to represent his country).

---

* Vaché died of an opium overdose.

CHAPTER TEN

LA PELOTA NUNCA SE CANSA

(The Ball Never Tires)

1994–
Latin America and the Global Game

Own goal, own goal, thanks for the own goal.

—The last words Colombian defender
Andrés Escobar heard before his assassination

They're [the Argentines] a den of thieves from the very top to the bottom.

—Jorge Batlle, president of Uruguay

Maracanã is a cathedral. The temple of football. It is a place to even hold mass.

—FIFA president Sepp Blatter

The tragedy would read like a novella by García Márquez. Though, in view of their country's propensity for violence, Colombians had long grown used to such things.

Middle class and eloquent, Andrés Escobar had had a healthy attitude toward his chosen profession: "This sport illustrates the close relationship between life and the game. In football, unlike bullfighting, there is no death. In football no one dies; no one gets killed. It's more about the fun of it, about enjoying."[1] In May 1988, the young Colombian defender had slipped his marker and headed a fine equalizer against England at Wembley Stadium. Six years later, on the day the 1994 World Cup entered its knockout phase, Escobar was assassinated outside a Medellín nightclub. His only crime: to have steered the ball into his own net.

The player had been taunted the night of his death. That evening Escobar had gone out with friends, though by all accounts he had exercised enough self-control not to respond to the insults. Four days before, he had written in *El Tiempo*, "Please, let's not let the defeat affect our respect for the sport and the team. See you later, because life goes on." Once again, he apologized for the goal, but had asked to be respected. Two brothers, Juan Santiago and Pedro David Gallón Henao, self-styled "entrepreneurs" whose main line of business involved narco-trafficking, were the main provocateurs. Rumor had it that they had lost money gambling on the country's performances. It was believed that other cartels, with betting on defeat in mind, had engineered the poor showing.

"Señor Autogol" was to be expected. "You're a nigger just like Asprilla" was a different matter. Escobar was also accused of having thrown the game for money. At 3 a.m. Escobar was about to leave the parking lot, when one of the brothers got into the player's car and turned up the volume on the radio before exiting the car. His driver, Humberto Muñoz, then murdered Andrés Escobar. It is rumored that the assailant shouted, *"Gracias por el autogol"* (Thanks for the own goal) before shooting the player. Each of the six shots carried with it the cry of *"AUTOGOL!"* That night forty other people were shot in the city. Escobar's death had left the writer Enrique Santos Calderón with a sense of devastation—more so than the assassination of liberal politician Luis Carlos Galán at a rally five years before—and shame in being Colombian.

Although Escobar's *autogol* (own goal) would not be forgotten, few would remember anything else about Colombia's brief sojourn in the United States. In her opening match, Colombia took the game to Romania, but a mixture of shrewdness and fine goalkeeping would thwart the exuberance of the Latin Americans. The match ended 3–1 to Romania, with Colombia being caught out by two clever first-half goals—one of which was Hagi's beautifully weighted chip that eluded the goalkeeper Córdoba. Before the next game, Colombia's coach, Francisco "Pacho" Maturana, received yet another death threat from a death squad. If Maturana picked Atlético Nacional's midfielder, Barrabás Gómez, not only would the player and coach be killed, so too would their families. Gómez did not play, and opted for early retirement. Understandably the Colombians looked agitated when they took to the field against their American hosts. As the teams lined up during the national anthems, Faustino Asprilla thought a shot might be fired. Ten minutes from the halftime whistle, Escobar made his error. As he lay on the turf, after having guided the ball past a startled Córdoba, the expression on his face seemed to foretell his fate. After Earnie Stewart scored again for the USA, Valencia's second goal of the tournament came too late in the game and failed to save Colombia from successive defeats. In *El Tiempo*, one fan was quoted as saying, "If we aren't capable of beating the gringos, then we aren't worth anything."[2] Any hope of progressing to the next round was now dependent on a victory over Switzerland and a Romanian defeat. It was not to be. The autumn before, things had been very different. Colombia had been hailed as potential world champions. The country had become the victim of her own success.

Unlike European (UEFA) qualification for the World Cup—which entailed its fair share of questionable ties against nations with no discernible footballing talent—there were very few straightforward matches in its South American equivalent. Venezuela apart, a country that conceded thirty goals in eight matches, it was becoming the toughest competition in world football. Colombia had been pooled with Argentina, Paraguay, and Peru, all of whom were unpredictable. Nevertheless, Colombia enjoyed a golden month, one in which she did not lose a single qualification match. Having beaten Peru 4–0 in Barranquilla, the Colombians traveled to Buenos Aires, where the team only needed a draw to secure qualification. Argentina had already been beaten by Colombia in mid-August. On September 5, 1993, a date forever etched in the memory of Argentines and Colombians alike, Buenos Aires was witness to one of the greatest matches in the history of the Latin American game. Colombia massacred Argentina. Colombia looked like Brazil in her pomp and danced around the Argentine defense to the tune of five goals (two apiece for Rincón and Asprilla, and one for Valencia). With defeat imminent, even the Argentinians cheered. In Bogotá that night, eighty people died violently, whereas in Cali, where the mayor had had the foresight to have the city's bars close, the body count was only three.

The Colombian media called it "parricide." Argentina's manager, Alfio Basile, was ashamed. "I never want to think about that match again. It was a crime against nature, a day when I wanted to dig a hole in the ground and bury myself in it."[3] Ever brazen where such matters were concerned, Maradona stated that "Colombia can't break history. Argentines have to continue as we are. Argentina on top, Colombia underneath."[4] The way the game had established itself in the region had created a psychological hierarchy that had remained intact, even if results would prove otherwise. For Argentina, there was Brazil, her eternal rival, and then the other republics; for Brazil it was vice versa. Uruguay, by virtue of her early dominance, saw herself part of a triumvirate, though her neighbors had long banished her to that demimonde between them and the other republics. (Detractors of the Uruguayan game never failed to mention that her titles had been won before the introduction of color television.) The Colombians were now quick to respond—the spell had been broken—with an advertisement that captioned a picture of the footballing god himself with the words "Diego Armando; zero in history" written underneath.

Shortly after Escobar's murder, Gabriel García Márquez was told, "In this century, only three important things have taken place in

Colombia: in 1948, the 9th April [El Bogotazo]; in 1967, the publication of *One Hundred Years of Solitude*; and in 1993 the 5–0 [win] of
Colombia against Argentina in Buenos Aires." To which the Nobel
laureate responded, "And you know what the terrible thing is about
what you say? That it's true."[5] The win against Argentina had been
the highlight of the country's footballing history, the execution of
Andrés Escobar its lowest point. That Colombia believed herself to
be among the Latin America greats was understandable. In the semifinal of the 1993 Copa América, the Colombians only lost to Argentina, against whom she had drawn in the group stage, on penalties.
Qualification in grand style had also attracted the endorsement of
Pelé—something certain to spell misfortune—who predicted that
the country would go far at the next World Cup.

In the view of the Colombian journalist Eduardo Arias, Colombian football had hitherto suffered from a lack of identity. "*Selección
Colombiana de Fútbol* [Colombian national football team]. These
three or four words mean much, little, nothing, make us laugh or cry,
embarrass, are a source of pride . . . But history as such does not exist.
It is a quilt of fragments, stitched [together] with contradictory
threads, patches that, for the most part, have been minor stories of
success and defeat, ephemeral and isolated, to start over again. To
start over again. Above all, to start over whenever we leave the stadium dejected and with lowered flags; or whenever we turn off the
radio or television embittered by defeat, but with the secret conviction that the Colombian players are good."[6]

For a country so lacking in a positive self-image, any praise was
likely to distort the reality. With no real history on which to rely for
sober guidance, Colombian football believed that it had conquered a
game that had taken her neighbors years to tame. There were rumors
of excess (predominantly women and alcohol) incompatible with the
routine of a playing professional. Colombia now played matches of no
consequence—*à la brésilienne*—in order to please her sponsor and the
Federación Colombiana de Fútbol. Maturana had once explained

Colombia's dilemma: "Club football comes before international football in Colombia. It always has and always will. This is because the federation is rather poor."[7] But under Maturana, who would coach Colombia four times, the national game flourished, albeit briefly. (In 1995, the year in which Peru and Ecuador engaged in a brief conflict, known as the Cenepa War, he would be appointed coach of the latter. After a 2–1 victory against Peru in the Copa América later that year, he would famously say, "We've won a football match, we haven't won a war.")[8] In a country that had long favored the foreigner, especially players from the Río de la Plata, Maturana's time at Atlético Nacional early in his career stood out for his reliance on domestic talent. *La Prensa* said of him, "More than drug money, it was drug imagination. [Pablo] Escobar had the instinct that Maturana was a great coach. Nobody knew [that] then."[9] Maturana's faith would be repaid both domestically and on the continent's most prestigious stage. When Atlético Nacional faced down Paraguay's Olímpia in the deciding match of the 1989 Copa Libertadores, it was the first time in the competition's history in which the final failed to feature a team from any of the triumvirate of Argentina, Brazil and Uruguay. Atlético Nacional managed to secure the title after four rounds of "sudden death" in a penalty shoot-out in which René Higuita saved four and scored one.

The tragedy of Colombian football was that by the time it had started to be taken seriously by the traditional powers of the sport, its domestic game was already riddled with drug money and corruption. For the drug cartels, running a club was an attractive way of laundering narco-dollars, just like other "businesses" such a real estate, construction, hospitality, and the media. Moreover, it would afford the drug elite popularity among the fans. When Hernán Botero Moreno, president of Atlético Nacional, was charged with laundering $57 million and extradited to the United States, matches were suspended for a week. In 1988, in response to accusations of corruption, Juan José Bellini, president of América de Cali, said, "Why should this club need bad money? We have 2,000 rich members plus a group of legitimately successful businessmen who don't need that sort of operation. People put two and two together and get five. Maybe they are jealous of our success."[10] Nine years later he would be jailed for money laundering.

The tedium of Pablo Escobar's incarceration at La Catedral prison—or Club Medellín—was alleviated by visits from various football teams. Roberto Escobar, the infamous head of the Medellin cartel's brother, remembered, "René Higuita's Nacional team arrived first, on the celebration of Las Mercedes, the patron saint of prisoners. Pablo wanted us to play a real game against them, except as he warned them, 'Games here last about three or four hours, without rest and only two changes are allowed. A tie is settled by penalties.' They wore their official uniforms; we wore the colours of the German national team. Pablo was a good player but he was [marked] hard by Leonel Álvarez [the notoriously combative defensive midfielder], and when Pablo complained, Álvarez told him, 'This is how we play soccer, brother.' . . . Within a few days the professional teams from Medellín and Envigado also came to the Cathedral to play against us."[11]

In October 1983, during the administration of Belisario Betancur, the minister of justice, Rodrigo Lara Bonilla, exposed six of the nine teams in the Colombian league as having connections to drug cartels. Lara Bonilla, who had pursued the cartels with vigor, would be gunned down the following year. The assassin had been sent courtesy of Pablo Escobar. The kingpin's vengeance would make no exceptions, not even for the minister of justice. The judiciary and legal profession became a prime target for the drug elite during the 1980s with forty from their ranks executed per annum. One investigating judge was sent a message that read: "We are friends of Pablo Escobar's and we are ready to do anything for him . . . We are capable of executing you at any place on this planet . . . in the meantime, all the members of your family will fall, one by one . . . For calling Mr.

Escobar to trial you will remain without forebears or descendants in your genealogical tree."[12]

Bribery, needless to say, had become an everyday occurrence. In the semifinal of the 1989 Copa Libertadores between Nacional de Medellín and Montevideo's Danubio, the three Argentine officials were given a master class in Colombian coercion. A day before the match a group of men, carrying machine guns, entered the hotel in which the referee and linesmen were staying. According to one of the linesmen, Juan Antonio Bava, "They offered us money and threatened us and our families with death. They told us that Nacional *had* to win and added: 'The money's there. If you want it, take it! . . . Nacional wins or you're all dead meat.'" Luckily Danubio was thrashed 6–0. A year later Alvaro Ortega was not so fortunate. After refereeing Independiente Medellín vs. Club América, he was shot twenty times after being told, "That'll teach you to disallow a fucking Medellín goal."

In 1956, Colombia's minister for education, Abel Naranjo Villegas, stated that the people from the Atlantic coast "never could understand that language of violence, because their ways have always been fed by that 'fair play.'"[13] By the end of the century, it was the only language many Colombians understood. Eduardo Galeano believed that Colombians suffered violence as one would a disease. At times it seemed incurable.

La Pelota No Dobla (The Ball Doesn't Bend)

In the diary he kept of his travels in South America, later rewritten as *The Condor and the Cows*, Christopher Isherwood noted of Bolivia, "This unhappy country is cursed with the most inflamed kind of nationalism. Bolivians seem to hate and fear all their neighbors. They have their reasons, of course; every hater has."[14] In the closing decades of the century, the low-lying republics in the south of the continent hated having to play at altitude where Bolivian football had created something of a fortress from the thin air of the Andes.

Bolivia had more in common with Colombia than an interest in coca. The footballing improvement of both countries in the early 1990s made the other, grander republics in the region reassess long-held prejudices. Hitherto Bolivian football had been considered a joke—in 1949, Brazil had inflicted a 10–1 defeat on the country, before Uruguay scored eight goals without reply in the World Cup a year later. It would, however, be the World Cup qualifiers, rather than the tournament itself, that added luster to the country's somewhat unexceptional sporting history.

In July and August 1993, Bolivia won the first five matches in her campaign. Few would have given them any chance in a group that included Brazil, Uruguay, Ecuador, and Venezuela. But in Puerto Ordaz, a proto-American, ersatz city in the Venezuelan interior, they achieved the unthinkable: after going a goal behind after fifteen minutes, the Bolivians scored seven by the seventieth minute. Carlos D. Mesa Gisbert, an historian who would assume the presidency a decade later, felt the cycle of tie-saving draws and honorable defeats—"We played like never before and lost as always"—had been broken.

A week later, against Brazil in La Paz, Bolivia secured one of the greatest victories of her sporting history. The brilliant Marco Etcheverry—otherwise known as "El Diablo" (the Devil) for his demonic dribbling—covered half of the pitch before forcing a mistake from Taffarel, who let Etcheverry's shot dart through his legs. A minute later another Bolivian goal, and Brazil's unblemished record had come to an end: it was the very first time the country had lost a World Cup qualifying match. Afterward, two players, Rimba of Bolivia and Zetti of Brazil, failed a drug test. Rimba's excuse was that he had drunk tea made from coca leaves. Victories against Uruguay, Ecuador, and Venezuela (this time 7–0 in La Paz) followed. Nevertheless, in Recife, Brazil showed up Bolivia's inability to deal with crosses,

scoring six goals without reply. After Bolivia, it was Uruguay's turn
for a run of victories, though in her final match she had to contend
with Romário, who had been recalled to the Seleção despite a disciplinary record that was less than exemplary. "I already know what's
going to happen," said Brazil's prodigal son. "I'm going to finish Uruguay." Two late goals from Romário sent Brazil to the World Cup as
group winners. The Bolivian team was the runner-up, securing their
first berth at the tournament since 1950. "El Diablo" Etcheverry
would later recall, "There's a real change in your image when you
make the finals of the World Cup. I remember when Colombia qualified for the 1990 games. It was like, 'Wow, the country's reputation
soared overnight to another level.' We were in awe of them. That's
what we're hoping will happen to us."[15]

In the opening match of the tournament, Bolivia had to face the
reigning world champions, Germany. For much of this uninspiring
match, the Bolivians proved equal to the Europeans. In the end a
Klinsmann goal, in an otherwise tight game, defeated Bolivia, whose
prospects suffered when they lost Etcheverry to a red card four minutes after he had come on as a substitute. Another Bolivian expulsion
followed in the draw against South Korea, before a second defeat,
this time to Spain, put an end to Bolivia's dreams of progressing to
the next round.

The problem posed by fixtures carried out at altitude refused to go
away. Between 1996 and 2007, FIFA tried to ban all matches played
at altitudes of more than 2,500 meters. The reasons given ranged
from the perceived health risk the altitude posed to players to the
belief that the unfair advantage gained by the home team went
against FIFA's notions of "fair play." Argentina—who had not won
since 1973 in Bolivia, and would not do so until 2005—had been one
of the most fervent objectors, with Passarella famously refusing to
allow his team to play the 1997 Copa América quarterfinal in La Paz.
Not that this was the first time the Argentinian had complained. The
year before, after Argentina had lost 2–0 to Ecuador in Quito,

Passarella found a new excuse for their defeat. He claimed that *"En la altura la pelota no dobla"* (At altitude the ball doesn't bend). The veto incensed not only Bolivia, but also Ecuador and Peru. Chile and Mexico would also be affected. President Evo Morales resorted to playing a match on Nevado Sajama, six thousand meters above sea level, as proof that altitude had no serious physical consequences.

In 1997, Bolivia hosted the Copa América for the second time. With the tournament being played so close to the World Cup, qualification for which remained a priority for many in the region, certain republics chose to send weakened squads. High altitude favored the Bolivians, who played all their matches at the lofty Estádio Hernando Siles in La Paz. Brazil demanded to be based in Santa Cruz, 416 meters above sea level, otherwise she would withdraw from the competition. Bolivia could not afford a tournament without the reigning world champions and granted the Brazilians their wish.

Bolivia made light work of her opponents until she met Mexico in the semifinals. Mexico opened the scoring after eight minutes. Just before halftime the Paraguayan referee assisted the hosts by sending a Mexican off, and despite her team losing a player of their own to a red card, Bolivia's passage to the final was secured with three goals. On the other side of the draw, Peru were having a successful tournament, beating Argentina 2–1 in the quarterfinals. Peru's cause had been helped by Argentinian impulsiveness. The teenage Marcelo Gallardo, having missed and scored a penalty, was sent off after a fracas with the Peruvian goalkeeper. For the last eight minutes Argentina, who had succumbed to the vices that had dogged her game over the years, had to play with eight men. Peru now had to face Brazil. "We will make the best use of Brazil's weaknesses," said the Peruvian coach, Freddy Ternero. Denilson's goal in the first minute did not augur well for their prospects. Seventy-six minutes later Brazil had scored seven goals without reply. Brazil now made the journey to La Paz for the final, where her victory at 3,640 meters dispensed with the theory that it was impossible to win at altitude.

In truth, medical evidence has found little difference between acclimatized and nonacclimatized teams, though playing at altitude proved a physiological challenge for any team. Bolivia's Basque coach in 1993–1994, Xabier Azkargorta, believed "the psychological aspect . . . plays a lot in favour and contra the opposing team, and also against our team because it is often believed that altitude wins a match and that is not the case. You have to play."

Tetracampeão

In retrospect, "World Cup USA 94" was always going to be a case of hype over expectation. Ostentatious though the opening ceremony was—the marketing budget dwarfed any previous World Cup—USA '94 would end up delivering very little. But then the World Cup had for a long time flattered only to deceive; the mediocrity of Italy's tournament far from being an exception. The four-year cycle was perfect: it gave the world enough time to forget the disappointments of the last tournament while allowing it to look forward to the next edition. The game had become an exercise in nostalgia.

Before the tournament, even the Americans, usually so positive in such matters, were skeptical. Tom Weir, writing in *USA Today*, gave his reason in no uncertain terms. "The World Cup draw is Sunday and admit it, you don't care. And no matter how much this event gets crammed down your throat . . . you still won't care. But don't feel guilty about it. There's a good reason why you don't care about soccer, even if it is the national passion in Cameroon, Uruguay and Madagascar. It's because you are an American, and hating soccer is more American than mom's apple pie, driving a pickup or spending Saturday afternoon channel-surfing with the remote control."[16] For Americans, sports happened above the waist rather than below it. Even on the two occasions the World Cup was held in neighboring Mexico, they took little interest in the planet's greatest sporting event. Nevertheless, the American appetite for spectacle should not have been underestimated. The competition would have the biggest audience of any World Cup, drawing 32 billion television viewers. After the event Sepp Blatter boasted, "The 1994 World Cup produced a turnover of $4 billion . . . I mean no disrespect to other sports by saying that even the Olympic Games cannot compare. The World Cup was a fabulous success."[17] The football was not.

Brazil was no longer exceptional. She may have been the first country to win the World Cup on three occasions, but in the intervening years Italy and Germany had equaled her record. The pressure to win a fourth title was suffocating. Carlos Alberto Parreira would later say, "There was unbearable, almost inhuman pressure bearing down on me because Brazil had not won it since 1970. My god, that was mentally and physically exhausting for years, even during the qualifiers for the World Cup! Winning the World Cup simply meant I had accomplished my mission. I suddenly felt a ton weight drop from my shoulders."[18]

Brazil's campaign reflected this exhaustion. There was nothing carefree in her style of play; it was not Brazilian, nor was it wholly European, as certain Latin American detractors would have it. The team was now powered by two defensive midfielders in Mauro Silva and the gaucho Dunga. They won their group comfortably, the only hitch a one-all draw against Sweden. The country was unimpressed. Not that this should have surprised the Brazilian coach. The year before, Parreira had complained, "It got to the point where we beat Bolivia 6–0 and one newspaper in São Paulo accused us of playing defensively."[19]

In their game against the USA in the second round, that kind of accusation would be justified. Once again Brazil demonstrated— though because its team was the world's favorite, this was something that was always quickly and conveniently forgotten—that it could play rough. Nils Middleboe, the Danish amateur footballer who played for Chelsea in the 1910s, wrote of the 1958 World Cup: "The foul that upset me most was the one committed by a Brazilian against the French center half and captain in the semifinal at Stockholm. [. . .] In a level game with the score 1–1, the center half in question was tackled so recklessly, and so badly hurt, that the French team was reduced virtually to 10 men for the remainder of the match, after which the Brazilians had little difficulty in winning."[20] When the elegant Leonardo elbowed Tab Ramos in the face—the Brazilian must have thought he was playing against Uruguay—the ferocity of the assault felled him. The Uruguayan-born Tabaré Ramos, who had been the USA's most creative player, was taken off the pitch and sent to a hospital. Leonardo was suspended as a result and would watch the rest of the tournament from the substitutes' bench. The game was finally sealed when Romário's fine pass gave Bebeto no choice but to score. Leonardo's enforced absence allowed Branco to start in the quarterfinal against Holland. The game was made for schoolboy heroics on occasions such as these. With the match tied at 2–2, Brazil having squandered a hitherto secure two-nil lead, Branco secured a free kick. With a run-up nearly the length of the ball's distance from goal, the Brazilian drilled the ball into the bottom left-hand corner. "Before hitting the ball I looked up at the scoreboard," he would say. "There were 10 minutes to go. And I got it into my head it was the right moment, the just moment, and I had God's help to make it happen at that moment."[21]

Sweden would prove harder to break down, not least because of the prowess of the Swedish goalkeeper, Thomas Ravelli. Ultimately, though, the diminutive Romário found a pocket of space amid the towering Swedish defenders and scored the header that proved the only goal of a closely fought match. Brazil had reached the final for the first time in twenty-four years. The culmination of the tournament was a disappointment. Although they deserved their victory, in the end it was more that the Brazilians had wanted—or needed—the trophy more than the Italians. Ninety minutes ensued: no goal. Extra time: no goal. For the first time in the tournament's history, the World Cup would be decided through penalties. This in itself was no dishonor; the fact that the game had concluded goalless was shameful. When the exhausted Roberto Baggio, who had played so valiantly in spite of the injury he'd suffered in an earlier round, skied his penalty, the trophy went to Brazil. Baggio would later recount in his memoir, "When I went up to the spot I was pretty lucid, as much as one can be in that kind of situation . . . the ball went up three metres and flew over the crossbar . . . I was knackered . . . I failed that time. Period. And it affected me for years . . . If I could erase a moment from my career, it would be that one."[22]

The exhaustion that led to that miss seemed to sum up the tournament. Fifty-two matches had been played in a month, with little time for the players to rest in between games. (The final was played just four days after the semifinals.) The scheduling of matches in the midday heat, so as to allow for European broadcasting, did little to enhance the spectacle. Moreover, the comprehensive coverage of the event seemed to compound this feeling of ennervation. "People are demanding to know who's hurt, what the players are saying, every detail, every word," said a Bolivian television sports director. "And not just from Bolivia, they want to know how the other teams are doing . . . who's in form and who is not."[23] FIFA had made a concerted effort to seduce the American public with the "beautiful game." The stadiums may have been filled, but there was something missing. If anyone had been unsure before, it was now obvious for all to see—the game had lost its soul. Nevertheless, Brazil was once again world champion, returning the country to what it believed to be its rightful preeminence in the international game. In the words of the musician and critic José Miguel Wisnik, the period between 1974 and 1994 remained "a long intermezzo without victories, in which the central issue discussed in Brazil became the dilemma between 'soccer-art' and 'soccer-force.'"[24] If Brazil believed they had solved that conundrum, events four years later would prove otherwise.

. . .

The last time Uruguay had hosted the Copa América, it was still officially the Campeonato Sudamericano. Peñarol may have been reigning world club champions, but the country was in steep decline. Whereas in 1967, the Estádio Centenario had hosted all matches—only 1,500 had paid to see Chile vs. Bolivia and Paraguay vs. Venezuela—the 1995 edition took the tournament out into the country. Stadiums in Maldonado, Paysandú, and Rivera were modernized with the aid of $20 million.

The hosts opened the tournament with a 4–1 win over Venezuela, but their subsequent progress would be steady rather than remarkable. Their River Plate neighbors, having already qualified for the quarterfinals, were humiliated 3–0 in their last group match by the USA in Paysandú, a small city that sat on the Argentinian border. This was no fluke: a month before the Americans had thrashed Mexico 4–0 in Washington, D.C. Against Brazil, however, Argentina would put out her strongest eleven. After nine minutes the match was one-all, both teams having taken the offensive. Then a clever counterattack led by Ortega unleashed Batistuta, whose violent shot prompted a mistake from Taffarel. Even playing with ten men in the second half, Argentina withstood Brazil until the finish line was in sight. But the footballing gods had long memories. Nine minutes from the Peruvian referee's final whistle, Jorginho's lofted pass into the area was controlled by the elegant Túlio and flicked into the net. It was clear for everyone, apart from the referee, to see that the Brazilian had used his hand in bringing the ball down. Not even in the penalty shoot-out would there be justice. Taffarel saved twice. The "Hand of the Devil" had prevailed.

The Argentinians were quick to forget Maradona's handiwork.

Balbo felt cheated and disillusioned. One representative from the Argentinian federation stated, "This is robbery, it was an irreverence and an outrage." Even Héctor Núñez, the Uruguayan coach who had spent most of his managerial career in Spain, took the side of the Argentinians: "All that was missing was for the referee to applaud the goal."[25] In the view of *La Prensa*, it was a simple equation: "Brazil, with the hand of God." Ten years later, the Argentinian writer Pablo Vignone would construct an apologia for the handball:

> *When it comes to reproaching sins, it must be admitted that both the hand of Tulio in the* Copa América *in 1995 and that of Diego in the Mexico's World Cup, almost a decade before, were the product of an instant craftiness, steeped in the* potrero, *outside the law in regulatory terms, although characteristic of a folklore linked intimately with the spirit of football.*[26]

In the final against Uruguay, Túlio would score again, though this time with his chest. But the inclusion of Pablo Bengoechea by La Celeste would prove decisive when the Peñarol number 10 scored a perfect free kick that left Taffarel staring into his own net. With no more goals forthcoming, the ubiquitous penalty shoot-out followed. Túlio's luck ran out, and his penalty was the only one to be saved. Uruguay had maintained her record; she had never lost a championship as host. Four years later Brazil would have her revenge in a one-sided encounter which ended three-nil. Between 1997 and 2007, the Seleção would be the team to beat, winning four out of five titles.

Two months after the tournament, Colombia played England in an international friendly of no consequence at Wembley. The match remained goalless, though one brief passage of play alone was worth the price of admission. Of course, it did not come from the English. (The Northern Europeans had no call for such luxuries.) When Jaime Redknapp tried to chip René "El Loco" Higuita, the Colombia goalkeeper was more than up to the challenge. He treated the attempt on goal with the disdain it deserved. Waiting with the patience of a juggler, Higuita sprang forward and, with his body parallel to the ground, flicked the ball back over his head with the studs of his boots. The "scorpion kick" demonstrated that spectacle had not died: that the game, in spite of its many flaws, could provide moments of glory that had little to do with just victory or defeat.

Judgment in Paris

There had always been trouble with money. In the opening decades of the century, the game had been afflicted by the question of "false" or "brown" amateurism, which had hastened the advent of professionalism in the early 1930s. With official payment came accountability. Spectators, who had paid their entrance fee, now demanded a certain level of competency from their players, which usually took the form of victory. With the advent of professionalism, Marcos Carneiro de Mendonça, Fluminense's goalkeeper throughout the 1910s and 1920s, felt he could longer put up with the insults and profanities that had started to be directed at him when he conceded a goal. He soon gave up the game.

Over forty years later, however, players were no longer solely reliant on club wages. While the 1954 World Cup in Switzerland provided the first live television broadcast, it would be another sixteen years before Technicolor and satellite broadcasts would truly globalize the game. (In the interim, England's victory at home sounded the "Last Post" for the end of the empire.) Pelé was one of beneficiaries of this brave new world; swiftly earning a $120,000 contract for wearing Puma football boots. At the 1970 World Cup, with the cameras on him, the Brazilian deliberately tied his laces. But then he was a company man.

By 1996, the stakes were higher. Late that year the Brazilian Football Federation entered into a ten-year contract with the sportswear conglomerate, Nike, for $200 million. The catch was that the Seleção had to play fifty friendlies. Not that this was much of an issue for Brazilian football. It had long grown used to a byzantine fixture list, in which compulsive modification had become the norm. It took some time to establish a national league in a country so riven with strong regional identities, and its final instigation came via an unexpected source. In 1969, the creation of the Loteria Esportiva (Sports Lottery) allowed the government to exploit the republic's passion for the game. Profits were divided between the Ministries of Education and Culture and Social Security. Such was the lottery's success that, according to the sociologist Janet Lever, "[it] led to a direct change in the structure of Brazilian soccer. The government urged the CBD to establish a national championship so there would be lottery games all year long. In return for extending the soccer season from forty to eight-five games, the Ministry for Education and Culture offered money to CBD."[27]

It helped that, even before the foundation of the Campeonato Brasileiro in 1971, the lottery had helped unify the Brazilian game in the public's mind. Establishing a league was one thing, deciding even simple issues like the number of clubs that would participate was another. Twenty clubs played in the inaugural season; two years later this figure had doubled. Quantity put paid to quality. As soon as 1977, the number of clubs had escalated to sixty, though most league games were low on goals and skill. By the end of the decade, the Campeonato comprised ninety-six teams, though it was clear by now that the entrance of many of the smaller sides was little more than an exercise in inclusive politics: something that, like it or not, the paying public understood. Not only was there a proliferation of teams, but even the structure of the season was unnecessarily complex. In *Futebol*, Alex Bellos identified the Brazilian penchant for crescendos. "When there is a league, the best teams *always* proceed into a knockout stage. Brazilians do not understand championships without a 'final.'"[28]

Unsurprisingly, by the mid-1980s attendance had declined by 30 percent. The nation's loss of enthusiasm was compounded by a change in tactics: coaches told their charges not to dribble the ball into the net but to shoot from outside the area. This may have been more "efficient," but it did little to enhance the spectacle, and the prestige of the Brazilian League suffered accordingly. *World Soccer* described the 1988 Campeonato as being "marked by tedious football, microscopic attendances and more violence than a Charles Bronson film."[29] It was an all too true reflection of the state of the domestic game.

No wonder that those who had the opportunity to leave did so, especially if they could enjoy the more civilized schedules of Europe. Many believed the coming of professionalism, and the fundamental changes to the way clubs were run that it brought in its wake, was to blame. The humanitarian lawyer Heráclito Sobral Pinto, who had been born in the final decade of the previous century, gave his verdict on the game he loved as he sadly watched the struggles of América, the side he supported. "It seems to me that bad administrations of the team have been the responsibility for its collapse . . . We need to replace these directors with men of character, such as those in the directorships in the old days. Today no one in *futebol* merits my respect."[30]

Violence, against players and referees, and indiscipline blighted a game in which the offenders regularly found their punishment being downgraded from a suspension to a fine. As if this tacit endorsement for infraction was not enough, the CBF proved itself disturbingly willing to break its own rules. In 1996, Fluminense and Bragantino were both relegated, only for the CBF to show clemency and reinstate the clubs the following season. A match between Palmeiras and Vasco da Gama a few years before would epitomize the chaos that had befallen Brazilian football. Palmeiras took to the field at the Estádio Parque Antarctica, though there was no one against whom to play. Vasco da Gama, having won a court order that suspended play for twenty-four hours, had stayed in their hotel. The club was entitled to sixty-six hours rest, but had played a match forty-six hours earlier. When the Rio team arrived at the stadium the following day, it was refused entry. Palmeiras's coach, Vanderlei Luxemburgo, casually remarked that this kind of incident demonstrated why the country had failed to win a World Cup in over twenty years. But he would be no more successful than any of the others who had failed before him. The 2000 Olympics in Sydney, at which he coached the national team, brought a swift end to his brief international career. Olympic gold, a medal that Uruguay had won twice in the 1920s, had eluded Brazil for over eighty years, and her quarterfinal defeat to a nine-man Cameroon team that would go on to win the competition kept the honor frustratingly out of reach.

The proliferation of games—exacerbated by international club competition—required São Paulo to play two games on the same day. The club sent out reserves against Lima's Sporting Cristal for the Copa CONMEBOL—an ill-conceived and short-lived tournament for those that had failed to qualify for the Copa Libertadores—and a senior eleven for a league match against Grêmio. "I've given up complaining about fixture congestion," said Têle Santana. "I'm just glad we didn't have to play in the morning as well."

But despite the disastrous state of her leagues, Brazil had nevertheless become defined by the game at which she had so excelled in the past. The Brazilian writer Betty Milan voiced what most Brazilians felt to be true. "Football reflected the nationality, it mirrors the nation. Without football we Brazilians do not exist—just as one could not conceive of Spain without the bullfight . . ."[31] Of course this was reductive, but it sounded good. Brazil had come to enjoy a somewhat symbiotic relationship with the World Cup. She had become everyone's favorite, a parody of herself. To those who examined the country closely, there was now something distasteful about her quest to win another World Cup. Not only did it suggest gluttony, there was also a degree of narcissism at play. At times, Brazil seemed to be competing against her own history rather than against another nation. (Unlike Brazil, Argentina not only enjoyed defeating an opponent but also the act of humiliation.) The 1998 World Cup would end in failure and prompt a series of questions for which there would be inadequate answers. Though for the anthropologist José Sérgio Leite Lopes, there was a very simple reason. "The defeats in the World Cups between 1974 and 1990, which were received with sadness, especially in 1982 due to the quality and performance of the team that went to Spain, did not in any measure reproduce the reaction to the 1950 defeat. There was no longer a threat to national identity."[32]

The last World Cup of the century was extended to include thirty-two squads from five confederations. In 1930, eighteen matches had been played; sixty-eight years later there would be sixty-four. Moreover, there were fewer surprises for the Latin Americans. Of 110 players from the five CONMEBOL nations—Argentina, Brazil, Chile, Colombia, and Paraguay—forty-one played outside the continent, mostly in Italy and Spain. One such was Ronaldo, a twenty-one-year-old prodigy who already had the sporting curriculum vitae of a journeyman. He had started his career at Cruzeiro, before being advised by Romário to join PSV. Bobby Robson would then bring him to Catalonia. The British coach, who knew something about footballing genius having seen and been stung by Maradona at first hand, would later remember, "He was still only nineteen but I told Barcelona we must have him . . . he was rare, different and exhilarating. He had different skills from other centre-forwards. He's an incredible dribbler; he dribbles like George Best . . . He has an amazing ability to just plough his way through. Part of that is his natural talent and part is his amazing physique. He's incredibly strong, tall and beautifully balanced. And, of course, he had astonishing pace. I have never seen a player as fast as him when he runs away from people on the turn, or turns into the ball. He just explodes."[33] It's tempting to imagine that Robson was probably still awestruck by the goal his young charge had scored against Compostela: not so much a wonder goal as a force of nature that drove through the opposition to score. A year later, having been named FIFA Player of the Year,

Ronaldo moved to Inter for $27 million. And yet, for all the Brazilian's talent, he had the air of someone who was out of place, isolated. He seemed somehow disconnected from the world around him. It would be the same look he would have in the World Cup final.

Mário Zagallo, who was back as national manager, had feared that "they will never let us win in Europe. In Brazil, there is a deep suspicion that outside influences, such as bad refereeing decisions, and other factors beyond the control of the players, will stop us."[34] The defeat against Norway in the first round offered a clue. The world champions were vulnerable after all, especially in defense. The psychological advantage Brazil held over Chile allowed her a 4–1 victory, but Denmark proved tougher opposition—the Scandinavians once again taking the game to the South Americans. Holland, after her brilliant victory against Argentina, seemed out of sorts, but nonetheless managed to hold out for penalties. Though they were hardly displaying the form of world champions, the Brazilians were still deemed the favorite ahead of the final.

Her opponents, the hosts, France, had come through a series of hard-won matches, especially against Paraguay. The plucky Paraguayans, who did not deserve to lose, were sent home through a "golden goal." (A ridiculous device that ended the match the moment the ball touched the net in extra time.) France was a genuine reflection of the new republic's multicultural nature, with players born in Senegal, Ghana, New Caledonia, and Guadeloupe. Cosmopolitan they may have been, but this didn't stop their captain, Didier Deschamps, from announcing that he did not want to hear the samba played during the final. He wanted the French crowd, usually prone to apathy where the national team was concerned, to give voice.

Although victory would be France's, after brutally exposing Brazil's defensive frailties in a three-nil win, Ronaldo's "fit" overshadowed the proceedings. Its impact was not dissimilar to Maradona's shocking expulsion from the tournament four years before, only this time it was unclear who was at fault. In the run-up to kick off, Ronaldo had been replaced on the team sheet by Edmundo, a man with a propensity for extravagance and violent conduct, only to be reinstated half an hour later. This, perhaps, was Zagallo's ultimate mistake. The rumors had begun to circulate. Had he had an epileptic fit? Had he been poisoned? Was there unrest in the Brazilian camp? Had Nike forced Zagallo to field their star player? Afterward Bobby Robson would say, "They are killing him. They are flogging the kid to death. He's played 80 matches in less than a year and no wonder his body has said enough is enough . . . Nobody can put up with the kind of pressure he's been under."[35] Mysteriously, Ronaldo had been examined by medical staff, and declared fit. When he stated that he wanted to play, Zagallo had not had the courage to say no. The veteran coach feared the criticism that would ensue had he not played Ronaldo, and still lost. In the event, the young star who was usually such a thrilling amalgam of power, skill, and speed wandered listlessly around the pitch looking for all the world like a child who was surprised to find himself on the world's largest stage. Brazil had always been adept at transmuting her frailties into a scapegoat: in the modern age it was not a player but a foreign-owned corporate entity. Brazilians could vent their ire at Nike without having to conduct any uncomfortable self-examination. Nevertheless, writing in *Jornal do Brasil*, Luís Fernando Veríssimo was not blind to what he had seen. "Maybe this was the final World Cup of nationalism. The supporters painted their faces with the colours of their flags in order to say a tribal farewell to any notion of a country. In the future the supporters will be composed of false savages and World Cups will be what this one was in a disguised manner, a tournament of trade-marks or *griffes* [labels]."[36]

In El Diego's Shadow

While Brazil struggled to carry out the marketing strategy imposed upon her, Argentina had had to face her own demons. First the first time since 1982, there was no Maradona to carry the nation, no mes-sianic talisman. Jimmy Burns argued that "it was the international projection of an Argentine success story that endeared Maradona to his fellow countrymen. To them he seems to make up for so many of the failings in their own history. Maradona has provided Argentines with a sense not just of identity but also of escape. They saw purity in his play and called it poetry."[37] Once Maradona finally left the field of play—his resurrections would be legion—others would be asked to fill the role. Among the unceasing and often undistinguished parade of "New Maradonas," Ariel Ortega and Juan Román Riquelme both stood out, but they, too, would fall short.

An uninspiring start to World Cup qualification—which for many coaches in the region remained the hardest competition in the world—had not augured well for their prospects in France. And yet Argentina eventually won the CONMEBOL group, having man-aged to limit her defeats to two matches and securing the highest number of draws over the eighteen rounds. The *caudillo*-like Pas-sarella had sought to impose order where there had been none. Mara-dona's fall from grace represented all that was corrupt in the Argentinian game. There was no longer room for the wayward; long hair and earrings would not be tolerated (the elegant midfielder Fer-nando Redondo refused to conform, and was thus exiled from the national side). Passarella's *weltanschauung* was at times narrow-minded on the pitch too, especially where the goal machine, Gabriel Batistuta, was concerned. Bastituta had been left out in the cold for almost a year, having been asked to fit his explosive playing style into Passarella's more restrictive tactical formula. Everyone concerned issued unconvincing denials that personal animosity lay at the root of the dispute. And yet there were undoubtedly favorites in the squad, especially those from River Plate. (Most notably Ariel Ortega, though he had moved on to Valencia by the time of the World Cup.)

In her opening match, Argentina could only manage a one-nil win against an organized but unremarkable Japanese side. Nevertheless, the dearth of goals was redressed against Jamaica, who had never before played in a World Cup. Batistuta took ten minutes to score a hat trick, while Ortega provided the balance in the 5–0 thrashing. The score line flattered the Argentinians, four of whose goals came after Jamaica had a man sent off. In the final group match, with Croatia and Argentina both already through to the next round, the two teams conserved their energies in the latter's one-nil victory. England lay in wait and Argentina would have to marshal all her resources.

While her group opponents may not have been of the highest caliber, the Argentinians had managed not to concede a goal for eight matches. (The high point, a one–nil victory over Brazil in Rio de Janeiro.) The English press welcomed the encounter with the usual jingoistic verve. (The Falklands War had been added to an armory that already included the Second World War and the 1966 World Cup.) The *Sun* echoed earlier headlines with WE GOTCHA—ARGIES NEXT UP AFTER COLOMBIA.[38] Not that the Argentinian press was any less chauvinistic. Editorials alerted readers to a succession of English flashpoints—Beresford, Whitelocke, Ruglio (the "Lion of Wembley") in '51, Grillo in '53, Rattín in '66, Las Malvinas, Maradona in '86. One newspaper ran the front-page headline CHUCK OUT THE PIRATES! Glenn Hoddle was less interested in dwelling on history. He had played against Maradona in that fateful match in Mexico, but was careful not to speak in terms of revenge. Argentina, in spite of two subsequent World Cup titles, had still not forgotten 1966. England had not beaten the South Americans for eighteen years.

In an era that badly needed excitement, England vs. Argentina did not disappoint. As *Le Figaro* was keen to point out, "People keep telling us: 'The idea of nations has been overtaken; it is dangerous, in the past. The future is about the construction of great groupings of peoples and the withering away of nation states. There is only one goal: a planet without frontiers.' Yet it only needs a national team to go on the pitch, a national anthem to be sung or a goal scored, for millions of people somewhere in the world to be as one, to unite in joy or disappointment. This is civilised chauvinism."[39] After the match, *Clarín* stated, "For the two and a half hours of the broadcast, from Saint-Etienne, the country was almost brought to a standstill."[40]

The match would begin as it would end, with penalties. Though, fortunately, there would be no "golden goal," the sporting equivalent of *coitus interruptus*. From the start there was little love lost between the teams. Within five minutes, Diego Simeone had been brought down by England's goalkeeper, the Argentinian captain having allowed his boot to drag on David Seaman's thigh. The Danish referee, with Simeone beside him gesturing that he should apply a yellow card, gave a penalty. Nearly four minutes later, after Batistuta's powerful shot eluded Seaman, Michael Owen went to ground at the other end as England counterattacked. Another penalty, and the match was evenly poised at one-all. Fortunately for England, Argentina knew very little of the young Michael Owen. By the fifteenth minute, the South Americans realized what he could do. The move was a simple one, but difficult to execute. Beckham's clever pass found Owen, who cut through the Argentinian lines at speed, evading Chamot and Ayala, both unable (or unwilling) to get close to him. The deft chip into the top left-hand corner of the goal stunned the Argentinians. One English commentator said of the eighteen-year-old, "Just think what he'll be like when he grows up." (There would be glory—especially the hat trick in the 5–1 thrashing of Germany—though he would never quite fulfill his early promise.) Even the Argentinian press applauded.

Before halftime, the Argentinians employed a dash of *la viveza criollo* (creole cunning) to bring them back into the game. With a free kick given just outside the penalty area, Zanetti lingered behind the England wall, whose players were expecting a thunderbolt from Batistuta, only to emerge and control Verón's pass. It took one touch and a left-foot shot to bring the score level. It was a very Argentinian goal, one that had been drilled into the players by Passarella. Jorge

Valdano sought to explain the *gambeta* in the context of Argentinian guile: "The first is ability: to show that I, with my foot, have the skill to do anything; the second is feinting, I have to deceive my opponent, make him believe exactly the opposite of what I'm going to do. This is also very Argentinian, the taste for deceit."[41] Simeone had been playing as if he wanted an English player sent off and would get his wish when Beckham petulantly flicked his boot out at him. Argentina seemed to gain little advantage from this, and in the end, a penalty shoot-out revealed England's inability to deal with a "sudden-death" situation.

Passarella praised the English for their passion. What neither team would have been willing to admit was that the two footballing cultures weren't so different after all. (That had always lain at the heart of the England-Argentine animus.) Unfortunately, the Argentinian manager could not rid the team of another *criollo* vice—temper. In the quarterfinal against Holland, Ortega would take offense at a comment from the Dutch goalkeeper, Edwin van der Sar. The traditional head butt that ensued was punished by a red card. Two minutes later, Bergkamp's exquisite right foot sent the Argentinians home. Only three days before, *Clarín* had sought to crown Ortega as "the heir to Diego [Maradona], there's no doubt about it. With Maradona's dynasty finished, it's good to have an Ortega on hand. A match like this one was necessary, especially against the English . . ."[42] Few would seek to make the comparison again.

Una Manga de Ladrones (A Den of Thieves)

By the new millennium, Argentina, that most European of Latin American republics, had become a parody of itself, suffering the kind of financial meltdown that results from over a century of political and economic mismanagement. Triggered by excessive levels of domestic and international debt, the country had become enmeshed in a stereotypical Latin American debt crisis. The 1997 Asian financial crisis, which unexpectedly hit the "tiger" economies of Indonesia, Korea, Malaysia, and Thailand, had had a severe impact on Latin America. Brazil plunged into recession in 1998, and as international lending dried up and interest rates on high-risk debt began to spiral, Colombia, Ecuador and Peru were also severely affected.

Argentina, never the most popular country in the region, became toxic in the eyes of her neighbors. Such was the ill feeling engendered by the crisis that in 2002 Jorge Batlle, then president of Uruguay, said what many Latin Americans—and even Argentinians—felt. Filmed, without his knowledge, by a Bloomberg journalist, Batlle let down his guard: "Don't compare Argentina with Uruguay, or you're a complete ignoramus in relation to the realities of Argentina and Uruguay . . . Are you acquainted with the Argentine administration? Do you know how things operate in Argentina? Do you know the volume and magnitude of corruption in Argentina? We are completely different countries . . . [The Argentines are] a den of thieves from the very top to the bottom." When the scandal broke, Batlle apologized on television in true Latin American fashion—hyperbole with tears.

Racism remained ingrained on the continent; a stain that could not be removed. Entrenched notions of nationhood, for the most part false, pervaded the region. In the qualification rounds for the 2002 World Cup, Paraguay's extrovert goalkeeper, José Luis Chilavert, spat at the diminutive Roberto Carlos after the Brazilian said, "Indian, we've beaten you 2–0. You're a disaster." Earlier in the match, Carlos had barked, "Indian, get up!" Chilavert remained unrepentant, proud of his heritage: "We are a small, humble and hard-working country. We have never been given anything, and the only satisfaction in our country is football since politics is full of corrupt [politicians]."

Chilavert had experienced racism before, in Argentina, where he played for San Lorenzo and then more successfully at Vélez Sarsfield.

He would score over sixty goals in his career, including a hat trick against Ferro Carril Oeste in a 6–1 thrashing. One of his greatest goals was scored against River Plate. Chilavert took a quick free kick—Francescoli was still apologizing to his victim—from inside his own half and lobbed his opposite number. He would later say that "the first insult there [in Argentina] is: go steal in your own country, starving [dying of hunger] Paraguayan."[43] His observation was prompted by a match between Independiente and Boca Juniors, in which the fans of the former had unfurled Bolivian and Paraguayan flags carrying the number "12" (La Doce)—the name given to fans of Boca—as a racial slight.

Even in the twenty-first century Latin America would remain an enigma. Lip service continued to be paid to the integration of its peoples, while entrenched notions of nationhood, for the most part false, pervaded the region. In *The Labyrinth of Solitude*, Octavio Paz questioned these very identities. "'National traits' . . . were simply the result of the nationalistic proclamations of the various governments. Even now, a century and a half later, no one can explain satisfactorily the 'national' differences between Argentinians and Uruguayans, Peruvians and Ecuadorians, Guatemalans and Mexicans. And nothing except the persistence of local oligarchies, supported by North American imperialism, can explain the existence of nine republics in Central America and the Antilles."[44] A common Iberian history prior to independence would only exaggerate any sense of identity. In 2013, a video of a group of Chilean marines, chanting xenophobic refrains whilst jogging, was posted on the Internet. "I will kill Argentines . . . I will shoot Bolivians . . . I will slit the throats of Peruvians" recited in unison did little to enamor Chile to her neighbors.[45]

. . .

Like some chronic malady, *la violencia* may at times have been manageable but it had never gone away. By the millennium, it had flared up again, though the participants had become numerous. Not only was Colombia's military engaged in warfare against terrorist groups, such as the Marxist FARC, but there were also the paramilitary groups funded by the cartels with which to contend. In 2001, Colombia sought to host her first Copa América. It was never going to be straightforward. Two months before the start of the tournament, a car bomb in Cali injured a number of Colombian players. They had been staying at the hotel where the Peruvian squad had booked their stay. The situation was made worse by a succession of explosions in Medellín and Bogotá, one near El Campín stadium. The Colombian president, Andrés Pastrana Arango, had been optimistic when he stated that the country would host the "cup of peace."

This promise became even more unlikely when the vice president of the Colombian federation, Hernán Mejia Campuzano, was kidnapped at a roadblock. The president of the federation tried to keep the momentum going: "If the federations decide to withdraw their support for Colombia, it would be a very serious question . . . a slap in the country's face." Argentina and Canada declined to participate for reasons of security, so Honduras and Costa Rica were invited to take their places. The Colombian press condemned the tournament even before it started. And yet, in spite of the underlying tension, the tournament proved immensely popular, something helped by the hosts running out eventual winners. The highlight: Honduras, who had barely time to prepare their scratch squad, beating Brazil 2–0 to reach the semifinal. Colombia's opponent in the final was Mexico, who opted for a defensive strategy that never quite came off. Two red cards following the Colombian center-back Iván Córdoba's goal extinguished her hopes of a first Copa América. But this triumph would be tarnished eight years later, when ten players from a Colombian amateur team called Los Maniceros (The Peanut Vendors) were found slaughtered in Venezuela. During the match, the kidnappers had marched onto the football pitch and asked the referee for a list of

Colombian players, who were then abducted. A motive for the murders was never found.

. . .

By the time of the 2002 World Cup in South Korea, normal service was resumed, with all the previous Latin American winners of the trophy in attendance. This provided some relief for those in the midst of economic crisis. Nevertheless, Uruguay had not played in the competition for twelve years, and it showed. The prospect of facing Denmark in her opening match was one she did not relish psychologically. A belief had become prevalent among Latin American republics that certain countries were more difficult to beat than others. It was felt that to encounter a team with a similar style offered a better chance of success. Uruguay would have far preferred a known quantity— such as Spain or Italy—than the intimidating Northern Europeans. Defeat courtesy of a brace from John Dahl Tomasson suggested this fear was in danger of becoming a self-fulfilling prophecy. A goalless draw against a poor French side only reinforced Uruguay's penchant for self-destruction. Only a win against Senegal would see her through to the next round. After thirty-eight minutes, the Uruguayans had conceded three goals without reply. Unpredictable as ever, Uruguay came back into the match: Morales scored a minute into the second half; fifteen minutes later, Diego Forlán scored an exquisite volley from range, demonstrating that he should have been brought on earlier; and Recoba's penalty tied the match. The Uruguayans might even have won the match in the last minute had Morales not failed to head the ball into an open goal.

Argentina's tournament would reflect the country's parlous social and economic state. Argentina's turbulent economic history had failed to engender any predilection to fiscal temperance in the modern age. This would be the country's worst economic crisis since 1891. Through the 1990s, the country's growth had given her a false sense of security, but by 1998, the country had entered into a recession. In

March 2001, it went through three ministers of finance in three weeks. By November 30, fears of devaluation led to a run on the banks. The following day, bank deposits were frozen (*corralito*), which effectively strangled the economy. Riots, demonstrations, and looting ensued; twenty-five people would die as a direct result. At the end of the year, with the country prone, three presidents took over the reins of power for two tortuous weeks. By 2002, inflation, which had been low for a decade, had risen to 41 percent, while the poverty rate escalated from 25.9 percent in 1998 to 57.5 percent four years later. According to Pablo Alabarces, "Argentina was known by some as Belinda: a third of its inhabitants lived as if they were in Belgium; two thirds as if they were in India."[46]

With Argentina coming into the competition as one of the favorites, along with France, some 85 percent of the population thought the country might become world champions. The national team had not lost a match for two years under Marcelo Bielsa, even though the manager had not been paid in eight months. Many Argentinians thought that, with the country *in extremis* (as had been the case in 1978), a victory was surely theirs. Such was the natural order of things in the Argentinian mind. The squad was beset by injury: Ayala, Verón, Caniggia, Batistuta, Almeyda all suffering injury. Nevertheless, three days before her opening match, Argentina played a Japanese eleven and Batistuta scored three of the four second-half goals. It looked as if the team might fulfill its promise after all. In an otherwise mediocre match against Nigeria, their first opponents in the tournament, Batistuta's winning goal provided some welcome relief. The grudge match against England was next. Four years on, however, England, guided by an inscrutable Swede, Sven-Göran Eriksson, was wiser, especially one player who was playing with atonement in mind.

Michael Owen had been unlucky not to score early in the first half; his shot had hit the post. Later on, he had looked for a penalty when, moving to his right, he was caught by Pochettino. The hapless Argentinian had thought better of making the challenge and tried to move out of way, but it was too late. England was awarded a penalty. Football has always openhandedly given its players chances to both win redemption and earn condemnation. For Beckham, who had been so appallingly vilified four years before, his time had come. His emphatically struck penalty would be the only goal of the game. Argentina sought valiantly to find an equalizer, but England shut them down. Sweden would prove similarly obdurate in a one-all draw. Argentina was heading home after just three matches. The press would accuse the team of having lacked flair and imagination. *La Nación* called it "mechanical." Argentina may have been disappointed, but, somewhat paradoxically, for a nation for whom football had become part of the daily fabric, the recriminations were fleeting. It was another illustration of the extent to which Argentina, unlike her neighbors, retained a complex relationship with her national team. Football retained its *barrio* allegiances, and remained a parochial game. In the late twentieth century, advertising, especially on national television, did provide the catalyst for national feeling. But the nationalist climate remained only as long as *la selección* succeeded in international competition. Failure returned the game to its barrio roots. Whereas Uruguay and Brazil looked beyond their borders for affirmation, the Argentinian game remained insular and inward-looking, obsessed by self. Fernando Niembro of Torneos y Competencias gauged the climate: "We are sad, but this doesn't change our lives. People in Argentina have the same problems as yesterday and continue to worry about getting a job and avoiding being mugged on street corners."[47]

It was now Ronaldo's turn for a long-deferred redemption. After his ghostlike performance in Paris, Ronaldo had to contend with a sequence of cruel injuries that put his career on hold. From certain quarters his return to the game was greeted with a degree of skepticism; it was too easy to invoke the inducements offered by his lucrative advertising contracts. Nevertheless, he would come close to recapturing his old form. He scored in every match in which he played, except against England. (Ronaldinho's audacious free kick embarrassed England's David Seaman, whose confidence would never recover.) In the final, against an uninspiring German side that had willed its way through the competition, Ronaldo performed as he might have been expected to four years before. The pragmatic German opposition flattered him somewhat, but he had already shown his worth in the tight semifinal against Turkey, with the only goal of the match. Brazil's mediocre qualifying campaign had lowered expectations ahead of the tournament and the lack of pressure suited Brazil and, perhaps, Ronaldo.

"If Kafka Were Latin American, He Would Be a Realist"

Politics had always been closely allied to football in the region, so it came as no surprise that by the new millennium corruption in the Latin American game had become all-pervasive. Brazil was one of the principal offenders, provoking the country's former attacking midfielder Sócrates to state, "Through football we are renowned for trafficking in minors, forging passports, conniving with cheats, fostering injustice, lacking in spirit and stealing dreams. It is repugnant to be represented by these people."

In 2000, the Brazilian congress established a committee to investigate corruption in the domestic game. The following year, the committee published an eight-hundred-page report, which sought to indict thirty-three offenders. First on the list was Ricardo Teixeira, president of the Confederação Brasileira do Futebol (CBF), who was accused of corruption, including, as the president of the CBF, taking on loans for over $30 million from a New York bank at an interest rate of about 53 percent annually. The Brazilian senate even indicted the former national coach Wanderlei Luxemburgo with seeking illegal payments from the transfer of players. In the eyes of Álvaro Dias, chairman of a Brazilian senate inquiry, the corruption was endemic: "There is hardly a form of illegal activity we haven't come across. Since there is no internal or external supervision or accountability in Brazilian soccer, dishonest team officials can do whatever they want."[48]

Financial jeopardy in one form or another was common across the region. Despite increased television revenue streams, clubs like Racing in Argentina—with debts estimated to have been between $32 million and $65 million—and Colo-Colo in Chile managed to evade closure. In 2002, San Lorenzo attracted ninety lawsuits and thirty requests for bankruptcy. This was nothing new; in the 1970s and early 1980s the dictatorships in the region had intervened financially on behalf of a number of distressed clubs: Pinochet saved Everton of Viña del Mar; Stroessner had recued Sol de América and Cerro Porteño; and the Uruguayan military bailed out Peñarol. By 2010, the top twenty-six Brazilian clubs were €1.2 billion in hock to the state. That most cerebral of Argentinian ex-players, Jorge Valdano, stated what was obvious to anyone interested in the game: "All the main teams are on the verge of bankruptcy and the stands are empty." (This was not unique to Latin America: in 2010, empty stadiums were costing the top Italian teams up to €100 million a year in lost revenue.) Disrupted seasons were also common—especially in Uruguay, Bolivia, and Peru—due to referee and wage strikes.

During the decade, football was transformed into an export industry, one at which Latin America outclassed everybody else. By 2010, Argentina supplied more professional footballers than any other country in the world, usurping Brazil's premier position. In 2013, some 3000 Argentine and Brazilian players were sold abroad, which translated into over $400 million in export business. This strategy of selling players—often at a very young age, as was the case with Lionel Messi—may yet have a deleterious effect on domestic leagues. Nevertheless, it remained a way for clubs in the region—historically unable to balance their books—to survive financially. Thus the sales and marketing operations became more sophisticated, often at the expense of stadium renovation and ticket sales. Brazilian and Argentinian clubs would continue to export players not only to Europe but also to less established football cultures such as Algeria, Vietnam, Indonesia, the Maldives, and even the Faroe Islands.

At least in the short term, Argentina's burgeoning export-led economy did not have a negative effect on its domestic or Pan–Latin American game. The decade in effect belonged to Boca Juniors, who won four out of its five Copa Libertadores finals, partly under the influential Carlos Bianchi. In 2001, Boca Juniors beat Mexico City-based Cruz Azul—the first Mexican team to reach a final—by a score of 3–1 in a penalty shoot-out. Nevertheless, it was the 2003 championship that produced one of the strongest fields in the tournament's history. The final was a replay of the historic 1963 final, in which Santos beat Boca Juniors. Boca Juniors overcame the exuberant Santásticos, which included Elano, Robinho and Alex, over two legs. The following year, Once Caldas, the Colombian minnows and the tournament's surprise package, beat Boca Juniors on penalties. (Once Caldas employed highly defensive tactics, while Boca failed to convert a single penalty in the shoot-out.) For the rest of the decade Brazil provided a finalist at each edition of tournament, and 2005 and 2006 were all-Brazilian finals won by São Paulo and Internacional respectively.

At the 2006 World Cup in Germany, Brazil was acclaimed as the overwhelming favorite. Few could look past an almost preternaturally talented forward line in which Ronaldinho, Kaka, Adriano, and Ronaldo looked set to rip opponents to shreds. But their campaign proved to be a curiously limp, disjointed affair that ended in a quarterfinal exit.

Four years after the farrago in South Korea, Argentina's performance would be very different, though it would still end in disappointment. The nation's economy had improved and so, it seemed, had its game. The country was enjoying over 6 percent growth per annum, in part facilitated by a low peso, which in turn had revived domestic industry. In Gelsenkirchen, Argentina, guided by José Pekerman, put Serbia to the sword 6–0 in what was one of the finest performances by any national side in years. It was the return of *la nuestra*. The twenty-five-pass move that defined the match followed "Maxi" Rodríguez's pass to Heinze, then Mascherano, Riquelme, Rodríguez, Sorín, Rodríguez, Sorín, Mascherano, Riquelme, Ayala, Rodríguez, Mascherano, Rodríguez, Sorín, Rodríguez, Cambiasso, Riquelme, Mascherano, Sorín, Saviola, Riquelme, Saviola, Cambiasso, a back-heel from Crespo, and Cambiasso scores. For Sorín, it was a *golazo* that was reminiscent of Argentina's goal in the FIFA World Youth Championship final of eleven years before when José Pekerman had also been the manager. Two minutes before the final whistle, Lionel Messi scored what remains at the time of writing the only World Cup goal of his career.

Spectacular goals had become the trademark of Pekerman's side. Against Mexico in extra time of the next round, "Maxi" Rodríguez would score the winning goal by controlling a long-hit cross on his chest and volleying the ball into the net. By the time Argentina met Germany in the quarterfinal, there was a sense that the team might just make it all the way. With Argentina leading by one goal to nil and just eighteen minutes of the match to play, Pekerman sealed his fate. He substituted his playmaker, Juan Román Riquelme. Jorge Valdano said of him that "Riquelme's brains save the memory of football for all time . . . he is a player of the time when life was slow and we took the chairs out on the streets to play with the neighbours."[49] He was a player of great beauty, though in this match he had failed to shine. Germany—instilled with the Teutonic vigor, shared with the Anglo-Saxons, that impelled them to never admit defeat—scored eight minutes later. Whether or not it was a result of Riquelme's substitution, Argentina had surrendered the initiative. When it came to the penalty shoot-out, the Germans were clinical; the Argentinians had lost faith. Ever the bad losers, the Argentinians lost their tempers and the traditional brawl ensued. Metersacker was kicked in the groin for good measure. Defensiveness had long become an Argentinian national trait. Hiram Bingham had seen it manifest itself in 1908. In Brazil, unlike her neighbor, "there is none of that 'chip on the shoulder' attitude which the Argentino likes to exhibit."[50]

A decade on from Maradona's ignominious retirement, Argentina was still looking for a new messiah. Lionel Andrés Messi may have been born in Rosario, but he had been taken to Barcelona at the age of thirteen. He would later say that the Catalans were the club that would pay for his growth hormone treatment. His formative years in Spain made Argentinians suspicious. Mariano Bereznicki, a journalist working for the Rosario daily newspaper, *La Capital*, put it succinctly: "That's Leo's unfinished business, never having played here."[51] Had he not left the country he might have played for his favorite team, Newell's, and formed the kind of suffocatingly close bonds with fans that caused less talented players like Tévez, who did have that blot on his record, to be more loved. Efforts would be made to Argentinian-ize the young man, who was so much a product of Barcelona. Some found him not Argentinian enough—never having played senior football in the country and perhaps being too clean-cut, having too little of the *barrio* about him—others anxiously sought to find some trace of *argentinidad*. In 2007, he had scored a sublime individual goal against Getafe that was uncannily similar to Maradona's second in 1986, and when Barcelona played Espanyol later in the year, one commentator saw the vision:

> *Now it's Messi.*
> *It's Messi who faces up to the opposition,*
> *Messi to Eto'o in the area.*
>
> . . .
>
> *Eto'o takes the ball out wide to the touchline.*
> *Zambrotta . . .*
> *Messi couldn't get there . . .*
> *With his hand, with his hand, like Diego.*

I'll yell it anyway:
Goaaaaal!
It's Diego! Tell me it isn't! To me it's Diego. It's the same guy . . .
He's reincarnated, I don't believe in that but . . . he's reincarnated.
There can't be so many coincidences . . . Messi, or Maradona
dressed as Lionel Messi, goes down, puts on a Barcelona shirt,
and levels the game with his left hand.[52]

By the quarterfinals of the 2010 World Cup, the tournament was beginning to take shape as an all–Latin American affair, proof that the region's football still reigned supreme. Uruguay was expected to squeeze past Ghana; Brazil, ever the favorites, would undo a solid Holland; a swaggering Argentina, with Maradona as her coach, was expected to overcome a young, dynamic German side; and Paraguay looked like it would give a tentative Spain a tough match. All eyes were on an Argentina-Brazil final. It was not to be. All the teams faltered—Argentina was given an especially arduous master class in tactical wisdom by Germany—except for Uruguay, whose creole cunning and cool penalty takers won the game. Eduardo Galeano felt that Luis Suárez's infamous "save" may have been the ultimate sacrifice for country, an act infused with the selflessness of a Sydney Carton. But there was, of course, another way of looking at it. Mario Kempes had similarly practiced his goalkeeping skills against Poland in the 1978 World Cup. Brian Glanville believed the Argentine to have blemished his excellent tournament through this one act. The English journalist even went so far as to quote Sir Stanley Rous in his column: "The player who handles the ball on the goal line and gives away a penalty which is missed may feel that he has lost nothing. He has. He has lost his reputation as a sportsman."[53] But the River Plate republic, even with its long footballing tradition, could not carry the torch for the region for much longer: Holland outclassed Uruguay in a one-sided affair in the semifinals. Latin

American hegemony would have to wait another four years to assert itself.

When Brazil hosts the FIFA World Cup in 2014, it will be the first time the tournament will have been played in Latin America for twenty-eight years. Not since Argentina secured its inaugural win in 1978, in a somewhat compromised campaign, will so much be at stake for a host nation. Argentina and the other Latin America republics will want to embarrass Brazil at home; Brazil will have no option but to win.

Carta de América

For much of its history, Latin America has been cursed by disappointment. From auspicious beginnings, the clash of civilizations coupled with the Spanish quest for gold proved too strenuous for these nascent societies. The cracks showed early and never healed. By the first decades of the nineteenth century, independence from Spain failed to bring the stability that its architects had envisaged. It came as no surprise that the rest of the century was fraught with wars, fought within the new republics and without. Even the continent's great *libertador*, Simón Bolívar, could not hide his disillusionment, when he wrote to General Juan José Flores, a month before his premature death on November 9, 1830:

> *You know that I have ruled for twenty years, and from these I have derived only a few certainties: (1) America is ungovernable, for us; (2) Those who serve a revolution plough the sea; (3) The only thing one can do in America is to emigrate; (4) This country will fall inevitably into the hands of the unbridled masses and then pass almost imperceptibly into the hands of petty tyrants, of all colours and races; (5) Once we have been devoured by every crime and extinguished by utter ferocity, the Europeans will not even regard us as worth conquering; (6) If it were*

possible for any part of the world to revert to primitive chaos, it would
America in her final hour.[54]

Although Latin American history is so much the story of failure—
the burden of unfulfilled promise has always weighed heavily on the
region—football remains one of its greatest successes. Latin America
remains the continent to which the rest of the world looks for the
romanticism and lyricism of the game.

And yet, by the close of the twentieth century, the very sport that
had helped give the continent an identity was losing its own. Football
was now ubiquitous. No longer the eagerly awaited culmination to
the end of a week, the game was broadcast on television without
letup. Through television millions of dollars were channeled into the
region's leagues. Club football, youth football, international football:
the ball never tired. The game was no longer distinguishable from its
various forms. More importantly, it had lost all meaning. Those who
went to the stadium were in for meager fare. Matches provided an
opportunity for the fans and *barras bravas* (hooligans) to participate
in a dubious communion, and the football on offer was at times irrelevant. If good football could not be counted on, then violence, which
had always been part of the Latin American game, was often guaranteed. In 2002, an investigation into the Argentine game reported
that hooliganism had become a national crisis with over forty murders in a decade. Gun and knife attacks were not uncommon at many
matches. Six years later, the Uruguayan Football Association suspended all first division matches after Danubio and Nacional fans
invaded the pitch and started beating each other with iron rods and
corner flags. The best football had long been played in Europe, often
by Latin Americans. It was still there, across the Atlantic—as had
been the case in the 1920s and 1930s—that players would make their
name.

In his seminal lecture "The Argentine Writer and Tradition,"
Jorge Luis Borges sought to free Latin American culture from the

strictures of the parochial in favor of the universal: "I believe that our tradition is the whole of Western culture and I also believe that we have a right to this tradition, a right greater than that which the inhabitants of one Western nation or another may have . . . I believe that Argentines and Latin Americans in general . . . can take on all the European subjects, take them on without superstition and with an irreverence that can have, and already has had, fortunate consequences . . ."[55] The same can be said of the region's football: that Latin America took on an English game, and improved upon it; in effect casting the game in the region's own image. Wherever it is played, well or badly, football for all Latin Americans remains an expression of culture and identity. As Galeano rightly believes: "Tell me how you play, and I will tell you who you are."

NOTES

COMO EL URUGUAY NO HAY (THERE'S NO PLACE LIKE URUGUAY)

1. E. Galeano (2003), *Soccer in Sun and Shadow*, p. 1.
2. Quoted in L. Bethell (ed.) (1991), *The Cambridge History of Latin America, Vol. VIII, 1930 to the Present*, p. 195.
3. *New York Times*, January 3, 1951, p. 175.
4. V. S. Naipaul (1981), *The Return of Eva Perón*, p. 135.
5. Ibid.
6. Quoted in *El País*, June 17, 1986.
7. E. Galeano (2003), *Soccer in Sun and Shadow*, p. 47.

CORTÉS AND THE BOUNCING BALL

1. Quoted in T. Frängsmyr and A. Sture (eds.) (1993), *Nobel Lectures in Literature 1981–1990*, p. 159.
2. Quoted in E. M. Whittington (ed.) (2001), *The Sport of Life and Death: The Mesoamerican Ballgame*, p. 89.
3. B. de Sahagún (1997), *Primeros Memoriales*, p. 200.
4. A. de Herrera y Tordesillas (1725), *The General History of the Vast Continent and Islands of America, Commonly Call'd the West-Indies, from the First Discovery Thereof*, Vol. II, p. 341.
5. T. Stern (1948), *The Rubber-ball Games of the Americas*, p.60.
6. D. Durán (1971), *Book of the Gods and Rites*, p. 316.
7. A. de Herrera y Tordesillas, *The General History*, Vol. II, p. 340.
8. D. Durán, *Book of the Gods*, p. 313.
9. Ibid.
10. Ibid., p. 316.
11. T. Stern, *The Rubber-ball Games*, p. 64.
12. D. Durán., p. 318.

13. F. López de Gómara (1965), *Cortés: The Life of the Conqueror by His Secretary*, p. 390.

14. Ibid., Vol. II, p. 340.

15. O. Paz (1999), *Itinerary*, p. 45.

16. Quoted in T. Frängsmyr and A. Sture (eds.), *Nobel Lectures*, p. 159.

17. D. Tedlock (trans.) (1996), *Popol Vuh: The Mayan Book of the Dawn of Life*, pp. 63, 198.

18. E. Galeano, *Soccer in Sun and Shadow*, p. 24.

19. J. F. Woodroffe (1916), *The Rubber Industry of the Amazon*, p. 26.

20. Ibid.

21. D. Durán, p. 319.

22. Ibid., p. 319.

CHAPTER ONE

1. T. W. Hinchliff (1863), *South American Sketches*, p. 63.

2. Ibid., pp. 63–64.

3. W. H. Bullock (1866), *Across Mexico in 1864–5*, pp. 143–144.

4. F. Lillywhite (1860), *The English Cricketers' Trip to Canada and the United States*, p. 44.

5. O. Marshall (ed.) (2000), *English-Speaking Communities in Latin America*, p. 125.

6. C. W. Domville-Fife (1910), *The United States of Brazil*, p. 85.

7. Quoted in R. Miller (1993), *Britain and Latin America in the Nineteenth and Twentieth Centuries*, pp. 3, 5.

8. E. Galeano, *Soccer in Sun and Shadow*, pp. 27–28.

9. Quoted in A. Hamilton (1998), *An Entirely Different Game: The British Influence on Brazilian Football*, p. 40.

10. Quoted in R. Miller (1993), *Britain and Latin America in the Nineteenth and Twentieth Centuries*, p. 35.

11. Major A. Gillespie (1818), *Gleanings and Remarks: Collected During Many Months of Residence at Buenos Ayres*, pp. 183–184.

12. E. Fernández Moores (2010), *Breve historia del deporte argentino*, p. 59.

13. J. A. Page (1983), *Perón: A Biography*, p. 272.

14. *The Standard*, May 6, 1867.

15. Heald Family Papers, the John Rylands University Library, the University of Manchester.

16. *The Buenos Ayres Daily News and River Plate Advertiser*, June 6, 1874.

17. Quoted in J. Wilson (2007), *Buenos Aires: A Cultural and Literary History*, p. 3.
18. *The Standard*, June 17, 1875.
19. Quoted in C. F. Yametti (2010), *Historia del Fútbol de AFA*, p. 13.
20. *The Standard*, November 26, 1901.
21. Quoted in V. Raffo (2004), *El origen británico del deporte argentino*, p. 187.
22. Quoted in D. Goldblatt (2006), *The Ball Is Round*, p. 36.
23. *The Standard*, June 26, 1887.
24. S. Bolívar (2003), *El Libertador: Writings of Simón Bolívar*, p. 27.
25. Quoted in B. Elsey (2011), *Citizens and Sportsmen*, p. 6.
26. Quoted in E. Santa Cruz (1996), *Origen y futuro de una pasión: Fútbol, cultura y modernidad*, p. 34.
27. *El Callao*, August 3, 1892.
28. V. Raffo (2004), *El origen británico del deporte argentino*, pp. 47–48.
29. Quoted in G. Meyer (1967), *The River and the People*, p. 93.
30. Quoted in M. A. Bestard (1996), *Paraguay: Un siglo de fútbol*, p. 18.
31. Quoted in C. Borja Bolívar and E. Paravicini Ramos (2004), *Oruro Royal Foot Ball Club: Decano del fútbol boliviano*, p. 41.
32. W. Scully (1866), *Brazil: Its Provinces and Chief Cities*, p. 7.
33. Quoted in O. Marshall (ed.) (2000), *English-Speaking Communities in Latin America*, p. 262.
34. Quoted in A. Hamilton (1998), *An Entirely Different Game*, pp. 36–37.
35. Ibid., p. 9.
36. M. G. Mulhall (1878), *The English in South America*, p. 560.
37. Quoted in A. Guttmann (1994), *Games and Empires: Modern Sports and Cultural Imperialism*, p. 18.

CHAPTER TWO

1. E. Hobsbawm (1994), *Age of Extremes: The Short Twentieth Century: 1914–1991*, p. 198.
2. *Buenos Aires Herald*, October 13, 1912.
3. J. E. Rodó (1988), *Ariel*, p. 77.
4. Quoted in J. A. Crow (1992), *The Epic of Latin America*, p. 693.
5. Quoted in J. Frydenberg (2011), *Historia social del fútbol*, p. 47.
6. Museo del Fútbol, Asociación Uruguaya de Fútbol. Quoted in J. C. Luzuriaga (2009), *El football del novecientos*, p. 176.
7. *Buenos Aires Herald*, June 16, 1906, p. 5.
8. *Buenos Aires Herald*.

9. Quoted in Cavallini (2007), *Play Up Corinth*, p. 107.
10. F. N. S. Creek (1933), *A History of the Corinthian Football Club*, p. 84.
11. *The Standard*, July 14, 1914, p. 4.
12. Quoted in E. P. Archetti (1999), *Masculinities: Football, Polo and the Tango in Argentina*, p. 64.
13. *El Gráfico*, March 8, 1930 (No. 566), p. 13.
14. E. Escobar Bavio (1953), *Alumni: Cuna de campeones y escuela de hidalguía*, pp. 9–10.
15. http://edant.clarin.com/diario/2003/04/24/d-549894.htm (retrieved August 9, 2013).
16. Quoted in E. Fernández Moores (2010), *Breve historia del deporte argentino*, p. 68.
17. Quoted in J. Wilson (2007), *Buenos Aires: A Cultural and Literary History*, p. 6.
18. R. Lorenzo (1946), *25 años en el deporte*, p. 51.
19. E. Archetti, *Machos, Mistresses, Madonnas*, p. 38.
20. J. A. and M. Magariños Pittaluga (1942), *Del fútbol heróico*, p. 82.
21. E. Galeano (2003), *Soccer in Sun and Shadow*, p. 1.
22. Quoted in A. Giménez Rodríguez (2007), *La pasión laica*, p. 52.
23. Quoted in A. Reyes (2010), *Historia de Nacional*, p. 98.
24. Quoted in C. R. Torres (2006), "'If We Had Had Our Argentine Team Here!': Football and the 1924 Argentine Olympic Team," *International Journal of the History of Sport* 23:7.
25. Quoted in H. Kraay (ed.) (2007), *Negotiating Identities*, p. 81.
26. Quoted in J. M. Wisnik (2006), "The Riddle of Brazilian Soccer: Reflections on the Emancipatory Dimensions of Culture," *Review: Literature and Arts of the Americas*, p. 201.
27. G. Gardner (1846), *Travels in the Interior of Brazil, Principally Through the Northern Provinces, and the Gold and Diamond Districts, During the Years 1836–1841*, p. 21.
28. Quoted in D. J. Davis (1999), *Avoiding the Dark*, p. 19.
29. Quoted in A. Hamilton (1998), *An Entirely Different Game*, p. 58.
30. Quoted in J. Lacey (2007), *God Is Brazilian: The Man Who Brought Football to Brazil*, p. 160.
31. *Crítica*, October 3, 1920.
32. *O Imparcial*, May 14, 1919. Quoted in L. A. de M. Pereira (2000), *Footballmania*, p. 305.
33. W. H. Beezley and J. Ewell (eds.) (2001), *The Human Tradition in Modern Latin America*, p. 157.

34. Quoted in D. E. Levi, (1987), *The Prados of São Paulo, Brazil: An Elite Family and Social Change, 1840–1930*, p. 121.

35. Quoted in Andrews (1991), *Blacks and Whites in São Paulo, Brazil: 1888–1988*, p. 214.

36. Ibid.

37. G. Freyre (1959), *New World in the Tropics*, pp. 97–98.

38. M. González Prada (2003), *Free Pages and Hard Times: Anarchist Musings*, p. 55.

39. R. Sawyer (ed.) (1997), *Roger Casement's Diaries: 1910: The Black and the White*, p. 248.

40. P. F. Martin (1911), *Peru of the Twentieth Century*, p. 130.

41. W. H. Beezley and J. Ewell (eds.) (1998), *The Human Tradition in Modern Latin America: the Twentieth Century*, p. 20.

42. Ibid., p. 23.

43. Ibid., p. 156.

44. *El Gráfico*, No. 1, 1919, p. 3.

45. Quoted in E. P. Archetti, *Masculinities: Football, Polo and the Tango in Argentina*, p. 57.

46. G. Zuluaga Ceballos (2005), *Empatamos 6 à 0*, p. 52.

47. S. Salinas Gaete (2004), *Por empuje y coraje: Los Albos en la época amateur 1925–1933*, p. 31.

48. Cited in E. Escobar Bavio (1953), *Alumni: Cuna de campeones y escuela de hidalguía*, p. 124.

49. Quoted in B. Elsey (2011), *Citizens and Sportsmen*, p. 56.

50. Quoted in P. Modiano (1997), *Historia del deporte chileno*, p. 100.

51. *El Gráfico*, No. 470, 1928. Quoted in E. Archetti, *Machos, Mistresses, Madonnas*, p. 38.

52. W. H. Hudson (1930), *The Purple Land That England Lost*, p. 333.

53. J. L. Borges (2000), *Other Inquisitions, 1937–1952*, p. 143.

CHAPTER THREE

1. Quoted in R. Lombardo (1993), *Donde se cuentan proezas: fútbol uruguayo (1920–1930)*, p. 44.

2. Quoted in R. Lombardo, p. 58.

3. Cited in L. R. Maiztegui Casas (2005), *Orientales: Una historia política del Uruguay. Vol. 2: De 1865 à 1938*, p. 262.

4. Quoted in E. B. Burns (1990), *Latin America: A Concise Interpretative History*, p. 193.

5. Quoted in J. C. Chasteen (2011), *Born in Blood and Fire*, p. 171.

6. Cited in P. R. Spickard (ed.) (2005), *Race and Nation: Ethnic Systems in the Modern World*, p. 60.

7. Quoted in A. Giménez Rodriguez (2007), *La pasión laica: una breve historia del fútbol uruguayo*, p. 9.

8. Galeano (1998), *Soccer in Sun and Shadow*, p. 45

9. Quoted in F. Morales (2002), *Andrade: El Negro de París*, p. 52.

10. *New York Times*, June 2, 1924, p. 21.

11. *Le Figaro*, June 2, 1924, p. 6.

12. *New York Times*, June 10, 1924, p. 17.

13. Quoted in T. Mason (1995), *Passion of the People*, p. 31.

14. Ibid., p. 31.

15. F. G. L. Fairlie, *The Official Report of the VIIIth Olympiad*, Paris, 1924, p. 189.

16. E. E. Buero (1932), *Negociaciones internacionales*, p. 12.

17. Cited in M. Frau (2007), "Fútbol e Historia: la esquizofrenia oriental," *Cahiers du Monde Hispanique et Luso-Bresilien (Caravelle)*, No. 89.

18. C. L. R. James (1966), *Beyond a Boundary*, p. 252

19. Cited in C. R. Torres (2003), "'If We Had Had Our Argentine Team Here!': Football and the 1924 Argentine Olympic Team," p. 16.

20. *La Nación*, June 12, 1925, p. 2. Quoted in J. W. Richey (2007), *White Mestizaje: Soccer and the Construction of Argentine Racial Identity*, 1924–1930.

21. Quoted in E. Giovannini (2003), *La gira de 1925*, p. 35.

22. Ibid., p. 34.

23. *Crítica*, March 17, 1925, p. 14. Cited in M. B. Karush (2003), *National Identity in the Sports Pages: Football and the Mass Media in 1920s Buenos Aires*, p. 26.

24. Quoted in A. Reyes (2010), *Historia de Nacional*, p. 113.

25. *Crítica*, February 1, 1925, p. 14. Quoted in J. W. Richey, *White Mestizaje: Soccer and the Construction of Argentine Racial Identity, 1924–1930*.

26. *La Nación*, February 4, 1925. Cited in M. B. Karush (2003), *National Identity in the Sports Pages: Football and the Mass Media in 1920s Buenos Aires*, pp. 20–21.

27. Cited in *La Maga*, January/February 1994, p. 13.

28. *La Razón*, April 17, 1925, p. 8. Cited in J. W. Richey (2007), *White Mestizaje: Soccer and the Construction of Argentine Racial Identity, 1924–1930*, pp. 21–22.

29. *L'Écho de Paris*, March 16, 1925, p. 4.

30. Quoted in T. Mason, *Passion of the People*, p. 33.

31. *L'Écho de Paris*, March 16, 1925, p. 4.

32. P. Guedalla (1932), *Argentine Tango*, pp. 87–90.

33. Quoted in A. Hamilton (1998), *An Entirely Different Game*, p. 136.

34. E. F. Every (1929), *Twenty-five Years in South America*, p. 22

35. M. A. Bestard (1996), *Paraguay: un siglo de fútbol*, p. 72.

36. Ibid., p. 74.

37. L. Bethell (ed.) (1993), *Chile Since Independence*, p. 27.

38. *El Gráfico*, No. 363, June 19, 1926.

39. E. Galeano (2003), *Soccer in Sun and Shadow*, p. 50.

40. *El Gráfico*, No. 366, 1926, p. 17. Cited in E. Archetti (1996), *Playing Styles and Masculine Virtues in Argentine Football*, p. 40.

41. E. Sábato (1965), *Sobre héroes y tumbas*, p. 97.

42. *ABC*, April 26, 1927, p. 11.

43. *Los Sports*, May 13, 1927.

44. *New York Times*, March 4, 1927.

45. *New York Times*, March 21, 1927.

46. *New York Times*, March 30, 1927.

47. Cited in M. Dyreson (2011), "Imperial 'Deep Play': Reading Sport and Visions of the Five Empires of the 'New World,' 1919–1941," *International Journal of the History of Sport* 28:17, p. 2427.

48. E. Marín (ed.) (2007), *Historia del deporte chileno*, p. 108.

49. *New York Times*, June 3, 1928, p. S4.

50. *Oberbadisches Sportblatt (Wochenbeilage der Freiburger Zeitung)*, June 4, 1928, p. 1.

51. *Estádio*, No. 511, February 28, 1953.

52. *La Stampa*, June 8, 1928, p. 5.

53. *El Mundo Deportivo*, June 11, 1928, p. 1.

54. *New York Times*, June 1928.

55. Quoted in A. Etchandy, *Reportaje a la celeste*, p. 61.

56. http://ramplajuniors.com/noticias/1929/1929-primer-gira-de-rampla-por-europa.

57. Quoted in J. C. Chasteen (2001), *Born in Blood and Fire*, p. 202.

58. *Folha da Manhã*, July 15, 1929, p. 1.

CHAPTER FOUR

1. Quoted in R. M. Levine (1980), *The Case of Brazilian Futebol*, p. 233.

2. Quoted in C. Hunt (2006), *World Cup Stories*, p. 8.

3. Quoted in P. J. Beck (1999), *Scoring for Britain: International Football and International Politics, 1900–1939*, p. 144.

4. Quoted in S. Howell (1997), *The Ethnography of Moralities*, p. 111.

5. Quoted in B. Glanville (2010), *The Story of the World Cup*, p. 15.

6. http://www.fifa.com/aboutfifa/organisation/bodies/congress/birthfifaworld-cup.html.

7. Quoted in C. Eisenberg et al. (2004), *100 Years of Football*, p. 104.

8. A. Carbonell Debali, H. Mancebo Decaux, and M. Corbo Sentubery (1930), *Primer Campeonato Mundial de Football*, p. 10.

9. Quoted in T. Mason (1995), *Passion of the People*, p. 39.

10. Quoted in C. Hunt (2006), *World Cup Stories*, p. 14.

11. Quoted in A. Carbonell Debali, H. Mancebo Decaux, and M. Corbo Sentubery (1930), *Primer Campeonato Mundial de Football*, p. 15.

12. Quoted in W. H. Beezley and J. Ewell (eds.) (1998), *The Human Tradition in Latin America: the Twentieth Century*, p. 21

13. *Folha da Manhã*, 30 July 1930, p. 7.

14. R. Márquez C. (2012), *Olímpicos*.

15. Quoted in S. Collier, *The Life, Music, and Times of Carlos Gardel*, p. 125.

16. J. Sasturain (2006), *La patria transpirada*, p. 15.

17. J. C. Onetti (2009), *Cartas de un joven escritor*, p. 39.

18. http://www.fifa.com/classicfootball/stadiums/stadium=34866/quotes.html.

19. Quoted in T. Mason (1995), *Passion of the People*, p. 42.

20. http://www.fifa.com/classicfootball/players/do-you-remember/newsid=1166517/.

21. Quoted in R. Giulianotti and J. Williams (eds.) (1994), *Game Without Frontiers: Football, Identity and Modernity*, p. 235.

22. http://www.revistacredencial.com/credencial/content/el-lado-oscuro-de-los-mundiales.

23. Quoted in A. Carbonell Debali, H. Mancebo Decaux, and M. Corbo Sentubery (1930), *Primer Campeonato Mundial de Football*, p. 117.

24. Ibid., p. 121.

25. L. R. Maiztegui Casas (2005), *Orientales: una historia política del Uruguay. Vol. II. De 1865 à 1938*, p. 296.

26. J. Sasturain (2006), *La patria transpirada*.

27. R. Forbes (1933), *Eight Republics in Search of a Future: Evolution and Revolution in South America*, p. 5

28. *El Gráfico*, No. 604, 1931, p. 16.

29. Quoted in S. Martin (2004), *Football and Fascism*, p. 195.

30. *El Gráfico*, No. 604, 1931, p. 16.

31. *El Gráfico*, No. 589, 1930, p. 37. Quoted and translated in E. Archetti (1999), *Masculinities*, p. 65.

32. Quoted in S. Martin (2004), *Football and Fascism*, p. 195.

33. Quoted in P. Lanfranchi and M. Taylor (2001), *Moving with the Ball*, p. 80.

34. Quoted in T. Mason (1995), *Passion of the People*, p. 51.

35. Quoted in M. Taylor (2005), *The Leaguers: The Making of Professional Football in England, 1900–1939*, p. 217.

36. Ibid., p. 217.

37. Quoted in B. Glanville (2010), *The Story of the World Cup*, p. 25.

38. Quoted in H. G. Warren (1949), *Paraguay*, p. 300.

39. Quoted in G. Pendle (1967), *Paraguay*, p. 26.

40. E. Martínez Estrada (1971), *X-Ray of the Pampa*, pp. 98–99.

41. P. Lambert and A. Nickson (eds.) (2013), *The Paraguay Reader*, p. 447.

42. *L'Écho de Paris*, March 20, 1936, p. 8.

43. Ibid.

44. Quoted in D. C. Large (2007), *Nazi Games: The Olympics of 1936*, p. 275.

45. http://www.la84foundation.org/6oic/OfficialReports/1936/1936spart6.pdf., pp. 1048–1049.

46. Quoted in F. Novak (2004), *Las relaciones entre el Perú y Alemania: 1828–2003*, p. 114.

47. *Time*, August 24, 1936.

48. G. Thorndike (1978), *El revés de morir*, p. 158.

49. *Daily Mirror*, August 11, 1936, p. 2.

50. Quoted in J. Eslava (ed.) (2011), *Bien jugado*, p. 340.

51. Quoted in D. C. Large (2007), *Nazi Games: The Olympics of 1936*, p. 277.

52. Quoted in C. R. Boxer (1962), *The Golden Age of Brazil: 1695–1750*, p. 1.

53. Quoted in T. E. Skidmore (1998), *Black into White: Race and Nationality in Brazilian Thought*, p. 102.

54. Quoted in C. N. Degler (1971), *Neither Black nor White: Slavery and Race Relations in Brazil and the U.S.*, p. 121.

55. Cited in T. Maranhão (2007), "Apollonians and Dionysians: The Role of Football in Gilberto Freyre's Vision of Brazilian People," *Soccer & Society* 8:4 (October 2007), p. 514.

56. G. Freyre (1959), *New World in the Tropics*, pp. 111–112.

57. E. Martínez Estrada (1971), *X-Ray of the Pampa*, p. 320.

58. Quoted in P. French (2009), *The World Is What It Is: The Authorized Biography of V. S. Naipaul*, p. 308.

59. F. da Silva and R. dos Santos (eds.) (2006), *Memória social dos esportes: futebol e política*, p. 71.

60. G. Freyre (1945), *Brazil: An Interpretation*, pp. 86–87.
61. Quoted in D. J. Davis (1999), *Avoiding the Dark*, p. 130.
62. Quoted in P. M. Beattie (2004), *The Human Tradition in Modern Brazil*, p. 154.
63. Ibid., p. 155.
64. A. Bellos (2003), *Futebol*, p. 35
65. Quoted in P. M. Beattie (2004), *The Human Tradition in Modern Brazil*, p. 160.
66. Quoted in http://www1.folha.uol.com.br/fsp/mais/fs0102200403.htm.
67. Quoted in R. Daflon and T. Ballvé, "The Beautiful Game: Race and Class in Brazilian Soccer," *NACLA Report on the Americas* (March/April 2004), p. 24.
68. Quoted in S. Stein (1987), *Lima obrera, 1900–1930*, p. 234.
69. K. Loewenstein (1973), *Brazil Under Vargas*, pp. 304–305.
70. P. J. Beck (1999), *Scoring for Britain*, p. 261.
71. Quoted in I. Sharpe (1952), *40 Years in Football*, p. 185.
72. Ibid.
73. Ibid.
74. Ibid., p. 83.

CHAPTER FIVE

1. http://edant.clarin.com/diario/2002/05/04/d-01601.htm.
2. C. Peucelle (2011), *Fútbol todotiempo*, pp. 128-129.
3. Ibid., p. 128.
4. Quoted in B. Glanville (2010), *The Story of the World Cup*, p. 104.
5. *Folha da Manhã*, March 19, 1940, p. 12.
6. A. Bellos (2003), *Futebol*, p. 34.
7. Quoted in P. Modiano (1997), *Historia del deporte chileno*, p. 154.
8. *Estádio* 1:1 (September 12, 1941), p. 1.
9. W. Caldas (1990), *O pontapé inicial*, p. 88.
10. Ibid., p. 90.
11. Quoted in P. L. Alberto (2011), *Terms of Inclusion: Black Intellectuals in Twentieth-Century Brazil*, p. 110.
12. Quoted in J. Lever (1983), *Soccer Madness*, p. 56.
13. *El Gráfico*, No. 1163, October 24, 1941.
14. *World Soccer*, April 1962, p. 15.
15. Quoted in R. J. Santoro (2007), *Literatura de la pelota*, p. 127.
16. Quoted in C. Peucelle (2011), *Fútbol todotiempo*, p. 148.
17. Quoted in D. Fucks (1999), *El libro de River*, p. 130.
18. *Estádio* 1:8 (December 26, 1941).

19. Quoted in *Clarín*, March 30, 2002, http://edant.clarin.com/diario/2002/03/30/d-01601.htm (retrieved August 1, 2013).

20. *El Gráfico*, No. 1050, August 25, 1939.

21. C. Peucelle (2011), *Fútbol todotiempo*, p. 93.

22. Quoted in M. Melhuus and K. A. Stølen (1997), *Machos, Mistresses, Madonnas*, p. 46.

23. Quoted in J. Sebreli (2005), *La era del fútbol*.

24. Quoted in D. Fucks (1999), *El libro de River*, p. 100.

25. Quoted in O. Bayer (1990), *Fútbol Argentino*, p. 67.

26. Quoted in J. Wilson (2013), *Inverting the Pyramid*, p. 224.

27. E. P. Archetti (2005), "El deporte en Argentina (1914–1983)," *Trabajo y Sociedad* 7:6, p. 6.

28. *El Mundo Deportivo*, January 2, 1947, p. 1.

29. Quoted in J. Burns (2012), *La Roja*, p. 159.

30. Quoted in E. P. Archetti (2005), "El deporte en Argentina (1914–1983)," *Trabajo y Sociedad* 7:6, p. 7.

31. Quoted in G. P. T. Finn and R. Giulianotti (eds.) (2000), *Football Culture: Local Conflicts, Global Visions*, p. 124.

32. Quoted in L. Álvarez (2010), *Historia de Peñarol*, p. 209.

33. Ibid., p. 212.

34. Quoted in A. Reyes (2010), *Historia de Nacional*, p. 149.

35. Ibid., p. 169.

36. http://www.elgrafico.com.ar/blog_detalle.php?id_post=596 (accessed June 1, 2013).

37. J. Wilson, *Inverting the Pyramid*, p. 133.

38. Quoted in L. Álvarez, *Historia de Peñarol*, p. 326.

39. Quoted in G. Zuluaga Ceballos, *Empatamos 6 a 0*, p. 109.

40. Ibid., p. 17.

41. Quoted in V. L. Fluharty (1957), *Dance of the Millions*, p. 99.

42. E. Galeano (2009), *Open Veins of Latin America*, p. 103.

43. R. Lorente (1954), *Di Stéfano: Cuenta su vida*, pp. 88–89.

44. A. Reyes (2010), *Historia de Nacional*, p. 186.

45. G. Zuluaga Ceballos (2005), *Empatamos 6 a 0*, p. 54.

46. *El Tiempo*, February 5, 1948. Quoted in G. Zuluaga Ceballos (2005), *Empatamos 6 a 0*, p. 133.

47. *El Tiempo*, November 22, 1948. Quoted in G. Zuluaga Ceballos, p. 145.

48. G. Zuluaga Ceballos (2005), *Empatamos 6 a 0*, p. 54.

49. Ibid., p. 55.

50. Ibid.
51. Quoted in C. Eisenberg et al. (eds.) (2004), *100 Years of Football*, pp. 85–87.
52. N. Franklin (1956), *Soccer at Home and Abroad*, p. 89.
53. Ibid.
54. *World Soccer*, June 1971, p. 23.
55. G. García Márquez (2003), *Living to Tell the Tale*, p. 118.
56. Quoted in http://www.fifa.com/classicfootball/history/news/newsid=1608582/index.html (retrieved June 1, 2013).
57. G. Garcia Márquez (1981), *Textos costeños*, p. 463.
58. Quoted in C. Eisenberg et al. (eds.) (2004), *100 Years of Football*, p. 87.

CHAPTER SIX

1. Quoted in N. C. de Oliveira Santos (2009), *Brasil x Argentina*, p. 188.
2. *Jornal dos Sports*, June 17, 1950. Quoted in C. T. Gaffney (2008), *Temples of the Earthbound Gods*, p. 71.
3. Quoted in F. Morales (2000), *Maracanã: los laberintos del character*, p. 312.
4. *El Mundo Deportivo*, July 10, 1950, p. 4.
5. Quoted in B. Glanville (2010), *The Story of the World Cup*, p. 55.
6. Quoted in L. Prats (2011), *La crónica celeste*, p. 110.
7. *La Mañana*, July 9, 1950. Quoted in F. Morales (2000), *Maracanã*, p. 300.
8. Quoted in L. Prats (2011), *La crónica celeste*, p. 114.
9. Quoted in F. Morales (2000), *Maracanã*, p. 363.
10. Quoted in A. Giménez Rodríguez (2007), *La pasión laica*, pp. 136–137.
11. Ibid., p. 136.
12. Quoted in C. T. Gaffney (2008), *Temples of the Earthbound Gods*, p. 72.
13. http://www.auf.org.uy/Portal/NEWS/1170/ (retrieved 2 June 2013).
14. Quoted in T. Mason (1995), *Passion of the People*, p. 81.
15. Quoted in F. Morales (2000), *Maracanã*, p. 406.
16. N. Rodrigues (2002), *A pátria em chuteiras: novas crónicas de futebol*, p. 51.
17. Quoted in L. R. Maiztegui Casas, *Orientales 3, de 1938 a 1971*, p. 168.
18. Quoted in T. Heizer (2010), *Maracanazo*, p. 98.
19. http://www.fifa.com/classicfootball/players/player=174739/index.html (retrieved June 2, 2013).
20. Quoted in T. Heizer (2010), *Maracanazo*, p. 94.
21. Ibid., p. 99.
22. Quoted in F. Morales (2000), *Maracanã*, p. 383.
23. A. Bellos (2003), *Futebol*, pp. 63–64.
24. Paulo Perdigão (2000), *Anatomia de uma derrota*, pp. 27–28. Cited in J. M.

Wisnik (2006), *The Riddle of Brazilian Soccer: Reflections on the Emancipatory Dimensions of Culture*, p. 203.

25. N. Rodrigues (1994), *À pátria em chuteiras: novas crónicas de futebol*, p. 116.

26. Ibid., p. 117.

27. Quoted in S. Sosnowski and L. B. Popkin (1993), *Repression, Exile, and Democracy: Uruguayan Culture*, p. 81.

28. M. Benedetti (1996), *Andamios*, p. 126.

29. *El Gráfico*, 21 July 1950, p. 13.

30. Quoted in F. Morales (2004), *Reyes, príncipes y escuderos del fútbol nuestro: desde los años '40*, p. 98.

31. *The Times*, May 10, 1951, p. 9.

32. Quoted in E. P. Archetti (2005), "El deporte en Argentina (1914–1983)," *Trabajo y Sociedad Indagaciones sobre el empleo, la cultura y las prácticas políticas en sociedades segmentadas* 7:6.

33. Quoted in S. Inglis (ed.) (2006), *The Best of Charles Buchan's Football Monthly*, p. 13.

34. Quoted in A. Hennessy and J. King (eds.) (1992), *The Land That England Lost*, p. 165.

35. A. H. Fabian and G. Green (eds.) (1960), *Association Football*, p. 213.

36. *Estádio*, May 23, 1953.

37. *Estádio*, June 20, 1953.

38. Ibid.

39. Quoted in B. Glanville and J. Weinstein (1958), *World Cup*, p. 168.

40. *The Times*, June 28, 1954, p. 12.

41. A. Ellis (1963), *The Final Whistle*, p. 27.

42. *The Times*, June 28,1954, p. 12.

43. A. Ellis (1963), *The Final Whistle*, p. 156.

44. Ibid.

45. Quoted in G. Armstrong and R. Giulianotti (eds.) (1997), *Entering the Field: New Perspectives on World Football*, pp. 83–84.

46. A. Ellis (1963), *The Final Whistle*, p. 51.

47. Quoted in M. Godio and S. Uliana (eds.) (2011), *Fútbol y sociedad*, p. 80.

48. Ibid.

49. P. Alabarces (2007), *Fútbol y Patria: el fútbol y las narrativas de la nación en la Argentina*, p. 79.

50. Quoted in N. C. de Oliveira Santos (2009), *Brasil x Argentina: Histórias do Maior Clássico do Futebol Mundial (1908–2008)*, p. 206.

51. Ibid., p. 215.

52. Quoted in J. Foot (2007), *Calcio*, pp. 433–434.
53. Quoted in J. J. Sebreli (1998), *La era del fútbol*, p. 115.
54. *El Gráfico*, No. 2024, June 27, 1958, p. 21.
55. Quoted on http://www.dfb.de/?id=509766 (retrieved June 15, 2013).
56. Quoted in D. Bowler (2013), *Danny Blanchflower*.
57. *El Gráfico*, No. 2022, June 13, 1958, pp. 10–11.
58. *El Gráfico*, No. 2023, June 20, 1958, p. 7.
59. Ibid.
60. Ibid.
61. Quoted in S. Ferraro (1998), *Argentina en los mundiales*, p. 58.
62. N. Rodrigues (1993), *À sombra das chuteiras imortais: crônicas de futbol*, p. 26.
63. Quoted in J. A. Page (1995), *The Brazilians*, p. 391.
64. A. Stratton Smith (1963), *The Brazil Book of Football*, p. 34.
65. Ibid., p. 37.
66. Quoted in R. Castro (2005), *Garrincha*, p. 101.
67. Quoted in K. Foster (2009), *Lost Worlds*, p. 155.
68. J. Valdano (1997), *Los cuadernos de Valdano*, p. 91.
69. *World Soccer*, July 1963, p. 23.
70. *El Gráfico*, No. 2027, July 18, 1958, p. 56.
71. Quoted in M. Natali (2007), *The Realm of the Possible: Remembering Brazilian Futebol*, p. 280.
72. Quoted in P. Alabarces (2001), *Football and Patria: Sport, National Narratives and Identities in Argentina 1920–1998*, p. 143.
73. Ibid., pp. 127–128.

CHAPTER SEVEN

1. *El Gráfico*, No. 2154, January 4, 1961, p. 5.
2. Ibid.
3. *El Gráfico*, No. 2180, July 12, 1961, p. 66.
4. Ibid.
5. *El Gráfico*, No. 2156, January 25, 1961, p. 56.
6. *World Soccer*, February 1963, p. 31.
7. A. Stratton Smith (1963), *The Brazil Book of Football*, p. 64.
8. Pelé and R. L. Fish (1977), *Pelé: My Life and the Beautiful Game*, p. 114.
9. E. Galeano (1992), *We Say No*, p. 22.
10. Ibid, p. 23.
11. T. Mason (1995), *Passion of the People*, p. 89.

12. *World Soccer*, December 1960, p. 18.
13. *The Times*, May 11, 1961, p. 4.
14. Ibid.
15. *El Informador*, May 11, 1961.
16. *World Soccer*, September 1962, p. 16.
17. Quoted in M. Godio and S. Uliana (eds.) (2011), *Fútbol y sociedad*, p. 73.
18. Ibid., p. 54.
19. J. G. Castañeda (2011), *Manana Forever? Mexico and the Mexicans*, pp. 5–6.
20. Quoted in M. Dyreson, J. A. Mangan, and R. J. Park (eds.) (2013), *Mapping an Empire of American Sport*, p. 152.
21. *El Gráfico*, February 10, 1950, p. 38.
22. Cited in A. Hennessy and J. King (eds.) (1992), *The Land That England Lost*, p. 89.
23. Quoted in K. Brewster (ed.) (2010), *Reflections on Mexico '68*, p. 49.
24. Quoted in C. Ramírez Berg (1992), *Cinema of Solitude*, p. 43.
25. S. Collier and W. F. Sater (2004), *A History of Chile, 1808–2002*, p. 184.
26. Quoted in E. Marín (2007), *Historia del deporte chileno*, p. 212.
27. Quoted in B. Elsey (2011), *Citizens and Sportsmen*, p. 200.
28. *World Soccer*, August 1962, p. 8.
29. A. L. di Salvo (2000), *Antonio Ubaldo Rattín: "El Caudillo,"* p. 116.
30. *World Cup '62*, p. 128.
31. *World Soccer*, May 1963, p. 25.
32. Quoted in *World Cup '62*, pp. 157–158.
33. Quoted in A. L. di Salvo (2000), *Antonio Ubaldo Rattín: "El Caudillo,"* p. 118.
34. Quoted in S. Collier and W. F. Sater (1996), *A History of Chile, 1808–1994*, p. 260.
35. Quoted in R. J. Alexander (1958), *The Bolivian National Revolution*, p. 17.
36. *El Diario*, May 8, 1961; quoted in M. A. Peñaloza Bretel (1993), *Historia contemporánea del fútbol boliviano*, p. 46.
37. Quoted in C. D. Mesa Gisbert (1994), *La epopeya del fútbol boliviano: 1896–1994*, p. 94.
38. Quoted in J. A. Crow (1992), *The Epic of Latin America*, p. 826.
39. M. A. Peñaloza Bretel (1993), *Historia contemporánea del fútbol boliviano*, p. 94.
40. Quoted in E. Marín (ed.) (2007), *Historia del deporte Chileno*, p. 184.
41. *Time*, June 5, 1964.
42. *Clarín*, June 27, 2000 (http://edant.clarin.com/diario/2000/06/27/d-04201.htm).
43. Ibid.
44. *The Times*, June 1, 1964, p. 4.
45. Ibid.

46. *World Soccer*, October 1964, p. 4.

47. Ibid.

48. *World Soccer*, July 1965, p. 6.

49. H. McIlvanney (ed.) (1966), *World Cup '66*, p. 29.

50. D. Bowler (1998), *"Winning Isn't Everything . . .": A Biography of Sir Alf Ramsey*, p. 211.

51. Quoted in *The Football Association World Cup Report 1966* (1967), p. 165.

52. *La Prensa*, March 2, 1948. Quoted in B. Derrick, "General Perón and the Nationalisation of Railways in Argentina," *Magazine of the Friends of the National Archives*, 23:1 (April 2012).

53. A. L. di Salvo (2000), *Antonio Ubaldo Rattín: "El Caudillo,"* p. 274.

54. Ibid., p. 215.

55. *The Times*, July 25, 1966.

56. Cited in Fabio Chisari (2000): "'Definitely Not Cricket': *The Times* and the Football World Cup 1930–1970," *Sports Historian* 20:1, pp. 44–69. *The Times*, July 25, 1966.

57. *The Times*, July 26, 1966, p. 13.

58. Quoted in *The Football Association World Cup Report 1966* (1967), p. 294.

59. Quoted in C. Taylor (1998), *The Beautiful Game*, p. 46.

60. R. Kapuściński (1991), *The Soccer War*, p. 166.

61. Quoted in N. Clack (2010), *Animals! The Story of England v Argentina*, p. 102.

62. Confidential Report to London from the British Embassy in Montevideo (FO 953/2334), July 27, 1966.

63. A. L. di Salvo (2000), *Antonio Ubaldo Rattín: "El Caudillo,"* p. 213.

64. J. Sasturain (2006), *La patria transpirada: Argentina en los mundiales 1930–2006*, p. 51.

65. *The Times*, July 28, 1966, p. 1.

66. Quoted in A. Scher and H. Palomino (1988), *Fútbol, pasión de multitudes y de elites*, p. 113.

67. Quoted in *Copa Libertadores de América, 1960–2010*, Tomo 1, p. 17.

68. Quoted in L. Álvarez (2010), *Historia de Peñarol*, p. 395.

69. Quoted in *Copa Libertadores de América, 1960–2010*, Tomo 1, p. 18.

70. *ABC*, September 6, 1960, p. 41.

71. *El País*, February 10, 1961. Quoted in L. Álvarez (2010), *Historia de Peñarol*, p. 401.

72. Quoted in L. Álvarez (2010), *Historia de Peñarol*, p. 414.

73. Quoted in A. Giménez Rodríguez (2007), *La pasión laica*, p. 157.

74. Quoted in R. Mamrud (ed.) (2000), *40 años Copa Libertadores: 1960–2000*, p. 41.

75. Quoted in *World Soccer*, May 1964, p. 12.

76. Quoted in H. Brands (2010), *Latin America's Cold War*, p. 99.

77. G. Pendle (1965), *Uruguay*, p. v.

78. Ibid.

79. Quoted in B. Belton (2008), *The Battle of Montevideo: Celtic Under Siege*, p. 126.

80. *The Times*, November 6, 1967, p. 11.

81. Ibid.

82. Ibid.

83. *World Soccer*, January 1968, p. 23.

84. *World Soccer*, December 1967, p. 22.

85. Quoted in B. Belton (2008), *The Battle of Montevideo: Celtic Under Siege*, pp. 7–8.

86. Quoted in P. Alabarces (2001), *Football and Patria: Sport, National Narratives and Identities in Argentina, 1920–1998*, p. 136.

87. *World Soccer* 24:1 (October 1983), p. 19.

88. G. Best (2001), *Blessed: The Autobiography*, p. 158.

89. *Daily Mirror*, September 27, 1968, p. 32.

90. G. Best (2001), *Blessed: The Autobiography*, p. 159.

91. *Daily Mirror*, October 15, 1968, p. 29.

92. Quoted in P. Alabarces (2001), *Football and Patria: Sport, National Narratives and Identities in Argentina, 1920–1998*, p. 139.

93. *El Gráfico*, October 22, 1968, p. 1.

CHAPTER EIGHT

1. *New Yorker*, July 18, 1970, p. 70.

2. Quoted in H. McIlvanney and A. Hopcraft (1970), *World Cup '70*, p. 260.

3. E. M. Estrada (1933) (1971), *X-Ray of the Pampa*, p. 12.

4. T. P. Anderson (1981), *The War of the Dispossessed*, p. 2.

5. Quoted in C. Krauss (1991), *Inside Central America*, p. 59.

6. Víctor Manuel Méndez y Reyes (1972), *La "guerra" que yo viví*, p. 56.

7. http://elpais.com/diario/2009/07/20/deportes/1248040816_850215.html (retrieved October 10, 2013).

8. Quoted in R. L. Scheina (2003), *Latin America's Wars, Volume II*.

9. Quoted in O. Starn, C. I. Degregori and R. Kirk (1995), *The Peru Reader: History, Culture, Politics*, pp. 265–269.

10. Quoted in S. Ferraro (1998), *Argentina en los mundiales*, p. 88.

11. *World Soccer*, October 1969, p. 20.

12. Quoted in N. C. de Oliveira Santos (2009), *Brasil x Argentina*, p. 286.

13. *World Soccer*, November 1969, p. 18.
14. *La Prensa*, January 8, 1969, p. 26. Quoted in C. Aguirre (2012), "Perú Campeón: Fiebre futbolística y nacionalismo en 1970," in Carlos Aguirre and Aldo Panfichi (eds.), *Lima siglo XX. Cultura, socialización y cambio.*
15. *El Comercio*, January 8, 1969. Quoted in C. Aguirre (2012), "Perú Campeón: Fiebre futbolística y nacionalismo en 1970."
16. *The Times*, June 16, 1970, p. 13.
17. T. E. Skidmore (1988), *The Politics of Military Rule in Brazil, 1964–1985*, p. 111.
18. Pelé (2007), *Pelé: The Autobiography*, p. 175.
19. Quoted in J. Lever (1983), *Soccer Madness*, p. 68.
20. Quoted in H. McIlvanney and A. Hopcraft (1970), *World Cup '70*, p. 21.
21. Pelé (2007), *Pelé: The Autobiography*, p. 183.
22. Ibid., p. 184.
23. Ibid., p. 185.
24. D. Miller (1978), *World Cup: The Argentina Story*, p. 39.
25. *O Estado de São Paulo*, 21 June 1970.
26. T. Mason (1995), *Passion of the People*, p. 64.
27. Quoted in L. Bethell (ed.) (2008), *The Cambridge History of Latin America, Volume IX*, p. 198.
28. *World Soccer*, May 1971, p. 47.
29. Quoted in V. S. Naipaul (2002), *The Writer and the World*, p. 376.
30. J. C. Onetti (1965), *El pozo*, p. 45.
31. Quoted in A. Labrousse (1973), *The Tupamaros*, p. 146.
32. *World Soccer*, January 1972, p. 3.
33. *O Estado de São Paulo*, July 11, 1972, p. 35.
34. Quoted in F. Chaine (2003), *Matador: Mario A. Kempes*, p. 32.
35. Quoted in E. Bradford Burns (1990), *Latin America*, p. 305.
36. Quoted in K-H. Heimann (1976), *1974 FIFA World Cup*, p. 23.
37. Ibid.
38. Ibid., p. 25.
39. Quoted in *World Soccer*, January 1974, p. 17.
40. A. Dorfman (2002), *Exorcising Terror: The Incredible Unending Trial of General Augusto Pinochet*, p. 11.
41. M. Cooper (2002), *Pinochet and Me*, p. 61.
42. *World Soccer*, July 1974, p. 10.
43. Quoted in L. Edwards (2001), *Mediapolitik: How the Mass Media Have Transformed World Politics*, p. 243.

44. *Clarín*, January 13, 2011, http://www.clarin.com/deportes/futbol/stylecolorB F1424Planeta-RedondoibrElias-Figueroa-dueno-area_0_406759581.html (retrieved October 31, 2013).

45. Quoted in J. Cristóbal Guarello and L. Urrutia O'Nell (2012), *Anecdotario del fútbol chileno*, p. 19.

46. Quoted in N. C. de Oliveira Santos (2009), *Brasil x Argentina*, p. 338.

47. Ibid., p. 255.

48. Quoted in R. M. Levine and J. J. Crocitti (eds.) (1999), *The Brazil Reader: History, Culture, Politics*, p. 257.

49. *World Soccer*, April 1972, p. 7.

50. R. Castro (2005), *Garrincha*, p. 378.

51. V. S. Naipaul (2002), *The Writer and the World*, pp. 436–437.

52. J. Simpson and J. Bennett (1985), *The Disappeared*, p. 34.

53. *Buenos Aires Herald*, April 22, 1976. Quoted in B. L. Smith (2002), "The Argentinian Junta and the Press in the Run-up to the 1978 World Cup," *Soccer & Society* 3:1, pp. 69–78.

54. R. J. Walsh (1977), *Open Letter to the Argentine Military Junta, March 24, 1977*, p. 7.

55. C. Hitchens (2011), *Hitch-22: A Memoir*.

56. *World Soccer*, October 1972, p. 34.

57. Quoted in A. Scher and H. Palomino (1988), *Fútbol: pasión de multitudes y de elites*, p. 157.

58. Quoted in E. Aliverti (ed.) (1987), *El archivo de la decada/2: la dictadura*, p. 152.

59. *New Yorker*, August 7, 1978, p. 46.

60. *El Gráfico*, June 6, 1978. Quoted in R. Rein (2010), *Argentine Jews or Jewish Argentines?*, p. 234.

61. *El Gráfico*, August 1, 1975, p. 2. Quoted in A. Tomlinson and C. Young (eds.) (2006), *National Identity and Global Sports Events: Culture, Politics, and Spectacle in the Olympics and the Football World Cup*, p. 139.

62. Quoted in D. Miller (1978), *World Cup: The Argentina Story*, p. 158.

63. Quoted in O. Ardiles and M. Langley (1983), *Ossie: My Life in Football*, p. 30.

64. R. Villa and J. Miller (2010), *And Still Ricky Villa: My Autobiography*, p. 41.

65. D. Miller (1978), *World Cup: The Argentina Story*.

66. *World Soccer*, September 1978, p. 4.

67. O. Ardiles and M. Langley (1983), *Ossie: My Life in Football*, p. 30.

68. S. Kuper (2006), *Soccer Against the Enemy*, p. 219.

69. P. Alabarces (2001), *Football and Patria*, p. 161.

70. *World Soccer*, June/July 1975, p. 12.

71. Quoted in D. Miller (1978), *World Cup: The Argentina Story*, p. 10.

72. Quoted in M. Feitlowitz (1998), *A Lexicon of Terror*, p. 37.

73. E. Aliverti (ed.) (1987), *El archivo de la decada/2: la dictadura*, p. 163.

74. *World Soccer*, August 1978, p. 10.

75. P. Alabarces (2001), *Football and Patria*, p. 160.

76. Quoted in E. Fernández Moores (2010), *Breve historia del deporte argentino*, pp. 163–164.

CHAPTER NINE

1. *El Gráfico*, No. 3195, December 30, 1980.

2. *World Soccer*, February 1981, p. 7.

3. Television interview with Maradona, 1981.

4. Quoted in L. Prats (2011), *La crónica celeste*, p. 165.

5. J. Burns (2010), *Maradona: The Hand of God*, p. 24.

6. D. A. Maradona (2005), *El Diego*, p. 1.

7. Ibid., p. 4.

8. Ibid., p. 6.

9. D. Arcucci (2001), *Conocer al Diego*, p. 60.

10. L. Zanoni (2006), *Vivir en los medios*, p. 181.

11. *El Gráfico*, No. 3161, May 6, 1980.

12. *El Gráfico*, No. 3218, June 9, 1981.

13. C. Darwin (2001), *Charles Darwin's Beagle Diary*, p. 228.

14. Quoted in P. Armstrong and V. Forbes (1997), *The Falkland Islands and Their Adjacent Maritime Area*, p. 9.

15. http://www.elmundo.es/america/2009/11/22/argentina/1258929360.html (retrieved January 10, 2014).

16. Quoted in S. Menary (2007), *Outcasts: The Lands That FIFA Forgot*, p. 52.

17. *World Soccer*, February 1982, p. 20.

18. Quoted in J. Burns (1987), *The Land That Lost Its Heroes*, p. 270.

19. Quoted in J. Burns (2010), *Maradona: The Hand of God*, p. 94.

20. Quoted in J. Burns (2002), *The Land That Lost Its Heroes*, p. 271.

21. *El Gráfico*, No. 3271, June 15, 1982.

22. *La Prensa Gráfica*, June 28, 1982. Quoted in C. Urbina Gaitán (2009), "Desorganización y fracaso deportivo. La participación de El Salvador en el Mundial de Fútbol de España 1982."

23. Quoted in J. Burns (2010), *Maradona: The Hand of God*, p. 95.

24. M. Vargas Llosa (1996), *Making Waves*.
25. Ibid.
26. *El Gráfico*, No. 1338, February 15, 1946.
27. N. Femenia (1996), *National Identity in Times of Crises*, p. 64.
28. M. Vargas Llosa (1996), *Making Waves*, p. 168.
29. *The Economist*, Vol. 274.
30. *Placar*, July 9, 1982; quoted in L. Turchi Pacheco (2010), *Tragédias, batalhas e fracassos*, pp. 103–104.
31. Ibid, p. 89.
32. *New Yorker*, November 1, 1982, p. 121.
33. *El Gráfico*, No. 3150, February 19, 1980.
34. Quoted in J. S. Leite Lopes, "Transformations in National Identity Through Football in Brazil: Lessons from Two Historical Defeats," in Miller and Crolley (eds.), *Football in the Americas*.
35. *A Gazeta Esportiva*, July 6, 1982.
36. *The Times*, December 14, 1981, p. 16.
37. *El Mundo Deportivo*, November 22, 1979.
38. *New Yorker*, November 1, 1982, p. 115.
39. Interview in *Mundialito* (2010).
40. A. Bellos (2003), *Futebol*, p. 367.
41. *World Soccer*, January 1983, p. 6.
42. Quoted in D. Goldblatt (2008), *The Ball Is Round*.
43. Quoted in D. Yallop (2011), *How They Stole the Game*.
44. *New Yorker*, September 29, 1986, p. 46.
45. *El Gráfico*, No. 3477, May 27, 1986.
46. A. Ferguson (2000), *Managing My Life: My Autobiography*.
47. D. Maradona (2005), *El Diego*, p. 126.
48. B. Robson (1986), *So Near and Yet So Far: Bobby Robson's World Cup Diary 1982–1986*, pp. 38–39.
49. Quoted in N. Clack (2010), *Animals! The Story of England v Argentina*, pp. 159–160.
50. *La Razón*, June 20, 1986.
51. Quoted in J. Wilson, *Inverting the Pyramid*.
52. Quoted in M. Guterman (2009), *O futebol explica o Brasil*, p. 222.
53. S. Hodge (2010), *The Man with Maradona's Shirt*, pp. 104–105.
54. Ibid, p. 105.
55. B. Glanville (2010), *The Story of the World Cup*, p. 290.

56. G. Meyer (1967), *The River and the People*, p. 26.

57. *El Gráfico*, June 25, 1996; quoted in J. L. Arbena and D. G. LaFrance (eds.) (2002), *Sport in Latin America and the Caribbean*, pp. 68–69.

58. Quoted in *La Maga*, February 1994, p. 55.

59. Ibid, p. 30.

60. *World Soccer*, April 1986, p. 20.

61. *Clarín* (2002), *Argentina mundial: historia de la selección 1902/2002*, p. 142.

62. Quoted in C. S. Bilardo (1986), *Así ganamos*, p. 139.

63. D. Arcucci (2001), *Conocer al Diego*, p. 59.

64. *El País*, June 22, 2006.

65. A. Panfichi and V. Vich, "Political and Social Fantasies in Peruvian Football: The Tragedy of Alianza Lima in 1987," *Soccer and Society* 5:2 (Summer 2004), pp. 285–297.

66. Quoted in B. Elsey (2011), *Citizens and Sportsmen: Fútbol and Politics in Twentieth-Century Chile*, p. 235.

67. Quoted in E. Marín (ed.) (2007), *Historia del deporte chileno*, p. 449.

68. *Los Angeles Times*, Sepember 4, 1989.

69. N. Boyle (1992), *Goethe: The Poetry of Desire*, p. 464.

70. Quoted in P. Lanfranchi, "Italy and the World Cup," in J. Sugden and A. Tomlinson (eds.) (1994), *Hosts and Champions*, p. 153.

71. J. Sasturain (2006), *La patria transpirada*, p. 94.

72. P. Alabarces (2007), *Fútbol y patria*, p. 109.

73. D. Maradona (2005), *El Diego*, p. 171.

74. J. Villoro (2006), *Dios es redondo*, p. 75.

75. P. Gogarty and I. Williamson (2009), *Winning at All Costs*, pp. 25–26.

76. *New York Times*, July 1, 1994.

CHAPTER TEN

1. *La Semana*, July 3, 2009.

2. Quoted in T. Mason (1995), *Passion of the People*, p. 143.

3. http://www.fifa.com/classicfootball/matches/qualifiers/match=2791/index.html.

4. *World Soccer*, November 1993.

5. Erna Von Der Walde (1997), "De García Márquez y otros demonios en Colombia," *Nueva Sociedad* 150 (July/August 1997), pp. 33–39.

6. Quoted in P. Alabarces (ed.) (2003), *Futbologías*, p. 133.

7. *World Soccer*, May 1988, p. 24.

8. *World Soccer*, September 1995, p. 43.

9. C. Taylor (1999), *The Beautiful Game*, p. 163.

10. *World Soccer*, May 1988, p. 24.

11. R. Escobar (2009), *Escobar*.

12. Quoted in G. Livingstone (2003), *Inside Colombia*, p. 83.

13. G. Zuluaga Ceballos (2005), *Empatamos 6 a 0*, p. 36.

14. C. Isherwood (1949), *The Condor and the Cows*, pp. 161–162.

15. *New York Times*, August 23, 1993.

16. *USA Today*, December 17, 1993. Quoted in A. Tomlinson (2005), *Sport and Leisure Cultures*, p. 113.

17. Quoted in A. Tomlinson (2005), *Sport and Leisure Cultures*, p. 105.

18. *Soccer Journal*, May/June 2006, Vol. 51, No. 3, p. 45.

19. *World Soccer*, November 1993, p. 52.

20. *Soccer Journal*, May/June 2006, Vol. 51, No. 3, p. 22.

21. *New York Times*, July 11, 1994.

22. Quoted in the *Observer*, May 19, 2002.

23. Quoted in T. Mason (1995), *Passion of the People?*, pp. 141–142.

24. J. M. Wisnik (2006), "The Riddle of Brazilian Soccer: Reflections on the Emancipatory Dimensions of Culture," in *Review: Literature and Arts of the Americas* 39:2, pp. 198–209.

25. *World Soccer*, September 1995, p. 43.

26. http://www.pagina12.com.ar/diario/deportes/subnotas/46571-15793 -2005-01-25.html.

27. J. Lever (1983), *Soccer Madness*, p. 66.

28. A. Bellos (2003), *Futebol*, p. 305.

29. *World Soccer*, January 1990, p. 20.

30. Quoted in J. W. F. Dulles (2007), *Resisting Brazil's Military Regime*, pp. 213–214.

31. Quoted in T. Mason (1995), *Passion of the People?*, p. 130.

32. J. S. Leite Lopes, "Transformations in National Identity Through Football in Brazil: Lessons from Two Historical Defeats," in Miller and Crolley (eds.), *Football in the Americas*.

33. Quoted in J. Burns (2009), *Barça*, p. 334.

34. Quoted in W. Clarkson (1998), *Ronaldo!*, p. 241.

35. W. Clarkson (1998), *Ronaldo!*, p. 292.

36. Quoted in J. S. Leite Lopes, "Transformations in National Identity Through Football in Brazil: Lessons from Two Historical Defeats," in Miller and Crolley (eds.), *Football in the Americas*.

37. J. Burns (2010), *Maradona: The Hand of God*, p. 3.

38. *Sun*, June 27, 1998.
39. *Independent*, June 16, 1998.
40. *Clarín*, July 1, 1998.
41. *Observer*, January 8, 2006.
42. Quoted in P. Alabarces, A. Tomlinson, and C. Young, "Argentina versus England at the France '98 World Cup: Narratives of Nation and the Mythologizing of the Popular," *Media Culture Society* 23:547 (2001).
43. *El Comercio*, March 13, 2009.
44. O. Paz, *The Labyrinth of Solitude*.
45. *Clarín*, February 7, 2013.
46. R. M. Miller and L. Crolley (eds.) (2007), *Football in the Americas*, p. 98.
47. Ibid., p. 105.
48. *New York Times*, March 24, 2001.
49. *Guardian*, May 6, 2008.
50. H. Bingham (1911), *Across South America*, p. 15.
51. Quoted in L. Caioli (2010), *Messi*, p. 47.
52. Ibid., p. 167.
53. *World Soccer*, August 1978, p. 10.
54. Quoted in J. Lynch (2006), *Simón Bolívar: A Life*, p. 276.
55. J. L. Borges (2000), *The Total Library*, p. 426.

INDEX